The Foundations of Visishtâdvaita

Commemorating Millennium Ramanuja
(1017 – 2017 A.D)

By
Veeravalli P Jagannathan

Table of Contents

1. Religion: The Monument of Hope

From time immemorial, Vedic culture dominated our peninsular India i.e. Bhârat. The Tamil saints (Azhwârs) have made mention about the chorus oral rendering of the hymns of Vedas in their respective poems (*pâsuram* is the Tamil equivalent of 'verses') which are collectively known as Divya Prabandam. The loud voice raised in chorus during the Veda *ghosha* was like the roaring of the sea. Barring the few pilgrimage centers of North India, the rest of the 108 Divya Desams scattered over South India followed the *âgama* mode of worship. If the information contained in the verses of the said Prabandam is any indication, there were thousands of Brahmin families residing in many of those Divya Desams who were dedicated to the study (*adhyâyana*) and recitation of Vedas in temples while performing service to the deity (*sevâs*) and during ceremonies at home and social functions involving Vedic rituals and practices. Thirumangai Azhwâr's refrain would quite often be a rhythmic flow in numbers referring to the Vedic culture then existing –3 fires, 4 Vedas, 5 mahâ yajñas, 6-fold Vedic profession / 6 limbs (*angas*) of Vedas, 7 fundamental notes (*swaras* of music) and at times the sequences would extend with the mentioning of the 8 directions of propagation of Vedic culture.

முறையால்வளர்க்கின்ற முத்தீயர் நால்வேதர்
ஐவேள்வியாறங்கர் ஏழினிசையோர்

The vestige of the Vedic culture prevailing during British Rule (p8 Ref 1): "Sanskrit is still spoken as the tongue of the learned by thousands of Brahmins, as it was centuries before our era .... The Vedas are still learnt by heart as they were long before the invasion of Alexander and could even now be restored from the lips of religious teachers if every manuscript or printed copy of them were destroyed... The wedding ceremony of the modern Hindu, to single out but one social custom, is essentially the same as it was long before the Christian era."

The beauty and freshness of ideas in Rig Vedas, ceremonial mantras of Yajur Veda, the musical rendering of Sâma Veda, and prayers couched in lilting melody of the useful lore of Atharva Veda – by their fervid devotion, boundless optimism and moving faith have been providing the redeeming response from above like "Manna from Heavens".

This rich Vedic tradition or culture has suffered a setback in recent times if we go by the observation made by Sri. Krishnaswamy Iyengar in his article written in the year 1940: "The study of the Vedas according to strict rules of orthodox prescription is fast disappearing and the circle of persons that can repeat faultlessly the whole of the samhitas is fast diminishing. It is the Vedas that are the foundation of the Hindu religion and no devout Hindu can neglect the preservation of such a noble heritage. There are a few savants of *Krishna yajus*, but in the case of *Shukla yajus* or Sâma or Atharva, scholars have become so rare that they have now to be sought after and with them if there are a few anywhere, such learning will soon become extinct!" Seventy years later the situation now in 21st century is no better than what it was. If the following lines are any indication of the good old times that is referring to the heydays of the Azhwârs there existed as many as three thousand Brahmins, at one pilgrim center alone, who would rend the air with Veda ghosha. The relevant verse is quoted at the appropriate context.

6

In the ancient times people were reciting the entire Vedas (verse 331 of Tattva Mukta Kalapa) but the capacity diminished with the passage of time.

The one primary cause for the decline may be for the lack of support for Brahmins themselves. The State or the Government has miserably failed to support the rich Vedic culture. David Fawley squarely blames it on anti-Brahmanism - "the new communalism of Modern India". Vamadeva Sastri (alias David Fawley) makes the following candid observation: "they are the real false Brahmins who, devoid of spiritual values use their influence in the Government, media and educational systems to denigrate the great spiritual traditions of the land.... The blaming of Brahmins is a good play for groups who stand to make political gains through anti-Brahmanism ...They (Brahmins) have not disappeared. This is because behind the Brahmin class, are spiritual values which however often people fail to live up to them, cannot be ignored. The idea of a class of society devoted to the spiritual pursuits standing above financial and political motive is a great idea that needs to be instituted again in one form or the other all over the World.

"It is time for anti-Brahmanism to be questioned. Anti-Brahmanism is no more acceptable than anti-Semitism or negative stereotyping of any class, religion or ethnic group. The basic values that the idea of Brahmin class represents, like truthfulness, simplicity and compassion - are good and laudable in any enlightened culture."

The priceless ingredients of Hinduism are the three V's- Veda, Vipra and Vishnu.

विष्णुं क्रान्तं वासुदेवं विजानन् विप्रो

विप्रत्वं गच्छते तत्त्वदर्शी ॥

We may ask what constitute the adorable qualities of a Brahmin. The answer is given by Gitâchârya in Bhagavad Gita chapter 18 verse 42. (BG 18.42): they are the nine qualities such as control of the senses and the mind, austerity, purity forbearance, uprightness, general knowledge, spiritual knowledge and indomitable faith in religion. The ninth one, namely faith (âstikhyaṁ), according to Ramanuja's Gitabhasyam is a priceless virtue of a Brahmin and is explained very beautifully with copious references, taken from Bhagavad-Gita itself. He has followed it up by making a special mention about it in *Sriranga-gadhyam*. A penitent appeal to God for forgiveness is indeed "a cry from the depths".

॥ सात्त्विकतास्तिक्यादिसमस्तात्मगुणविहीनः ॥

Religion: "A Cry From The Depths"
Religion can be defined in many ways but the one given by the Christian monk is most telling. According to him, *"religion is a cry from the depths.* The noblest nature among men has been a religious one. No souls of mighty faculty of sensitivities are strong enough to sound the depths, fine enough to feel the heights, of this world history and grandeur, has been an indifferent, irreligious soul. They have bowed to the royalty of religious truth, either by joyful possession of it or by their cry for it. Only the surface of our nature can nourish an atheistic plant. When its depths are ploughed the latent seed of faith begins to germinate".

However, we should explore the meaning of religion from its fundamentals. We will start with the word 'holy'. Its root in the Anglo-Saxon word 'hal' or 'holig' means 'to be whole or united'. Religion is derived from the Latin roots 're' and 'legere' meaning 'bind together' or 'make a whole'. The question as to what things are to be made whole and how is answered by the scriptures of all the major religions. The Hindu word nearest to the root meaning of religion is 'yoga' which means union of man with God. Yoga derives from the Sanskrit root 'yuj', 'to join' (compare 'yuj' to the Anglo Saxon 'yoke'). Hence yoga is the doctrine or the method of joining man with God. The essential theme, according to the Hindu religion is God-realization as typified in the word 'dharma' which is synonymous with religion. "Religion is defined as the realization of the connection with the Divine Reality, conceived as a personality of highest value. It is a ligature or connecting again with Him from whom we have strayed away. Yoga also means connecting oneself with God (from *'yuj'* to connect). Thus, they mean the same thing. Undoubtedly later yoga meant the disjunction from outer nature of the world or separation from it to be able to connect oneself with God" (p203 of Ref 2).

In its essence religion is the search (*jijnyâsa*) for God and when one finds Him, only then one becomes whole and therefore 'holy' (VP 6.7.31).

॥ तस्या ब्रह्मणि संयोगो योग इत्यभिधीयते ॥

Refer also to Sahasranamam, the *nâmâvalis* '*Yogah*' (18) and '*Yogavidam neta*' (19). Lord Vishnu serves as the means and escort for God-realisation.

Bhagavad-Gita itself is the outcome of "a cry from the depths" of Arjuna whose heart was grief stricken with the prospects of mindless massacre of near and dear ones in the battle field at Kurukshetra. He pours out his depression thus: "I see nothing but greed in waging this war. I feel better to beg and live the life of a mendicant than kill and enjoy the comforts of a kingdom. I am confused about what is righteous and what is not. O Krishna, decide and tell me what is ultimately good for the soul. I surrender unto Thee".

|| यच्छ्रेयः स्यान्निश्चितं ब्रूहि ||

According to Ramanuja's Gitabhasyam, even Duryodhana suffered depression although for different reasons. That is why the first chapter of Bhagavad-Gita is titled as *visâda* yoga taking into consideration the depression of Duryodhana as well. For a full-length discussion see page 15 of Ref 3.

Religious Tolerance

This problem is nothing new to us in India. Swami Ranganathananda discusses it in his book (p32 of Ref 5).

"Hindu tolerance continued during Muslim intolerance because the tolerance was the product of a spiritual vision and philosophical conviction bequeathed by the Upanishads, which has become an inseparable part of the Indian outlook and way of life. There is uniqueness about Indian tolerance in that it has always been the product of religious faith, unlike the tolerance developed by the modern West resulting from its waning of faith in religion. Explaining this Indian approach, Dr S Radhakrishnan says (p317 of Ref 6): "tolerance is the homage which the finite mind pays to the inexhaustibility of the Infinite."

The vote-bank politics has not spared the Hindus. Now there is an attempt by the politicians, who in collusion with certain religious leaders, want to steamroll and bring all the Hindus under one banner – *sarva samaya samarasam*. This can only destroy faith and with the loss of faith, values are bound to vanish. What is desirable and what has been invoked from time immemorial past is time-honored tolerance. Artificial unity mongering is fatal to the religion (Ref 7). Close on the heels of the menace posed by equalization within Hinduism is the threat of conversion from outside. This sensitive issue will be found thoroughly discussed in the book on conversion which has several articles contributed by leading religious leaders who are still doing yeoman service to protect Hinduism and enlighten the Hindus (Ref 8).

Ashish Nandy, the well-known scholar, questions the concept of secularism as enshrined in the Constitution: "South Asian enigma: limits of religion" (Ref 9). He argues that "ideas of tolerance in ordinary people and everyday life are tinged with popular religious beliefs, however superstitious, irrational and primitive they may seem to progressive secular Indians."

An eminent sociologist T.N.Madan writes that secularism in South Asia is impracticable because it fails to recognize the importance of religion in people's lives. Gandhi was a deeply religious person and has left an indelible imprint on our society and polity, but he never brought his faith into politics. Today's leaders, whatever their personal religious beliefs may be, must profess a secular approach lest they find themselves debarred from the electoral process by the Election Commission (Ref 10).

In various judgments, the law courts of India have upheld that Hinduism is a way of life. The manual for the way of life is the ancient book Manusmrti and the code of conduct of humans is popularly known as *Mânava dharma* or *Sanâtana dharma*. Its ideal is enshrined in the life of renunciation known by the jargon *Sanyâsâshrama*. The life of a *sanyâsin* is well established in Ahimsa. The word Hindu is derived from two words *"himsa"* and *"dûyathe"* which means the one, who feels aggrieved at or causing injury (himsa) to others (vide Merutantra).

॥ हिंसायां दूयते यस्माद्धिन्दूरित्यभिधीयते ॥

Regard for Women in Manusmrti

What a pleasant contrast that Hindu women enjoy the highest status and respect sanctioned by the *shrutis* and *smrtis*! A mother should be adored like God (*mâtr devo bhava*). The father comes second only to mother. Manusmrti (3.36) states that "god's delight where women are respected." A woman after marriage leaves her home and enters the home of her husband. She should be accorded a ceremonial welcome and she should be properly treated with tenderness and love. Disrespect to her would spell disaster to the family of her husband, says Manu.

About ill treatment to women among several religions, even Christianity must share the blame. What Friedrich Nietze had said bears this out. He contrasts Bible with Manusmrti: "I know of no book in which so many tender and kind remarks are addressed to women as in the law books of Manu. The author has a way of being polite to women which has never been surpassed...All things upon which Christianity vents its abysmal vulgarity, procreation for example, women, marriage, are in Manusmrti treated seriously with reverence love and trust. How paltry the New Testament is compared to Manu, how it smells."

The ultimate God-Head, according to the Philosophy of Ramanuja, is the Divine Couple, and even in the prayer he has accorded prominence to Shree, as per the 'ladies first' principle.

लक्ष्मी नाथ समारंभां नाथ यामुन मध्यमाम्।

अस्मदाचार्यपर्यन्तां वन्दे गुरु परंपराम्॥

And Swami Deshika, in Sri Stuti, follows suit by extolling Lakshmi as the Mother and Vasudeva as the Father constituting the Ultimate inseperable God-Head.

॥ माता देवि त्वमसि भगवान् वासुदेवः पिता मे॥

12

The Modern 'Chaos'

The deep malaise afflicting the modern society is analyzed and expressed thus (Ref 2): "Our present world has been more tried than the past because of the chaos introduced by science. What is the pattern of chaos? It is indeed the triumph of technique over the values of life which refuse to conform to the scientific pattern of law. These are values more important than what science has been able to assure. Law indeed is the promise of science and whilst giving us laws it has also made the higher fountains of human life lawless.

Man has been cheated out of his freedom by the growth of outer system of law…The forces that he has unleashed and can unleash yet, are precisely the forces that can also smother him, entirely. Further, the values so very necessary for his individual comfort and solace also seem to wither away under the strain of the modern search for mechanical power yoked to the ulterior demands of vital and political power. This then is the peculiar nature of modern chaos.

For a typical example of 'Modern Chaos' we may peruse the paper (Ref 4) written from the standpoint of the neuroscientific view of life: "brain imaging was invented for medical diagnosis. But its far greater importance is that it may very well confirm, in ways too precise to be disputed, certain theories about 'the mind', 'the self', 'the soul' and 'free will' that are already devoutly believed by scholars in what is now the hottest field in the academic world, neuroscience. Granted, all those skeptical quotation marks are enough to put anybody on the qui vive right away, but Ultimate Skepticism is part of the brilliance of the dawn I have promised."

For all the milestones achieved the appalling conclusion arrived at is that man is no better than a dog! "The consensus was that since the human mind is, after all, an entirely physical apparatus, a form

13

of computer, the product of a particular genetic history, it is finite in its capabilities. Being finite, hardwired, it will probably never have the power to comprehend human existence in any complete way. It would be as if a group of dogs were to call a conference to try to understand The Dog. They could try as hard as they wanted, but they wouldn't get very far. Dogs can communicate only about forty notions, all of them primitive, and they can't record anything. The project would be doomed from the start. The human brain is far superior to the dog's but is limited nonetheless. So, any hope of human beings arriving at some final, complete, self-enclosed theory is doomed, too."

The above arguments tinged with pessimism put forward by Tom Wolfe are from the stand point of a die-hard scientist but a spiritualist would analyze it more constructively and optimistically. The living entities, according to our theory of karma, are arranged in a hierarchical level, man occupies the highest level in the hierarchy while beasts and plants occupy lower and lower levels.

"That there are no philosophies or religious ritualism in the world of flora and fauna seems to be one of the wondrous and intelligent looking arguments of guided atheists, when they justify their reluctance in accepting religion" (p139 of Ref 11).

The reader may refer to the commentary of Ramanuja for the two verses 17 and 18 of Gita chapter 14 which provides the rationale for grading the living beings. *Sattva guNa* would entitle a living entity to occupy the higher level while *rajo guNa* and *tamo guNa* would be for lower and lower levels.

The *Sattva guNa* would develop the capacity of the intellect for knowledge. Theoretically speaking there is no limit to the growth of knowledge. We may compare the difference between an ordinary intellect and an advanced one to the difference between an ordinary

14

copper conductor and the super conductor made of special material. At low critical temperatures, the super conductor conducts enormous currents much, much greater than the ordinary conductor. The intellect attains enormous capacity for knowledge when Sattva guNa gets purified by *sâdhana* with the elimination of rajo and tamo guNa. Abridgment of knowledge results in bondage or samsâra (*Jnâna sankochah samsâra*) whereas boundless expansion or blossoming of intellect leads to *Jnâna vikâsah mokshah* or liberation.

Why should the Jnâna expand to infinity? It facilitates to commune with the Absolute. "The Absolute of thought is Bhagavan, the God of religion. Brahman is the 'infinite' not in the sense that it is quantitative endlessness or the infinite that is conditioned by the finite and is therefore finite, but it is the infinite that dwells in the finite with a view to convert the self to infinite (*brhattvât cha brahmanattvât cha*) and give it the eternal value at mukti." "The term 'infinite' in the philosophy of religion corrects the tendency of thought to abstract itself from the thinking process or the pulsation of intelligence and gives a positive meaning to the infinite as actual and determinate." To get Brahminized, one should deserve. It is true that non-deserving nature makes one feel that he is no better than a dog and it goes a long way to eschew ego.

தண்குடந்தைக் கிடந்த மாலை
நெடியானை அடிநாயேன் நினைந்திட்டேனே.

Proceeding with the discussion (Ref 2): "Freedom is the price that man has to pay for security. Freedom is the price that man must pay for survival in the modern dictator-ridden world of scientific men. Mephistopheles did not offer a greater gift than the Modern dictator. And what does he offer? To keep the animal needs alive and abolish the spiritual and the individual …Religion got the first death blow when the value of the individual was abolished, his freedom condemned in the name of the collective and the universal."

Of what avail is achievement in the world of mortals? A good soul is bound to get dejected after critically examining the ways of the world. All activities done in the past resulted only in momentary pleasures. For a good soul, a feeling of despair is inevitable leading to a routing of the senses. This disgust for the ways of the world is "a cry from the depths" (Mundakopanishad 1.2.12; Isa 9).

परीक्ष्य लोकान् कर्मचितान् ब्राह्मणो निर्वेदमायान्नास्त्यकृतः कृतेन।

तद्विज्ञानार्थं स गुरुमेवाभिगच्छेत् समित्पाणिः श्रोत्रियं ब्रह्मनिष्ठम्॥

A strong feeling of remorse for leading a worldly life is the essential requirement for switching over to a spiritual way of life. Gitâchârya calls it as 'nirveda' which is nothing but "a cry from the depths" (BG 2.52).

பழுதே பல பகலும் போயினவென்று அஞ்சி அழுதேன்.

An individual's tryst with destiny is indeed "a cry from the depths". Either we evolve into a divine being or we perish. As Coleridge puts it, "if man is not rising upward to be an angel, he is sinking downward to be a devil. He cannot stop at the beast." Again, referring to KCV's writings, "man can triumph over animal as he has already done so far, even in this race for universal love and power. The power so far has been through love of his body but the prophets and rishis envisaged this day when there is more need to save the soul and the individual than his body. Culture is the preparation for the great emergence of the divine and not as man.

"In all chaos, there is the persistent partiality – fragmentariness of these values. They catch hold of someone value – *artha* or *kama* – economic materialism or hedonistic materialism or the cross

16

between them which is today known to the world as the industrialism of the capitalists or communistic variety – and so distort the soul and understanding of man and by a procrustean method almost annihilate the one thing that culture seeks to preserve, the freedom in the world by a superior realization of the freedom that belongs to the essence of existence of oneself.

"It is only when man becomes really man or human that he can be trusted to use the knowledge and powers that science grants wisely and for all. Else it can become a menace not only to humanity and civilization but to life itself. Such a disaster to civilization must at all events be averted and finally be made impossible. To avert we have the niggardly League of Nations and compromising League of Intellectual Co-operation. But to make it impossible is wanted a genuine culture of the individual, the discovery of his immortal essence, Supreme Spirituality and integrality and humanity. In other words, what is required is the finding of the uniqueness of everyone, his self which is Supremely Divine. This is the Supreme truth, 'the ancient ideal of Indian philosophy'. Not all the centuries that has rolled by can retract that Supreme value and their promise is the guiding hope of Indian thought through millennia."

"The whole of the Vedic civilization is the effort started at the very dawn of history to prepare for this great future step that mankind must make: the study of the Upanishads, the Aranyakas and the Brahmanas in this light of the preparation of man. Building up man in the Divine by the Divine light and force and delight is a revelation to which there is no parallel in history or pre-history. This is the sacred literature of the Aryans capable of being and in fact calculated to be the sacred Revelation of all humanity – Veda. Vedas can be many but there is only one Veda. The integral four-fold Veda of the Hindus" (p 357 of Ref 2).

The supreme Vedic culture is ingrained in the epics and purânas as the following verse from Adi Parva (1.293) reveals:

इतिहासपुराणाभ्यां वेदं समुपबृंहयेत्।

बिभेत्यल्पश्रुताद्वेदो मामयं प्रतरिष्यति॥

Rajaji, whose books on the two epics are the most popular ones, expains the sum and substance of the epics in a lucid manner. "Sorrows of human life are painted with sublime beauty and rolled out in a grand panorama. Behind the story of errors and sorrows the poet enables us to have a vision of Transendent Reality. Thus it is that Mahabharatha, though a story, has come to be a book of dharma. This book in style and substance is altogether different from tales and romances. In modern novels, dramas and pictures, exciting scenes are enacted, the hero passes through dangers and difficulties and finally marries the woman he loves, or else everything seems to go on happily but suddenly things go wrong and a terrible misfortune happens and the curtain drops. This is the art-scheme of ordinary sensational stories. The Ramayana and Mahabharata are quite a different kind of artistic creations. When we read them our inner being is seized and cleansed, so to say by being alternately passed through joys and sorrows, and we are finally lifted above both and taken to the Transcendent and Real."

Take for example the biography of Rama. The story demonstrates that in this impermanent (*anityam*) painful world of mortals, one cannot escape the sorrow caused by the forces of evil. Rama cries at the loss of Sita (vide the sarga titled, '*Râghava vilâpah*'). Again he mourns for the death of the bird king Jatayu who sacrificed his life fighting the evil Ravana (Ram 3.67).

राज्याद्भ्रंशो वनेवासः सीता नष्टा द्विजो हतः

The sufferings of the soul are enacted through the example of Sita, the heroine of Srimad Ramayana. It is not so much the fire but tears from her "cry from the depths" that burnt the city of Lanka.

॥ यः शोक वह्निं जनकात्मजायाः ॥

Kulasekar Azhwar adopts the vein of 'a cry from the depths' to express the sorrows of Dasharatha who suffers the pangs of seperation from his son Rama when Rama leaves for the forest to fulfill the pledge given to his step mother Kaikeyi.

The lamentations of Mandodari, wife of Ravana, forms a big *sarga* in Ramayana. She comes to the battlefield and after seeing the deadbody pours out her agony —"cries from the depths" –in terms not that of an ordinary woman. She was conscious that Rama, who was present, was an *avatara purusha*. Ironically she waxes lyrical and admires and praises Rama in vedantic jargon before she condemns the heinous misdeeds of Ravana (Ref 12, VS 216).

Now coming to Mahabharat, the book (Ref 13 opens with a two-page account of the story of Mahabharat): "the tragic and heroic figure of Queen Kunti emerges from an explosive era in the history of ancient India. As related in the Mahabharata, India's grand epic poem of 110,000 couplets, Kunti was the wife of King Pandu and mother of five illustrious sons known as the Pandavas. As such, she was one of the central figures in a complex political drama that culminated fifty centuries ago in the Kurukshetra war, a devastating war of ascendancy that changed the course of world events."

The story is described in the several paragraphs that follow and we shall fast forward to the events narrated in the concluding paragraphs.

"Having delivered the Pandavas from this last calamity (Kurukshetra war) and seeing that all His plans were fulfilled, Lord Krishna was again preparing to leave. For years Duryodhana had tormented Queen Kunti's family, but Krishna had protected them at every twist & turn- and now He was leaving for Dwaraka. Kunti was overwhelmed, and she prayed to Krishna from the core of her heart… Kunti's spontaneous glorification of Lord Krishna consists of just 26 verses and in the following couplet quoted below she appeals for re-occurance of calamities so that she would always remember Him" (Bhagavatam 1.8.25).

विपदः सन्तु नः शश्वत्तत्र तत्र जगद्गुरो।

भवतो दर्शनं यत्स्यादपुनर्भवदर्शनम्॥

"I wish that all those calamities would re-visit again and again so that we could see You again and again, for seeing You means that we will no longer see repeated births and deaths."

Tirumangai Azhwar went from one temple after another (more than 80 that spread from the Himalayan regions to the south) longing for vision of the Lord and His Consort. "Please give me a darshan of Yours which will free me from *samsâra*."

ஆண்டாய் உனைக் காண்பதோர் அருள் எனக்கருளிதியேல்
வேண்டேன் மனைவாழ்க்கையை விண்ணகர் மேயவனே

Who can forget the outcries of Draupadi when her modesty was outraged (Sabha 90.44)?

हा कृष्ण द्वारकावास क्वासि यादवनन्दन। इमामवस्थां अनाथां किमुपेक्षसे॥

शङ्ख चक्र गदापाणे द्वारकानिलयाच्युत। गोविन्द पुण्डरीकाक्ष रक्षमां शरणागतम्॥

The last two lines of the above verse are prescribed as part of daily prayers to be recited at the conclusion of Sandhyavandana.

An event that was the turning point in the life of Mathoor Krishna Murty was reported on the eve of his death on 6th oct 2011. "Mathoorji (as he was affectionately called) would have slid into oblivion 35 years ago itself had he been successful in his attempt to commit suicide in London." He gave up his attempt when he providentially read the lines in the book on Mahabharata (which also contains a brief account of Ramayana) in which a frustrated Hanuman gave up his suicide attempt in the nick of time when suddenly Hanuman realized that he had not searched for Sita in Ashokavana. It is customary among Hindus to read Ramayana, particularly Sundara Kândam when one is faced with acute problems in life.

In sum, longing for God is the mother of all cries from the depths. 'But how do we love God? Love for the pleasures from the senses we have. But love for God who is *atindriya* or beyond the senses, how are we to acquire it? We are not accustomed to that sort of love and how are we going to cultivate it? Sri Kuresha, known also as Azhwar, beautifully bemoans this unfitness for God-love. "I have got a large desire" says he, "for all the pleasures of the body, but none whatever for Your Feet. My mind is every moment tormented by diverse things such as disease, poverty, want of joy, getting things I do not desire, not getting things I hanker after and my irritating inferiority complex; but never once have I been worried by the thought that I do not bear any love to Thee." An Azhwar says, "I have not a single qualification in me to God-love and still like a blind man I grope in the dark for a God whom my untutored heart longs to love. Lust is of the flesh, but love is of the spirit. A gracious God ever watchful of His devotees' interests hears this wail and fills the hearts of the devotees, who can thus cry out in agony and despair out of their deep and abiding love towards His Feet" (Ref 14).

It would be appropriate to close this section by highlighting the trying circumstances that lead to the rise of Sri Ramanujâchârya who rose above the firmament to fulfill the crying need of the hour.

As we look back into our religious history to a period thousand years before, we find that the Advaita of Shankara was the dominant religious philosophy ruling the roost. The dominance was to the extent that the teachers of Advaita were averse to *Para Tattva* (Ultimate God-Head) of Vishnu and would even deride Vishnu in terms not acceptable to the Vaishnavite community. For a specific instance in point we may cite an incidence that occurred in Ramanuja's life: "When his teacher Yâdavaprakasa interpreted the word "*kapyasam*" with unbecoming low simile, Sri Ramanuja's soft heart, tender by nature and softened by devotion, melted and as he was massaging, tears rolled down from the corners of his eyes like flames of fire and fell on the thigh of Yâdavaprakasa." It was indeed "a cry from the depths" of Ramanuja!

The only remedy for the soul, drowning in the sea of greed of materialism, is to look away from it and become a follower of the Philosophy of Ramanuja. This is typified in the *thanian* dedicated to him.

॥ तदितराणि तृणायमेने ॥

Advaita derived its strength from Shankarâchârya's commentary on Brahma Sutras and at the time when the above painful incidence occurred, there was no other commentary which critically examined the highly-biased views of Shankara and the Vaishnavites were groping in the dark for want of a better alternative. "It ultimately took a Ramanuja to check the spread of this idealistic theory, question its validity based on both logical reasoning and scriptural exegesis and offer a concrete philosophy that meets the demands of the head and the heart, at once" (Ref 15). The following 59th pâsuram (Ref 16).

கடலளவாய திசை எட்டினுள்ளும் கலி இருளே
மிடைதருகாலத்து இராமானுசன் மிக்க நான்மறையின்
சுடரொளியாலவ்விருளை துரத்திலனேல், உயிரை
உடையவன் நாரணன் என்று அறிவாரில்லை உற்று உணர்ந்தே.

The above *pâsuram* should be read along with shlokas 56 & 65 of (Ref 18).

These verses describe the scenario that existed before the advent of Ramanuja. The age of Kali had spread its darkness of ignorance. It was the time when utter chaos and confusion prevailed, what with untenable faiths ruling the roost. The Vedic tradition suffered a serious set-back. Great saints of yore –Valmiki, Vyasa, et.al –became the object of ridicule. Shukha was a laughing stock as he was treated like a play thing, like a parrot. The crooked-minded gave faulty interpretations and adverse comments on the sacred texts. It was at this dark period the light known as Yatiraja (Ramanuja) arrived on the scene to drive away the darkness. Yatiraja is described as the Light of Vedânta. It is because of this *avatara purusha* that the people were saved from subscribing to false system of thoughts.

Religion: The Monument of Hope

The agony of being mean-minded is again 'a cry from the depths'. Acharyas and azhwars have expressed such feelings of remorse in fine poetry to serve as a medium of appeal before God. Yamunâchârya, for example (Ref 19), expresses his ungodly nature thus: "I'm the seat of a thousand crimes and I have fallen into the depths of the terrible ocean of worldly existence (48 ibid); I have swerved from the path of spiritual life and have fallen into the gloomy world of ignorance (ibid 49); discipline my mind, O Lord, so that I can be fit enough to serve you (ibid 59); I have been a transgressor, vile, fickle-minded, the breeding ground of envy, ungrateful, arrogant, lascivious, deceitful, cruel and most wicked (60 ibid). In your avatar as Krishna you showed extreme tolerance and pardoned the wicked Shishupala who uttered a hundred derogatory remarks against you. You should likewise pardon and accept my dog-like behaviour (63 ibid); When I say, "I am yours" I should be shown mercy. Did you not assure (*charama shloka* of Gita) that surrender once is enough? You have another weighty reason not to ignore me as I'm the grand-son of the highly adored Nathamuni" (65 ibid).

Azhwars feigning penitential mood have called themselves as dogs. Refer to Peria Tirumozhi (1.9.1) & Tiruneduntandakam 29. These verses can also be considered as "a cry from the depths". The maximum number of such verses uttered calling himself as 'dog' have come from Tirumazhisai Azhwar. See verse numbers of Tiruc chanda Viruttam –46, 47, 84, 98, 110 and 111 (Ref 20). Perhaps the rationale can be deduced from verse 90 (ibid): "O Lord! I have not conquered my senses. I am not fortunate to have been born in any one of the four castes. I have not learnt any of the four Vedas. Thus, most unqualified (no better than a dog) as I am, I have no other go except to hold on your lotus feet for my salvation."

If these verses are any indication, even a dog's life can result in freedom from bondage, when the appeal is made directly to God in the manner shown by the azhwars. One need not feel sunk like Tom Wolff, mentioned earlier!

Tirumazhisai Azhwar: "This wretched dog is not blessed to enjoy you like your devotees. However, have pity on me and tell me how I should get freed from the death-birth cycle and reach thy Abode of Bliss" (46 ibid).
நாயினேன் வீடுபெற்று இறப்பொடும் பிறப்பறுக்கு மாசொலே

24

"O Lord, you dwell in several places. But tell me where this dog can approach you" (47 ibid). "Has the Lord earmarked another life for me after the termination of the present one (*pinpiRakka vaiththanan koR*); I tremble to think of it. Or is he in his munificence has fixed a time when I would develop bhakti (*anbu*) towards Your lotus feet? This ignorant dog is at a loss to know what is there in store?"

நாயினேன் என் திறத்தில் என் கொல்? எம்பிரான் குறிப்பில் வைத்ததே?

"This dog is no longer what it was before. It has undergone a sea-change. It has given up anger. It is no longer the slave of the senses. I think of you always and I have developed liking for you. Having come this far, you should not let me down. Free me from rebirth. Grant me eternal service at your Lotus Feet (98 ibid).

"I am still vulnerable, likely to be swayed by the mean-minded people. Before I succumb and fall astray you should save me and instill *bhakti* for you (100 ibid).

பெறற்கரிய நின்னபாத பத்தியான பாசனம்
பெறற்கரிய மாயனே யெனக்கு நல்க வேண்டுமே

"I may not be pure judged from absolute standards of *yogins* who contemplate on Thee. Let the despicable behavior of this dog pass for as penance fit enough for the grant of liberation (110 ibid). It is said that you tolerated even Shishupala, a sworn enemy of yours, and you had put up with his unruly behavior but favored him at last (111 ibid)" (compare with Stotra Ratna 63).

"Days are like swords which have chopped off major part of my life. Old age and infirmity dog my footsteps and has considerably weakened my body. The day of death is fast nearing. O Mind! Make haste, offer your prayers and sing his glory and request for the absolute bliss (*miLvilâtha bhogam nhalga vendum* -112 ibid). The Lord is a problem solver as he relieved Shiva from the curse (113 ibid).

25

"O Mind! The eight factors which cause bondage get removed by His grace and you are destined to rule like a king in Paramapâdam," (vânamâLa -114 ibid). "O Mind. Remember the promise of the Lord (Varaha charama shloka). Your bright future is certain to be realized sooner than later (115 ibid). You are not only going to get rid of rebirth but you are going to be under His benign care. He will serve as your father mother and all relations rolled into one and take good care of you. With so much hope, why should you feel sunk in the ocean of misery (115 ibid).

"The dog-like existence is coming to an end. Fear, disease, afflictions of the mind, old age –all these maladies will be a thing of the past since there will be no more embodiment to experience the sufferings (117 ibid). O Ranganatha! My mind at last succeeded in staying firm on your Lotus Feet. What a transformation –from a wandering street dog to a devotee of you (119 ibid). To conclude, today I have attained my goal: My Lord has put a full stop to my rebirths. He made His auspicious form shine in my mind. He wiped my mind clean of all *vâsanas* and gave me the abode of Infinite Bliss for me to enjoy forever!"

இயக்கறாதபல்பிறப்பில் என்னைமாற்றி இன்றுவந்து
உயக்கொள்மேகவண்ணன் நண்ணி என்னிலாயதன்னுளே
மயக்கினான் தன்மன்னுஜோதி ஆதலால், என்னாவிதான்
இயக்கெலாம் அறுத்து அறாத இன்பவீடுபெற்றதே.

The reader should take note of the words *inRu* and *vīdu peRRathE*. The former means 'today' and it is so appropriate that there was no more 'tomorrow' for the Azhwar and further proof of his attainment is indicated by the latter which is in the past tense!

Incidentally the prescription for softening the 'hard-core' is uttering the names of Acharyas (43 of Ref 16 & 6 of Ref 17).
Service to God in Paramapâdam is the goal. But this feeling of servitude, one may object, is opposed to mundane experience since

dependence on others is always painful and is counter to the philosophy of freedom (*para vasham duhkham*). However, those who are enlightened about the nature of the soul know that the only one who ought to be served is God.

In the Shakespeare's play "The Life of King Henry the Eight', there occurs a dialogue wherein Cardinal Wolsey regrets his service to the king:
"Had I but served my God with half the zeal
I served my king, he would not in my age
Have left me naked to mine enemies."
Any service other than God is demeaning, sinful (Peria Tirumozhi 1.9.7).
பெரியேனாயினபின் பிறர்க்கே உழைத்து ஏழியானேன்.

Service to God undoubtedly means service to Lord Vishnu. Gitâchârya has made this point clear (BG 14.26): "He who serves Me with unalloyed *bhakti* (*avyabhicharena bhakti-yogena sevate*) transcends the qualities of *prakrti* and attains Me".

Having invoked Gita, it is natural to recall the shloka on mukti and Ramanuja's commentary on the two verses 18 &19 also of chapter 14. The one desirous of *mukti* should undergo self-discipline and the discipline involves eschewing *tamo guNa* and *rajo guNa*. It involves improving *sattva guNa* by partaking *sattvik* food. In interpreting these verses Ramanuja quotes hymns from the Upanishads. Hence Gita is Gitopanishad par excellence!

The Role of Religion
A few points may be noted down from the book (Ref 11).
When the mind is agitated, sorrow is experienced and when it is tranquil, there is joy. Happiness therefore is measured by the tranquility of one's mind. Man, the roof and crown of creation, has the unique capacity of quietening his mind without helplessly

depending upon the objects around him... Our great religious books help us to awaken and promote this dormant faculty in man. Our firm belief today is that the joys we experience through our senses lie in the objects of the world. Consistent with this belief, we are constantly engaged in acquiring, possessing and aggrandizing more and more wealth. But a little reflection reveals to us that the acquisition and possession of wealth is no measure of one's happiness. We are but too familiar with the striking contradictions in life between a millionaire sitting and mourning in his palatial apartments and an ill-clad peasant roaring in ecstatic joy amidst his poor circumstances. A line from the great Jnâna Vairagya Bhushana should be recalled here.

नास्ति पित्राऽऽर्जितं किञ्चित् न मया किंचिदार्जितम्।

अस्ति मे हस्तिशैलाग्रे वस्तु पैतामहं धनम्॥

If the joy is inherent in the sense objects, then each object should provide the same quantum of joy to all those who come in contact with it. Obviously this is far from the truth. For instance, a cigarette fills one with joy and satisfaction, while it drives another mad with annoyance.

Objects of the senses do not behave consistently even in relation to the same individual. The same object which please at one time (sugar, for example) comes to cause pain at another time (after contacting diabetes); the same causes anger at one time and at a later moment brings about tranquility. Pleasure or pain is not in matter. All objects are pleasurable or painful due to one's karma. On the liquidation of karma, pleasure and pain disappear (see Vedartha Sangraha, VS 249).

The Dual Path: The Path of the Pleasant (*preya*) and the path of the Good (*shreya*). *Religion* can be likened to a kindly policeman directing mankind to the path of the Good, but the irresolute mind tries to gain immediate flickers of joy, by choosing the other. Man is thus denied an opportunity of having a greater and serener happiness which the scripture provides (see Kathopanishad for the import of the words *preya* and *shreya*).

Notwithstanding one's knowledge of good and bad, and the guidance provided by religious doctrines, one seems to constantly gravitate to the lower and vulgar actions of life. It is so amazing that man knowingly chooses a path which is detrimental to his ultimate prosperity. The *thanian* (homage) on Periâzhwar and his message are worth recalling. He condemns even bread labor!

கீழ்மையினிற் சேரும் வழியறுத்தோம் நெஞ்சமே வந்து.
கூழாட்பட்டு நின்றீர்களை எங்கள் குழுவினில் புகுதலொட்டோம்.

Religion holds a mirror up to man's real nature within and provides him with the ways and means for chastening his emotions and edifying his thoughts, thereby enabling him to live a more dynamic and cheerful life.

Religion is like a friendly policeman who guides man through this 'traffic of life', to reach the goal of a perfectly happy and successful life.

Religion is not a mere mechanical worship, but a scientific formula for right living (*ujjivanam*). By adhering to it, man develops himself and enjoys a better and more purposeful life.

Religion prescribes certain eternal values −*brahmâchârya* (self-control), *ahimsâ* (non-injury) and *satyam* (truthfulness) −which are prescribed for regulation of our physical, mental and intellectual personalities respectively.

Religion helps us to the life of harmony and gain poise in personality. Religion is a happy and intelligent blending of philosophy and ritualism.

There are three categories of men of baser type: stone-men, plant-men and animal-men –their activities are guided by feelings and impulses rather than discrimination and understanding. They don't make use of their great capacity in them.

The fourth variety is 'man' –the best in creation. He can not only discriminate extrovertly in the realm of the gross world, but can delve into the subjective layers of his personality until he reaches the spiritual core in himself.

Japa Yoga: Japa, properly done can more effectively bring about a sustained single pointedness than all the hasty methods of meditation. A mind seasoned with japa is like tinned food, which is ready for consumption after a few seconds warming up on the fire. A short period of meditation can take japa-conditioned mind to unimaginable heights in an impossibly short time.

Tiruppavai
The essence of the teaching of Gita lies in the sattva guNa since only a sattvik person will aspire for liberation. We may say the exact opposite of sattva is tamo guNa. The best way to get rid of tamas, according to Andal, is by rising early in the winter month since it is God's own month.

॥ मासानां मार्गशीर्षोऽहम् ॥

Andal spearheads the campaign on tamoguNa by sending the early morning wake-up calls. The calls get graded in severity of expression from pâsuram to pâsuram. It is calculated to bestir even the most adamantly somnolent of the gopis (refer verses 6 to 15 of Tiruppavai; a brief outline, from this standpoint is given below.)

"Don't you hear the chirping sound of the birds? Haven't you heard the conch radiating from the temple? Wake up and enjoy listening to the loud uproar of Hari Nâma being uttered in chorus by munis and yogis whose hearts are purified by constant contemplation on the Lord reclining on adisesha?" (pullum - Tiru.6).

Parenthetically speaking how fortunate are those who experience the Suprabhata Seva (at brahma muhurta) at Tirumalai, Guruvayur or any other Perumal kovil!

"Don't you hear the sound of the valiya birds (*ânaicâttan*) and the churning sound of curds?" (*kîcu kîcu* -Tiru.7).

"It is getting late. The eastern sky is brightening and the buffaloes are fanning out for their morning graze. Wake up!" - (*kîzh vânam* - 8).

"O mother! Please wake up your sleeping daughter! Is she dumb, deaf or dull witted (to ignore all the noise outside)? (*tümani* - 9).

"Seeing you asleep it appears that the proverbial Kumbakarna has bequeathed his great sleep to you? (*notru* -10).

"We have come to wake you up so that you may join us in our praise of Krishna, the cloud coloured Lord. Should you still curl up in bed without a murmur of a response to our crying calls? (*katru karavai* - 11).

"Unmindful of the hustle and bustle around, you continue to sleep! What is behind this great sleep of yours? All have woken up already." (*kanaithilam* -12).

31

"Venus has risen and Jupiter has set. Noise of the birds pervade everywhere. Instead of having a plunge in cool waters, you are immersed in deep slumber (what a shame!) Cast off your sleep and join us (*pullin vai* - 13).

"Pray come and have a look at your backyard. The Nîlotpala has blossomed (because of sunshine) and the lily (*âmbal*) has closed its petals (which opens only in the absence of sun). It is already quite late. Wake up! (*ungal puzhakadai* - 14).

"O sweet young parrot! Are you still sleeping!" (*elle ilankiliye* - 15).

The last (10th gopi) is very sensitive as she is touched to the quick. She cuts them short by a quick retort; "don't throw such chilling words at me. I am already awake and will be joining you".

The essence of management is contained in this pithy saying: "Procrastination is the thief of time". It applies equally well to a spiritualist.

॥ शुभस्य शीघ्रम् ॥

In the 29 pâsuram, Andal has given the time schedule for sowing the seed of God love, nurturing it and reaping its benefits. "In the wee bit of the early morning hour prostrate unto Him" - *citram ciru kâle vandu unnai sevittu*" (29). Esoterically, it (*ciru kâle*) refers to the interim period between *prapatti* and the last moment when life ebbs out for good. The whole past for a *mumukshu* is one long night and the future an eternal day. This interval is like the morning twilight which though lasts for a short while, is full of hope (A Monument of Hope at that!) of a bright future in the joyous conclave of Divine Amity i.e. in the company of *Divya Dampathi and Nityasuris in Paramapâdam*.

सायुज्यं प्रतिपन्ना ये तीव्र भक्तास्तपस्विनः ।

किङ्करा मम ते नित्यं भवन्ति निरुपद्रवाः ॥

The above verse (Parama Samhita 30-94) is an assurance from God Himself: "Those who are fervently devoted to Me in bhakti-yoga and those who stay rooted in the penance of prapatti will attain Me. Once having come here (Srivaikuntam) they will ever be at My service. They will never return to karmabhumi again. Tiru-mazhisai Azhwâr's expresses his pinnacle of optimism thus: (Nân. Tiruvandadi 95).

ஏன்றேன் அடிமை யிழிந்தேன் பிறப்பிடும்பை
ஆன்றேன் அமரர்க்கு அமராமை -ஆன்றேன்
கடனாடும் மண்ணாடும் கைவிட்டு மேலை
இடநாடு காணவினி.

We may conclude this 'Monument of Hope' expressed in the verse (Ref 21).

Blessed is the one who is earmarked for liberation (sandrshhTah). With the munificence of an Acharya he gets initiated to pursue the spiritual path. He receives the three mantras from the Acharya (sara-vak-vit). He develops a sharp discriminative mind to understand the three fundamental realities. He cuts off connection with those of the worldly. He firmly establishes himself on the chosen path thanks to his constant touch with the Acharya and his noteworthy disciples. He leads a divine life. He prevents himself from committing sins and atones for lapses. Thus, he makes himself deserving to enjoy brahma-anubhava (Godly-experience) not only during his stay in this world but for ever after breathing his last.

Tirumangai Azhwar lists the benefits that would accrue to the one who contemplates on the Lord while doing japa (on the greatness of Tirumantiram).

குலம் தரும் செல்வம் தந்திடும் அடியார்படுதுயராயினவெல்லாம்
நிலந்தரஞ்செய்யும் நீள்விசும்பருளும்
அருளொாடுபெருநிலமளிக்கும்
வலந்தரும்மற்றுந்தந்திடும் பெற்றதாயினும் ஆயினசெய்யும்
நலந்தருஞ்சொல்லைநான்கண்டு கொண்டேன்
நாராயணாவென்னும்நாமம்.

The grace of God showers benefits in multitudes of ways: one can get rise in status; get enormous wealth; get one's worries wiped out in a trice; get emplacement in His Blissful Abode; one can get ownership of a mighty estate; one can get immense power; one can gain anything one wants; one can get devotion to Him. All these benefits accrue to one who contemplates on the word Narayana. Can there be a greater hope for mankind?

2. The World Monument: Sanskrit

The most ancient language, universally accepted, is Sanskrit. Tamil comes next and English is certainly of recent origin. Several scholars from India and abroad have labored hard to trace the history of our ancient Vedic Civilization and the period of emergence of the Vedas, but they could not arrive at a consensus on this issue. B.G Tilak, for example, in his 'Arctic Home In The Vedas', divides the whole period from the commencement of the Post Glacial era (assumed as the commencement of Krta Yuga) to the time of birth of Buddha into five time domains spanning from 10,000 B.C to 500 B.C. But the Tilak's classification would not be acceptable to Western scholars who place the creation of Earth itself to about 4004 B.C. With that kind of mind set they wouldn't agree to the existence of Aryan race earlier than 2000 B.C. MacDonnell summarized about the uncertainty prevailing in the various speculations, thus: "History is the one weak spot in Indian literature. It is in fact non-existent. The total lack of historical sense is so characteristic, that the whole course of Sanskrit literature is darkened by the shadow of this defect, suffering as it does from the entire absence of exact chronology. Early India wrote no history because it never made any." If the history of English literature is any indication to go by, Macdonald's unfair and unqualified comment on our own history would amount to 'a fish talking like a whale'!

Let us have a close look at English history itself. There was hardly any English in existence prior to 500 A.D, i.e., for the first five centuries after the birth of Jesus Christ! The earliest one which of course cannot be called English in the real sense of the term is believed to be the epic Beowulf, the poetry of Anglo-Saxon language. Frankly speaking Beowulf is even difficult to read, not to speak of the strain in deciphering its meaning. That is invariably the case with the few pieces of the so called old English literature. But the Englishman holds it in high esteem: "The unselfish heroism of Beowulf, the greatest prototype of King Alfred... and the pure poetry of which marks every line." (p17 of Ref 22). The author continues: "concerning the history of Beowulf, a whole library has been written, and scholars still differ too radically for us to express a positive judgment." These lines occur in the second chapter captioned "The Anglo-Saxon or old English period, 450 A.D - 1050 A.D". If even this recent event should be mind boggling, what to say about the antiquity of the Vedas and Sanskrit literature?

The name Anglo-Saxon is derived from Angles and Saxons, tribes, who, in the fifth century left their homes on the shores of the North Sea and the Baltic to conquer and colonize distant Britain.

The author William J Long traces the development of English from scratch and divides the period of its development into several ages- age of old English just mentioned, The Anglo-Norman Period (1066-1350), The age of Chaucer (1350- 1400), The Revival of Learning (1400-1550), The Age of Elizabeth (1550-1620), The Puritan Age (1620- 1660), Period of the Restoration (1660-1700), Eighteenth century literature (1700-1800), The Age of Romanticism (1800-1850), The Victorian Age (1850-1900).

Regarding the factors that led to the present form of English, let us turn to page 63 of (Ref 22): "In the tenth century the Normans conquered a part of northern France, which is still called Normandy, and rapidly adopted French civilization and the French language. Their conquest of Anglo-Saxon England under William, Duke of

Normandy, began with the battle of Hastings in 1066. The literature which they brought to England is remarkable for its bright, romantic tales of love and adventure, in marked contrast with the strength and somberness of Anglo-Saxon poetry. During the three centuries following Hastings, Normans and Saxons gradually united. The Anglo-Saxon speech simplified itself by dropping most of its Teutonic inflections, absorbed eventually a large part of the French vocabulary, and became our English language." That explains the popularity of Chaucer's masterpiece "Canterbury Tales" written in readable English of the fourteenth century. The first complete Bible in English was written in 1382. Printing was brought to England by Caxton in 1476 and almost all English literature came to be written after the advent of the printing press. That is all about the history of English!

The author Long presents a stimulating discussion about the utility of literature which is worth noting down:

"Literature is the expression of life in words of truth and beauty; it is the written record of man's spirit, of his thoughts, emotions, aspirations; it is the history and the only history of human soul. It is characterized by its artistic, suggestive and permanent qualities. Its two tests are its universal interest and its personal style. Its object, aside from the delight it gives us, is to know man, that is the soul of man rather than his actions; and since it preserves to the race the ideals upon which all our civilization is founded, it is one of the most important and delightful subjects that can occupy the human mind. "It is a curious and prevalent opinion that literature, like all art, is a mere play of imagination, pleasing enough like a new novel, but without any serious or practical importance. Nothing could be farther from the truth. Literature preserves the ideals of a people; and ideals- love, faith, duty friendship, freedom, reverence- are part of life most worthy of preservation... Literature makes us play truant with the present world and run away to live awhile in the pleasant realm of fancy".

Barring the first hundred pages, the rest of the book of 450 pages of William Long's history concerns with English literature of the last three centuries only i.e., 18th, 19th and 20th century and in the words of the author, Milton's famous sentence "A good book is the precious life blood of a master spirit" might be written across the whole of Victorian era. For a biography of Queen Victoria, the reader can enjoy reading '*Victoria Charitram*' written in beautiful Sanskrit prose and poetry by Pundit Sri Gopalâchârya who died at the young age of 27 in the year 1907. He has also written Aryâ Saptashatî (a poem of 717 verses) on the life of Sri Vedânta Deshika.

History of Sanskrit
Admittedly, English literature is dwarfed before the Monument of all languages, Sanskrit and the Englishman realized it rather late during the British Rule of India. The self-same Macdonald mentioned earlier gives vent to his admiration thus: "Since the Renaissance there has been no event of such worldwide significance in the history of culture as the discovery of Sanskrit literature in the later part of the 18th century... Charles Wilkins, who, having at the instigation of Warren Hastings acquired a considerable knowledge of Sanskrit at Benares, published in 1785 a translation of the Bhagavad Gita or "The Song of the Adorable One"... Sir William Jones published in 1789 a translation of Sakuntalam, the finest Sanskrit drama which was greeted with enthusiasm by such judges as Aerder and Goethe... Among the ancient literatures, Sanskrit gives a clearer picture of the development of religious ideas than any other monument of the world."

We may reproduce here the glowing tribute given by Max Muller who is famously known as *Moksha Mûlar* (literally meaning the man who knew the roots of liberation from bondage!)

38

"Yet such is the marvelous continuity between the past and the present of India that despite repeated social convulsions, religious reforms and foreign invasions, Sanskrit may be said to be still the only language that is spoken over the whole extent of the vast country."

Hindu Superiority: "No country except India and no language except Sanskrit can boast of a possession so ancient or venerable. No nation except the Hindus can stand before the world with such a sacred heirloom in its possession, unapproachable in grandeur and infinitely above all in glory. The Vedas stand alone in their solitary splendor, serving as a beacon of divine light for the onward march of humanity."

Stephen Knop: "Sanskrit is a Divine language, the parent of all other languages. Similarly, the Vedic literatures are Divine scriptures meant for the assistance and advancement of all living beings. Likewise, with the Vedic Aryan culture. It has existed from before the time of universal creation in the spiritual realm. It has been given to the world and is in existence since the creation. And it will continue to exist after the annihilation of this cosmic creation. This is the spiritual nature of the Sanskrit language and Vedic knowledge. It exists as a frequency through which pure spiritual knowledge travels into and through the material creation, yet retains its natural existence beyond it. In other words, it reveals the nature of Absolute Truth, and the Absolute Truth exists within it, with or without any material cosmic manifestation. As the consciousness of people reaches the frequency level of the Vedic knowledge, as has been the experience of great sages who are on this spiritual path, the insights and understanding that Vedic literature offers will become self-evident" (p9 of Ref 23).

अनादिनिधना नित्या वागुत्सृष्टा स्वयंभुवा।

आदौ वेदमयी दिव्या यतस्सर्वाः प्रवृत्तयः ॥

The eternal Veda is a treasure trove of words or *sabda*. Vâg means vocal expression of *Sabda*. *Sabda* in Vedic parlance is not merely sound but expresses a word conveying a certain meaning. *Vâk* is speech composed of several words. Sayana in his introduction to Rig Veda defines shruti:

॥ वाचा विरूपनित्यया इति श्रुतिः ॥

Vedas are known as shruti, literally 'what is heard' and from what is heard, follows what is understood; that is from sabda follows bodha or understanding. Between *sabda* and *bodha* there is *sphota* (or *dhvani*) which is the characteristic capacity of a word to signify its import. Words have a natural power of imparting knowledge (Vedârtha Sangraha para 227).

॥ शब्दस्यापि बोधकत्वशक्तिः स्वाभाविकी ॥

The deeper significance of speech is highlighted by Maharishi Patanjali while commenting on the Rig Veda (hymn X. 6,71) in his famous work, Mahabhashya, said to be the Mother of all commentaries. He provides an insight into the magic of words. To attain divinity (Brahma Sayujyam) one should take up the art of 'Sabda Sâdhana' or sound culture and in the considered opinion of the Maharishi the sâdhana will be effective only when the perfection is achieved through a sound knowledge and application of grammar. It is a proven fact (Taittiriya Samhita of Yajur Veda, 2.4.2) that a discordant note in *swara* can cause havoc. *Sabda* is not a lifeless mechanism but a vivid materialisation of higher consciousness –a consciousness that at once resolves into sabda and artha and "what we call *vâk*, as the vehicle of communication is nothing but an expression of Chaitanya lying within."

Evil forces can cause havoc to *vâk*. The demons Madhu and Kaitabha stole the Vedas and thanks to Lord Madhusudhana (Hayagriva) the Vedas were restored to Chatur Mukha Brahma. Swami Deshika's adoration of Vedas is translated into worship of Lord Hayagriva, the Chetanas- Chetana. In the Stotra dedicated to Him, several pithy phrases are coined to eulogise Him-Vâjîvaktra, Vasudeva, Vâgîshâkya, Vâgîshvara, Vâgadhîsha and so on. "Let the words be a shower of ambrosia-sweet, delicious and beneficial. Let it serve like the wish yielding Kamadhenu." The concluding verses 27 to 32 serve as mantra for the seeker of good speech.

॥ सरस्वतीं संश्रितकामधेनुम् ॥

The same poet demonstrates a good speech set in metrical melody of Sanskrit expressed through the 'Voice of Krishna' (*shauri-vaktrendu*). The speech of Lord Krishna addressed before an august assembly of kings, is compared to nectar-producing rays of the moon. The Swami demonstrates the soul filling effect of a brilliant speech purified by grammar - *parishuddhâm sarasvatîm* (Yad. 22.53).

तृषितैरिव ते श्रोत्रैः संभूत श्रुतिसौरभाम्।

पपुः प्रिय हितां तस्य परिशुद्धां सरस्वतीम्॥

The Aryan Tradition

"The old Aryans were a different kind of builders. Instead of granite, precious stones or metals, they used the most elusive substance of all- the spoken word. The human mind was the architect of their grand design and mantras (literally mind instruments) were their tools. They built philosophical systems such as, the Vedânta, the Sankhya and the Yoga. They immortalized their achievements of the spiritual world in hymns and elegant prose. For, the Vedas, the oldest text on religion will remain intact as long as humans communicate through the spoken word."

तदुपगतसमाससन्धियोगं सममधुरोपनताथर्ववाक्यबद्धम्।

रघुवरचरितं मुनिप्रणीतं दशशिरसश्च वधं निशामयध्वम्॥

If the above verse is any indication, the fine composition of the saint Valmiki describing the biography of Sri Rama has shaped the life and psyche of the people of Bharat over the millenniums. The above verse is quoted in the author's book on Ramayana (Ref 24).

Eternal Vedas

The fact that Vedas existed before creation implies that Vedas are eternal. When at the time of creation, God the Supreme, recalls to His mind, the universe as it existed before (*yathâ pûrvam*) and wills to become many. To carry out His own wish, He creates the Four Faced Brahma first. By being the *antaryâmin* (indweller) of Brahma, He prompts, directs and assists Brahma during the process of creation. In other words, the God empowers Brahma to proceed with the creation.

When Brahma utters the Vedic word '*Bhūh*', the word intuits the mind of Brahma to imagine what the word ''stands for (as we said before, the connection between the sound and what it represents is Nitya, eternal). The Earth represented by Bhūh springs into existence –the Earth is created before the very eyes of Brahma! This wonder Earth appears like in a magic show and hence is called *mâyâ* (wonder) or *prakrti*. Similarly, when he utters Bhuvah, the intermediate world is created, and so on. Though Vasishta and other Rishis are created by Brahma, the said Rishis go into meditation to get instructions in trance from their Indweller (*antaryâmin*). The Rishis jot down the instructions in written format as Vedas, passing for as the Gospel Truth which is termed *apaurusheyam*, meaning 'not of human origin' (Hayagriva Stotram 6). The Rishis in turn carry out their instructions. Thus, solely intuition (*yogi pratyaksham*) plays the part of creation. Living entities, of four different kinds - gods, humans, animals and plants - begin to inhabit the Earth (Shveta 6.11).

The One God gets pervaded and is hidden in all beings as *antaryâmin*. The said Upanishad at the end unequivocally states that God creates the Creator Brahma first while equipping him with the Creation Manual, namely the Vedas.

यो ब्रह्माणं विदधाति पूर्वं यो वेदांश्च प्रहिणोति तस्मै।

A wide-ranging discussion on the above lines is gone through in Sri Bhâshyam under the sub-topic Devatâdhikaranam and in this context identical texts from Manusmrti (1.5 to 10) and Vishnu PurâNa are brought to focus for explaining the phenomenon of creation as found in the original texts, Vedas. In this context, several verses from Hayagriva Stotra may also be recalled: the concept of apaurusheya (6), He as a redeemer of Vedas (8), Vedas as huge trees (11), He as unmanifested cause of Creation (12) jingling sound of His anklets serving as a repository of Shabda or Vedagira (22).

Though it is difficult if not impossible to know the time of origin of the Vedas, it is definitely possible to determine the times of the classical Sanskrit literature. The extant grammar texts, according to scholars (Ref 26), throw light on the history of Sanskrit. Three distinct periods can be assigned to the development of Sanskrit. First, the Vedic period when Vedas reigned supreme: "The world of the Veda is a world by itself; and its relation to all the rest of Sanskrit literature is such, that the Veda ought not to receive but to throw light over the whole historical development of the Indian mind. The phonetic condition of Sanskrit remains almost exactly the same as that of the earliest Vedic. In the matter of grammatical forms, the language shows itself almost stationary."

Yaska's Nirukta and Panini's Ashtadhyayi provide, so to speak, an intermediate link between the Vedic and non-Vedic literature. The former lays down correct principles of the derivation of words while the latter serves the twin purpose of providing the grammar of the Vedas (*chhandas*) and that of the language (*bhâsha*).

Panini introduces the alphabets in a novel way. The sounds comprising vowels and consonants are the sounds which emanated from Shiva's *damaru* (drum). The alphabets are expressed through 14 sutras (aphorisms) which are given the special terminology, *Maheshvara Pratyahara* Sutras. The 8 chapters (each of 4 quarters) comprise in all about 4000 sutras (to be precise 3995).

चतुः सहस्त्री सूत्राणां पञ्च सूत्र विवर्जिता।

अष्टाध्यायी पाणिनीया सूत्रैमहिेश्वरैः सह॥

Sûtra means a string and viewed in this sense the whole work is one chain of short sentences linked together in a most concise fashion. Chapter 6, first pâda, alone contain 64 sutras devoted to the science of recitation of vedas, known as Svara Siddhanta. It is said that Panini's rules are nowhere more scrupulously observed than in such an ancient work as the Aitreya Brahmana, a portion of the vedas. "Aitreya Brahmana shows some *gâthâs* which are obviously more archaic than the rest of the work. Notwithstanding these irregularities, the Brahmanas are the best representatives extant of the verbal portion of the language of which Panini writes the grammar though he did not mean these when he spoke of the *bhâsha*."

Panini's text is also an important historical source of cultural and geographical information. His work takes cognizance of important Vedic words: such as Vasudeva (sutra 4.3.98). His concept of dharma is attested in sutra 4.4.41 as *'dharmam charati'* - 'he observes dharma' (duty, righteousness) relating to Taittiriya Upanishad.

Intense interest is being shown in the field of computer-software. "Panini's theory of morphological analysis was more advanced than any equivalent western theory. His treatise is generative and descriptive and has been compared to the Turing Machine wherein the logical structure of any computing device has been reduced to its essentials using an idealised mathematical model."

After Vedas, commences a period at the threshold of which we find the Brahmanas, which so to speak look backwards to the preceding, that is, present the Vedic language in the last stage of its progress towards Panini's *bhâshâ*; and later, we have Yâska and Panini. This may be called as the period of Middle Sanskrit.

"Times had advanced and with it the language. The operation of the concurrent causes of linguistic progress had by the days of Kâtyâyana and Patanjali modified Panini's grammar. The verbal forms such as those of the Perfect which are taught by Panini as found in the bhâsha of the current language, not the chandas or obsolete language, had gone out of use in the time of Kâtyâyana and Patanjali and particles had come to be used. A close examination of Vârtika (grammar text of Kâtyâyana) shows that certain grammatical forms are not noticed by Panini, but are taught by Kâtyâyana and it can be concluded that they did not exist in Panini's time. "If to Kâtyâyana's eyes 10,000 inaccuracies are discernible in Panini, the only explanation must be that to Panini they were not inaccuracies but by Kâtyâyana's time the language had progressed and necessitated a fresh appendix to Panini's grammatical treatise. The period of intervention must be sufficiently long to allow old grammatical forms to become obsolete and even incorrect and their meanings to become antiquated and even un-understandable." The saying currently in vogue among scholars is, when in doubt, follow the rule given in the updated text.

For an illustration, we may refer to a familiar verse for the discussion. Panini clearly prohibits the use of mâ with an augmented tense. His injunction is '*na mâng yoge*' (Ashtâdyâyi 6.4.74), with *mân* the thematic '*a*' is to be avoided. But there are several forms in the Ramayana ("*mâ nishâda*, for example) where this thematic 'a' is added even when the preterit is preceded by *mân*. This is in clear disregard by Panini's rule as quoted.

<u>Was Kâtyâyana a Tamilian?</u>

Scholars (Ref 27) believe Kâtyâyana could be a Tamilian: "Being a southerner Kâtyâyana naturally noticed that the Tamil words Pandya, Chola and Chera which had been naturalized in Sanskrit literature in the forms Pandya, Coda and Kerala, had not been dealt with by Panini and proceeded to make rules to explain their formation... Tamil tradition is that the three kings (*mūvendar*) as they were always called by the Tamils, reigned in the Tamil land from the time of creation." Certainly, as per Yâdavâbhyudaya of Swami Deshika, Mūvendar existed in Sri Krishna's time (Yad 22.209).

चोलकेरलपाण्ड्यानां पश्यन् अनुगतिं प्रभुः

चकार पुनराधानं धर्म्यं हुतभुजामिव ॥

If the Tamils had existed during Dvapara yuga, it goes without saying that they should have existed in Rama's time of Treta Yuga. Valmiki had recorded the meeting of Agastya (the author of Tamil) at Panchavati with Rama. Moreover, there is no need for deduction as there is specific mention of it in Ramayana itself (Ram 4.41.3).

तथैवान्ध्रांश्च पुण्ड्रांश्च चोलान् पाण्ड्यान् सकेरलान्।

In Swami Deshika's Hamsa Sandesha, the regions where the Karnataka and Andhra meet (I.20), the Chola country (I.36, 37), the rivers Kaveri (I.42, 43) and Tamraparani (I. 51, 52) and the Pandya country (I.50) get glorious description.

46

पुण्यावासैः पुरजनपदैर्मण्डितान्पाण्ड्यदेशान्॥

Patanjali gives but a few forms which differ from Kâtyâyana's and hence for all practical purposes, the two grammarians are deemed to be belonging to the same period. The form which the language assumed now became the standard for later writers to follow and Kâtyâyana and Patanjali are now the generally acknowledged authorities on all points concerning the correctness of Sanskrit speech. It is customary to begin the study of grammar with a prayer addressed to the three exponents, known as Munitraya:

वाक्यकारं वररुचिं भाष्यकारं पतञ्जलिम्।

पाणिनिं सूत्रकारं च प्रणतोऽस्मि मुनित्रयम्॥

Grammarians have taken note of two kinds of words, *nitya* (eternal) and *kârya* (created). Bhartruhari calls them as divine and colloquial. Patanjali's language is most simple. It is said that one, to get fulfillment in life should rule a kingdom like a king or read the majestic treatise of Patanjali.

"Patanjali's language is most simple, lucid and impressive. The sentences really consist of a series of dialogues, often smart, between one who maintains the *pûrvapaksha*, and another who establishes the siddhanta. Hence the language is plain and simple and the sentences are short, and such as a man may naturally use in ordinary conversation or oral disputation.

"Patanjali used to look upon *sabda* as great divinity (*mahân devah*) that makes its presence felt by every act of utterance. His work portended the birth of a form of *sâdhana* in which sabda or Eternal Verbum should be worshipped with all the reverence shown to a Divinity. He was a true follower of the tenet outlined in the Chandokhyopanishad 7.2.2.

॥ स यो वाचं ब्रह्मोपास्ते ॥

The said Upanishad declares thus: "Vâk is greater than a name or word. Verily speech manifests as Yajur Veda, Sama Veda, Atharvana Veda, Itihasas, PurâNas (Panchamo Veda) and so on. But for speech, the pairs - dharma/adharma, truth/untruth, good/bad, pleasant/unpleasant - cannot be known. So, contemplate Vâk as Brahmam.

Now it will be appropriate to know the times to which these grammarians belong. Since Apastambha did not follow Panini's grammar it is quite likely that he lived earlier than Panini. By convincing arguments, the scholars Sir R.B. Bhandarkar and Goldstucker have unequivocally established that Panini's age belongs to seventh century B.C and that of Patanjali to the second century B.C.

Time of Lord Krishna

Regarding the place and time of birth of Lord Krishna, we have sufficient supporting verses from the lore and astronomical data for certain to determine the age to which Krishna belongs.

First, let us quote the verse from Harivamsha (113.62). The reader should also refer to Tani Shloki for a soul filling exposition of the verse.

एषनारायणः श्रीमान् क्षीरार्णव निकेतनः ।

नागपर्यङ्कमुत्सृज्य ह्यागतो मधुरां पुरीम् ॥

The above verse refers to the Avatar of Lord Krishna and the place of birth is mentioned as the city of Madhura, located on the banks of the sacred river Yamuna. Lord Sriman Narayana whose abode located in the Milky Ocean, left His serpent couch Adisesha and

48

came down in the embodiment of child Krishna. Just as the dawn gives birth to the Sun whose rays touch the lotus bud to blossom, Mother Devaki gave birth to the child Krishna to dispel the darkness enveloping the world in misery and brought about joyful bloom of the inner lotus (*hrth pundarikam*) of the hearts of the sages and saints.

The time of birth is the most auspicious moment in astronomical calendar as vouchsafed by the Brhat Jatakam. At this point of time five planets had attained their zenith. Swami Deshika casts the horoscope, as it were, couched in fine poetry.

अथ सितरुचिलग्ने सिद्धपञ्चग्रहोच्चे व्यजनयदनघानां वैजयन्त्यां जयन्त्याम्।

निखिलभुवनपद्मक्लेशनिद्रापनुत्त्यै दिनकरमनपायं देवकीपूर्वसन्ध्या॥

The above data has enabled the modern Pundits in Astrology to decipher the exact d.o.b of Krishna! "At the time of K's birth, vernal equinox was at 47 degrees and the Dakshinayana was at 137 degrees. So as per Vyasa's statement, K must have been born just after July 21st equivalent to Nabas. Now the foreigners try to fix up Kali Yuga as 18th Feb. 3102 B.C Chitra Shukla Pratama; since on that day they were not able to find the five planets they concluded that Vyasa's statement was wrong. Unfortunately, they had not understood Vedic Panchanga and so they took Varahamihira's into consideration. If they had gone back to 26 lunations they could have found out that on the 10th Jan. 3104 B.C five planets were hanging at Dhanishta star, Magha Prathama. Ancient Rishis had their zodiac starting from Dhanishta star Magha masa. Now for calculation purposes we take 28th Dec 3101B.C Maga masa Prathama as beginning of Kali Yuga. Now K was born in Dakshinayanam near the meeting place of Dvapara and Kali Yuga. We know exactly that the international figure viz. Feb 18th, 3102 B.C has been recognized by all astronomers in the world as the beginning of Kali. Based on this we can easily calculate the d.o.b of K as July 27, Friday, 3112

B.C, Bhâdrapâda masa, Krishna paksha, tropical month Nabas"
(Ref 28).

Two important milestones in the life of Krishna can be cited. He
lived in Nanda's house till he was 11 years (Bhag. 3.2.26). The other
one indicate the completion of Avataric mission. This completion is
invariably indicated by Chatur Mukha Brahma himself. It happens
in Ramavatar also. (after the slaying of Ravana and in the concluding
section of Uttara Kânda). In the following verse, Krishna is
reminded of His age (that He was 125 years at that point of time) by
Vibudeshwara i.e., Brahma (Bhag.11.6.25; also see p 35 of Ref 29).

यदुवंशेऽवतीर्णस्य भवतः पुरुषोत्तम।

शरच्छतं व्यतीताय पंचर्विंशाधिकं प्रभो॥

Lord Krishna's biography is meticulously documented in several
books of yore such as Visnu PurâNa by its author Parashara,
Mahabharata, Harivamsha and Bhâgavata PurâNa of Veda Vyasa, to
cite only a few of the most important ones.

Even in Ashtadhyayi, there is reference to Krishna (Sutra 4.3.98).
Bhandarkar has pointed out several references to Krishna occurring
in the Mahabhashya of Patanjali (Ref 30).

"The longevity of Krishna worship is attested from time to time by
antiquarian finds, like those of the monolithic column dedicated to
Vasudeva, at Besnagar near Bhilsa in Central India, by a Greek
envoy named Heliodoros, which scholars date between 140 and 130
B.C."

The Refinement of Tamil

We can broadly divide the extant Tamil literature into the earlier Tamil which some scholars call as natural Tamil and conventional Tamil. "It will not be an exaggerated estimate to ascribe a period of five centuries to the development of what one might call the natural poetry which preceded the conventional poetry on which Tolkâppiyanâr based his grammar. We thus reach 1000 B.C as the later limit of the birth of Tamil poetry".

The above finding is from the research treatise, (conducted during 1928-9, Ref 27): "The Tamils accepted the seen world and were satisfied with the joys of the living present. The ineffaceable sex-urge and the delirious joys of fighting, love of women and hatred of enemies, respectively called Agam and Puram, were enough subjects for their songs. These poets flourished in the sunshine of royal favor. The kings were lavish in the distribution of meat and liquor to bards and their kinfolk. The early Tamil poets were of the earth earthy. This was exactly the way in which the Tamil muse came to be born" (Ref 27. Chapter XII, "Earliest Tamil Poetry Extant").

The style of living of old Tamils as found in Agam and Puram compares well with that of the Anglo- Normans: "Love, chivalry and religion- these are the three great literary ideals which find expression in the metrical romances. Read these romances now, with their knights and fair ladies, their perilous adventures and tender love-making, their minstrelsy and tournaments and gorgeous cavalcades- as if humanity were on parade –and you have an epitome of the whole childish, credulous soul of the middle east" ("The Anglo-Norman Period" Ref 22).

These primitive languages earned the dubious distinction of being called as "*Mleccha Bhâshâ*". The languages lacking in refinement were best suited for those who were solely attracted by the external glamour of the material world. (*mlâ*=low, *iccha*=desire).

51

Aryanisation called for a thorough revision or refinement of the language and culture. The first step to soul-centered life is by resorting to 'Ahimsa' and avoiding eating flesh and drinking liquor. According to Gitâchârya (BG 5.22) the wise do not give themselves up to rejoicing in the pleasures of the senses. In a materialistic society where the blind leads the blind, there is no question of soul life. Higher life, according to the Kathopanishad (2.5, 6), does not exist in that society of spiritually blind people. Hence the grammar of the language should cater, primarily, to the demands of the spiritual minded.

Natural Tamil gave way to conventional Tamil thanks to the overpowering influence of Vedic culture and Sanskrit grammar (see Chapter XV of Ref 27).

"Sanskrit culture first began to affect Tamil literature when Agattiyanâr composed his Tamil grammar. It is a fact that he made a careful investigation of the facts of Tamil speech and framed a grammar of that tongue. Following Panini, he discovered or later invented seven cases in Tamil and his disciple Tolkappiyanar, following Aindra school of Sanskrit grammar made it eight.

"The momentum gathered by the poems of the Puram / Agam class during the ages which intervened between the rise of Tamil poetry and the period of Agattiyanâr, carried on that class of literature to five centuries after his time, when the old literature began collapse and a new Tamil literature inspired by the Sanskrit muse was born and largely eclipsed the older fashion of poems. However, it needs to be mentioned that Tolkappiyam as a complete handbook on grammar has a separate chapter called Poruladhikâram which does not ignore the then extant Tamil poetry, including Agam and Puram" Probably the continued prevalence of this old practice was seriously condoned and ridiculed by Nammâzhwar himself. For, he

52

has devoted one full set of ten verses which severely criticize the practice of praising humans, *nara stuti* (Tiruvâi Mozhi 3.9).

என்னாவில் இன் கவி யான் ஒருவர்க்கும் கொடுக்கிலேன்

"Later legend said that Agattiyanâr invented Tamil; there is this kernel of truth in this legend that later Tamil literature was the ultimate intrusion of Aryan literature into Tamil under the auspices of this first grammarian of the language. Tamil literature acquired preeminent status thanks to the induction of Vedic culture into Tamil grammar.

"Not that Tolkappiyanar rises above the temptation of importing Aryan ideas into his grammar of Tamil poetry... But often he is oppressed by his knowledge of Sanskrit literature and his belief that the Aryan social policy and religious system were divinely appointed ones. Thus, to Tolkappiyanar, the ideal social organization was the division of people into four varnas, with the three higher enjoying besides social privileges, literacy, privilege of being heroes of poems."

Not only the Varna dharma but ashrama dharma also continued to be the prevailing norm. Valluvar echoes Manu. Compare Manusmrti 3.77 & 78 with the Kural: "members of the three ashrama(s) depend on the munificence of the house holder" (See 41 of Ref 31).

இல்வாழ்வான் என்பான் இயல்புடைய மூவர்க்கும்
நல்லாற்றின் நின்ற துணை.

A true householder is a steadfast friend
To the other thee orders in their virtuous path.

It appears that certain scholars have jumped to wrong conclusions without making a complete study and PTS criticizes them in his "History of the Tamils" (page lv): "Great Tamil scholar as he

(V.Kanakasabhai) was, he was suffering from a disability; in his time, many of these ancient books had not been printed." Arokyaswamy gives a specific instance in his article "The Religion of Tamils 1800 years ago": "The poems generally designated as the 'Sangam Works' have their feet on religion and as such provide us with an instructive window on the religious state of their times... Kanakasabhai gives the reader altogether a wrong impression when he refers to the fewness of the Brahmins during this period (vide p 55,56) : "Tamils 1800 years ago")... Two lines of the tenth canto (142, 3) of the Silappadikâram gives a beautifully suggestive evidence of the great number of the Brahmins during this period when they describe the volume of smoke ever seen rising up into the skies in the city of Puhar, as dark cloud-like smoke, sweet in smell, rising from the yagas of the Brahmanas, here characterized as 'men of religion' (*maraiyor*)...a vast panorama of cults and religions, ranging from that of Indra and of the nature gods to that of Bhakti or fervent devotion to Shiva or Vishnu, which has now found a settled home in the Hindu mind. This is as much a mark of the "unchanging East" as a tribute to the broad-minded tolerance of our forefathers." Azhwar's pâsuram quoted below establishes this truth unequivocally:

தில்லைநகர்த்திருச்சித்ரகூடந்தன்னுள்
அந்தணர்களொரு மூவாயிரவர் ஏத்த
அணிமணியாசனத்திருந்த அம்மாந்தானே.

There are also instances when a Shiva bhakta got converted into a vaishnavite. Chembian, also known as Chenganân, in his previous life was a spider known for its great devotion to Shiva. PeriaPurâNam, authored by Chekizhar, is a poem devoted to the lives of the devotees of Shiva (the devotees known as Nâyanmârs), and the spider episode figures in that PurâNa. Verses in Peria Tirumozhi (6.6) describe the factors that led to Chembian's conversion to a Sri Vaishnavite. Apart from the above evidence, Tirumangai Azhwar also provides solid proofs for the existence of pundits well versed in Sanskrit as well as Tamil (ibid 7.8.7).

Regarding the founding-fathers who exercised powerful influence to maintain the uniform cultural unity and identity of India, reference is invited to page 326 of Ref 27: "Hence the antiquity of ancient Sanskrit works, ought not to be decided on the strength of stray allusions which were added in later times. But whatever be the merit of the theory that Chanakya wrote on Artha, Nyâya and Kâma and that he was also the Dramidâcharya referred to by Ramanuja in his Sri Bhâshya, it cannot be denied that that he was one of the most learned men of his age and the first of the series of great South Indian scholars e.g., Nâgârjuna, Dinnâga, Buddhadatta, Dharmapâla, Shankara, Ramanuja, Ananda tîrtha, Mâdhava, Shâyana and others who were leaders of Indian thought and the torch bearers of culture throughout the whole of India from pre-christian times. This fact more than others, emphasizes the unity of India and the continuity of its culture, though the land was always broken up into "fifty-six" states, so far as the administration of public affairs are concerned."

The author dwells at length on the Aryanization and Sanskritization of the south and it is worth noting down here his views on the latter (p213 ibid): "Agattiyanâr and Tolkappiyanar introduced into Tamil a few tadbhavas, i.e. Sanskrit words which have been fitted into the phonetic framework of Tamil. They are found in the sutras of Agattium that are quoted in the commentaries of the medieval age and in the grammar of Tolkappiyanar, but Agattiyanâr respected the genius of Tamil sufficiently, to invent Tamil words for most of the technical terms of grammar. The percentage of words borrowed from Sanskrit is few or nil in the earliest extant poems, but goes on gradually increasing as time passes; so much so that the percentage of Sanskrit words in a poem may be taken to be roughly indicative of its age."

Towards the latter half of the first millennium AD, a new style of Tamil writing known as Manipravâla, became popular. (Mani= diamond, pravala=coral) It is essentially Tamil language with Sanskrit words interspersed, in such an easy and flowing manner that the Tamil words are written in their own ligatures while the Sanskrit words are retained using alphabetical Sanskrit letters either in the devanâgiri script or the grantha-akshara. This style facilitates large scale induction of Sanskrit vocabulary into the medium of Tamil. Manipravâla, for the Tamil speaking people, is a vara-prasâda, indeed a boon. It has the ease of communication facilitated through the simple Tamil grammar and immense value added with the inclusion of words in original Sanskrit. Rahasya Traya Sâra, of Swami Deshika is a work written in Manipravâla.

Deshika pointedly refers to Agattiyanâr by his other name, Kumbhî sûnu (Paduka Sahasram 2.9), and lists the spectacular achievements of this diminutive sage who had performed super human wonders. He sipped the ocean. He swallowed and digested the demon Vatapi. Such a marvelous sage's powerful language became the vehicle for Shatakopa to convey the Vedas. In fact, the Tiruvâi Mozhi of Shatakopa throws light on the difficult sections of the Vedas which are otherwise difficult to comprehend. Tamil Prabandam acquired the status of the Vedas and what is more the Azhwars made the otherwise intractable Vedic content accessible in Tamil to all men and women (Daya-Shatakam 3). The Tamil poems of Nammâzhwar became universally accessible (Dravidopanishad TR 4).

|| अगस्त्यप्रसूतात्विति परिजगृहे भूमिकाभेदयोग्या ||

The Discovery of Tamil Prabandam
It appears Ranganatha Muni, popularly known as Nâtha Munigal, grandfather of Yamunâchârya, was enthralled to listen to the panegyric sung in praise of the lord Aravamudan at Sarangapani Temple, Kumbakonam, drinking deep the ten verses sung by the

temple priest and particularly his attention was drawn by the concluding line in the 11th verse which states that the ten verses form a part of the thousand (Tiruvâi Mozhi 5.8).

குழலின் மலியச்சொன்ன ஒராயிரத்துள் இப்பத்தும்
மழலைதீரவல்லார் காமர்மானேய்நோக்கியர்க்கே.

Nâtha Muni wanted to know the remaining 990 verses but he was informed by the priest that they were not available and that further enquiry should be conducted at the place Kurugûr, the place of origin of the author of the verses viz. Shatakopa.

Nâthamuni came to Kurugûr in pursuit of the verses but was informed that they were lost. However, he was fortunate to get a small poem in Tamil composed by Madhura Kavi, who was none other than the disciple and a contemporary of Shatakopa himself. Nâtha Muni was filled with joy and hope and resolved to go for the search in right earnest. He worshipped Shatakopa just as Madhura Kavi Azhwar had done and he used Madhura Kavi's own composition (the poem beginning with கண்ணிநுண்சிறுத்தாம்பு) to invoke the munificence of Shatakopa, who, after having fulfilled his mission as a world teacher (as an *Avatara Purusha*), and after executing his role as the *Prapannajana Santâna Kûtasthar* (in response to an order from the Divya Dampati), had gone back by then to Sri Vaikunta with his status restored to that of a Nitya Sûri viz. Vishvaksena.

The crowning example of Acharya Bhakti (*âchâryopâsanam-* BG 13.7) is that of Madhurakavi Azhwâr's. To him even the mention of the name of his Acharya viz. Tenkurukur Nambi, would bring back pleasant memories and therefore, would trigger the springs of nectar in his mouth (*amudu ûrum*-1). He would often roll over the name in his tongue and derive immense pleasure from it. It is an ardent Vedic prayer for one to be blessed with intellectual vigour, sweet speech and nectar-like music to experience the *Brahmânubhava* of Vedic chanting (e.g. *"jihvâ me madhumattamâ"*). Madura Kavi derived such pleasure by reciting Tiruvâi Mozhi. It is the music of Tiruvâi Mozhi (யாழின் இசையே அமுதே) which, incidentally, brought Nâtha Muni to Tenkurukur.

He recalls how fortunate he was to get a glimpse of the Lord's lustrous physique (*karia kola tiruvuru-3*) thanks to his belonging to Kurugûr Nambi. How fortunate he was to come under the influence of Shatakopa when helplessly he stood rejected by the high-ranking Vedic pundits (*mikka-4*). Hence for him, Shatakopa acted as father, mother, friend, philosopher, guide and master. He turned a new leaf with his wayward behavior becoming a thing of the past thanks to his devotion (*anbu-5*) for Kurugûr Nambi. The transformation is for good and it has imparted eligibility to him to sing the glory of his master. (*tan pugazh-6*) A glance from his master has wiped clean of all the old sins (*pandai valvinay-7*) and he would take efforts to popularize the Tamil compositions to all the people living in all the eight directions. Giving wide publicity is justifiable since the compositions reveal the central teachings of the Upanishads and are couched in a metrical melody of a thousand-verse meant for immersing the devotees of God in a sea of joy. (*adiyavar inbura-8*). What is more, the teachings, given in simple Tamil and set in soul-stirring music (*nirka pâdi*), stays put in my mind forever (*nenjul niruttinân-9*)! The chastising influence of Tiruvâi Mozhi is so great that even the brute among men can get benefitted since it has the power to correct (*tirutti pani kolvân-10*) and instill devotion. And make the devotee enjoy the Bliss of Vaikunta.

நம்புவார் பதி வைகுந்தம் காண்மினே

Swami Deshika has highlighted the significance of the poem of Madhura Kavi (by casting them in ten epithets such as *inbattil* etc. see Ref 32), and has provided copious references to Tiruvâi Mozhi for those epithets. The Ref (ibid) traces the line of Guruparampara: from Nathamuni onwards upto Ramanuja.

How Madhurakavi discovered his guru is an interesting episode to narrate. It appears, he, a Brahmin, had gone to Kashi in quest of higher learning but was disappointed for not getting an appropriate guru whom he was looking for. He was feeling ill at ease for having wasted his time and energy in coming over to Benares. When he was thus bemoaning his plight, he saw suddenly a bright hallow-like effulgence of light in the southern sky beaconing him to move southwards and he did follow the path of "the lead kindly light'. The light brought him all the way down south to Azhwar Tirunagari and after reaching the intended destination the light is said to have disappeared. He saw the bright face of Shatakopa seated in the hollow of a tamarind tree. He was captivated by the pleasant fragrance of vakula- flower-garland (*vakula sumanah vâsanâm-udvahantîm*) adorning the shoulders and the bright face of Shatakopa, with eyes drawn inward in contemplation and mind lost in divine experience. He saw a different sun so to speak: *vakula bhûshana bhâskara*.

Madhura Kavi achieved the object of his search. He saw before him the very embodiment of knowledge he was looking for. It was a meeting of two great minds, a disciple and a guru in waiting. Swami Deshika while showcasing this picture of Shatakopa offers his salutations to him (Shatâri), in the third verse of Paduka Sahasram.

आम्नायानां प्रकृतिमपरां संहितां दृष्टवन्तम्।

Now we can very well appreciate the anxiety of Nâtha Munigal to get the complete works of Kurugûr Nambi. He drew inspiration and motivation from the poem, *kanninun chiruthambu* mentioned earlier, and it served him as a mantra to achieve his objective. He is said to have embarked upon a yogic exercise to establish contact with Shatakopa and thanks to Providence and the Divine Will, his efforts were crowned with success. Shatakopa is said to have appeared before him during trance (*yoga sâkshâtkâra*) and imparted to him not only Tiruvâi Mozhi but also verses including that of other Azhwars totaling about 4000, the entire collection known as Nâlâyira Divya Prabandam. A major portion of the 4000 is contributed by two Azhwars alone- Nammâzhwar's 1296 verses and Tirumangai Azhwâr's 1253 verses i.e. a sum of 2549 verses. Tiruvai mozhi (TVM) is the manual for Prapatti and one of the four books (*Grantha Chatushtayam*) prescribed for study. It is dealt with in chapter 14, titled Bhagavad Vishayam.

In Guruparampara Sâram, Vedânta Deshika, while tracing the line of Acharya(s), makes it clear that the Tamil Divya Prabandam would serve as the equivalent of the philosophy of Vedânta for everyone in this kali yuga. In Swami's own words:

பராங்குச பரகாலாதி ரூபத்தாலே அபிநவமாக ஒரு
தசாவதாரம் பண்ணி மேகங்கள் சமுத்ர ஜலத்தை
வாங்கி ஸர்வோபஜீவ்யமான தண்ணீராக உமிழுமா
போலே வேதார்த்தங்களில் ஸாரதமாம்சத்தை ஸ்ர்வரும்
அதிகரிக்கலான பாஷையாலே ஸங்க்ரஹித்து காட்டினார்.

The Swamy goes to the extent of saying that the 18 books belonging to the domain of vidyâ-sthâna, listed earlier have not only become redundant but even burdensome-*chumai* (vide Adhikara-Sangraham). Is the Tamil Prabandam inferior to Sanskrit in any way because of the tag that Tamil is a mleccha bhâsha? No, certainly not. Even the Nitya Sûris have never got tired of listening to it (*kettu ârâr*) though the poetical composition is intended as a listening-pleasure to the devotees (*thondar*). Why should the devotees suffer an inferiority complex? On the contrary they should feel immensely elated and proud of the language for its capability to communicate Vedânta. Nammâzhwar was not taught by anybody but he was blessed with the knowledge directly from *Sriyah-Pati* and he for his part served only as a medium for the flow of the verses from his sacred lips (*tiruvâi*).

Madurakavi's andâdi is one of the 24 poems that go up to make the Divya Prabandam. It is included in the First Thousand (representing Pranava Mantra) as the last prabanda. The short poem is recited before and after the recitation of TVM, even as the sacred Pranava in relation to Vedas. The four works of Nammâzhwar are considered as representative of the four Vedas and the six poems of Tirumangai Azhwar are the equivalent of the six limbs (*angas*) of Vedas. The Tamil Vedas replaced the Sanskrit. Nammazhwar became the Guru for Kali Yuga even as Veda Vyasa was the Preceptor for Dvapara Yuga. The following extract is from Ref 33.

இப்படி அநுசூயாதி குணயுக்தராய் "ப்ரணிபத்யாபி வாத்யச" இத்யாதிகளிற் படியே ஸம்யகுபஸந்நரானவதிகாரிகளைப்பற்ற யதார்த்த தர்சிகளாய் யதாத்ருஷ்டார்த்தவாதிகளான வ்யாஸ போதாயநாதிகளாலே யதாதிகாரம் ப்ரவ்ருத்தமான வேதாந்த ஸம்ப்ரதாயத்திற்கு இந்த யுகாரம்பத்திலே ப்ரம்மநந்யாதிகளுக்கு பின்பு நம்மாழ்வார் ப்ரவர்த்தகரானார்.

Prophecies Galore

Srimad Bhagavatam (11.5.38, 39) predicted the birth of azhwars on sacred river banks and it came true. For example, Nammazhwar and Madurakavi took birth on the banks of river Tamraparani at Tirukkurugur and Tirkkolur respectively. Bhavi-shyat PurâNa (vide the section Kurukapura Mahathmyam) envisaged the birth of Nammazhvar. The prophesies did not stop there. Nammazhvar himself had predicted the birth of Ramanuja as suggested in the following verse of T.V.M.

பொலிகபொலிகபொலிக போயிற்றுவல்லுயிர்ச்சாபம் நலியும்நரகமும்நைந்த நமனுக்குஇங்குயாதொன்றுமில்லை கலியும்கெடும் கண்டுகொண்மின் கடல்வண்ணன்பூதங்கள்மண்மேல் மலியப்புகுந்துஇசைபாடி ஆடியுழிதரக்கண்டோம்.

The birth of Ramanuja at Sriperumbudur brought immense pleasure and relief to Alavandar. However, he became anxiety stricken once again when he came to know that the young lad was under the tutelage of Yadava prâkâsha, a staunch Advaitin. The bright lad disagreed with the teachings of his guru and parted company (p114 of Ref 34).

"After giving up his discipleship to Yadava-prâkâsha, Ramanuja is now studying the scriptures by himself, and according to the behest of Sri Kanchi-purna, he everyday fetches a jar of water from the sal-well (62 of Ref 35) for the worship of the Lord". Yamuna's joy knew no bounds on hearing this (see 420 onwards of Ref 36). Then and there he composed eight hymns of salutation to the Lord. And adressing Mahapurna he said, "My child, without delay please bring Ramanuja here. It is good to have him included in our group." On hearing this, Maha-purna saluted the holy feet of the Guru and started for Kanchipuram. Rest of it is history.

The Cardinal Message
It would be appropriate to conclude this chapter on languages by highlighting the two most important advantages of knowing the Tamil language. The whole world admires Tirukkural as it is the finest book on the Art of Living in the society. The second more important than the former is of course the Poem TVM, the reading of which not only gives pleasure here in this world but in the world beyond as revealed in the following lines.

நாவினால் நவிற்று இன்பமெய்தினேன்
கேட்டு ஆரார் வானவர்கள் செவிகினிய செஞ்சொல்லே.

3. English Influence: Boon or Bane?

Great Britain has played the pioneering role in cherishing and nourishing democratic ideals throughout the World in general and India. For, Britain ruled India for more than a century and taking into consideration the trade relations the connection stretches far back in time to 1600. However, to put the records straight, the government of India was assumed by the crown in 1858. We must go eight centuries back in time reckoned from the present when England had put forward her first step in empowering people the right to govern themselves. It was in the year 1215 AD that the monarch, King John, granted liberty through the Great Charter, Magna Cârta, signing under pressure from his barons, at Runnymede. Among the chief provisions of the charter was that no free man should be imprisoned or banished except by the law of the land and that supplies should not be exacted without the common council of the realm.

From then on, Civil Liberties was the main topic of discussion in the Royal and political circles. Liberty was in the melting pot of heated debates and the great luminaries, through their forceful writings and powerful speeches, shaped the course of political history. We may mention a few of the landmark events and books "from the mighty minds of old" that have left "foot prints on the sands of time".

"The Prince"

In the study of politics, the 'New Learning' finds clearest expression in Nicolo Machiavelli's (1469 -1527) work 'The Prince' (1513). Should a ruler keep faith? This is the famous question raised in that book and answered by the author himself.

The author admits that everybody knows how laudable it is for a ruler to keep faith. However, in the world of actual politics, such laudable intentions may be irreconcilable with expediency and interest. "Therefore, a prudent ruler ought not to keep faith when by doing so it would be against his interest and when the reasons which made him bind himself no longer exist. If men were all good, this precept would not be a good one; but as they are bad, and would not observe their faith with you, so you are not bound to keep faith with them". The predicament of a king is very well brought out through an analogy: "The ruler must imitate the fox and the lion, for the lion cannot protect himself from the traps and the fox cannot defend himself from wolves!"

"Institutes of Christian Religion" 1535) by Jean Calvin (1509 –'64)

This book was translated, after a lapse of two centuries, into English by John in 1813. The author expounds the doctrine of original sin and defines conscience.

"Man is under two kinds of government: one spiritual by which the conscience is formed to piety and the service of God; the other political by which a man is instructed in the duties of humanity and civility which are to be observed in an interaction with mankind. They are generally and not improperly denominated the spiritual and the temporal jurisdiction, indicating that the former species of government pertains to the life of the soul and the latter relates to the concerns of the present state not only in the provision of food and clothing but to the enactment of laws to regulate a man's life among his neighbors by the rules of holiness, integrity and sobriety.

For the former has its seat in the interior of the mind while the latter only directs the external conduct: one may be termed a spiritual kingdom and the other a political one ...

The definition of conscience must be derived from the etymology of the word. For as, when men apprehend the knowledge of things in the mind and understanding, they are thence said *scire* 'to know' whence is derived the word '*scientia*', science or 'knowledge' so when they have a sense of Divine justice as an additional witness which permits them not to conceal their sins or elude accusation at the tribunal of the Supreme Judge, this sense is termed *conscientia* , 'conscience'. For it is a kind of medium between God and man, because it does not suffer a man to suppress what he knows within himself but pursues him till it brings him to conviction "having no more conscience of sin".

But he who knows how to distinguish between the body and the soul between this present transitory life and the future eternal one, will find no difficulty in understanding that the spiritual kingdom of Christ and civil government are things very different and remote from each other.

For since the insolence of the wicked is so great and their iniquity so obstinate that it can scarcely be restrained by all the severity of the laws, what may we expect they would do if they found themselves at liberty to perpetuate crimes with impunity whose outrages even the arm of power cannot altogether prevent?

Holy scriptures do teach that God reigns by His own proper authority and kings by derivation, God from Himself, kings from God, that God has a jurisdiction proper, kings are His delegates. It follows then that the jurisdiction of God has no limits, that of kings bounded, that the power of God is infinite that of kings confined, that the kingdom of God extends itself to all places that of kings is restrained within the confines of certain countries."

These ideas of Calvin are noble and divine and can as well pass for as the tenets of the Upanishads. These ideas of Calvin of 16th century held sway over two or three centuries, but no further. In the middle of the 19th century the famous economist John Stuart Mill pooh-poohed Calvinism in no uncertain terms and if his essay "On Liberty' is any indication, the era of hedonistic culture was already in place sidelining and ignoring subtle feelings of religion divine in nature. This will also be discussed later at the appropriate time when it was written.

Puritan Age

There is a period in British history called the 'Puritan Age' (1620-1660) when the people no longer tolerated the oppression of the king. So to speak there was a moral awakening (p187 of Ref 22). The political upheaval could be summed up in the struggle between the king and Parliament which resulted in the death of Charles at the block and the establishment of the Common Wealth under Cromwell. Changing ideals caused trauma and misery to the people who longed for personal liberty. Even the great poet Milton (1608-1674) cherished the supreme Puritan principle, the liberty of individual soul before God. It is said that the poet cut short his travels in Europe when he came to know about the uprising in England: "For I thought it base to be traveling at my ease for intellectual culture while my fellow countrymen at home were fighting for liberty."

'Leviathan'

The first general theory of politics in English language appeared in 1651. The author of the book Hobbe (1588 -1679) and this great work "is not an apology for the Stuart monarchy nor a grammar of despotic government".

"Two Treatises of Government" by Locke (1632-1704) –English empirical philosopher who had a great influence on the 18th century philosophy; he was also the author of, "Essay concerning the human understanding" and several works on education, government and religious toleration.

In this history of literary contributions, we should take pride to include the translation of Tiruk Kural into foreign languages. The earlist was from Fr. Beshi of the Society of Jesus (1700 -1742) who translated it into Latin. White Ellis, of the East India Company, who came to India in 1796 translated some of them (120 couplets) into English. Among others who translated the Kural into English are Dr.G.U.Pope (1820 -1908), the Rev.W.H.Drew and the Rev John Lazarus. There are also versions in the French (Ariel) and German (Graul) (see Ref 31).

Bhagavad Gita was translated into English during the rule of Warren Hastings (1732 -1818), the First Governor General of British India. Edgerton is credited to have published a two-volume edition of the Gita, with text and translation, recommended it as an introduction not only to Indian thought but also to Sanskrit language even for beginners.

Jean Jacques Rousseau (1712 -78) –French philosopher, advocate of return to natural state in which man is both good and happy; "Contract Social" (1762) explained the view that society founded on a contract and that the head of a state is not the people's master but their mandatory had profound influence on French thought and prepared the way of the 'French Revolution'.

Voltaire (1694 -1778) spent 3 years in England from 1726 to '29 and his letters on "The English" (1734) showed the French and European reading public, (England) "a land of freedom and common-sense, secular in outlook, tolerant in religion and respectful of the rule of law."

Like Voltaire, Montesquieu (1688 -1755) went to England. The writings in English and French mutually benefited the two nations. In the second half of the 18th century political criticism and philosophical expression became more daring and outspoken. The monument to that era is the 'Encyclope die' (1751 -1772) which synthesized all knowledge representing philosophical outlook.

French Revolution: In May 1786, the French Monarchy was overthrown and the First republic was established. Then followed England's war with France (1793 -1832).

Tracing the further course of history of France, She came under the dominating influence of Napoleon Bonaparte (1769 -1820)."The defeat of Napoleon and the revival of the old European order at the Congress of Vienna (1815) seemed to put an end to the nightmare of revolution and democracy."

There was a sea-change in political awareness of the people of England.

The first to raise the issues of the French Revolution was Edmund Burke (1729 -1797) whose 'Reflections on the Revolution in France'(1790) was an immediate literary success in England and on the continent. The idea that civil government borrows from ecclesiastical ideals was taken note of. There was consensus in the belief that the ideals of religion and government are closely linked. Rational enquiry into political institutions as well as religion was not encouraged since the critical spirit of rationalism is bound to challenge, question and attack and finally destroy the civil and religious foundations of the society.

Burke at the age of 37 entered parliament. He was English Whig statesman, political and philosophical writer and orator. He profiled a statesman in these terms: "A disposition to preserve and an ability to improve, taken together, would be my standard of a statesman." He particularly warned the callous attitude of England towards India: "Great empires and small minds go ill together!" Out of his enquiry emerged the bible of Modern Conservatism.

Year 1776 is an important landmark in the history of the modern world. It was on 4th July 1776 that American Continental Congress declared North American Colonies to be free and independent of Great Britain; the discovery of Steam Engine by James Watt in England also took place in this year; besides in this year two most significant books (one on politics and the other on economics) were brought out by two luminaries –Bentham and Adam Smith both from England.

Jeremy Bentham's life (1748 -1832) spanned a long period of transition in British history; while experiencing the 18th century autocracy at its worst, he could perceive the firm outlines of 19th century democracy. His life reflects the transformation of his country. Bentham was a Tory until 1808 and he became a radical democrat at the age of 60. He was more interested in reforming the law than practicing it. He considered no justice was too small and no human being unimportant. His voice of liberal humanity combined a rare degree of devotion to general humanitarian causes and his willingness and capacity to do small chores and attend to petty details.

Bentham wrote the book 'Fragment' in 1776. He pragmatically describes the nature of political society in terms of obedience: the indestructible prerogatives of mankind have no need to be supported upon the sandy foundations of a fiction. In this early work of Bentham there is more than a touch of Burke.

Government is not based on metaphysical generalities –it is more psychological than logical. It is governed by interest and advantage –advantage being understood in relation to empirical needs of the individual in society where as Burke looked upon interest as the product of historic groups, the individual occupying a subordinate position by comparison.

First law of nature is to wish your own happiness; and in the prevailing atmosphere of united voices of prudence and pervading benevolence, "seek your own happiness in the happiness of others."

Bentham was among the principal founders of the University of London. He was a strong admirer of US which he considered as the only 'pure democracy'. He believed matchless constitution can work wonders – any formula devised by men could meet all contingencies of real life –greatest happiness of the greatest number; object standard by which individuals could agree on personal happiness; passions and prejudices divide men; great principles unite them.

Incidentally, the most famous book, "Democracy in America" was written by Tocqueville during 1835 –'40. This work and the next book that follows can be considered as modern version of Charvaka founded by Bruhaspati, guru of devas.

<u>"The Wealth of Nations" (1776)</u>
The author of the above book, Adam Smith (1723 –'90), is regarded as the founder of Economics as an area of study used for production. The book was the first of its kind giving a full-scale treatise on political economy covering production, distribution and consumption. Adam Smith in this treatise analyzed the past and drew conclusions with practical implications for policy frame work. The basic thrust of modern economic thinking is not different from what Smith had covered in his treatise. The main thrust is how the

wealth of a nation increased. He found the engine of economic growth in the division of labor and specialization which led to increased production; technical progress and accumulation of capital. According to Smith the prosperity of a nation is determined by two important factors: the degree of productivity of labor and the amount of productive labor that is being employed. The treatment includes related aspects such as exchange, capital, value and distribution. He maintained that the division of labor is not a result of human generosity but an outcome of the natural tendency of human beings to opt for mutual exchange and cooperation purely out of self-interest and the desire to possess the goods of others.

The other important factor for promoting growth, according to Smith, is capital accumulation which determines the degree of division of labor and specialization: The more substantial the available capital, the greater the degree of division of labor and of specialization possible. The extent of markets also places a limitation on the extent of division of labor. His reputation firmly established when he published another major treatise, "The Theory of Moral Sentiments". He had the far-sighted vision to discuss different systems of political economy and vehemently criticized the 'mercantalists' and 'physiocrats' and he made a strong case for foreign trade which he believed would maximize the basket of goods and services available to the people. He was in fact advocating a system of free enterprise economy having its own regulatory mechanism which can lead to an optimal allocation of resources. He recognized the need for state intervention to protect the domestic infant industry from foreign competition. For example, Dacca-mull was very popular in those days. To stifle its growth and to protect her industry in Britain the government thought it fit to 'cut the thumb' of the makers to kill the native textile industry. How can 'Moral Sentiments' prevail in a business environment when the norm is *'vyâpâram droha chintanam'!*

Smith might have underestimated malevolence of the Raj". However, one cannot find fault with the laudable intentions of Smith as he took cognizance of other functions of the state –such as security, justice and the provisions of infrastructural facilities. His "Theory of Moral Sentiments" written earlier (1759) was a work devoted purely to those standards of ethical conduct that can sustain the cohesion of society. He also wrote many essays on philosophical and literary subjects and over the years his writings on justice and rhetoric have been found to be evolving towards a complete system of social sciences. His profound ideas could not be accomplished in his life time but had greatly influenced the dominant intellectual outlook of the western world and the history of economic thought. By the end of the 18th century far reaching institutional reforms had taken place reducing the role of governments in many areas and throughout Western Europe. It was in this environment of economic liberation that the 19th century turned out to be a period of industrialization and economic prosperity.

By the time of his death in 1790, five volumes of "The Wealth of Nations" had been published. Vol I & II deal with the theories of production, value and distribution; Vol III depicts the economic history of Europe; Vol IV gives a critical account of the then mainstream ideas of physiocracy (the government that advocates by political economists; the Europeans in those days considered that the soil is the sole source of wealth and only proper object of taxation and mercantilism. Vol V which accounts for more than one quarter of the book is devoted to public finance including a discussion of his famous canons of taxation.

This excellent work of Adam Smith can pass for as the Creator's Manual! Thus, the modern era of materialism too firm roots with "wealth of nations".

प्रवृत्तिलक्षणं धर्मं प्रजापतिरथाब्रवीत्।

The contributions of three Europeans belonging to the 19th century should be mentioned before we conclude since they had tremendous impact on the modern mind: John Stuart Mill (1806 – '73), Alfred Bernhard Nobel (1833 –'96) and Thomas Babington Macaulay (1800 - '59).

"On Liberty"

The author of the above essay John Stuart Mill, was the son of James Mill who was the disciple of the illustrius Jeremy Bentham , a pandit in politics mentioned earlier. The essay of 37 pages, published in 1859, had a tremendous impact on the European's in general and the English speaking people in particular. The issue of 'Liberty' is analyzed from three standpoints:

1. Liberty and authority

A few extracts from the essay would show the concerns of the author to the extent to which society can benefit from high standards of liberty.

The subject of this essay is not the so called 'Liberty of Will', so unfortunately opposed to misnamed doctrine of Philosophical Necessity; but Civil or Social Liberty: the nature and limits of power which can be legitimately exercised by society over the individual. The struggle between Liberty and Authority is the most conspicuous feature in the portions of history with which we are earliest familiar, particularly in that of Greece, Rome and England.

The aim, therefore of patriots was to set limits to the power which the ruler should be suffered to exercise over the community; and this limitation was what they meant by liberty.

What was now wanted was, that the rulers should be identified with the people; that their interest and will should be the interest and will of the nation. The nation did not need to be protected against its own will. There was no fear of tyranny over itself.

The notion that the people have no need to limit their power over themselves, might seem axiomatic, when popular government was a thing only dreamed about, or read of as having existed at some distant period of the past. But according to Manusmrti 7.3, a people need a ruler to be free from fear. But an arrogant king (Vena, for example) was a menace. What is expected of a king (like Prthu) is *vinaya*, humility (41 & 42 ibid).

French Revolution, was an aberration –a sudden convulsive outbreak monarchical and aristocratic depotism. In time however, a democratic republic came to occupy a large portion of the earth's surface, and made itself felt as one of the most powerful members of the community of nations ("the sun never sets in the British Empire").

Phrases such as "self government" do not express the true state of the case. The "people" who exercise the power are not always the same people with those over whom it is exercised; and the "self-government" spoken of is not the government of each by himself, but of each by all the rest.

Like other tyrannies, the tyranny of majority ("mobocracy") was at first, and is still vulgarly, held in dread, chiefly as operating through the acts of public authorities.

There should be a limit to the legitimate interference of collective opinion with individual independence: and to find that limit, and maintain it against encroachment, is as indispensable to a good condition of human affairs, as protection against political depotism. The practical question, therefore, is where to place the limit –how to make the fitting adjustment between individual independence and social control –is a subject on which nearly everything remains to be done.

The likings and dislikings of society, or of some powerful portion of it, are the main thing which has practically determined the rules laid down for general observance, under the penalties of or opinion (that powerful portion in the Indian context, according to Manusmrti was the Brahmin community).

The only case in which the higher ground has been taken on principle and maintained with consistency, by any but an individual here and there, is that of religious belief. Those who first broke the yoke of what called itself the Universal Church, were in general as little willing to permit difference of religious opinion as that of church itself…minorities seeing that they had no chance of becoming majorities, were under the necessity of pleading to those whom they could not convert, for permission to differ.

The great writers to whom the world owes what religious liberty it possesses, have mostly asserted freedom of conscience as an indefeasible right, and denied absolutely that a human being is accountable to others for his religious belief. Yet so natural to mankind is intolerance in whatever they really care about, that religious freedom has hardly anywhere been practically realized, except where religious indifference, which dislikes to have its peace disturbed by theological quarrels, has added its weight to the scale.

The object of this essay is to protect the individual's freedom… In the part which merely concerns himself, his independence is, of right, absolute. Over himself, over his body, the individual is sovereign. An individual should air his opinion or thought without fear or favour.

I regard utility as the ultimate appeal on all ethical questions: but it must be utility in the largest sense, grounded on the permanent interests of man as a progressive being.

The only freedom which deserves the name, is that of pursuing our own good in our own way, so long as we do not attempt to deprive others of theirs, or impede their efforts to obtain it. Each is the proper guardian of his own health, whether bodily, or mental and spiritual. Mankind are greater gainers by suffering each other to live as seems good to themselves than by compelling each to live as seems good to the rest. I regard utility as the ultimate appeal on all ethical questions (hedonistic views are based on the animal faith that the physical well-being lies in being utilitarian and it is a refined form of egoism as it is founded on enlightened self love and prudence. Humanism can help in promoting social order, but when it prefers better worldliness to other worldliness it is a secular view and has no stability as better worldliness is still a form of worldliness without any spiritual value —vide p348 of PNS).

Religion, the most powerful of the elements which have entered into the formation of moral feeling, having almost always been governed either by the ambition of a hierarchy, seeking control over every department of human conduct, or by the spirit of Puritanism.

Liberty of thought assumes paramount significance and a thorough consideration of this part of the question will be found the best introduction to the remainder. Those to whom nothing which I am about to say will be new, may therefore, I hope, excuse me, if on a subject which for now three centuries has been so often discussed (reckoning from the time of John Knox, Protestant reformer, 1505 -72), I venture on one discussion more.

2. Liberty of Thought and Discussion.

Strange it is, that men should admit the validity of the arguments for free discussion, but object to their being "pushed to an extreme"; not seeing that unless the reasons are good for an extreme case, they are not good for any case...Is the belief in a God one of the opinions, to feel sure of which, you hold to be assuming infallibility? But I must be permitted to observe, that it is not the feeling sure of a doctrine (be it what it may) which I call an assumption of infallibility.

We can illustrate the argument of Stuart by relating to one of our own experience. The same Brahma Sutras have been the basis of diverse interpretations and the growth of doctrinal variety and richness all of which evolved out of the pregnant and suggestive nature of the original aphorisms of BS. This is the reason why Sri Bhâshyam is polemical in nature.

In order to illustrate the mischief of denying a hearing to opinions because we, in our judgment, have condemned them, it will be desirable to fix down the discussion to concrete cases.

It is among such bold men we find the instances memorable in history, when the arm of the law has been employed to root out those bold men and the noblest doctrines on which they firmly stood their ground. The author cites not one but three cases –that of Socrates, the event at Calvary and Marcus Aureleus (we can cite Vibhishana who expressed his disapproval of the conduct of his elder brother Ravana right on his face, for which he was asked to leave the country instantly. We cannot forget 'The Father of the Nation' during the freedom struggle). History teems with instances of truth put down by persecution and they show that this country (England) is not a place of mental freedom.

For a long time past, the chief mischief of the legal penalties is that they strengthen the social stigma. Socrates was put to death, but the Socrates philosophy rose like the sun in heaven, and spread its illumination over the whole intellectual firmament.

The same can be said of Vibhishana. He criticized his elder brother Ravana for keeping Sita in captivity, at considerable risk to his life. (p350 Ref 24). The couplet in Tiruk Kural (Ref 31) puts it succinctly as quoted below.

இடிப்பாரை இல்லாத ஏமரா மன்னன்
கெடுப்பார் இலானுங் கெடும்.

A king unguarded by trenchant counsel
Needs no foes to come to grief.

No one can be a great thinker who does not recognize, that as a thinker, it is his first duty to follow his intellect to whatever conclusion it may lead. It is as much and even more indespensable, to enable average human beings to attain the mental stature which they are capable of. Where there is a tacit convention that principles are not to be disputed, we cannot hope to find that generally high scale of mental activitywhich has made some periods of history so remarkable.

The German phenomena provides a stirling example. The impulse given at three epochs in the 18th century was important enough to kindle enthusiasm and stirred up the Germans from their foundation. They raised even persons of the most ordinary intellect to something of the dignity of thinking beings.

The rise of intellect alluded to by Stuart has to be perceived in the light of later developments in Germany. The 'rise in intellect' increased the rapid rise in level of S&T and rise in S&T did not augur well for mankind if the writings (and the predictions in particular) of Friedrich Wilhelm Nietzche (1844 -1900) were any indication. In the year 1882, on a particular day he took everyone by surprise by announcing that "God is dead". The news was that educated people no longer believed in God, as a result of rise in rationalism and scientific thought, including Darwinism, over the preceding 250 years. "The story I have to tell," wrote Niezche, "is the history of next two centuries," and went on to predict that the 20th century would be a century of "wars such as have never happened on earth," wars catastrophic beyond all imagining (Ref 4).

Continuing with "Liberty": Learning mathematics makes a mind 'stereotyped'. Geometry for example. There is nothing at all to be said on the wrong side of the question. The particularity of the evidence of mathematical truths is that all the argument is on one side. There are no objections, and no answers to objections. But on every subject on which difference of opinion is possible, the truth depends on a balance to be struck between two sets of conflicting reasons.

The greatest orator, save one of antiquity, has left on record that he always studied his adversaries case with as great, if not with greater intensity than his own. Cicero (106 – 43BC) practiced as the means of forensic success, requires to be imitated by all who study any subject to arrive at the truth (Ramanuja arrived at the truth of Visishtâdvaita only after pointing out all the flaws in the doctrine of Advaita).

Stuart highlights the need for a sound argument: he must know them in their most plausible and persuasive form; he must feel the whole force of the difficulty which the true view of the subject has to encounter and dispose.

If the teachers of mankind are to be cognizant of all that they ought to know, everything must be freely discussed, written and published without restraint.

The fact however is, that not only the grounds of the opinion are forgotten in the absence of discussion, but too often the meaning of the opinion itself. It is for this reason Swami Deshika versified the critisisms on Advaita in his Shata dushani. One must merely utter the verse in clinching the point at issue).

The words which convey it, cease to suggest ideas, or suggest only a small portion of those they were originally employed to communicate.

For want of active debate and discussion the faith or belief suffers. From this time may usually be dated the decline in the living power of the doctrine (to keep alive the doctrine Ramanuja insisted that Sri Bhashya should be studied and discussed by every one).

We often hear the teachers of all creeds (especially Visishtadvaitins) lamenting the difficulty of keeping up in the minds of the believers a lively apprehension of the truth so that the truth may penetrate the feelings and acquire a real mastery over the conduct... The belief in that creed (*siddhant*) ought to produce in a mind thoroughly imbued with it.

The author argues that one's faith should be made of stirner stuff. Then the author undertakes a lengthy discussion on what constitutes the belief of Christians. Laws or morals remain only on paper – all Christians believe the blessed are the poor and those who are ill used by the world; that they should love their neighbour as themselves and so on. They have an habitual respect for the sound of them, but no feelingwhich spreads from the words of the things signified, and forces the mind to take them in, and make them confirm to the formula. Whenever conduct is concerned, they look around for A and B to direct them how far to go in obeying Christ.

The sayings of Christ coexist passively in their minds, producing hardly any effect beyond what is caused by mere listening to words so amiable and bland (this point of Shankara —*shabda janya jyana* —is strongly opposed by Ramanuja).

There are many reasons, doubtless, why doctrines which are the badge of a sect retain more of their vitality (Ramanuja Siddhanta) than other sects (those of Advaita siddhanta).

There are many truths of which the full meaning cannot be realized, until personal experience has brought it home. But much more of the meaning even of these would have been understood, and what was understood would have been far more deeply impressed on the mind, if the man had been accustomed to hear it argued pro and con by people who did understand it (Azhagiya Shingar would convene a meeting – *sathas* - of pandits and conduct heated debate over a particular topic. This form of open discussion will educate the audience in no small measure).

The Socratic dialectics, so magnificently exemplified in the dialogues of Plato, were a contrivance of this description.

From where the Christian morals originate from? Stuart traces the history of Christianity from the times of Old Testamant: a system elaborate indeed, but in many respects barbarous, and intended only for a barbarous people. St Paul, a declared enemy to this Judaical mode of interpreting the doctrine and filling up the scheme of his Master, equally assumes a pre-existing morality, namely that of the Greeks and Romans; and his advice to Christians is in a great measure a system of accomodation to that; even to the extent of giving an apparent sanction to slavery. What is called Christian, but should rather be termed theological, morality, was not the work of Christ or the Apostles, but is of much later origin, having been gradually built up by the Catholic church of the first five centuries, and though not implicitly adopted by moderns and Protestants, has been much less modified by them than might have been expected (the reader may compare our own religion's high water-mark that was extending to far earlier Vedic times).

From several standpoints, Christian morality is incomplete and one-sided. It has all the characters of a reaction; it is, in great part, a protest against Paganism. Its ideal is negative rather than positive; passive rather than active; Innocence rather than Nobleness; Abstinence from Evil rather than energetic Pursuit of Good; in its precepts (as has been well said) "thou shalt not" predominates unduly over "thou shalt". In its horror of sensuality, it made an idol of asceticism, which has been gradually compromised away into one of legality. It holds out the hope of heaven and the threat of hell, as the appointed and appropriate motives to a virtuous life; in falling far below the best of the ancients and doing what lies in it to give it to human morality an essentially selfish character, by disconnecting each man's feelings of duty from the interests of his fellow creatures, except so far as a self interested inducement is offered to him for consulting them. It is essentially a doctrine of passive obedience.

I believe that other ethics than any which can be evolved from exclusively Christian sources, must exist side by side with Christian ethics to produce the moral regeneration of mankind; and that the Christian system is no exception to the rule, that in an imperfect state of the human mind, the interests of truth require a diversity of opinions (the ISKCON movement has gone a long way in realizing the idealsof Stuart!) Stuart closes the second section by show casing 'the real morality of public discussion'.

3. Individuality as one of the Elements of Well-being

The need for individuality is stressed. It is desirable in short, that in things which do not primarily concern others, individuality should assert itself.

If it were felt that the free development of individuality is one of the leading essentials of well-being. This will not be acceptable to us who seek freedom from "the fetters of sensuous, spurious individuality and elevate ourself to the noble level of adhyâtma". This kind of an awareness is too much to expect from a westerner! However we have to learn the mind of a westerner!

Wilhelm von Humbolt: "The Sphere & Duties of Government" – the end of man, or that which is prescribed by the eternal or immutable dictates of reason, and not suggested by vague and transient desires, is the highest and most harmonious development of his powers to a complete and consistent whole; that, therefore, the object towards which every human being must ceasely direct his efforts, and on which especially those who design to influence their fellow men must ever keep their eyes open, is the individuality of power and development; that for this there are two requisites, freedom and variety of situations; and that from the union of these arise individual vigor and manifold diversity, which combines themseves in originality.

His attack on customs and customary practices would be the equivalent of the native criticisms on varNa ashrama dharma.

Though the customs be both good as customs, and suitable to him, yet to conform to customs, merly as custom, does not educate or develop in him of the qualities which are the distinctive endowment of a human being. The human facilities of perception, judgment, discriminative feeling, mental activity, and even moral preference, are exercised only in making choice.

83

Human nature is not a machine to be built of a model, and set to do exactly the work prescribed for it, but a tree, which requires to grow and develop itself on all sides, according to the tendency of the inward forces which make it a living thing.

One whose desires and impulses are not his own, has no character, no more than a steam engine has a character. If, in addition to being his own, his impulses are strong, and are under the government of a strong will, he has an energetic character.

Materialist Stuart rides rough-shod over spiritual Kelvin

The author traces the contour of the religious minded who guard themselves from falling a prey to hedonism and he directs his attack on them. There is an unmistakable atheistic tinge in his attack. Let us continue with his essay.

"I do not mean that they choose what is customary, in preference to what suits their own inclination. It does not occur to them to have any inclination, except for what is customary. Thus the mind itself bowed to the yoke: even in what people do for pleasure, conformity is the first thing thought of; they like in crowds; they exercise choice among things commonly done: peculiarity of taste, eccentricity of conduct, are shunned equally with crimes: by dint of not following their own nature, they have no nature to follow; their human capacities are withered and starved; they become incapable of any strong wishes or native pleasures, and generally without either opinions or feelings of home growth, or properly their own. Now is this, or is it not, the desirable condition of human nature?

It is so, on the Calvinistic theory. According to that, the one great offense of man is self will. All the good of which humanity is capable, is comprised in obedience. You have no choice; thus you must do, and no otherwise: "whatever is not a duty is a sin." Human nature being radically corrupt there is no redemption for any

84

one until human nature is killed within him. To one holding this theory of life, crushing out any of the human faculties, capacities, and susceptibilities, is no evil: man needs no capacity, but that of surrendering himself to the will of God: and if he uses any of his faculties for any other purpose but to do that supposed will more effectually, he is better without them. This is the theory of Calvinism; and it is held, in a mitigated form, by many who do not consider themselves Calvinists; the mitigation consisting in giving a less ascetic interpretation to the alleged will of God; asserting it to be His will that mankind should gratify some of their inclinations; of course not in the manner they themselves prefer, but in the way of obedience, that is, in a way prescribed to them by authority, and therefore, by the necessary conditions of the case, the same for all.

We have italicized the passage to show that Calvinism is close to our Vedânta. Its equivalent with respect to our context would read thus: Every individual as a rational being, has the self legislative will to free oneself from the fetters of sensuous, spurious individuality and elevate oneself to the autonomy of the pure soul. The true meaning of spiritual freedom thus won by moral effort consists in the knowledge that our actions are governed by the Divine sanctions of God (who is the Inner Ruler) and dedication of every act of ours (*krishnârpanam*) as the adoration (*ârâdhana*) of God which in essence is the equivalent of the Latin phrase –*ad majorem dei gloriam* (Jesuit motto).

What a pity that instead of admiring the time honoured Calvinism, Stuart chose to condemn it. Read what he says further:

Stuart: In some such insidious form there is at present a strong tendency to this narrow theory of life and then the author lays bare his complete ignorance on the principle of spirituality. Asceticism, just as Calvinism is a noble way of life rooted in *nivrtti* dharma. The normal humans much less a westerner steeped in hedonism can hardly be expected either to know it or rarer still practice it. If it is

Calvinism Vs. hedonism, only the latter will win in the west! After all, East is east and west is west!

Stuart's wavelength of thought conforms more to the down to earth pravrtti dharma: In proportion to the development of his individuality, each person becomes more valuable to himself, and is therefore capable of being more valuable to others. There is a greater fullness of life about his own existence, and when there is more life in the units there is more in the mass which is composed of them (men of noble mind would rather keep aloof, if we go by the advice of Kural).

சிற்றினம் அஞ்சும் பெருமை சிறுமைதான்
சுற்றமார் சூழ்ந்து விடும்.

The great avoid the low in whom
The low find their kin.

Stuart lays bare his materialistic leanings: "there is always need of persons not only to discover new truths, and point out when what were once truths are true no longer. Simply said, it is obsolosence.

It is true that this benefit is not capable of being rendered by everybody alike: there are but few persons, in comparison with the whole of mankind, whose experiments, if adopted by others, would be likely to be any improvement on established practice. But these few are the salt of the earth; without them human life would become a stagnant pool.

"Persons of genius, it is true, are, and are always likely to be, a small minority; but in order to have them it is necessary to preserve the soil in which they grow. Genius can only breathe freely in an atmosphere of freedom."

Then the author devotes some space for 'originality of thought and action' and condemnation of 'mediocrity'.

86

<u>Concluding Stuart's essay "On Liberty"</u>

If we keep the criticism of Burke against the then ruling British viz "Great empires and small minds go ill together' then Stuart's writing convey a telling message advantageous to India: "a state which dwarfs its men (Indians working in the administration) in order that they may be more docile instruments in its hands even for beneficial purposes –will find that with small men no great thing can really be accomplished; and that the perfection of machinery to which it has sacrificed everything, will in the end avail it nothing, for want of the vital power which, in order that the machine might work more smoothly, it has preferred to banish."

<u>Impact of 'English' on Indians</u>:

As far back as 1792 there was one Sir Charles Grant whose sole object of ushering in English education, it seems, was to impart the knowledge of Christian religion. Take for instance the efforts of Macaulay (1800 -59) to implement it. In 1835 he made English language compulsory in schools and colleges. It seems he used to boast: "If our plans of education are followed up, there will not be a single idolater among the respective classes in Bengal thirty years hence." In order to carry out the plan of crucifixion he armed himself with the mandate from the British Parliament. Here is his speech delivered on Feb 2, 1835.

"I have travelled across the length and breadth of India and I have not seen one person who is a beggar, who is a thief.

"Such wealth I have seen in this country, such high moral values, people of such caliber, that I do not think we would ever conquer this country, unless we break the very backbone of this nation which is her spiritual and cultural heritage, and, therefore, I propose that we replace her old and ancient education system, her culture, for if the Indians think that all that is foreign and English is good and greater than their own, they will lose their self esteem, their native culture and they will become what we want them, a truly dominated nation".

The telling effect of the aforementioned legislation and its follow up unleashed on the people of India can be gauged from what the 'Father of the Nation' had said at Chatam House in London on 20th Oct, 1931: "India today is more illiterate than it was 50 or 100 years ago."

Pandit Madan Mohan Malaviya (1861 – 1946) had conveyed his note of dissent as a member of the Indian Industrial Commission (1918), "about education, the neglect of which by colonial power largely accounted for the backwardness of India. British India would not have lagged behind but for the omission on the part of the government where it had not agreed even to the modest 'Primary Education Bill' sponsored by Gokhale and supported.

Books suggested for further reading relevent to the present context (Ref 37): "An example of this sort of invasion has caused such a difference in Indian culture, history and its status in the world is that of the British. The English attempted to divide and conquer India to ruin the Vedic Aryan Civilization and to demean Indian culture even to the point of trying to make its own people hate everything that is Indian. Dr.S.V describes (p165-6 ibid) that on 3rd July 1835, Lord Macaulay suggested that the only statesmanship of the Britishers to establish permanent imperialist sovereignity over their richest colony India, was to make the Indians Englishmen by taste. This was accomplished through English education."

Before concluding this chapter, we may say a few words about the impact of "On Liberty" on the mind of man. The reader should note the year when it was published. It was in 1859, the later half of the 19th century, considered as the beginning of the era of Industrial

Revolution and it originated from England. Those were the days when inventions and discoveries were the order of the day. There is no doubt that the writings of Stuart must have inspired and motivated many budding European scientists and engineers to contribute, and the well documented developments are any indication, there was indeed a mammoth output in the field of S&T.

We may mention the great Alfred Nobel (1833 -1896) who was, incidentally a contemporary of Stuart Mill himself. It is said that Nobel held 355 different patents, dynamite being the most famous. He must have got the shock of his life wnen he read his own premature obituary which condemned him for profitting from the sales of arms. This report was instrumental in prompting him to bequeath his fortune to institute the Nobel Prizes. The proceeds of the corpus fund, is used to award five prizes, awarded anually to the persons adjudged by the Swedish learned societies to have done significant work during the year in physics, chemistry, medicine, and literature and the person who is adjudged by the Norwegian parliament to have rendered the greatest service to the cause of peace.

"These few persons" (viz. the award winners), according to Stuart, "in comparison with the whole of mankind, are the salt of the earth; without them, human life would become a stagnant pool" : Intellectual giants and emotional pygmies!

In sum, the influence of English education has resulted in the production of youths who go west in search of affluence of the white world! It is justified since 'brain drain is better than brain in the drain'!!

It is worthwhile to conclude, in the words of the English poet Wordsworth who felt heart-sunk about the growing materialism and the absence of plain-living:

"The world is too much with us

   Getting and spending we lay waste our powers".

It is not that 'the world is too much with us' rather we are too much with the world – we expect too much from the world. We have become money maniacs. Simple living cherishing noble ideals are no more. Our high-thinking is reserved only for money-making for expensive living.

As far as the livelihood is concerned it is easily met: "Will not the grains collected from the left overs after in the paddy field sufficient to douse the fire in the stomach? Will not a few helpings of hand-full of water quench the thirst? Will not some old clothe serve as a decent wear?" asks Deshika in his Pentad hymn. When all these are got fair and free, where is the need for money (Ref 61)?

4. The Founders of The Philosophy of Upanishads

Those familiar with Vishnu Sahasranama would recall the third verse from the beginning which mentions the ancestors of Veda Vyasa including his son. He is the great-grandson of Vasishta, grandson of Shakti, son of Parashara and the father of Shuka. Of interest for us here are the works of Parashara and his son Vyasa. The father proudly talks about his son to his disciple Maitreya (vide Vishnu PurâNa 3.4).

"In the beginning the Vedas existed as a massive tree of hundred thousand branches and the hymns having four pâdas. It was unwieldy and very difficult to memorize. It was my son who classified and sorted them out into four broad divisions to facilitate easy bihearting and for this reason he came to be called as Veda Vyasa. Those are the four branches of Vedas popularly known as Rik, Yajus, Sama and Atharvana. He propagated the four through his disciples: Paila for Rig Veda, Vaishampayana for Yajur Veda, Jaimini for Sama Veda and Sumantu for Atharva Veda. The brilliant Romaharsha was made incharge of Itihasas and PurâNas".

Let us briefly outline the contents of the Vedas.

When a hymn has four *pâdas* cast in one or the other *chandas* such as *anushtup*, *trishtup* etc. it is called a rik and since it abounds in riks it got the name Rig Veda. And when the same riks are sung with music, then it is called Sama Veda. Gitâchârya calles Himself as Sama Veda: *"vedânâm sâma vedosmi"* (for an interesting commentary, see Tatparya Chandrika for BG 10.22).

Research scholars, particularly the western types, obsessed with fixing a time frame for the Vedas, have come to the conclusion that Rig Veda is the most ancient one among the four Vedas, and within Rig Veda itself the scholars have supposedly identified several epochs as those of earlier and later ones (Ref 38). Professor Max Muller wrote a brilliant translation of Rig Veda and it was so popular that a second edition was published, along with Shayana Bhashya, under the auspices of Maharaja of Vijayanagaram. A broad outline of the contents of Rig Veda can now be given. The vedas are the very breath of the Supreme Being and have been preserved through the oral tradition.

॥ तस्यै तस्य महतो भूतस्य निश्वासितमेतत् यदृग्वेदः ॥

The Rig Veda contains 10,552 hymns set in different meters spread over1017 groups (Ref 39). They are brought under ten books called Mandalas. Seers or rishis (known as mantra drashtas) are about 700 in number and the most important among them are the seven Rishis given in a particular order, Grtsamada, Vishvamitra, Vamadeva, Atri, Bharadwaja, Vasishta and Kanva and the contributions from these seven main rishis form the contents respectively of Mandala II to VIII. It is the tradition that the two biggest Mandalas occupy the beginning and the end i.e., Mandala I and X and they contain 191 hymns each. Mandala I deals with sacrifices and the tenth one abounds in secular and philosophical hymns.

The oft quoted hymn of Rig Veda (I.189-1) is below.

अग्ने नय सुपथा राये अस्मान् विश्वानि देव वयुनानि विद्वान्।

युयोध्यस्मज्जुहुराणमेनो भूयिष्ठां ते नम उक्तिं विधेम ॥

Incidentally the above hymn is the last mantra of Ishavasyopanishad. The meaning given in (Ref 39): "O Agni! O Lord! Being verily a knower of all things to be known, lead us by an auspicious path to the attainment of desired wealth. Remove from us all deceitful sins. We offer unto Thee profuse words of obeisance."

The word *yajus* means sentences consisting of two or more words. Invariably it is meant for fulfilling the desire of a person, *yajamâna*. Among the Vedas, Yajur Veda occupies a preeminent position. This gets revealed in Narayana Upanishad: Rig Veda occupies the domain of the Sun. The bright rays of the Sun are the Sama Veda. The Purusha occupying the central disc of the Sun is Yajur Veda. (vide the hymn *'adityo va'*). It stands revealed in the conceptualization of Vedas as a bird in Brahmavalli (Anandavalli). The head of the bird is Yajur Veda. The two wings are Rig and Sama Veda. The tail of the bird is Atharvana Veda. This section of the Taittiriya Upanishad is the sixth adhikaraNa of Brahma Sutra – known as Anandamaya adhikaraNam.

There are two branches of Yajur Veda : Krishna and Shukla. The former is also known as Taittiriya shaka. This branch contains 82 sections or *prashnas*: samhita (44), ashtakas (25), latakam (3), aranyakam (8) and mantra prashna (2). The Shukla Yajur Veda was received by Yagnyavalkya directly from the Sun as he was forced to part company from his guru, Vaishampayana whose name was mentioned earlier. This branch has 15 shakas.

Broadly speaking each Veda has three sections –Samhita, Brahmana and Upanishad (Aranyaka). In the mantra section, we find the ecstatic admiration of nature's beauty and bounty expressed in lyrical metrical hymns by the contemplative seers. The Brahmana section deals with rituals and sacrifices, meant for mental integration and self purification. The last section contains the philosophic wisdom known as Vedânta.

In general, there are three forms of Vedic passages —*vidhi* (injunction), artha vâda (recommending prescribed actions and preventing prohibited actions) and mantras. The Vedas teach us the nature of the Supreme Brahman, Sriman Narayana, the mode of worshipping Him and the fruits accruing therefrom (section 231 of Ref VS).

परमपुरुष तत्स्वरूप तदाराधन तत्फल-

ज्ञापक वेदाख्यं शब्दजातं नित्यमेव।

Purusha Sukta (PS)

दद्यात् पुरुषसूक्तेन यः पुष्पाणि अप एव वा।

अर्चितं स्यात् जगदिदं तेन सर्वं चराचरम्॥

The fact that Purusha Sûkta (PS) figures in all Vedas (*sarva vedeshu anugatam*) is cited in Moksha Dharma of Mahabharat accounting for its eminence (Ref 40). The Sukta epitomize philosophical and cosmological thoughts, relating to the genesis of the worlds. The Rig Vedic version describes just the emergence of the world from a sacrifice (*yagnya*) performed by the Devas. With slight variation, the same sequence is present in the Sama and Atharva Vedas. In Shukla Yajur Veda, the Purusha is exalted, stating that the knowledge of the Purusha leads to liberation (*moksha*). Supplementary hymns recounted by Twashta, give details of Purusha's evolution.

Purusha according to the cosmology of the Vedas, is the primordial man and the first principle of the emerging world. He was glorified by the rishis and identified as Lord Maha Vishnu.

In the first part of the Sûkta, the Purusha is described in the philosophical background, in relation to the worlds. In the second part of the Sûkta is recounted the emergence of Purusha, from a huge mythical principle, known as Virat and of His expansion enveloping the earth and other worlds.

॥ तस्माद्विराडजायत ॥

The third part of the Sûkta presents an allegorical sacrifice performed by the Devas, where Purusha is offered totally, as oblation. The world and all the creations sprang forth, out of this offering. In the Rig Vedic version, the emergence of the world from the yagnya is alone described; but, the Purusha, we must note, is described, not as Creator, but as an offering. The Devas helped Purusha become the world, as an outcome of the yagnya. The narration of the birth of Agni and other devatas, and of horses, and of other animals, follow.

"Narayana is not referred to by the name in the Sûkta. But Apastamba identifies Purusha with Narayana.

॥ उपहितं पुरुषेण नारायणेन उपतिष्ठते ॥

"The identification of Purusha with the world would appear to warrant an explanation. As Purusha is transcendental and a distinct one, the rik declares that the visible world is but the Purusha (2nd rik).

॥ पुरुष एवेदं सर्वम् ॥

"The Vedas connect the perceptible world with the unseen Purusha. In the Sûkta, we come across four apparently different relationships between the world and the Purusha. The first is, that of the Purusha with thousand (many) heads, eyes and feet. Then His transcendental character is demonstrated."

॥ स भूमिं विश्वतो वृत्वा ॥

"As also His immortality:"

॥ उतामृतत्वस्य ईशानः ॥

"It is also recited that the expanding universe is fed by Purusha, but He is greater still."

॥ अतोज्यायाँश्च पूरुषः ॥

"The fourth impression produced is that, all this visible world is but a fourth of Him and that three- fourths of Him is beyond the frontiers of the world."

॥ पादोऽस्य विश्वा भूतानि त्रिपादस्यामृतं दिवि ॥

The central message of Purusha Sûkta

The Supreme Being is referred to as Purusha in the first rik of Purusha Sûkta. Purusha is God and He is Purushottama, as per Bhagavad Gita. The heads, the eyes and the feet, in thousands are symbolic of referring to His infinite capacity, of infinite dimension. According to a sutra of Panini, thousand stands for infinity. He is Omnipresent. He existed in the past and He would ever exist in the future. He is, therefore eternal, Omniscient. In other words, He is not constrained by either ether or time. The Lord Almighty, God, pervades, to put it in the language of physics, in a space-time-continuum. What we see, this visible Universe is only a part or only a quarter of His glory. But the greater part, the major three fourths part, is the luminous eternal domain known as Parama Vyoma or Parama Pâda or Nitya Vibhûti. This visible universe, Lîlâ Vibhûti, undergoes continuous modification i.e., subjected to growth and decay since it is subjected to the physical laws of entropy. But His Nitya Vibhuti, His permanent headquarters, does not suffer change but remains ever bright, peaceful and blissful. And it is inhabited by Nitya Sûris or angels who possess auspicious characteristics such as being free from old age, death, sorrow, hunger, thirst etc.

The phenomenal world of ours is the manifestation of Aniruddha which literally means one who cannot contain Himself without being manifested in all things of all categories, animate and inanimate. From Aniruddha, Virat emerged. What was exceedingly subtle, the Virat grew into a Purusha, the creator Four Faced Brahma. The worlds emerged from all sides of the creator, behind and front.

स जातो अत्यरिच्यत। पश्चाद्भूमिमिथोपुरः ॥

The gods performed the sacrifice (*yagnya*) using Virat Purusha as the oblation (*havis*), spring season as ghee (*âjya*), summer as firewood (*idmah*) and autumn as the offering. For this sacrifice, there were seven fence sticks and twenty-one fuel sticks. As an indication of having commenced the yagnya, the primordial Purusha, serving as *yâga pashu* was bound and sacrificed with the participation of Devas, sadhyas and rishis. In this a great physical principle is demonstrated viz. the law of conservation, one is sacrificed for the sake of getting another. There is also the metaphysical truth governing living entities. Yaga is a 'mental yagnya' or '*Âtma Samarpana*' to benefit all. Gitâchârya has underscored this principle in BG 3.10. One should work out one's destiny through sacrifice. The products of the yagnya are spelt out in the following riks. Curds mixed with ghee came forth from the yagnya; then emerged the beasts of the forest and cattle of the country side; the books of rhyme and reason such as, Rik, Sama,

Yajur and chandas emerged; then horses, cows, sheep and goat appeared.

To underscore the importance of what follows, questions are posed in rik 12 and answered in 13. Brahmins came from the Purusha's mouth; the race of kshatriya from the arms; vyshyas from the thighs; and shudras from the feet; moon from the mind; sun from the eyes; Indra and Agni from mouth; Vâyu from breath; the upper worlds from the navel; heaven from the head; earth from the feet; directions from the ears. This is only a symbolic way of stating the fact that all objects proceeded from Virat Purusha, now gets the appellation Veda Purusha. The 16th rik extols the glory of the Purusha who completed the Srishti yagnya, complete with names and forms assigned to all things created.

Vedas underscore a sentient principle behind creation. This knowledge about the order of creation, *Srishti krama*, has come down through an unbroken tradition. Brahma, the Primordial Purusha, taught this to Indra and other gods. Then Indra enlightened by Brahma, taught in his turn to Pratardana and so on and so forth. He who desires immortality should know the Supreme Lord Narayana. The aspirant for immortality should know the purpose behind creation and why he has been created.

तमेवं विद्वान् अमृत इह भवति। नान्यः पन्था अयनाय विद्यते॥

To put it plainly, immortality consists in getting relieved from this world of *samsâra* or the world of *prakrti* known as *Lîlâ Vibhûti* and get transported or transferred or promoted to the *Nitya Vibhuti*. He should deserve and desire for the promotion. He should take up the methodology of *Upâsana* and this is possible only by Lord's grace. The key to secure his grace is through devotion (Bhakti) towards Him and not by any other means. And what is more the devotion can confer the benefits of immortality even here in this life, in this world itself!

The gods (the *prâna* of Brahma) worshipped the Purusha through *mânasa yagnya* which served as a fore runner for attaining final release. Noble souls who undertake *mânasa yagnya* reach the highest region (Sri Vaikunta), the world of the Nitya Sûris (eternally free souls) and enjoy divine communion.

In a brilliant passage in Vedârtha Sangraha (VS 126) Ramanujâchârya outlines the career of *mânasa yagnya* that would lead a devotee to the attainment of Purushottama.

॥ अनुध्यानरूप भक्त्येक लभ्यः ॥

It is customary to recite the Uttara Anuvâka after the completion of Purusha Sûkta. And in addition, two other Sûkta(s) – Narayana Sûkta and Vishnu Sûkta –are also recited along with Purusha Sûkta. It would still be incomplete, if the Shrî Sûkta and Bhû Sûkta are omitted. All in all, the five Sûkta(s), collectively known as Pancha Sûkta are the most important ones recommended for daily recitation. It would hardly take half an hour for complete recitation of Pancha Sûkta.

The Narayana Anuvâka, a sequel to P S, enunciates clearly and elaborately the truth that the Supreme Purusha is the ultimate cause of the prapancha, who pervades, sustains and directs all beings, sentient and non-sentient, who is the architect of names and forms, who is the abode of all glorious perfections, who is absolutely stainless, who is the embodiment of compassion, who is ever engaged bringing round wayward souls and who grants immortality, is none other than Sriman Narayana.

Panchamoveda

More significantly sage Veda Vyasa is considered as the avatar of Lord Vishnu.

॥ व्यासाय विष्णुरूपाय ॥

He is venerated as the treasure trove of the vedas, Brahmanidhi. He was named Krishna Dwaipayana because of his dark complexion and his birth in an island, '*dvīpa*'. Father's admiration mentioned earlier continues further on: "O Maitrya! Vyasa is none other than Lord Narayana Himself. Who else could have authored this great work Mahabharata" (VP 3.4.5).

कृष्णद्वैपायनं व्यासं विद्धि नारायणं प्रभुम्।

को ह्यन्यो भुवि मैत्रेय महाभारतकृद्भवेत्॥

Mahabharata acquired the unique distinction of being called 'Panchamo Veda' or 'The Fifth Veda'. The grand epic is composed of more than hundred thousand verses and it is said that what is found in this is to be found elsewhere (*yat iha asti tad anyatra*). What is not found here do not exist anywhere else (*yannehasti na tat kvachit*). It is encyclopedic!

Accolades galore abound in praise of Vyasa. "He is the lamp of wisdom brimming with the oil, Mahabharata". The wisdom for this mighty work, *Bhârata-Samhitâm*, is supposed to have got distilled through the knowledge he (son of his mother Satyavati, *Satyavati sûnu*) had gained from composing the eighteen purânas and the thorough grounding he had in grammar.

अष्टादश पुराणानि अष्टौ व्यकरणानि च।

ज्ञात्वा सत्यवतीसूनुश्चक्रे भारत संहिताम्॥

PurâNas wax lyrical about the greatness of Vyasa (Ref 41). According to Vâyu and Shaiva purânas, for example, "the venerable Veda Vyasa churned the ocean of the Vedas, using his intellect as the churning rod and produced for the good of mankind the moon called Mahabharata."

॥ जगद्धिताय जनितो महाभारत चन्द्रमाः ॥

Badarayayana (yet another name for Vyasa) did churning of the Upanishads too, to produce the cream called Brahma Sutras (BS). Ramanuja alludes to this amazing feat of Vyasa in his introductory verse of his magnum opus, Sri Bhâshyam.

॥ सुधां उपनिषद्दुग्धाब्धिमध्योद्धृताम् ॥

BS will be explored in greater and greater detail as we proceed.

About Mahabharat

In the two great epics, Srimad Ramayana and Mahabharata, the authors themselves had a significant role to play. Maharishi Valmiki had the blessing of securing a first-hand account of the story of the heroine Sita who had taken shelter in the maharishi's own hermitage while in the other epic but for sage Vyasa there is no story of Mahabharata at all. We shall make the latter clear through illuminating passages from a recent (year 2001) rendering of the story written "in the idiom of the day without affecting the dignity and treasures of thought and philosophical insights of Mahabharat" (Ref 42).

"The Poet: Traditionally, Veda Vyasa is regarded as the author of the Mahabharata. There is also a legend of Lord Ganapathi acting as his scribe. Interestingly Veda Vyasa plays an important role in the story of the epic... When the great Kuru Dynasty was on the verge of extinction, at his mother's request, Vyasa came to the rescue. The two wives of the dead monarch bore two sons, Drtharashtra and Pandu, a servant maid bore a son, Vidura. Vyasa remained on the periphery of the action... When a cataclysm seemed imminent he advised his mother to retire to the forest, and her daughters-in-law accompanied her. He visits the Pandavas and the Kauravas off and on, and offers wholesome advice.

"A few words must be said about the Bhagavad Gita... Its philosophy is based on excellent logic. And in the world of technology, industry, consumerism and speedy advances, peace of mind becomes more and more precious and more and more difficult to achieve. The philosophy of Gita makes it one of the treasures of the world of thought.

"The Mahabharata depicts a world in which values are derived from ideals; (but now in the present) we belong to a world in which values are derived from the satisfaction of the senses; in our world, this derivation is based on the experience of increasing numbers. To put it more clearly, the world of the Mahabharata is one in which a noble life, a pure life, a peaceful life, a pious life are ideals; from these values like truthfulness, self-sacrifice, valour, patience and piety are derived. Ours is an age in which the pleasure of the senses is supreme, and so wealth, worldly shrewdness, power, rudeness, pomp and consumerism become values. With the means of sensual pleasures and the seekers of pleasures multiplying, the pleasures themselves become cruder. The very concept of hero and heroism changes; (i.e., they have suffered a decline viewed from the stand point of the ideal value system).

"The history of nations which became free a few decades ago, including India, shows one thing clearly —above all, a country needs leaders of character. Gandhiji rightly put 'Politics without principles' among the Seven Deadly Sins. No other traits can save a leader if he does not have character. The Mahabharata not only drives home the supreme indispensability of character but examines 'character' itself.

"Brahmins are received with respect always, and society has also high expectations of a Brahmin. Bhishma says, "First and foremost, the king should look up to the gods and Brahmins with reverence". It is recognized that determining the caste by birth does not stand to reason. Nahusha, in the form of a python, asks Yudhishtra, "Who is a Brahmin? What should he know?" and Yudhishtra's answer is, "He is a Brahmin who has the qualities of truthfulness, charity, fortitude, character, non-violence, self-restraint and compassion. He should have the knowledge of *Parabrahma.*" The python questions: "If the Brahmin has no particular 'Karma' and he has to be identified by his character, then caste will have no meaning, will it?" Yudhishtra answers, "Already there has been intermingling among the people and so birth cannot be the criterion. Character is therefore primary... To the Brahmin Gayatri is the mother, the Acharya is the father. Until he studies the Vedas he is a Shudra." The python says, "Truthfulness, self- restraint, tapas, yoga, nonviolence and charity pave the way for salvation, not caste." There is also the story of Dharmavyadha to underline the idea that not caste but conduct is important.

"Vyasa Once More: *Vyasochitam jagat sarvam-* so runs a well-known saying; another well-known saying asserts that whatever is worth knowing is to be found in the Mahabharata and that whatever is not found in the Mahabharata is not worth knowing. It is easy to understand why such tributes have been paid. Our wonder is heightened when we reflect that the author of the Mahabharata was, probably, a man who led an austere life of total renunciation of worldly pleasures. But he has not shut himself up in solitude. The advice given by Kanika, Markandeya, Hanuman and Narada shows what insights this Sage had into the affairs of the world. He is in the world but not of it. He acknowledges his obligations; what is more important, he responds when Satyavati is in distress and thinks of him. All through the epic, we find him intervening when an appeal is made to him or when the course of life demands it. He is wise, clear-eyed, and compassionate. It is this that wins our admiration – that he, wise and detached, is yet compassionate and seeks to direct the course of the lives of those still involved in the affairs of the world. There is a passage which is seldom noticed. He narrates a curious story. Once Lord Indra finds the celestial cow, Kamadenu, in tears. He asks her the reason. She answers, "Lord, I weep at the plight of my son. Look, Lord Indra, there on the earth, a peasant has yoked one of my sons. The yoke is heavy and my son is weak. He has collapsed and he is dying. And yet the peasant is lashing him with his whip. My heart bleeds for the child." What a vision! Kamadenu, the celestial cow, watching her innumerable progeny from the heavens, weeps for the wretchedness of one weak son. Only the most compassionate of men, could have visualized this scene. Earth and heaven, the world of men and the world of nature, are ever present before his eyes. The very same analogy of Kamadenu will be found employed in Ramayana also. The pitiable plight of grief stricken Kausalya because of her separation from her only son Rama is highlighted by Bharata to Kaikeyi through the Kamadenu example, just described (refer sarga Ram 2.74).

"Vyasa is no radical, nor a revolutionary. In fact, the authority of the Vedas is cited again and again and the Varnashrama system is accepted. A revolutionary is concerned with a society in a phase. Vyasa is concerned with the fundamentals of human life itself- and that life a part of the life of the universe. As the spectator of a fast dying epoch, he is concerned with the problem of a moral society and a significant individual life."

The Brahma Sutras
We have said that Veda Vyasa classified the Vedas into the four divisions and churned the Vedas to produce the Fifth, Panchamo

Veda. He also churned the Upanishads and extracted the essence known as Brahma Sutras. It enjoys pre-eminence from the stand point of 'modernism' also. It contains in essentials a critical review of all patterns of philosophical thinking that took shape in the interval between the ancient Upanishads and the time when Vyasa formulated BS. He had taken into consideration the wide-ranging isms which we can put it in the order of "diminishing distance from it": Charvaka, Buddhism of all the principal variations in the tradition, Jainism, Vaiseshika, Nyaya, Sankhya, Yoga, Purvamimamsa, Saivism, Saktaism, and Vaishnavism.

A brief overview of BS is given below (introduction of Ref 43). "The Vedânta Sutras of Badarayana, identified with Vyasa are, by common consent, regarded as the most authoritative and systematic exposition of the Upanishads and recognized as the best manual of Vedânta. On a superficial view, the Upanishads appear to be conflicting and self-contradictory without any trace of logical consistency. But the Sutrakara, with his genius for synoptic knowledge, affirms the continuity and unity of all the texts (BS III.3.1).

॥ सर्ववेदान्त प्रत्ययाधिकरणम्॥

The sutras string together the teachings of the Upanishads and present them as a systematic whole. The Sutra is cryptic or laconic, and is defined as a clear, concise and comprehensive aphorism that should be faultless and free from repetition. The method of employing connected catch-words to arrive at systematic unity is planned and perfected in the BS. It is unrivalled for its metaphysical profundity and spiritual power. From the first Sutra to the last, the arguments develop rhythmically, step by step until the whole scheme is completed. The parts are so organically related with one another and with the whole, that, if a part is destroyed, the symmetry of the whole will also be destroyed. The central idea that pervades

105

the constituent elements in the truth that Brahman is real and spiritually realizable. The aphorist is also a supreme artist, and by the method of *samanvaya*, he reconciles the apparently conflicting Upanishads and harmonizes them into a *coherent* whole. The dominant motive of the Sutrakara is to combine philosophic speculation with spirituality and communicate the wisdom so gained to aspiring humanity. The sutras in their exposition start with the aspiration of the philosopher or *mumukshu* for *Brahmajnâna* and end with the attainment by the *mukta* of *Brahmânubhava*."

BS has other names –such as Uttara Mimamsa Sutra, Vedânta Sutra and Shârīraka Sutra. The first two designations thought apt are not in currency. The name Shariraka Sutra is a hoary title adopted by Shankara and more ancient writers such as Upavarsha and Bodhayana.

Bodhayana, a brilliant disciple of Vyasa is said to have contributed a massive commentary on the BS, known as Vritti grantha. This mammoth work (which Ramanuja had perused) had over ten lakh words for expounding in depth the sutras numbering 545. But this work is lost now.

Vyasa was not satisfied with all his contribution mentioned so far. Probanly what with the descriptions of the war scenes at Kurukshetra in volume after volume, could have unsettled his mind. And the words of Lord Krishna at the battle field would have been troubling him. "He who knows My divine birth and deeds gets freed from rebirth" (BG 4.9). Vyasa had not paid any attention in narrating the childhood of the wonder-kid Krishna – a great omission indeed!

Vyasa chose a secluded spot on the bank of river Saraswati and began ruminating over the cause for his melancholy. Mind-reader Devarishi Narada, the mind-born son of Chatur Mukha Brahma, got a wind of the depression and appeared before Vyasa. Whenever pain and anguish rack the brow, Devarishi Narada would invariably appear like a ministering angel and give the prescription like that of a psychiatrist. This episode occurs in Bhagavatam (1.5.5).

॥ अथापि शोचस्यात्मानमकृतार्थं इव प्रभो ॥

The sum and substance of Narada's analysis and prescription is as follows:

"O Learned Vyasa! You have not sufficiently expatiated on the greatness of the Lord Supreme. No doubt you are the author of great many works such as Brahma Sutra, Mahabharata etc. You are a gifted scholar. But scholarly works don't appeal to everyone. Bhagavatas are like the swan bird, a shade above the average. They are not like the crows, which revel in small dirty pools. Knowing fully well the dangers of samsára, the devotees would prefer to pour themselves in reading and reciting verses, which contain the names of Ananta. They know that by reciting and knowing the greatness of the Lord Mukunda, and by singing and dancing in ecstacy the sins get automatically washed out and facilitate to cross over the sea of samsára. For such people the work need not necessarily be scholarly. Therefore engage yourself in the task of writing the exploits of Mukunda. I am sure being a great scholar you would do poetic justice in portraying the biography of Krishna in particular and avatars of Lord Vishnu."

॥ तन्महानुभावाभ्युदयोऽधिगण्यताम् ॥

Vyasa complied with the prescription and wrote the book known as Bhagavata PuráNa. Veda Vyasa not only got rid of his depression for good but also attained a deep sense of fulfillment. It is worthy of mentioning here that Deshika has also taken Narada's suggestion in captioning his great poem as:

॥ यादवाभ्युदयः ॥

Bhagavatam, the book of avatars of Vishnu, contains twelve books. The first book records the events leading to the narration of Bhagavatam to Parikshit, the only surviving son of Pandavas, from sage Shuka, the son of Vyasa. The second book gives a thumbnail sketch of creation. Book three describes the Lord's descent as a divine Boar and Lord Kapila's teachings on liberation to His mother Devahûti. In book four, Shuka tells several stories, the story of Daksha's yaga, Dhruva charitra, and a glorious account of king Pratu and the parable of Puranjaya highlighting the danger of succumbing to sexual passion. Book five dwells on the awe-inspiring biography of Jada Bharata and his famous teachings on spirituality to king Rahûgana. This book also contains lessons on Geography and Astronomy. Book six has the story of Ajâmila; the disastrous consequences of king Chitraketu who attempted to undo destiny; a curse resulting in his birth as a demon Vrtra; the death of the demon at the hands of Indra; and Indra too rues the consequences of slaughtering Vrtra. Book seven describes graphically the trials and tribulations undergone by Bhakta Prahlada and his rescue by the Lord Himself in the avatar of Narasimha. The remainder of book seven is devoted to the delineation of the code of conduct of righteous living —*varna ashrama dharma.*

The eighth contains an account of Gajendra Moksha, churning of the Ocean of Milk, (*Kshîra Sagara*) for nectar, and an elevating account of Bali, whose staunchness in truth remained unshakable that he kept up his promise to Vamana, avatar of Vishnu. The ninth gives a brief history of the kings of the Solar and Lunar Dynasties; an account of Chyavana, the sage and Sukanya, his loyal spouse, of Ambarisha and Durvasa, of Harishchandra and Purûravas, of Yayâti and a brief account of Sri Ramavatar. But in the whole of Bhagavatam, it is Sri Krishna who holds the centre of the stage. The tenth and eleventh books, devoted to Sri Krishnâvatar occupy more than half the volume of Bhagavatam. Lord Krishna, the Divine child of Vrndavana, the darling of the Gopis, the protector and upholder of Dharma, the teacher of Moksha Dharma, the comrade of Kuchela; the myriad facets of God who descended as avatar of *Vishnu* living amidst men yet remained indisputably God.

Bhagavatam has an edge over Vishnu PurâNa in that there are a few more episodes of Krishnâvatar in the former but not found in the latter. They are, the deliverance of Nalakubara from Narada's curse, the killing of the asura who came as a whirl-wind, the slaying of Aghâsura, the stealing of the maiden's clothes, the gracious unbending to the wives of sacrificers and such charming episodes as those of the Lord's domestic life and the bestowal of His grace on Kuchela and Shrutadeva. There are other omissions as well, which may be deliberate since Parashara confined his teachings to those of Maha Vishnu and His consort Lakshmi and avoided non-Vaishnavite. The omission of Manu's daughter Devahûti in Vishnu PurâNa (1.7.18) has also resulted in considerable deletion of episodes involving her –especially her marriage with Kardama Prajâpati and the birth of her son Kapila as the 10th child and the elaborate Kapila's teachings (Sankhya Philosophy) to his mother. Above all Bhagavatam has the unique distinction of predicting the avatars of (*abhinava dashavatara*) of azhwars in this age of Kali. The first line of the oft repeated verse from Bhagavatam (11.5. 38 & 39) is given below.

॥ कलौ खलु भविष्यन्ति नारायणपरायणाः ॥

Both the purânas mention Purasha Sukta. In Vishnu PurâNa, for example, the highest place is accorded to Sri Purusha Sukta in the child Dhruva's *stuti* (praise) when the Lord appeared in response to the child's penance. It would not be an exaggeration to say that the riks of Purusha Sûkta are rendered into verses in Dhruva Stuti. The following verse occurring in that context will be found no different from the first rik of Purusha Sûkta. (VP 1.12.56)

सहस्रशीर्षा पुरुषः सहस्राक्षः सहस्रपात्।

A few salient points regarding the unique greatness of Vishnu PurâNa may be mentioned:

The Maharishi Parashara begins the narration after recalling the boon he had received from his grand-father Vasishta and the other celebrity Pulastya. There is a story which relates how Parashara came to know the divine secrets. This was the reward he got for abandoning the yaga which he undertook to wreak vengeance on the clan of asuras responsible for the murder of his father Shakti. His surpassing forbearance moved his mentors beyond measure and hence the award of the boon (VP 1.1.26; Sri Bhâshyam p104).

पुराणसंहिताकर्ता भवान्वत्स भविष्यति।

देवतापारमार्थ्यं च यथावद्वेत्स्यसे भवान्॥

VP is ranked highest among the 18 purânas. Yamunâchârya in his Stotra Ratna has praised VP as PurâNa Ratna (4 of Ref 19).

Ramanuja siddhanta rests squarely on the teachings of VP alone and there is not a whisper of a mention about Bhagavata. For, there is a polar contrast in the manner of teachings between VP and Bhagavatam: in the former the teachings follow the guru parampara tradition while the latter it is different. Vyasa equipped his son Shuka for the task of rescuing the King Parikshit from the curse. The said king was fortunate enough to listen to Bhagavatam for seven days and get purified before he was reduced to ashes by the king Tarkshya's bite.

However, Badarayana's BS follow the guru parampara tradition – Jaimini, Kashakrtsna and Audulomi were the disciples. Besides, in the guru-parampara tradition it was mandatory that father should impart his knowledge to his son in particular and then only to the chosen disciples. From these considerations, it is appropriate to compare VP & BS, the teachings of the father and son. And in addition, each of the Upanishads follow the time honoured tradition. Even today this tradition is followed especially with regard to learning Sri Bhashya.

The working of the two mighty minds becomes conspicuous when we take note of the similarity in the style of approach to the study of Brahmam undertaken by Parashara in his Vishnu PurâNa and Veda Vyasa in his Brahma Sutras. It is only proper to assume that the two works are complementary in nature since the topic dealt with is the same one: enquiry into Para Brahmam. There is every indication of the son's learning from the father. The former can pass for as a disciple as much as the latter's disciple Maitreya. Ramanuja pointed out the universal concordance of the two works between son and father, by equating the aphorism BS 1.1.2 with the verse VP 1.1.31 (VS 156).

ब्रह्म स्वरूपविशेषप्रतिपादनैकपरतया

प्रवृत्तं इति सर्वसम्मतम्।

Vishnu PurâNa begins with Maitreya posing a volley of 25 questions to his preceptor Parashara. Though the questions pertain to Brahmam, the surprising thing to be noted is that in all those questions, the word Brahman is conspicuous by its absence and the added surprise is that the addressee Parashara is addressed as Brahman instead! The knower is accorded the status of God who is to be known, the respect par excellence that a disciple can show to his Acharya! It is not without reason. After all the teacher was not new to the student. It is at the lotus feet of Parashara that Maitreya learnt the Vedas along with the six limbs and the dharma Shâstra. The student is clear about what he intends to know as the questions

111

he had posed is regarding the infinite Brahman. And he closes the questionnaire with the following humble request:

॥ ब्रह्मन्प्रसादप्रवणं कुरुष्व मयि मानसम्॥

Out of the 25 questions, the following 8 need to be answered in the order in which they are posed and the reply forms the first Amsha (canto) of Vishnu PurâNa which comprises of six Amshas in all. The subject is broached in a dialogue-like fashion and not a one-sided narration from beginning to end. The added significance is that the fifth amsha is devoted to a biographical sketch of Bhagavan Krishna and what is more this PurâNa is supposed to have been written during the reign of King Parikshit (VP 4.20.53).

Here are the eight questions: (Refer VS 157)
1. How did the world spring into existence?
2. What will happen to it in the future?
3. Who is the root cause of creation of the world?
4. Out of what this world was created?
5. Where was this material lying before creation?
6. Into what will it again disappear?
7. In what proportion the five elements exist?
8. What is the basis for creation of living beings?

Parashara gives answer in a single verse to all the questions. The answer would have been 'Brahmam' if he was not addressed with that word. The *samanvaya* principle comes handy to him enabling him to choose the word Vishnu instead of Brahman. Secondly, he made it unambiguous by specifying Vishnu in his reply and this verse is naturally accorded the pride of its place in SB. This verse is like the title song and here is the verse (VP 1.1.31; SB p105).

विष्णोः सकाशादुद्भूतं जगत्तत्रैव च स्थितम्।

स्थितिसंयमकर्तांऽसौ जगतोऽस्य जगच्च सः ॥

The world came into existence from Vishnu and it is sustained by Him. It is sustained and supported by Him alone. The world is Him, which means that the world is His body. In other words, BS is of a piece with VP in declaring the principle of *sharira shariri bhava* between the Lord and His creations. The relation between Brahman and the universe of chit and achit is that of the relationship between soul and body i.e., an organic inseparable relationship.

"All are parts of a stupendous whole
Whose body nature is and God the Soul."

Having answered succinctly and before proceeding to elaborate, the Maharishi pauses for a while to offer his obeisance to the Almighty God in several verses and he begins with the familiar one uttered during the recitation of Sahasranama —*avikârâya shuddhâya* ...

Manusmrti

वेदेषु पौरुषं सूक्तं धर्मं शास्त्रेषु मानवम्।

भारते भगवद्गीता पुराणेषु च वैष्णवम्॥

Reference was made to the above couplet (but not quoted) in Padma PurâNa which lists four texts, the most important ones in the lore. Purusha Sûkta ranks as the best part of Vedas, even as Manusmrti is the foremost among the dharma Shâstra(s), the Bhagavad Gita is the most cherished part of the Mahabharata and Vishnu PurâNa holds the highest place among the purânas.

We have discussed the Purusha Sukta and Vishnu PurâNa and now we shall bring our attention to focus on the Manusmrti.

Why is Manusmrti so important among the Dharma Shâstra(s)? A verse in Bhagavad Gita (BG 4.1) makes a direct reference to Manu

113

(this fact acknowledged by Maharishi Manu himself, vide Manusmrti 12.117. According to that Gita verse, Bhagavan Krishna says that the same teachings that are being given to Arjuna, were earlier (i.e. during the Krta Yuga) imparted to the first king of the Solar Dynasty viz. Vivasvân, who in turn passed it on to Manu. Patently Manu not only transferred it to his descendant Ikshwagu but has put it in the form of writing, and just as Bhagavad Gita, the text book of verses wrote by Manu, known as Manusmrti, has survived to this day. This book has served as a manual, also known popularly as Manava dharma for time out of mind, and in fact the English word 'man', itself is but a derivative of the word 'Manu'. Hence the teachings contained in Manusmrti are essentially the same as in Gita except that the teachings of Gita were fine tuned in order that it has universal appeal and the teachings which emerged from the lotus lips of Padmanabha at the end of Dvapara Yuga in the battle field at Kurukshetra, were intended, it appears, more for the succeeding Kali Yuga. The fact that today more than 3000 commentaries on Gita exist and are continuing to be written, vouchsafes for the timing of its propagation!

Veda Vyasa also has highlighted the importance of Manusmrti in no uncertain terms.

स्मृत्यनवकाशादोषप्रसङ्ग इतिचेन्नान्य

स्मृत्यनवकाश दोषप्रसङ्गात्॥

The fairly long sutra quoted above belongs to BS II.1.1. The meaning of the sutra is that if we admit the teachings of Kapila then it would mean the rejection of other more important smrtis –such as Bhagavad Gita, Manusmrti, Vishnu PurâNa –all of which uphold the existence of Sriman Narayana. We reject Kapila smrti which argues against the existence of Brahman- *Ishvara / nirîshvara vâda.*

That is what BS fights tooth and nail in rejecting Sankhya of Kapila (See chap 5 of Ref 44).

Manu has emphasized, in no uncertain terms, that a society well founded on the teachings of Vedas and a society consisting of Brahmins well versed in the recitation and interpretation of Vedas, should be the most ideal society one could wish for: "Memorize or perish" (Manu.5.4)! As many as 29 verses in the first chapter (92 to 110) are devoted to the high expectations from Brahmins and verses 111 to the last verse 119 specify succinctly the subject matter of the chapters that follow (chapter II through chapter XII). The first 12 verses of the second chapter of Manusmrti, for example, clearly establish that the teachings are founded on the bedrock of Vedas. Manusmrti is essentially an engine of motivation for the study of Vedas (2.165 to 168). Details such as when to perform Sandhya and the sins that are atoned are repeatedly stressed (2.101, 2). A long period of 36 years of study is recommended for a complete course of study of the Vedas (3.1). Study of Vedas enables one to remember even past lives and help one overcome the travails of *samsâra* (4.145-9). Brahmins are the brain-trust of the Vedas (9.316). The sixth chapter throws light on the practice of yoga (Ref 44).

The 126 verses comprising the last chapter underscore the preeminence of Vedas in unequivocal terms and according to Maharishi Manu no other source of knowledge can explain the rationale behind the pith and marrow of human existence and the purpose or goal of life as elegantly and as clearly as the Vedas. Non-Vedic systems (*vedabâhyâh*) are crooked in their perspective, since they would be found one way or the other established in *tamas* (XII. 96). According to a verse in Bhagavatam (6.1.40) what conforms to Vedas is dharma and what is not is declared as adharma.

The following is from Manusmrti 12.94.

पितृदेवमनुष्याणां वेदश्चक्षुः सनातनम्।

अशक्यं चाप्रमेयं च वेदशास्त्रमिति स्थितिः ॥

Among the several commentaries on Manusmrti, the two old ones in Sanskrit are popular. The earlier (900 AD) is the one contributed by Medhâtithi (for which an excellent English commentary is also available) and the later (1100 AD) one is that of Govindaraja, who, in addition, has written a commentary for Srimad Valmiki Ramayana. It appears that Govindaraja has critically examined the commentary of Medhâtithi as well. We have still a later one authored by Kullûkabhatta, who, in his commentary, has included the views of Medhâtithi as well as Govindaraja. See also Ref 45.

In praise of Manusmrti:
The Sanskrit text was first translated into English in 1794, and translation into other European languages swiftly followed. For Nietzsche, the humane wisdom of Manu far surpassed that of the New Testament... No understanding of modern India is possible without it, and in the richness of its ideas, its aphoristic profundity and its relevance to universal human dilemmas Manu stands behind the great epics, the Mahabharata and the Ramayana" (Ref 46).

"Manu is variously referred to as the father of humanity, as one of the ancient sages, as having established fire as a semi-divine being, who received from God Himself the laws and regulations, as a king in the Krta-yuga, as author of a work in Arthashastra. In the Manusmrti Manu is referred to as a king.

"Manu's work has been held in high esteem. Such remarks (as given below in Sanskrit) testify to the importance traditionally attached to this smrti since early times. The work of Manu is an epitome of the ancient culture of India" (Ref 46).

116

॥ मन्वर्थविपरीता या सा स्मृतिर्न प्रशस्यते ॥

॥ मनुर्वैयत् किञ्चाह तद् भेषजम् ॥

Is Manu relevant to the modern times?

"The principles of Manu's Scheme of Social Organization, repeated very briefly by Krishna in the Gita, and detailed by Bhishma in the Shânti Parva of the Mahabharata, if properly interpreted and applied in modern conditions, can solve all human problems and reconcile Individualism and Socialism, Capitalism and Communism, by pointing out the rational middle course between their irrational and erroneous extremes, and by obviating the psychological difficulties which are being ignored by all the belligerents in the present chaotic war and welter of isms. Psychological difficulties can be overcome only by psychological devices. Human affairs can be administered successfully only with the help of the laws and facts of human nature. Hence Manu applies the principles of psychology and philosophy in organizing human society. Western thinkers are beginning to realize that the difficulties, in the way of success of each scheme covered by the word Socialism, are psychological (Gettell, in his 'Political Science' and Bertrand Russell in his 'Roads to Freedom'), while it is also generally recognized that the extremes of so-called Individualism must be checked. And they are gradually approaching those psychological and metaphysical principles which alone can provide the remedy for the prevalent disease. Thus, Viscount Haldane's Introduction to Miss Follett's "The New State' (1926) and much of Part I of the work, may be regarded as a commentary on Manu's dictum:

॥ न ह्यनध्यात्मवित् कश्चित् क्रियाफलमुपाश्नुते ॥

"No one who ignores the principles of philosophy and psychology can bring any human activities to successful issue" (p 169 of Ref 29).

The fact that Manusmrti is being debated even in modern times goes to show the continued popularity of the book (Ref 47).

We have discussed so far about the importance of Manusmrti. Now we shall proceed with a discussion on the importance of Manusmrti in the *siddhanta* of Ramanuja.

Under whose command (*âdesha*) the universe is governed?

This question is answered candidly in Brhadaranyaka Upanishad (5.8.9) and in Manusmrti (12.122, 123). The reader may refer to Vedârtha Sangraha (para 98) specially reserved for Manu. Both sources cited contend that the chain of command proceeds from the God-Head who is without a second. Looking for identity of views from the lore, compare, for example, Manu (1.21) with VP (1.5.63) containing the same words as given below (Refer Vedârtha Sangraha 17):

॥ वेदशब्देभ्य एवादौ देवादीनां चकार सः ॥

Manusmrti and Vishnu PurâNa

In the former, sages approach Maharishi Manu, who is seated in a highly contemplative mood, expecting the arrival of his learned disciples for giving instructions on Manava Dharma. Quite expectedly the questions posed by the sages are in the realm of functions and duties of humans. In VP, Sage Maitreya approaches Maharishi Parashara and poses a whole set of 28 questions in one breath in which the earlier part of the set pertains to creation (the reader should refer to Tani Shloki for the graphic portrayal of the opening verse '*parâsharam munivaram*' of VP). Responses from Manu and Parashara contain identical views on creation but later diverge since Manu confines himself to a harangue on Mânava Dharma while Parashara dwells more on the Adhyâtma Shâstra. The views on creation are identical with the Purusha Sûkta. There are several

118

areas of commonality between the two books. The following verse in the section dealing with creation occurs in both the books. (Manu 1.10; VP 1.4.6)

आपो नारा इति प्रोक्ता आपो वै नरसूनवः ।

ता यदस्यायनं पूर्वं तेन नारायणः स्मृतः ॥

Bhagavadgîtâ

Among the four most important source books from the lore on *adhyâtma shastra* (as per the verse quoted earlier) we have so far discussed three of them namely, Purusha Sukta, Manusmrti and Vishnu PurâNa. We shall now briefly discuss the fourth remaining book, Gita. It merits mentioning here that Gitâchârya Himself vouchsafed for the unitary nature of the teachings by revealing that He had imparted the same teachings to Maharishi Manu in an earlier epoch far distant in time and hearing this revelation from the Lord, Arjuna became awe-struck (*tvam âdau proktavâniti*- BG 4.4). The reader may also refer to the authors book (Ref 3).

Gitâchârya mentions about the close link that exists between the teachings of shrutis and smrtis.

ऋषिभिर्बहुधा गीतं छन्दोभिर्विविधैः पृथक् ।

ब्रह्मसूत्रपदैश्चैव हेतुमद्भिर्विनिश्चितैः ॥

"The teachings (that are being imparted to Arjuna) have been sung by seers like Parashara and Manu in various ways (*smrtis*), in the various distinctive hymns of the shrutis, and also in the well reasoned and conclusive words of the Brahma Sutras."

The reader should understand the implication of the word '*vinishchitaih*' occuring in the above verse. Arjuna had asked Bhagavan to decide and tell (*nishchitam brûhi*) while Bhagavan

119

responds that a well reasoned (*vinishchitaih*) teachings such as BS already exists! That goes to show the great importance of BS.

Referring to (p.viii of Ref 48): "The Brahma Sutras come to the scene at this stage of evolution of Vedânta and they supply the dialectical and substantiating frame-work of thought underlying the Upanishads. Their function is to cordinate the teachings and set forth the logical justification of the doctrines advanced. They work out lines of interconnection and modes of critical vindication. Reason is the supreme instrument in this process. This characteristic of the work is manifest in the very nature of each section trying to solve a problem and develop a decisive conclusion in answer to the challenge of a prima facie view. It is for this very reason that the first aphorism characterises the work (BS) as the nature of Jignyasa or enquiry. It is perhaps this idea that the author of the Gita has in mind when he describes the BS as 'reasoned' and issuing in decisive conclusion. But something more by way of textual completion is needed. The Sutras embody the barest logical principles. They justify and coordinate, but the substance of thought as thus justified and coordinated remains unformulated. The central inspiration and the lofty poetry of the Upanishadic utterances have to be regathered and reduced to a single statement eschewing the dialectical and synthesising scaffold. There is a clear necessity for the condensation of the positive essence that emerges out of the justification. Only thus the Vedânta secure unity of effect and consolidation of theme. The Gita is the fulfilment of this fundamental necessity. It is a consolidated restatement of the vision of the Upanishads in their very style and living idiom. If the Upanishads represent revelation, and the BS represent the justifying philosophical argumentation, the Gita represents the re-revelation of the truth emerging out of the justification. In the language of Indian logic the Upanishads declare the *Pratignya*, the sutras add the *Hetu* and Gita gives the *Nigamana*. This in principle is the outlook governing the adoption and utilization of the three basal texts."

120

Regarding the three basal texts: The school of Vedânta accept the Triad as the fundamental or canonical or basal texts, known as *Prasthâna Traya*. The Upanishads are pre-eminently and in the primary sense the books of Vedânta and they constitute the Shruti Prasthana. BG is assigned the status of *Smrti Prasthâna* and BS is given the place of *Nyâya Prasthâna*. From the standpoint of checking the corrupting influence of other systems, especially the philosophy of agnostics and atheists so rampant in this Kaliyug, it is needless to mention that *Nyaya Prasthana* is accorded the highest importance in Visishtâdvaita.

The other two schools –Advaita & Dvaita – establish their respective philosophies in a similar manner. "All the philosophical schools are deduced from the authority of the *Prâsthana Traya*. Each an individuality which clearly marks it off from the rest. The orthodox method in India of a system by a refutation of the rival schools. This method of formal logic has so much stamped itself on the social life of followers of each system that an attempt at a sympathetic study of all systems with a view to discover the points of rapproachment is declared unphilosophical.

In India the view of life is one with the way of life and philosophical differences enter into the details of life and create their own tradition. This often sets free a spirit of exclusive institutional loyalty which is alien to the synthetic study of Vedântic thought. The Gita relies more on the way of synthesis than of siddhanta and the comparative method rests on the guidance of the Gita spirit (p122 of Ref49). The small book which highlights the differences between the three siddhantas is suggested for further reading (Ref 50).

In order to develop an unshakable intellect Ramanuja had insisted that every student should go through the 'reasoned' text of BS. When Ramanuja was about to leave this world he found his disciples

121

grieving so much that they had no interest to live after his passing away. Ramanuja chided them and asked them to stop worrying and start thinking as to how best to serve through the God-given instruments of mind, speech and body. His parting advice consisted of five kinds of service.

1. Study and propagate Sri Bhashya
2. If not competant to do (1), spend the time studying the Prabandam of azhwars.This is in keeping with azhwar's own advice.
3. If not qualified for (2) serve in the holy temples.
4. For any reason if (3) is also not possible reflect on the Dvaya Mantra.
5. If even (4) is not possible one need not worry. He or she can go in search of a Sri Vaishnavite of good conduct and live in his or her august presence. The Swamy has mentioned the above five in chapter 17 Nigamanadhikara (of RTS). The following words are his:

ஸ்ரீ பாஷ்யத்தை வாசித்து ப்ரவர்திப்பித்தல்

Concluding this chapter in the words of the great speaker and writer Prof K.S. Narayanachar (p276 of Ref 51): "A Vedic siddhanta like that of Ramanuja, which has its roots in the Vedas, is thus spread over several thousands of years, and has for its expression and explication, exegesis and expounding, not merely the whole of Vedic literature, but also a variety of writings:

1. the explicitly logically coherent writings of Vyasa, Bodhâyana, Tanka, Dramida, Bharuchi, Kapardi, Srivatsânka mishra, Nâthamuni, Yâmuna, Ramanuja, Deshika, Parashara Bhattar... and writers to date like Uttamûr Vîra Râghavâchârya Swâmi;

2. The implicitly coherent systems embodied in the poetic composition of the Ramayana, the Mahabharata, the Vishnu PurâNa, Bhagavata, the hymns of the Azhwars, the Stotra(s) or

hymnal literature of the Acharya(s), employing the highest modes of symbolic and mythical thought unifying religious, aesthetic and spiritual intuitions;

3. The literature of the Agamas, employing the language of worship, the rituals, the symbolic ceremonies, the myths and the practical mode of intuiting the spiritual highest thought form and concrete shape;

4. A fourth category of literature called Dharma Shastram is used as a test to see if this ethical literature and their values could be successfully derived from the basic metaphysical position of the system, and is used as a manual for daily conduct, character and code of behavior for the individuals as well as the society. It could also be treated as the ethical elaboration of the central thought of the system, sociology in keeping with the main metaphysics, embodying it in terms of social law and inherent social, ethical values.

"In other words, Ramanuja's is a system of thought whose intuitive expressions are scattered over a variety of wide ranging kinds of literature, logical, poetic, metaphorical, mystical, metaphysical, ritualistic, sociological, and aesthetic —each of which is a kind of system bearing cross-checking with the others, whenever required. This is an advantage which other systems do not enjoy…"

5. Sri Ramanujâchârya: The Founder of Vishishtâdvaita

Given the fact that Ramanuja in his young age was a student of Yadava-prâkâsha, a staunch Advaitin, it becomes necessary to know the history preceding his birth.

Historians are of the firm opinion that after a lot of bloodshed and heavy loss of life during the wars (Kalinga war for example), Emperor Ashoka became depressed over the futility of war. Whatever may be the outcome of the war, the means in no way justify the end —the mindless massacre of combatants leaves an unhealable scar in the minds of near and dear ones. The Buddhists seized the oppurtunity of the depressing scenario and preached Buddhism resulting in large scale conversion of Hindus into Buddhists, including the king himself. The great Vedic culture suffered a setback.

At this point of time Buddhism held India in its grip. Buddhism itself was, we are told, a revolt against the abuses which are said to have come in the wake of the Vedic period. In the name of the Vedas and under the guise of the Yagnas ordained by the Vedas, cruelty and selfishness probably reigned supreme. Lord Buddha's purpose in denying the validity and efficacy of the various sacrifices must have been only to protest such excesses in the name of the Vedas. But, as often happens, the purpose of the doctrines enunciated by the Acharyas, like Buddha, was missed by his followers, and the later schisms based upon Buddha's doctrines were essentially destructive, and posited nothing but Sûnyam or nothingness. Everything was denied. Even the *Charvaka* or the Materialist accepts the truth and validity of the world, though he denies them to God. The *Madhyamika* with his theory of *Sûnyavâda* denied everything, the world and God not excepted. Vedic culture suffered further and further decay.

Civilization of society increases with culture, and breaks down as cultural values deteriorate, as we have seen the fall of the Egyptian, Greek and Roman civilisations. When culture deteriorates, there is an increase in barbarism and immorality, philosophy is misinterpreted and utter disaster follows. Shankara appeared at such a stage and brought about the great renaissance in Hinduism (p 83 of Ref 11).

The emphasis that Shankara laid was, therefore, upon God or Brahman. The first and foremost thing was to establish the God who had been forced to hide Himself by the materialist and the

125

Buddhist. Sri Shankara, therefore, took this up as his mission, and we all know how successfully he has accomplished it. His several works on Vedântic wisdom and religious experience are a monument (read 'Edifice' as we have called it) to his great intellect, but for which God would have disappeared long ago from the minds of men. The swing of the pendulum now took it to the other extreme. Not only was Brahman affirmed and re-postulated, but as part of the same scheme, the validity of the world was denied. *Brahmam Satyam* and *Jagan mithya*, together formed the essence of the doctrine that Shankara preached. Not only the man of today, but even God Himself, must be thankful to Shankara for having thus re-established His existence, though without name, form or attributes, in a world which had completely denied Him (p 119 ofRef 14).

There are more than a dozen different commentaries on BS. The one written by Shankarâchârya was founded on *Mâyâ Vâda* (the theory of illusion) and *NirguNa Brahmam* (God without attributes). Shankara's work should be viewed from a historical perspective. Shankara's period- AD 788 to 820- is in accordance with the one given on page 57 of Ref 5.

Ramanuja came a few centuries after Shankara. He was born in the year 1017 A.D. Shankara's doctrine had come in for a lot of criticism in the later years. There was a crying need, therefore (felt centuries after the disappearance of Shankara), for a restatement of the Advaitic or monistic view, and question its validity.

The young Ramanuja had no alternative but to study Vedânta under the guru Yadavaprâkâsha, who was a popular Advaitin at Tiruputkuzhi, a close suburb of Kanchipuram. It should be mentioned here that Ramanuja took advice from Kanchipurna who was in the temple doing service to Lord Varadaraja. It was not mere service alone but he was in talking terms with the Lord –a supreme bhakta!

Many a time Ramanuja differed from the teachings of his guru (see p81 & 99 of Ref 34). Ramanuja's studentship under an Advaitin was the cause of great concern and worry to Yamunâchârya who, at Sri Rangam was holding the important position of being the chief promulgator of Vishishtadvaita (for his contributions see p513 -17 of Ref 43. The reader will notice that in that list a commentary on BS, the foundational text of Visishtâdvaita is conspicuous by absense. Incidentally he wanted it to be fulfilled by some one, and banking on the prophesy, he had pinned his hope on Ramanuja). The concern was not without reason.

When Yamunâchârya paid a visit to Kanchipuram to have darshan of the Lord, he is said to have seen Ramauja with the guru on the way, but thought that the time was not proper to contact and talk to

127

Ramanuja. He poured his gnawing concern and sorrow to the deity. "O Lotus-eyed one! Please do bring Ramanuja to your faith by bestowing your grace upon him." Yamunâchârya was not in the know of what a great Visishtadvaitin Ramanuja already was.

लक्ष्मीश पुण्डरीकाक्ष कृपां रामानुजे तव।

निधाय स्वमते नाथ प्रविष्टं कर्तुमर्हसि॥

The story goes that there was an attempt to drown Ramanuja in the river Ganges at Benaras where the guru and his shishyas went on a pilgrimage. Providentially Ramanuja was warned in time and saved from the murder attempt. Ramanuja strayed away from the group into the forests at Vindhya. He lost his way and his distress call evoked sympathy from none other than Lord Varadaraja and His consort Perundevi. Donning the role of hunter and wife, the Divine couple came to rescue him and miraculously brought him safe to the vicinity of Kanchi over the night! The couple vanished leaving him in wonder and thankful devotion after asking him to fetch water for drinking (this incident is recalled in 62 Ref 18).

Meanwhile, Yamunâchârya's health started deteriorating fast. He had sent Mahapurna (a disciple of his) to bring Ramanuja immediately to Sri Rangam. But even before the arrival, Yamunâchârya's pulses had stopped and the lifeless body had three of its fingers remaining folded, purportedly indicative of three messages to be conveyed perhaps posthumously to Ramanuja!

"Ramanuja, with eyes transfixed, kept gazing on that great one, as if the two were exchanging thoughts. All stood mute; no one in that gathering uttered a word. With amazement, they beheld the communion of the living with the dead."

In that communion, Ramanuja had comprehended that Yamunâchârya had three last wishes (or are they three commands?) to be fulfilled and when Ramanuja spelt out the three and gave his assurance that he would fulfill them, the three fingers took life, as it were, and unfolded. Thus, Ramanuja enabled the soul of Yamunâchârya to rest in peace!

The three vows taken by Ramanuja were (p 121 Ref 34):
1. To show gratitude to Veda Vyasa and Parashara by giving those names to suitable persons;
2. To pay a tribute to Saint Nammazhwar by arranging for a commentary to be written on the azhwar's poem, Tiruvâi Mozhi;
3. To bring out a Visishtadvaitic commentary on BS

श्रीभाष्यं च करिष्यामि जनरक्षणहेतुना ॥

Ramanuja was assailed by serious doubts on several vital points in the interpretation of the Vedânta and BS. He approached his mentor

129

Kanchipurna with a request to obtain the Lord's own answers to those doubts. Those answers were vouchsafed to Ramanuja, and through him to the world, in six vakyas or sentences (p127 of Ref 34).

"The works of Ramanuja are as valuable as his life, and they were the fulfilment of his promise in youth to carry out the message of Alavandar to systematize the whole teaching of Visishtâdvaita in its metaphysical, moral and mystical aspects. In his Vedârtha-Sangraha, he analyses the defects of Advaita, Bhedabheda and Saivaism and harmonizes the apparently conflicting texts of the Upanishads by his foundational principle of the *Sharira-Sharirin* relation. His magnum opus is the immortal Sri Bhashya (SB) which is an authoritative exposition of BS as Shariraka Shastra in the truest sense of the term.

Sri Varadaraja Swami at Kanchipuram
mokshopâyah nyâsa eva janânâm muktim ichchatâm
mad bhaktânâm janânâm cha nântima smrtirishyate

Apart from SB, Ramanujâchârya has written several commentaries on BS, ranging from the very simple to the advanced level, with a view to make it understandable for everyone. Vedârtha Sangraha, for example, (to be discussed in chapter 6) can itself serve as a sort of introduction to Sri Bhâshya.

A masterly gloss on both the works, viz. Vedârtha Sangraha and Sri Bhâshya, exist written by the celebrated scholar (belonging to 12/ 13th century), the most brilliant Sudarshana Sûri who says that Vedârtha Sangraha was expounded in the form of a lecture before Lord Srinivasa at the temple in Tirumala.

Sri Bhâshya, being a polemic work, is severely argumentative, highly technical and quite terse. Out of overflowing compassion Ramanuja has abridged Sri Bhâshya into Vedânta Dîpa in which much of the controversy and elaborateness of arguments are eliminated so that it may be easily understood and the book can serve as a beginner course. There is yet another simpler commentary by Ramanuja, known as Vedânta Sara, which, to borrow a modern phrase, meant for dummies desirous of studying BS.

We might discus the significance of this prefix 'Sri' in Sri Bhâshya. It is said that it was intended to distinguish SB from the other great commentary called Maha Bhâshya which is a work of Patanjali on Panini's Sutras (there is also a belief that Ramanuja is an avatar of the grammarian Patanjali)!

The BS is an intellectual exercise conducted to extract the import of the Upanishads. BS is the quintessence of the Upanishads (*uttamam Sâram*) and hence a closely guarded secret (*vibuda-guptam*) meant for the study of the scholarly. Upanishads are many and the diverse contributions of the major ones call for a systematic presentation of the philosophy in a unified and coherent manner. They seem to need a consolidation of statement. As Ramanuja puts it, the BS is the

131

nectar churned out from the milky ocean of the Upanishads by Veda Vyasa, the son of Maharishi Parashara.

॥ पाराशर्यवचस्सुधामुपनिषदुग्धाब्धिमध्योद्धृताम्॥

The next great wish of Alavandar was a gloss on Tiruvâi Mozhi and Ramanuja was instrumental in its execution. "The Aarayirapadi, the first Visishtadvaitic commentary on the TM of Nammazhwar, is traced to his (Ramanuja's) inspiring influence. This was composed by his chief disciple Kurukesha (Tiruk-Kurugai-Piran-Pillan). A commentary on the Vishnu-sahasranama was written by Parashara Bhatta in compliance with Ramanuja's instructions. In this way and by these works the dream of Yamunâchârya to formulate Visishtadvaitic Vaishnavism became an accomplished fact. These great works are ever-enduring monuments of Ramanuja's synthetic genius" (p520 of Ref 43).

"The dream and wish of Yamunâchârya got its fullest realization in the person of Sri Venkatanatha.", says Dr K.C.V (p140 of Ref 52). If we compare Sri Ramanuja's period (1017- 1137AD) with that of Swami Deshika (1261-1362 AD) it becomes apparent that more than 150 years had elapsed before the latter's contribution began to appear after the exit of the former. In this interval of 150 years, Ramanuja's Philosophy was subjected to criticism from all sides and to establish Sri Bhâshya on a firm footing, Ramanuja himself had appeared, it seems, in the avatar of Sri Venkatanatha (vide Saptatiratnamâlika, verse 12).

बाह्यांश्चापि कुदृष्टिकान् भुवि पुनः भाष्यप्रतिष्ठाशया

श्रीमद्वेङ्कटनाथदेशिकशिरोरत्नात्मनाऽऽविर्बभौ

The abstract can be explained through a concrete analogy. Ramanuja painted the vast canvas of Visishtâdvaita, but it was left to Vedânta Deshika to finish the painting by filling in the details. "This difficult task to which he addressed himself required prodigious labor and

132

persistent attention to details." Another analogy is also adduced. Deshika's works serve as a strong fence to the crops of Ramanuja.

பூமன்னுமாதுபொருந்தியமார்பன் புகழ் மலிந்த
பாமன்னு மாறன் அடிபணிந்துய்ந்தவன், பல்கலையோர்
தாம் மன்ன வந்த இராமநுசன் சரணாரவிந்தம்
நாம் மன்னி வாழ நெஞ்சே! சொல்லுவோம் அவன் நாமங்களே.

"O Mind! Keep muttering Ramanuja since it can do wonders. While doing so let not the esoteric image leave you even for a moment: The Poet Nammazhwar sang profusely in praise of the Lord whose chest was adorned by the presence of Maha-Lakshmi. She switched from Her dwelling place of the large lotus flower to the chest since the latter was softer and cosy! And Ramanuja took refuge unto the poet's holy feet, singing his songs to lead a peaceful and blissful life. This lesson, the secret of joy of living from Ramanuja, was imbibed by the noble souls and they in turn took shelter in him. You should also follow suit and lead a blissful life under the shelter of Ramanuja."

The devotion towards his âchârya contained in the above verse of Anudanar is made explicit in letter and spirit and highlighted by Nayinâchârya when he extols his father cum âchârya, Vedânta Deshika (Thuppul Pillai) in an identical manner. This is the special feature of the beginnings of both the Tamil andadis. What a fine tribute and praise for the builders of the monument Visishtâdvaita spanning over four centuries!

மாமலர் மன்னிய மங்கை மகிழ்ந்துறை மார்பினன் தாள்
தூமலர் சூடிய தொல்லருள் மாறன் துணையடிக்கீழ்
வாழ்வை உகக்கும் இராமாநுச முனி வண்மை போற்றும்
சீர்மையன் எங்கள் தூப்புல் பிள்ளை பாதமென் சென்னியதே.

"My head adorns the feet of Tuppul Pillai whose mission was to sing in ecstasy the glory of Ramanuja for his eddyfying contributions for the beneit of the world. Please note that while Amudanar included Nammazhwar and Ramanuja, Nainâchârya added Thuppul also in addition to the earlier two âchâryas, acknowledging the fact that while the bed-rock foundation was laid by Ramanuja, the grand super-structure was raised by Vedânta Deshika!

Ramanuja as Yatiraja

The word Yati is synonymous with sanyâsi and Ramanuja earned the title Yatiraja i.e. king among Yatis. What an irony of fate that the self same Yâdavaprakasa who was Ramanuja's guru once, turned a new leaf and became a vaishnava sanyasi and an ardent disciple of Ramanuja himself (13 of Ref 18). At the instance of Ramanuja, a treatise on the code and conduct of an ascetic (*Yati dharma Samucchayam*) was written by Yâdavaprakasa. Swami Deshika, in his poem Yatiraja Saptati waxes lyrical on the life, works and philosophy of Ramanuja in seventy-four lilting verses, the number indicative of the Maths established by Yatiraja. The following verse describes his pleasing form.

उपवीतिनमूर्ध्वपुण्ड्रवन्तं त्रिजगत् पुण्यफलं त्रिदण्डहस्तम्।

शरणागतसार्थवाहमीडे शिखया शेखरिणं पतिं यतीनाम्॥

In the above verse four distinguishing marks adorning the self as Yatiraja. It starts with the sacred thread (*yajñopavīta*), which is the hallmark of a *trivarnika*. The Tridanda or the staff held in the hand is the distinguishing feature of the order of a Sanyâsi (the *Tridanda* formed by combining three vertical splices from a bamboo staff and the same is said to represent symbolically the three restraints of a practicing ascetic viz. penance of thought *manó danda*, control over speech *vâg-danda* and control over the body, *kâya-danda*). Gitâchârya as defined the three penances in specific terms in the 17th chapter of Gita. The forehead adorned with pundra is the distinguishing feature of a Sri Vaishnavaite. The upward pundra is symbolic of the ever-expanding intellect in consonance with the growing feet of Lord Trivikrama. The avatar of Yatiraja is the result of good deeds (*punya*)

134

accrued by countless inhabitants of the three worlds. The purpose of this avatar is to show the path of surrender as the means for salvation. All these can only pertain to a Vaishnava sanyâsi and as typified in king among the order of sanyasins viz. as Yatiraja.

The Fall of Advaita

Dr.K.C.Varadachari, who was holding the chief post of Sri Venketeshwara Oriental Institute until his retirement in 1962, had contributed immensely to the philosophy of Vishishtâdvaita. In the good old days two prominent scholars, K.C. Varadachari the student and his master P.N. Srinivasachari (retired principal and professor of philosophy, Pachaiappa's College, Madras), like the disciple and the guru, enriched the literature on Vishishtâdvaita by presenting the philosophy of Ramanuja to the English knowing public. PNS admires the student when he says that "the book (Ref 2) as a whole shows that the writer has Philosophical gifts". Dr. KCV begins his introduction in an awe-inspiring manner:

"The system of Ramanuja occupies a significant and paramount place in the History of Vedântic philosophic thought. Starting from the Vedic fountain, to use the orthodox phrase or metaphor, the rivers of interpretation flooded unrestrained in the very division and diversion of Sankhya, Yoga, Vaiseshika, Nyâya, Mîmâmsâ, the Jaina and Buddhistic schools till finally every one of them was accepted and rejected in turn by the Philosophic Mind, and in exhaustion turned to the solacing grounds and surging oceanic expanse of the Vedântic thought. But neither did it find there what it vainly sought, for wave within wave and inundation after inundation revealed an unlimited and illimitable depth and interior. It could not (dropping the metaphor hereafter) sullenly closet itself to the fundamental assumptions, for never were they easy. It was alluring; pleasing in the extreme was the quiet rest in the initial revelation of the Vedântic aspiration in the Advaita of Mâyâvada. But such a rest was apparently shortlived. It was bound to be so, it could not be otherwise. It promised potencies of immense magnitude and it heralded the death of ego-centrism in life, its bitter and garnering fruits, in the ocean of a pure chaste and illumed and absorbing Experience of the Eternal Absolute Bliss. But the demand of the world was not replied; after all, the lure to thought was the world from which and for which it sought to exalt itself. So, in its effort to conquer what it would enjoy, it could bear no divided rest, nor bear with quietude the hymn of hate against life in its furious on march of time; it wanted to subdue rather than deny, to accept rather than reject; for power needs acceptance and overcoming, possession and glory, not the puny and impotent way of surrender and gloom, quietism and feebleness. But the lure was strong and remains strong, not only was the recoil from life was real and psychological, its votary was a great man, a pure and magnificent flower of humanity-Shankara."

Before proceeding further, we may bring forward what KCV has said about illusion and the philosophy of Shankara in the chapter, "Theism and Illusion": "The approach to a proper understanding of the theistic thought must be sought in the actual postulations of the seers who have in some measure enjoyed the Holy Presence. It will be admitted that the two great seers Shankara and Ramanuja have diverged sufficiently regarding the experiences of the Ultimate or the Absolute or the Brahman, and the theistic mind of both the Saiva and Vaishnava varieties has grasped at the truth of the Ramanuja's statement rather than that of Shankara. The main bone of contention between the two can easily be said to be the theory of Maya or 'World illusion' or total illusion which the one denied and the other affirmed...Our struggle is real in this world. The facts of our bondage and our consciousness of it are also facts of capital importance. The need for crossing over the turmoil of life, tortures of bondage, and limitations of intelligence are decisively clear. The promise of the illusion theory is that these are all unreal and that one should discover the inner Being, the Self of transcendent light,

136

which is ever shining in our hearts. This metaphysical reality of the Self in us does one thing, it somehow grants us that strength of possession already of that which has to be attained, and as it were, shows out a suggestion that untruths and falsities and illusions are more easily got rid of rather than real obstacles."

What was mentioned in parenthesis is Advaita in brief. Now continuing with the 'Introduction' where the author KCV traces the post Shankara developments: "but something ought to be done, that was the will of the Zeitgeist (which in German means, 'the spirit or tendency of the times'). Truth accepts no divided rule between itself and unreality. Understanding could be satisfied, if life would not be thwarted by mere denial. It may be called true and real and not a mere dream, for in as much as it exists should it not be called real and true, for, what is the criterion of reality but existence?

"It may have the attribute of significant meaning, yet there is no need to reject finally unity or identity, *ekatva*... Thus, the half-hearted concession of the *Bhedabheda vadins* was not accepted. It strained to be counted as an entity, real absolutely and without any reserve or not at all. It was perhaps better to be treated as eternally unreal rather than be treated as real and unreal by fits and starts. In Ramanuja it found its leader, its voice and effectuality...The utterances of the Vedic Realists found its logical culmination and echoes in the system of Ramanuja. Ramanuja was the first to claim eternality and reality of the world in Vedânta. (for Vyasa mentions that the world is real in his commentary on the Yoga Sutras). He was the first to recognize the fundamental unity of Truth, Goodness and Beauty. As it was expressed "they are the threefold cord by which our wagon is hitched to a star".

"The hope of every philosophical attempt has been and is, if it be worth its name, the ultimate analysis and synthesis of our experience, giving legitimate hopes that may be attained by us in our

137

effort to master nature which somehow we feel fetters. This is what Ramanuja attempts to do in his Philosophy which we shall trace taking as his authoritative statement the BS commentary known as Sri Bhâshya."

Attempts to belittle Visishtâdvaita and discredit Ramanuja

This can be traced to Shankara himself who sowed seeds of dissension when he postulated two Brahmans –the higher *NirguNa Brahman* and the lower *SaguNa Brahman*. Ramanuja was at pains to prove that the former does not exist through a long-drawn polemics about which we are not concerned now at present. The point at issue is that an uncalled-for bias / allergy against Visishtâdvaita exists even amongst public figures such as god-men and academicians. This bias, despite their efforts to conceal, surfaces in their writings. The reader will be shocked to know the prejudice they harbour in their heart of hearts. Take for example the great Swami Vivekananda. When the time suits him, he would pay rich compliments to Ramanuja: "Ramanuja … with a most practical philosophy, a great appeal to the emotions, an entire denial of birthrights before spiritual attainments, and appeals through popular tongue, complely succeeded in bringing the masses back to the Vedic Religion."

Swami Vivekananda is said to have written a letter to Alasinga Perumal, on 6th May 1885. The bias is obvious in the letter: "All of religion is contained in the Vedânta, that is, in the three stages of Vedânta philosophy, the Dvaita, Vishishtâdvaita and Advaita; one comes after the other. These are the three stages of spiritual growth in man. Each one is necessary… Now in your journal write article after article in these three systems, showing their harmony as one following after another…" If one understands the explanation of Ramanuja, where on earth, is the need for Shankara's ill conceived Advaita at all in the first place and in that event, there is no stage left beyond Vishishtâdvaita! In the process of *reductio-ad- absurdum*, the

Advaita stands rejected and a fallen Advaita has no more face to lead! One can imagine the kind of humiliation Alasinga Perumal would have suffered. One should never countenance blessings from another who does not belong to one's faith.

Even the great Dr Radhakrishnan was not free from bias:
Some of our people whose faith in the Vedas is suspect were prepared to bend backwards by giving up their allegiance to Vedas and it suited them to hoist the flag of Shankara's Advaita in a bid to claim the status of philosophy from the foreigners and in the process Ramanuja was sidelined and ignored. Even the all-knowing Radhakrishnan displayed his bias in his book "Indian Philosophy" (two volumes published in 1927) by captioning the chapter on Shankara as "Advaita Vedânta of Shankara" whiles the one on Ramanuja's as merely "The theism of Ramanuja" (Vol II p445). Apart from denying Ramanuja even the status of a Vedântin, he went on to criticize the founding father of our ancient Vedic tradition, Veda Vyasa himself. His cryptic comment is that "his (Vyasa's) work is not so much systematic philosophy as theological interpretation" (p431 of the same volume).

A question arises whether there was no one to defend Ramanuja when scholarly critics from the opposite camp, chiefly Radhakrishnan, traded such unsavory comments. A fitting response was indeed in the offing thanks to a very competent academician who made an in-depth analysis of the criticisms and objections levelled against and stoutly defended Ramanuja's Vishishtâdvaita in unequivocal terms. We are referring to Prof P.N. Srinivasachari who fulfilled the need of the hour through his lectures and writings (preface Ref 43).
"The main purpose of this work is to give a critical and comprehensive exposition of the central features of the philosophy of Vishishtâdvaita and its relation to other schools... I published in 1928 'Ramanuja's Idea of the Finite Self' in a very concise form. My

later work, 'The Philosophy of Bhedâbheda, published in 1934, was designed to serve as an exhaustive introduction to the study of Ramanuja and the development of his system in the history of Indian Philosophy. (In this book PNS advances a detailed criticism of 'Mâyâ Vâda'). The present work is a comprehensive but modest survey of the system of Vishishtâdvaita as outlined in a series of eight lectures delivered by me under the auspices of the University of Madras."

The first chapter of PNS's book is devoted to a discussion on Philosophy versus Theology, the contentious issue raised by Radhakrishnan. The war between the two is verily the war between reason representing Philosophy pitted against faith represented by Theology and PNS in his masterly treatise conducts it at five different levels. A few points arising out of the discussion are noted below.

Theology is based on faith in truths regarded as infallible because of scriptural authority or divine disclosure and is therefore antagonistic to the free exercise of reason on the facts provided by human experience.

Theology, therefore condemns the rootless, wayward drift of philosophy and takes refuge in faith. Religion shuns philosophy as mere theory, dry as dust formulations, abstract and obscure, while philosophy rejects religion as arbitrary and intuitional. No man can be a free thinker in philosophy and at the same time a believer in religion.
"Vishishtâdvaita strikes a compromise between the extremes of Philosophy and Theology. It is neither pure Philosophy nor pure Religion but is really a Philosophy of Religion! As such it offers a contrast, on the one hand, to mere philosophical speculation overall of reality, especially of the western type, and on the other hand, to

religion in the sense of a faith in revealed theology based on the evidence of miracles (p1).

Point of Dispute between the West and the East

"The relationship between religion and philosophy has been one of the most important points of dispute between the East and the West. For a proper understanding of the relationship that exists or is established between these two, it would be necessary to cover a large ground. The aim of any understanding in this respect would be to clear the grounds of confusion. In this paper, I intend to survey the various views of Western writers and to point out that the Eastern view in respect of the relationship is as much important as theirs." With these remarks Dr KCV proceeds to analyse the said relationship and steers clear of all confusion and misunderstanding (p221 Ref 2).

For the different view points for discussion he has chosen Jacques Maritain: "Introduction to Philosophy", Rene Guenon: "Introduction to the study of Hindu Doctrines", Dean Inge: "Contribution to the Contemporary British Philosophy" and Nicolas Berdyeav: "Solitude and Society". The author has chosen these since, to put it in his own words, "I have taken the most clearly expressed statements of the representative writers on philosophy... Nicolas Berdyeav, one of the most distinguished writer philosopher of this century writes about the relationship between Religion and philosophy as one of antagonism, because religion claims to possess in theology a cognitive expression, a field of knowledge... In the conflict between religion and philosophy, truth is on the side of religion when philosophy claims to replace it in the sphere of salvation and eternal life, but truth is on the side of philosophy when it claims to higher degree of knowledge than that attained by the elements of naïve knowledge incorporated in religion." In this sense philosophy helps purify religion by protecting it against the objective and natural processes assailing religious truths."

141

"All persons are not endowed with the philosophic spirit of reasoning that seeks the knowledge of reality as rationally constructed unity. Philosophy as the science of knowledge of reality is *tattva-darshana*... Indian thought makes *darshana* a metaphysical approach to reality, rather than a philosophic approach as such...Philosophy or *tattva-darshana* means not merely human knowledge but knowledge that is granted to the individual human being and which, by a process of interpenetrative understanding, leads us to the ultimate consciousness aimed at by the human soul...That is the reason why Indian thought had from the beginning of history always sought to find a basis in the truly Metaphysical or *Paratattva Darshana*, the Vedânta to which all the other systems tend, which is the firmest synthesis of all perspectives, but regulated by the truly universal Wisdom, the knowledge of the One which makes life a consecration, a righteous one and a full one and a liberated one."

Now it would be appropriate to present a parallel view of the same Darshana from PNS (p19): "A Darshana is a body of eternal and impersonal spiritual truths enshrined in shruti which can be logically tested and verified, by personal experience...The Vedântic Darshana affords insight into the nature of Brahman, and the ultimate proof of the existence of Brahman is the experience of Brahman. It is not *tarka drshti* or the natural light of reason and dialectic thinking on all things, but is *tattva-drshti* or the soul-sight of Brahman by knowing which everything is known. The Upanishadic rishis were specialists in spirituality and were philosopher seers...divine experiences of the Azhwars have Vedântic validity and value. Vishishtâdvaita as a philosophy of religion reconciles revelation, reason and intuition, and claims to be universal and accepts whatever is coherent with its cardinal truths. It summons humanity to participate in the riches of Brahmânubhava or the experience of Brahman, and its spiritual hospitality knows no geographical or racial barriers."

We may sum up in the words of Gitâchârya that a philosopher (Jnâni) is a seer of reality or *tattva-darshi* (BG 4.31).

॥ ज्ञानिनस्तत्त्वदर्शिनः ॥

The lofty view of Vedânta as presented by Ramanuja is known as Ramanuja Darshana or Vishishtâdvaita. Ramanuja is indeed a tattva-darshî in the light of observation made by Gitâchârya. For an in-depth understanding of not only the Upanishads but also the Gitopanishad, Ramanuja's works serve as the beacon light and the only indisputable guide (the difficulties faced in studying the other commentaries on Gita is highlighted by SS Raghavachar in his work, "Ramanuja on the Gita").

For any clarification or doubt in understanding any of the verse in Bhagavad Gita one should necessarily consult Ramanuja's Gita Bhâshya, observes Swami Deshika in his Tâtparyachandrika. In the song celestial (Gita) Bhagavan Krishna had to avoid dilating on the wide ranging metaphysical issues because of the time constraint and He had left it to Arjuna to find it out for himself at leisure by approaching a tattva-darshi. Nonetheless as far as the teachings on the practical salvational aspects are concerned, Gita is a complete Adhyâtma Shâstra.

॥ यज्ज्ञात्वा नेह भूयोऽन्यज्ज्ञातयमवशिष्यते ॥

ஸர்வேச்வரன் தானும் தானுபதேசித்த ஜ்ஞானத்தை பின்னேயும் "தத்விந்தி" என்று பலஞானிகள் பக்கலிலே கேழ்க்கவித்தானிறே - ஸம்ப்ரதாய பரிசுத்தி

But Ramanuja, in his Gita Bhâshya, made the teachings complete by making repeated references to the Upanishads, thus bringing Gita in line with the Upanishads. Of mention is his Gita Bhâshya for BG 13.2 which includes a collection of passages from the Upanishads and the longest commentary in the whole of Gita Bhâshya. In keeping with the unitary teachings of Prasthâna Traya, the long passage of Gita Bhâshya for BG13.2 is reproduced in the Maha siddhanta of Sri Bhâshya under the heading, with a view to homogenise the teachings:

॥ संग्रहेण सिद्धान्तोपन्यासः ॥

The Vedic course over the millenniums acceptable to Ramanuja (130 of Ref 60) is the pathway treaded by exponents, such as Bhagavan Bodhayana, Tanka, Dramida, Guhadeva, Kapardi, Bharuchi and others while non-Vedic schools, and Vedic schools having perverted vision are refuted and rejected by Ramanuja. Schools discountenanced by Ramanuja are those of Charvaka, Shâkya, Aulûkya, Akshapâda, Kshapanaka, Kapila, Patanjali and others (38 of Ref 35).

॥ श्रुतिनिकरनिदर्शितोयं पन्थाः वेदावलम्बि कुदृष्टिभिस्सह निरस्ताः ॥

Another 'missile' from Advaitin (Ref 54)
The war between the two isms goes on unabated even in the current times in order that the modern minds are vigil: "be informed than armed".

"Over the past thousand years many polemical works have been written by Pundits... Some years back Sri Jagadîswara Sastri of Madras Sanskrit College wrote a small work purporting to refute Ramanuja's Sri Bhâshya. I published a reply to this work entitled 'Vishishtâdvaita Vijaya' written by the late revered Kozhiyalam Ranganathâchârya swamy, with my Tamil translation. Sri Jagadîswara Sastri wrote to me that he will write a work refuting

144

'Vishishtâdvaita Vijaya' and he is unable to do the same even though 23 years have elapsed since the publication of the work."

Close on the heels of the above publication was another: during 1975-76, Dr. R Balasubramanyam, then Director of the Dr S. Radhakrishnan Institute for Advanced Study in Philosophy, delivered three lectures, under the title, "Some problems in the Epistemology and Metaphysics of Ramanuja". This time, the rebuttal was provided by Prof K.S. Narayanachar on a request from the editor Krishnaswamy Iyengar himself and was published through Sudarsanam. A few passages from the book "The Epistemology and Metaphysics of Sri Ramanuja-Vindicated" are given below.

"Dr R. Balasubramanian has found fault with Ramanuja's philosophy and *pramana* concept from the Advaitic standpoint, repeating the same old arguments of Shankara, in a parrot-like manner, which have been torn to shreds by Ramanuja and his followers over the centuries... Philosophical Advaita came to die its true death in the 13th century A.D only, when Acharya Vedânta Deshika dealt it with a fatal blow in his great and magnificent Shata-Dûshani. Refer to the (verse 70 of Ref 18 & 99 0f Ref 16): With the advent of the king among ascetics Yatiraja, all the then existing systems vanished into thin air- such as the ones founded by Buddha, Kapila, Kanada, Kumarila and Prabhakara. And the utterances of Brahma and Shiva also lost their flavor and fragrance. When such big heads had rolled and vanished into thin air, is there any need to mention separately the fate of the system of Shankara? "The booklet under question has no new arguments against Ramanuja's position, his exegesis of shruti texts, of his concepts of evidences, and is worth ignoring, as the old arguments have already been answered."

"From such contemptuous references (nine of them listed) to Ramanuja and over-praising of Shankara, these 'interpreters' of

Indian thought to the west consider that a system of thought is 'pure' and 'philosophic' if it excludes God, Theology and Theism, and verbal testimony from serious consideration and where these are considered seriously, they make the philosophy 'impure' and its propounder a mere theologian' and 'theist'.

"This is an arbitrary and even opportunistic distinction unwarranted by facts. It is invented only with the mischievous motive of deprecating Ramanuja's thought and to convert the very deficiencies of Advaita into virtues! If Ramanuja is a theist and by the same standards we describe Shankara as an atheist, would Radhakrishnan, Hiriyanna or Balasubramanyam accept it? What is philosophy if its job is not the harmonization of all types of intuitions, moral, spiritual, aesthetic and scientific? What is the use of 'pure philosophy' (if it ever existed!) if it "marches indifferent to the hopes and beliefs of man"? Why should religious concern be dubbed as 'theological obsession'? Look at Radhakrishnan's atheism when he writes: "prayer and worship of the Supreme as Iswara do not lead to final release" ('Brahma Sutra', p38).

The polar contrast that exists between Advaita and Vishishtâdvaita lies in the interpretation of BS and hence any book on Vishishtâdvaita or Advaita should necessarily project the criticisms fairly without any ambiguity. Now that so many waters have gone under the bridge, the Advaitins conveniently overlook or skip the controversies for reasons best known to themselves. Their bias prevents them from uttering even the name 'Ramanuja'! For, the moment they utter 'Yatiraja' their siddhanta is gone (*yatinrpati shabde viramati* -51 of Ref 18).

We give an instance in point. This pertains to a book of theirs (Ref 55). The review extends over 6 columns of 'The Hindu' and it does not contain a whisper of a mention of Ramanuja. The reviewer seizes the opportunity to exaggerate the antiquity of Shankara's

146

period. He says, "Before proceeding further, it has to be stated that while Sage of Kanchi put the year of Shankara's birth to 509 BC (proved by the long and unbroken lineage of the Pontiffs of Sri Kamakoti Peetam from its first Shankarâchârya, Adi Shankara, to its illustrious 69th and 70th pontiffs of our own day), some contributors to this volume accept the later dates assigned to Shankara by the British historians and foreign Indologists." There is no need to consider the contents of this book for any mentioning of Ramanuja's role in the development of philosophy or culture of our civilization. There cannot be a narrower perspective than theirs!

Charge Against Ramanuja

All said and done there is still a serious issue, in the opinion of modern-day scholars, that is pending to be addressed. The issue is stated clearly in Ref 56.

"Of the three Acharyas well known as Vedânta systematisers, it is well known that only Sri Ramanuja did not write full length or systematic commentaries on the Ten Principal Upanishads, while the other two, Shankara and Madhva have attempted them. This has left an unfortunate impression on later day Vedântins that the Upanishads taken by themselves as independent cannon do not much support Ramanuja's views, and hence the Acharya must have avoided writing independent commentaries!"

Even the well known western critic, George Thibaut (Ref 57) had to contend that while Ramanuja is more faithful to the BS, Shankara is more faithful to the Upanishads. This is an elementary conclusion that anyone would arrive at. However, a scholar comes to defend Ramanuja (p3 of Ref 58).

Writers who discard Shankara's interpretation of the BS and the Gita with considerable heat pay him the compliment that his interpretation of the Upanishads is more faithful than that of

147

Ramanuja. Thibaut and Zaehner are typical examples of this tendency. To know Ramanuja's understanding of the Upanishads in general and of specific passages therein, we should study relevant statements in his SB, VS and the Gita Bhashya. The prejudicial verdict of Western scholars and the absence of ready and direct material tend to create a difficult situation on this question.

It is not to be supposed that Ramanuja did not recognise the primacy of the Upanishads. For him God Himself is to be named 'Aupanishada-Parama-Purusha', the Supreme Spirit revealed in the Upanishads. God is also sruti-sirasi vidīpta specially expounded by the Upanishads, the crown of the Vedas. The BS simply bring out the essence of the Upanishads. The words of Badarayana constitute the nectar churned out of the milky ocean of the Upanishads: "parasharya ... madyoddhrtam". The Gita also teaches, according to him, bhaktiyoga, which, he says, was already taught in the Vedânta.

॥ वेदान्तोदितं भक्तियोगं अवतारयामास ॥

However, Rangaramanuja furnished the system of Ramanuja with full length commentary on all the Upanishads. This addition can hardly be supposed to have done anything by way of scholarship and philosophical depth that was beyond Ramanuja. In his commentaries, Rangaramanuja is responsible only for the interpretation of the less significant and less controversial portions of the Upanishads. In the elucidation of all the peak passages and all that call for dialectical determination of import, he invariably incorporates Ramanuja's own elucidation from Sri Bhashya and the Vedârtha Sangraha.

Evaluation of Advaita

Sri S.S. Râghavâchârya, in his masterly thesis, evaluates Shankara Bhâshya thoroughly and dispassionately before highlighting the merits of Sri Bhâshya (Ref 59). A few passages are recalled here to

148

know the underlying scheme with which the author has proceeded to facilitate the evaluation. "The first available commentary is that of Shankara. It is magnificent in point of style, thoroughness of execution and philosophical excellence. I engaged myself in outlining the vast and neatly arranged thesis of the original under the guidance of this masterly commentary. As I completed the synopsis of Shankara's commentary (this forms the major content of the book extending up to the page number 156 of the book), a problem presented itself with some force.

"Shankara manipulates the theme of the original within the framework of two levels of thought.
1. A system of theism absorbing the realistic modes of thought.
2. A claim to go beyond that level to propound a philosophy of a cosmic spirit-centered Monism. The two directions are sharply distinct and Shankara affirms that the central purport of the BS lies in the latter doctrine. Thus, the commentary sets up a new problem. "This led to an analysis of the principal points of the preferred understanding of the text as well as an examination of the BS to discover in it the basis for these points. In the chapter entitled 'Reconsiderations' (this section extends from p157 to p210) it has been established conclusively that the supposedly higher teaching attributed to the text as its authentic purport is entirely without evidence.

"At this point of frustration, the study had to look for another commentary, capable for salvaging the philosophy of the BS. Of the same dimension as that of Shankara and of equally high literary excellence and philosophic depth was the commentary of Ramanuja. My study of the BS focused itself on this solid classic of interpretation.

"The Sri Bhâshya of Ramanuja forcefully confirms the findings of the chapter, 'Reconsiderations'. It was felt at this stage that Shankara

149

did not handle the Sutras purely from the standpoint of textual fidelity. But he perhaps thought that he was producing a sounder philosophical system than the theistic version of the Sutra doctrine. The situation appeared to call for a philosophical evaluation of the doctrine advanced by Shankara. The perspective widened and rose beyond the exegetical Vedânta to Vedânta as a logical and cogent system of philosophy. Happily, Ramanuja's Sri Bhâshya superbly met the requirements of this purely philosophical evaluation of Advaita Vedânta. It offered a rational criticism of the Advaita of Shankara. Particularly, the concept of NirguNa Brahman and the doctrine of cosmic illusionism, received thorough criticism, hardly equaled in the later polemics of Vedânta. The later refutations of these basic tenets are a vindication of the stand of Ramanuja in the idiom of the complicated sophistications of a more formal age of dialectics.

"Some further questions arise. The refutation of Shankara's stand on the BS and the connected ratiocination leave out one important issue. The BS is a derivative of classic and its fountain-head is the Upanishads. If Shankara did full justice to the Upanishads, the deviation from the import of the BS is no major error. This line of thinking is put forward by the great commentator of Shankara, Vachaspati Misra. The trend receives powerful expression from Madhusudana Sarasvati in his refusal to revere Vyasa, the author of the BS. The question is whether the Upanishads propound the notion of Brahman as an impersonal abstraction or as the supreme and concrete divinity in which the individual finds its enrichment. Ramanuja sets forth an interpretation of the Upanishads, in his Sri Bhâshya and Vedârtha Sangraha (incidentally, the author SS Râghavâchârya has also translated Vedârtha Sangraha), which establishes a concrete and theistic view of the Upanishadic Brahman without the abstractness of NirguNa Brahman and the drastic reductionism concerning the individual and the cosmos. His interpretation of the Upanishads confirms his understanding of the

150

BS. There is no disowning of the Upanishads in the interests of loyalty to the BS.

"There is another important point. Shankara's commentary cannot but expound the theistic element in the BS, which is rather inconveniently extensive. The original text of the Sutra seems to err in its range of attention to what is to be superseded by what the commentator holds as the ultimate concern. It is doubtful if the full scope and merit of what is superseded receive legitimate expansion and just substantiation in the Bhâshya of Shankara. This situation imposes on Ramanuja the task of working out the supposedly lower version of Vedânta into the fullness of its formulation.

"Ramanuja follows up his refutation, philosophical and exegetical, of Shankara's higher version of Vedânta with an extensive exposition of the purport of the BS in terms of a concrete spiritual monism, bringing out the supremacy of Brahman, assimilating into it, in an adjectival status, the finite realities of nature and the individual self. The present study concludes with a summary of Ramanuja's philosophy of the BS. The brief note added in conclusion helps to identify the philosophy of the BS and clarifies its methodology and substance."

The following passages outline Raghavâchârya's exhaustive thesis (see page 214): "Ramanuja in his Sri Bhâshya sets for himself certain fundamental objectives and his work of adequate dimensions is a steady and progressive achievement of them.

He marks the deviations of Shankara's interpretation from the direct and almost self-evident import of the text in the various crucial sections. The deviations, he argues, render it self- contradictory. Thus, there is deviation and the deviation mars the coherence of the philosophy propagated. In this he consolidates and completes the criticism of Shankara by the previous critics such as Bhaskara.

151

An additional point of strength (as claimed by Shankara) would be that the basic authority of the sutra, which it (Shankara Bhâshya) endeavors to clarify and justify, is the body of the principal Upanishads and they, as Shankara's commentaries on them seek to demonstrate, in addition to the demonstration during the Sutra Bhâshya itself, are claimed to establish the Shankarite version of Vedânta.

In answer to this quite intelligible defense of Shankara, Ramanuja undertakes a three-fold task.

Firstly, Ramanuja works out a complete examination of the view of reality in the interests of which Shankara deviates from the straight forward import of the BS, in a measure far exceeding anything in that direction by previous critics of Shankara in terms of completeness and quality. He maintains that it is <u>fallacious</u> to the core. This refutation of Shankarite Advaita is one of the major ingredients of Sri Bhâshya.

For Ramanuja the philosophy directly following from the sutra is imperfectly and poorly sketched by Shankara, for purposes of eventual cancellation by the view that he himself upheld. As a matter of fact, that philosophy properly presented and developed in all its legitimate extent and implications, it is asserted by Ramanuja, is an unassailable structure impossible of supersession by any philosophy, Shankara's or any other. He undertakes the reconstruction of it in all its comprehensiveness, depth and intricacy. This is second major element in the Sri Bhâshya.

And thirdly, Shankara reads his higher view in the sutras, which found themselves on the Upanishads, and demonstrates during his commentary on the sutras how the view follows from what the Upanishads promulgate in their peak declarations, in addition to his demonstration of the same in his interpretation of the several

152

Upanishads. Ramanuja reacts to this exegetical position by an alternative interpretation of the Upanishadic texts, particularly the ones on which Shankara rely most for his specific philosophic conception supposedly higher. He also offers a total view of all texts and sees in them an integrated view of the nature of reality. This twofold exercise of re-interpretative philosophizing, according to him, sets aside the view of Shankara as a misconstruction and erects in its place the standpoint he discerns in the sutras as authentically emanating from the Upanishads. The substantiation of the claim to the fidelity to Upanishads is a further constituent of Sri Bhâshya.

This in brief, is the statement of Ramanuja's objectives. We may sum them up in the following words (p 216):

1. The detection of deviation from the sutras and the consequent attribution of self-contradictory doctrines to the author of the BS;
2. The examination of fundamental principles of Shankara's Vedânta;
3. The fuller statement of the philosophical view that springs directly from BS;
4. The perfect fidelity of this view to the Upanishads, the primordial scriptures of Vedânta"

This section as analyzed above is captioned as 'The significance of Sri Bhâshya' (pages 211 to 231). The lucidity in the exposition is such the author instead of generalizing, cites the sutra / adhikaraNa of BS where Shankara has <u>forced his ideas to prevail</u>.

After so much of his own presuppositions, that Shankara should move on to the doctrine of the unreality of the world startles us with unexpected advent. There are only two adhikaraNas (2.1.6 & 2.1.9) where this exit is executed.

"The procedure imports to the text enormous incongruity. It seems, as if, the view of the unreality of the world is made to storm into BS (this is regarding Adhikaranas 2.1.6 & 2.1.9) unsettling the intellectual coherence of the work and brings it down to a state of chaos. This section ends with the following observations (p230 ibid):

"Shankara's interpretation of the BS errs in its deviations such as the major instances considered above and the deviations are not merely insupportable in themselves but the reconstruction of the philosophy of the BS in the hands of Shankara renders it grievously inconsistent and divided within itself." It is said that, amidst the oasis of SaguNa Brahmam, Shankara was bent upon discovering a desert within the oasis and to this day his followers would prefer to remain in the desert! To express it in terms of the modern idiom, Shankara surreptitiously inserted a virus, as it were, into his commentary on BS and annulled / ignored/side-lined Veda Vyasa's teachings. "This may be the reason for Madhusudana Saraswati's extraordinary refusal to praise Vyasa and to prefer offering his adoration only for Shankara and Sureshwara."

To proceed further with the analysis of criticism of the doctrine of Advaita, the author devotes one more chapter, entitled 'The Significance of Sri Bhashya' continued from pages232 onwards to the end of the volume. Ramanuja has formulated his indepth attack on Advaita under two broad headings- Mahapurvapaksha and the seven objections against the concept of avidya of Advaita. The author has accordingly treated the former briefly in 16 pages (232 to 247) and the latter in 14 pages (248-261). The reader keen on getting a full grasp of the criticism should read the full text.

"In the exposition of Ramanuja's polemics, we have to note two findings of importance.

1. In Ramanuja's presentation of the Advaitic thesis and his criticisms, there is a clear demarcation between the philosophical argument and scriptural substantiation. Hence

154

the isolation of the purely rationalistic substance of Advaita offers no difficulty. The seperation of philosophical elements from the exegitical material is clearly maintained both in the Mahapurvapaksha, the statement of Advaita, and Mahasiddhanta, its refutation...

2. Ramanuja directs his critticism fundamentally and directly on Shankara, whom he does not name, but does not fail to take into account other Advaitins of great stature, such as Mandana, Padmapâda, Sureshwara, Vimuktâtman, Vachaspati Mishra and Prakashâtman, who have contributed to the buiding of the mighty edifice of the Advaita doctrine.The position attacked is taken in the fullness of formulation including these great elucidations and supplementations. The cardinal principles of Advaita are brought out in systematic development in the Mahapurvapaksha and are similarly examined in faultless logical sequence in the Mahasiddhanta. It is necessary to go through these discussions in their essentials in order to understand Ramanuja's critical survey of Advaita."

Fast forwarding to the end of the discussion (p247): "This part of the Mahapurvapaksha and its solid examination by Ramanuja is a supreme example of what philosophical dialectic can be in the hands of the great builders of Indian philosophy. There is the additional excellence that the entire *Purvapaksha* is reconstructed by Ramanuja himself into a magnificent edifice much more impressive than the originals it condenses. The *Purvapaksha* so far considered by Ramanuja's critique performs a valuable service in so far as it can be in terms of reason, and its examination is also conducted in the same style. If the resulting critical estimate is sound, it would appear that Shankara's deviation from the plain and natural philosophical import of the BS was effected in service of a philosophy that did not merit such a sacrifice. The sutras are construed in a distorted direction in the interests of an intrinsically untenable philosophy."

The passages below pertain to the seven objections (*sapta vidha anupapatti*) mentioned earlier, against Advaita (for a full account of the treatment the reader should refer to the book (pages 249 - 261 of Ref 59).

"The theory of spiritual monism or Advaita postulates that 'avidya' is the principle or factor or mechanism by which the unreal presents itself as real. In other words avidya conceals the real and projects the unreal before consciousness. It is not merely the process of concealment and misleading projection but that inexplicable something which engineers the deception. This entire explanation is subjected to a seven-fold refutation. A brief recapitulation of the arguments is necessary… So runs the seven-fold refutation in Sri Bhashya."

SSR makes a brief reference to the work of Swami Deshika also (p258 ibid). "But what Ramanuja accomplished was a systematic formulation of the criticism in a comprehensive shape inclusive of some additional line of attack. There is no rigidity about the number of arguments in connection with avidya as seven as each lends itself to many ramifications. This, perhaps, motivated Vedânta Deshika's naming of his polemics as Shatadûshani (we have devoted a separate section for Shatadûshani, later in this book). The Madhva school further expanded its destructive movement in works such as Nyaya Sudha and Nyayâmrta. The consequence was that the metaphysical edifice of Advaita was forced into a defence position as witnessed in works such as the Advaita Siddhi of Madhusudana and many minor works of that kind. The other consequence was that the many refinements and complications were introduced in the statement of the beleagured structure of thought going far beyond the confident and sharp nucleus of the originating masters." The reader may also refer the book of PNS (p52–60 of Ref 43): "Ramanuja devotes a special section to the criticisms on the theory of 'avidya' held by Shankara … Ramanuja in his masterly introduction to his Sri

156

Bhashya subjects this theory (of *avidya*) to severe criticism and his classical refutation of it is known as *Sapta-vidha-anupapatti* or the seven-fold-inadmissibility."

6. Vedârtha Sangraha

The very pacement of Earth in the Solar System reveals the master plan of the Creator, God. Had the Earth been placed on a little closer orbit to the Sun water would not have existed at all in the first place (it would have evaporated!) and had She been placed a little farther away from the present location, it would have been too cold to bear. In either case life would not have been possible. Add to this the Earth's tilt and rotation on Her axis. But for the tilt there would not have been the seasonal variations and but for the rotation there would not have been day & night. The earth is created mainly with a view to provide support and experience for the living beings governed by their individual destiny, to pulsate.

There are several parallels that can be drawn between the concepts of Modern Science about cosmology on the one hand and that of upanishadic cosmology on the other. But there is this one vital difference between the two. In the latter, there is the Creator according to whose will / plan (sankalpa) the Creation proceeds and evolves. Hence creation rests on a sentient principle. That Creator is none other than God Himself who is Sriman Narayana. The God is so named because there was no sentient being before Him. Unlike science, creation sans God has no interest for a Vedântin who is keen on his salvation. Hence Ramanuja begins his Vedârtha Sangraha with the following shloka.

अशेषचिदचिद्वस्तुषेषिणे शेषशायिने। निर्मलानन्तकल्याणनिधये विष्णवे नमः ॥

Modern science has developed the theory of cosmology (popularly known as the 'Big Bang Theory') to explain creation of the universe. Science explains everything in terms of the atom as the basic building block of matter and God is not in its reckoning. But in Vedânta the creation is brought about by the will of God and the ingredients that constitute the basic building blocks are three- *chit* (sentient principle), *achit* (non-sentient principle) and *Iswara* (God) – and not matter alone as in science. Creation is an oppurtiny given to the living being to better its destiny and man may work towards salvation.

Gitâchârya states that the living entities, particularly the humans should eke out their living by performing yagnyas which will eventually free them from the fetters of bondage. Yagnya is essentially selfless service.

सहयज्ञाः प्रजा सृष्ट्वा पुरोवाचप्रजापतिः। अनेन प्रसविष्यध्वं एष वोऽस्तु इष्टकामधुक्॥

The process of creation is known as Srishti and what is created exists for a definite period, though a long one, and gets dissolved during the phase known as praLaya. After praLaya once again Srishti takes place. The two alternate, Srishti- praLaya- Srishti and so on, ad infinitum (BG 9.7, 8).

सर्वभूतानि कौन्तेय प्रकृतिं यान्ति मामिकाम्। कल्पक्षये पुनस्तानि कल्पादौ विसृजाम्यहम्॥

Each time the creation resembles exactly like the previous one- *yathâ pûrvam akalpayat*. In *praLaya* the cosmos exists potentially without any distinction but during Srishti what remained enfolded becomes unfolded- the transition from *kârana* to *kârya-avasta*.

The modern science tells us that the Sun (a star) would cease to shine the moment the fusion reaction ends. This happens when there is no more fuel left to burn in the Sun, a gas giant (a massive LPG). All the reactions which happen in a sequence in the energy production were predicted and proved by the Nobel Prize winner, Hans Beth. So, the present Sun will not be shining for ever!

According to Visishtâdvaita, Sriman Narayana is not only responsible for Creation (*jagat karaNatvam*) but in addition He is the one who grants liberation (*moksha pradatvam*). Ramanuja has expounded the two roles in two of his major works viz. Sri Bhâshyam (SB) and Vedârtha Sangraha (VS). In the former work, which is the magnum opus of Ramanuja, cosmology is treated in Arambhana Adhikaranam (41) where the treatment is tough and rigorous. But here in this section we have taken the latter work for study since the treatment in VS is somewhat at the rudimentary level and somewhat (!) easy of understanding.

Vedântic Cosmology as in Vedârtha Sangraha (VS)
Creation begins at a certain epoch in time. The cosmos existed in the form of *Sat*. It was the primordial cause to start with. In sciemce the epoch is termed as the point of singularity. At first *Sat* existed in a subtle form, almost as a point which is dimention-less. The process of creation began from / at a point of singularity, time, t=0. We have intentionally used the indefinite article 'a' to mean that we can't be definite about occurrences of such epochs since the cycle repeats ad infinitum. In Vedic parlance, this point is praLaya. The Cosmas (World) existed in the subtle form as '*Sat*' during creation and the Sat was only one (Chandogya Upanishad 6.2.1).

॥ सदेव सोम्य इदमग्र आसीत् एकमेव अद्वितीम्॥

Tattvamasi

One of the most important application of *samanadhikaranya* is in respect of unravelling the import of the great expression (*mahavakya*) Tattvamasi as it occurs in the sixth chapter of Chandogya Upanishad. This long chapter consisting of sixteen sub-divisions (*khandas*) relate to the teaching of cosmology (science of creation) by Uddalaka to his son Shvetaketu. The dialogue begins thus: "Shvetaketu! It is our tradition that a *brahmacharin* should take up his studies in a gurukulam." After completing 12 years of study the boy returns home. The father asks, "Have you had the wisdom of enquiring that entity by knowing which all that was unheard of before becomes heard, all that was un-thought of before becomes thought and all that was unknown before becomes known" (Chand 6.1.3)?

येनाश्रुतं श्रुतं भवति अमतं मतमविज्ञातं विज्ञातमिति ।

The boy retorted, "How can such a thing be possible?", to which the father replied, "Why not? Just by knowing a lump of clay all the products of clay having the names pot, plate etc become known. If you know the cause, the clay, the effects such as pot, plate etc. become known. By knowing a nugget of gold all the ornaments made of it become known. By knowing one nail-cutter all that is made of steel become known." Shvetaketu endearingly responded this time: "The teachers did not teach me the deep implication of this concept. Father! Who else would teach me but your kind self. I am all ears. Please go ahead, with your lessons." The lesson begins with a bang (Chand 6.2.1)!

सत्त्वेव सौम्येदमग्र आसीदेकमेवाद्वितीतम् ॥

"There was only *Sat* at the beginning and it was only one without a second." '*Sat*' in the above sentence pertains to Brahman. The term 'only one' '*ekameva*' signifies that Brahman is the material cause as well as the instrumental cause, all rolled into one. In this respect it differs from the clay example wherein, apart from clay, accessories such as a potter, wheel etc are needed to transform the clay into pots etc. 'Idam' refers to the existing visible universe differentiated with names and forms. It goes without saying then (before creation) the universe was with Brahman without distinctions of names and forms.

The Upanishads unfold the science of cosmic evolution. It should appeal to the modern mind as it is in tune with the modern science of Cosmology, more particularly the 'Big Bang Theory': At $t=0$, the visible universe began to evolve, it seems, from a point of singularity. That means to say the expanded and still expanding universe we see today, was concentrated in a point, at the point of singularity which occurred some 20 billion years ago. The point contained all the matter held under infinite pressure. The Upanishads say that not only matter (*prakrti*) but even souls (*purushas*) were existing in Brahman in a subtle state before expansion. There is arbitrariness in modern science regarding the point of initiation, i.e., when the primordial beginning (at $t=0$) occurred but the Vedic science attributes the initiation process to the will of God (*tadaikshata*). Modern technology can hold a library of information within the tiny size of a pin head. If that is possible for a human why not for God Almighty to seal the fate of seven billion people (the current population of the world) in a zipper, as it were!

What is the rationale for this creation? It is mere sport or entertainment for God, according to Sutrakara. "The creation for the world is really an act of recreation in sportive spontaneity on the part of the divine Actor or Artist, God. The logical and moral ideas of Brahman as *upâdâna karana* and *nimitta karana* of the universe, is more transfigured in the aesthetic idea of *lîlâ*. This view was fully developed in the chapter on aesthetic philosophy. There it was shown that the creative art is the purposeless purpose of the Sat as

162

the Bhuvana Sundara to make beauties out of nature and the self and enjoy the art of beauty" (p271 of Ref 43).

We shall proceed with Uddalaka's teachings to Shvetaketu (Chand. 6.2.3).

तदैक्षत बहुस्यां प्रजायेयेति। तत् तेजोऽसृजत।

That 'Sat' deliberated, "May I become many? May I be born?". The Sat created Tejas or fire. An animated Tejas also thought, "May I become many? May I be born?" Tejas created, ap or water. The rik proceeds with a rationale. When the brain gets heated up (i.e., when tejas is overworked) perspiration (water) is produced. Perspiration follows inspiration, perhaps!

Those waters deliberated, "Let us become many"; "May we be born". Then *Ap* or water created *anna* or *Prithvi*. When there is rain there is plenty of food (6.2.4).

Chandogya goes into the elements composing physical embodiment. It begins with a colour code for the elements: Agni by its appropriate red colour, water by white; and food by black. Each of these elements gives rise to three components of graded consistency. Food decomposes into faeces (gross), flesh (intermediate) and mind (subtle); tejas into bone, marrow and speech; and water into urine, blood and vital air (6.5.4).

अन्नमय हि सोम्य मन आपोमय प्राणः तेजोमयी वागिति

There follows the anatomy of spirituality. The subtleties mentioned above could be understood by taking practical examples. The butter churned out of curds is light, hence moves up and floats. Mind is subtle like butter. Subtle oxygen in water supports life (prâNa). The subtle calories of exothermic reactions energize the speech producing organs of the body (6.6). The father asks his son to fast for 15 days to demonstrate to the son that at the end of the fast the mind becomes blank and therefore the son is neither able to remember nor recite the Vedas. This experiment proves that out of 16 parts of the mind 15 have become lost due to fasting. However, all the Kalas (parts) were restored after taking food and the memory and speech restored. (6.7) Mind is like a tethered bird which is being held by the hands of a hunter. In a similar manner, the mind is tethered to the prâNa. When the soul gets parted, one's speech unites with the mind. The mind gets merged into prâNa, prâNa into tejas and tejas with the Brahman (6.8) Water leads or conveys food and hence it is named *ashanâya* and similarly tejas is *udanâya*... This Sat is also known as Antaryâmin. "Thou art that" (6.8.7)!

One finds nothing inside a seed yet what a wonder that a huge Nyagodha tree has come from the seed. It appears the tree has come from nothing. So is the Universe! (6.12). Like salt in water the '*sat*' is here alone in this universe but can not be perceived. The refrain is that '*sat*' is subtle (6.13.3).

स य एषोऽणिमा एतदात्म्यमिदं सर्वम् । तत् सत्यम्। स आत्मा तत् त्वमसि

श्वेतकेतो इति ॥

Now regarding the meaning of *Tattvamasi*: Vedântin(s) differ widely in the interpretation of *Tattvamasi*. (For a cross-section of views refer p596 Ref 43) Ramanuja explains the amazing Vedântic concept 'Tattvamasi': The term '*tat*' expounds Brahman as the cause of the world, as the abode of all perfections. The term '*tvam*' (denotative of individual self) Brahman itself is signified as the Inner Ruler of the jîva, as possessed of its body, as existing within the jîva as its self and possessing the jîva as its mode. On all other theories, two glaring errors ensue, namely, that of giving up the governing principle of coordination and ascribing evil to Brahman itself (82 of Ref 60a).

तत् त्वं इति सामानाधिकरण्ये तत् इत्यनेन जगत्कारणं सर्वकल्याणगुणाकरं

निरवद्यं ब्रह्मोच्यते । त्वं इति च चेतन समानाधिकरण

वृत्तेन जीवान्तर्यामि रूपि तच्छरीरं

तदात्मतया अवस्थितं तत्प्रकारं ब्रह्मोच्यते ॥

Ramanuja says (15 of Ref 60a) that one should develop a vedantic mind to comprehend the import of the Upanishads. Take any word 'cow' for instance. For a vedantin, the word has three meanings, all primary and direct, namely, the bodily configuration of the cow, the self or soul of the cow and likewise the Inner Self or the Inner Ruler within the soul of the cow, which is Brahman. A layman, not acquainted with vedanta, is not likely to be aware of this third significance or meaning which is as direct and primary as the other two. This is the sum and substance of Antaryami Brahmanam (SB 152).

अतो गवादिशब्दवत् जीवात्मवाचिनः शब्दाः परमात्मपर्यन्ताः ॥

In his volume on Chandogya, NSA mentions the following important point: "Sudarshana suri points out in his commentary on VS that this statement *"tattvamasi"* establishes Visishtâdvaita alone and not nirvisesha Advaita. (refer to SB p145, the para beginning with *"tatvamasyâdivâkyeshhu"* and ending with *"paratvât sâmânâdhikaranasya"* quoted and translated. "The statements like 'Thou art that'…is meant to signify one thing alone subsisting in a two fold form."

Let us retrace to the point at t=0 i.e, at the beginning of 'Creation'there was no entity other than 'Sat" and 'at first' means before creation. Narayana mentioned earliet is denoted by the term 'Sat'. The subtlety implies that cosmos existing as 'Sat' could not be distinguished because, if 'Sat' were to be examined under microscope it would have consisted of three things – Brahman, 'souls' and matter. The three can be alternately put as Iswara, chit and achit' respectively. Like Hubble's Expansion in Modern Physics, the Sat underwent a transformation from the subtle to the gross. What was not distinguishable before, got transformed into distinguishable forms.

"Ramanuja explains cosmology in terms of *sharira – shariri* relation. Brahman in all its states has souls and matter for its body; when they are subtle, Brahman is in the causal condition, and when they are in the gross state, Brahman is in the effected state and it is called the world…Non-sentient matter is ever changing, sentient souls are liable to suffering and Brahman is ever pure and perfect. Brahman is Narayana" (p273 of Ref 43).

चितचितोः परमात्मनः च सर्वदा शरिरात्मभावं

शरीरभूतयोः कारण दशायां नामरूपविभाग अनर्हं

सूक्ष्मदशापत्तिं कार्यदशायां च तदर्हस्थूलदशापत्तिं

वदन्तीभिः श्रुतिभिः एव ज्ञायते ॥

In the Chandogya, Brahman is referred to as *Sat*. A few more terminologies are required for better comprehension. Sat is the material cause (*upâdâna kârana*). The word *advidīya* implies that Brahman alone is the instrumental or operative cause (*nimitta karaNa*) and denies the existence of any *nimitta karana* other than Brahman. An analogy is often cited for better understanding. In the case of making pots, mud is *upâdana karana* and potter the *nimittana karana*. The potter is different from the material. But in cosmic creation the two –*upâdana* & *nimitta* –are in one and the same entity viz. the Brahman. The Brahman willed: "I will multiply. I will be born as many" (Chand 6.2.3).

॥ तदेक्षत बहुस्यां प्रजायेय ॥

The word Sat is Brahmam who is endowed with absolute knowledge (*sarvajnyatvam*), absolute strength (*sarva shaktitvam*) and by His mere will he can accomplish anything He likes (*satya sankalpatvam*). Though He has everything accomplished (*avâpta samasta kâmannapi*), He idulges in Creation as a sport (*lîlârtham*). Bored being alone and for entertaining Himself, He decided to create, "Let Me multiply, let Me be many" and for the fulfillment of that purpose, from a part of Himself He created the elements like ether and so on. He entered each and every Jivâtman (10). The number within the bracket refers to VS unless otherwise stated.

अनेन जीवेनात्मना इति जीवस्य ब्रह्मात्मकत्वं

प्रतिपाद्य ब्रह्मात्मकजीवानुप्रवेशादेव

कृत्स्रस्याचित्वस्तुनः पदार्थत्वम् एवम्भूतस्यैव

अचिद्वस्तुनो नाम रूपभाक्त्वं इति च दर्शयति।

The reason for matter acquiring names and forms is mainly because of its association with sentient beings and the Brahman who pervades it. The Creation as entertainment sports is discussed in "*na prayojanattva-adhikaraNam*" –vide SB 2.1.10. The abbreviation SB stands for Sri Bhâshyam.

Several attributes of *Sat* can be listed. The world of chit & achid has Sat as its material cause and instrumental cause; *Sat* has its support (*sat âdhâratâ*); both are controlled by *Sat* (*sat niyamyatâ*); everything exists to serve the purpose of *Sat* (*sat sheshhadi sarvam cha*). All these beings (*prajâs*) emerge from *Sat)*, have their being in *Sat* and are ultimately absorbed into *Sat* (Chand 6.8.4).

सन्मूलाः सौम्य इमाः सर्वाः प्रजाः

सदायतनाः सत्प्रतिष्ठाः।

More and more attributes of *Sat* get added on as the creation process gets unfolded. For example, refer under sutra (*shrutatvâchcha* – SB1.1.12).

All embodiments –gods, humans, animals and plants –are modes and for this reason they have B (Brahman) as their soul. Any word in Sanskrit is formed as the combination of roots (*prakrti*) and suffixes (*pratyaya yogena*). Examples of words –god, man, yaksha, rakshasa, cow, deer, bird, tree, creeper, wood, stone, grass, pot, cloth etc. All the things in the world are the body of B and the existing world is real thanks to B, for B is the soul (*krtsnasya jagata: brahma-âtmakena satyam; krtsnasya jagata: sa eva âtma, krtsnam jagat tasya shariram*).

The term 'thou' is B having the individual self as His mode. The sentence 'tattvamasi' is a great principle taught by the father to his son (Shvetaketu).

तस्मात् त्वं शब्दवाच्यमपि जीवप्रकारं

ब्रह्मैव इति सर्वस्य ब्रह्मात्मकत्वं प्रतिज्ञातं

तत्त्वमसि इति जीवविशेषे उपसंहृतम्।

"Ramanuja expounds *"tattvamasī"* as the relation of *sharīra* and *sharīrin* and affirms that B, the cosmic ground, is the inner self of the jīva as its *sharīrin*. His interpretation reveals the meaning of the text in the light of illustrations employed in the Upanishad, fits in with the context and satisfies the ends of synthetic philosophy" (p597 of Ref 43). For illustrations see Ref 62.

Ramanuja clarifies *tattvamasi* by taking into account other shruti texts. Take the following statement:

॥ अन्तः प्रविष्टश्शास्ता जनानां सर्वात्मा ॥

B enters all living beings with a view to effect control (*shâstâ*) from within ie. by being within the âtma as Antaryamin. According to coordination or grammatical apposition principle (*samanadhikaranya*), 'that' and 'thou' ('that art thou' –*tattvamasi*) refer only to B. The word 'that' refers to B who is the ultimate cause and who is a repository of auspicious qualities and who is changeless and free from all imperfections. 'Thou' refers to B who has the individual self as His body, being the Inner Ruler of the individual self.

But Shankara reads differently. In his interpretation based on the same principle of *samanadhikaranya*, 'that art thou' means identity or oneness of the jîva and the B. Ramanuja contends that the said principle applies only when the two words having different meanings apply to the same thing and not when they signify identity.

तत् त्वम् इति समानाधिकरण प्रवृत्तयोर्द्वयोरपि

पदयोः ब्रह्मैव वाच्यम्। तत्र तत् पदं जगत्कारणभूतं

सर्वकल्याणागुणाकरं निरवद्यं निर्विकारमाचष्टे।

त्वम् इति च तदेव ब्रह्म जीवान्तर्यामिरूपं

सशरीरजीवप्रकारविशिष्टमाचष्टे।

The scholars have accepted the error committed by Shankara in applying the principle *samanadhikaraNa*. Dr. Radhakrishnan termed it as a 'learned error'. Nonetheless they assert that "theirs is a divorce between the grammar of reality and the grammar of language." Search the index *sâmânâdhikaranya* of Ref 43 for detailed discussions.

Several flaws in the doctrine of Advaita are brought forward for appraisal in the succeeding paras of VS. However a more rigorous and exhaustive account of it will be found in SB. (vide the title, '*Saptavidha anupapatti*'. Their greatest shortcoming is brought to focus in VS 46.

Advaitins poser: One must admit that âtman is consciousness (*vignyâna svarûpa âtma*) and it is self luminous (*sa cha svayam prakâsha:*). When a self is embodied as god or human, it will have to be admitted (by you also) that this self luminosity of the âtma undergoes obscuration (*svarûpa prakâsha tirodhânam*). To account for it an external agency, which is causing the obscuration has to be posited. This is not tenable. This is a serious doctrinal defect. It is more pronounced when the âtma-s are many. Relatively speaking the difficulty appears to be lessened in Advaita, since the âtmas are replaced with a single B.

भवतां आत्मा अनन्त्य अभ्युगमात्

सर्वेष्वयं दोषः परिहरणीयः।

"Avidya, according to Advaita, is said to be the innate obscuration of pure consciousness" (p53 of Ref 43).

The Advaitins dropped the hammer on their own leg by equating the jivâtma with B. That is why they have landed into serious problems. Wrong hypothesis leads to wrong conclusions. But we have no such difficulties since we follow the time honoured unbroken tradition –cultured and nurtured by such great exponents as Bhagavan Dvaipayana, Parashara, Valmiki, Manu, Yagnyavalkya, Gautama and Apastambha (VS 47). All these maharishis had great vision of the Supreme. One who has the backing of the great works left by them will face no difficulty at all in answering any question or handle any situation. Unfortunately, the Advaitins stand to lose by breaking away from the tradition of the a/m *maharishis*.

Ramanuja provides appropriate quotations from the works of the afore mentioned exponents to resolve the issue (48 –50).

PNS: p236, "The Visishtadvaitic philosopher with his loyalty to truth in all its levels finds no need to strain the texts to support his position" and on p599, "On the whole it is Visishtâdvaita as Shariraka Shastra that presents a synthetic view par excellence, of Vedânta, because its avowed aim is to harmonize the seeming contradictions of the shruti in the light of the *ghata* shrutis by employing the samanya method, and it is the supreme merit of Bhasyakara to wind up the discussion with a note of harmony in the highest sense of the term: "thus everything is satisfactorily explained (*iti sarvam samanjasam*)."

The obscuration issue raised by the Advaitins (vide VS 46) is now taken up and explained in VS 51& 52. The nature of âtman is knowledge and consciousness (*dharmabhûtajnâna*) is its attribute. It is *karma* which veils this consciousness. The âtma suffers contraction or expansion of consciousness thanks to karma or avidya. The shlokas in VP (6.7.61 – 63) explains this phenomenon and Ramanuja adds:

क्षेत्रज्ञानां स्वधर्मभूतज्ञानस्य कर्मसंज्ञया

अविद्यया सङ्कोचं विकासं च दर्शयति।

PNS: p27, "The concept of *dharmabhutaJnâna* is the foundational truth of Visishtâdvaita theory of knowledge... Consciousness cannot be aware of itself but presupposes a self of which it is the attribute."

Next, the issue of getting rid of avidya is addressed (*kena va avidya nivrtti*: --VS 56). Several misconceptions of Advaita –such as nirvachaniyam, adhyasa, svapna, shunya tattvam etc.–are taken up for appraisal and proved that they don't stand scrutiny. Those well versed in shastra will not accept those concepts (VS 73).

॥ शास्त्रविदो न बहुमन्यन्ते ॥

PNS: p55, "Ramanuja in his masterly introduction to his Sri Bhashya, subjects this theory (of *avidya*) to severe criticism and his classical refutation of it is known as '*Saptavidha Anupapatti*' or 'The Seven Fold Inadmissibility'.

After refuting the rival philosophies the arguments are brought to a close in VS 80.

The Omniscient Brahman

It was mentioned that at the epoch of deluge (*praLaya*) the cosmos exists in a subtle state and at srushti what remained enfolded becomes unfolded and becomes the gross (*sthula*). The Absolute broods and becomes the many by evolving the world-body) '*pariNamat*' the BS 1.4.27).

Here as in Modern Cosmology, the conservation law of Mass and Energy (the famous equation, $E=mc^2$) applies albeit in a different way. The content in the gross state is the same as that of the content in the subtle state. That is, nothing new is added and nothing of the old is subtracted. In other words, the cause is imminent in the effect. Brahman with *chit & achit* in a state of non-differentiation becomes *chit & achit* in a state of differenciation with an infinity of distinctions in name and form. It should be noted that the âtma-s are not in a pure state at the epoch of *praLaya*, according to Gitâchârya (GBG 13.12).

॥ परिशुद्धस्वरूपं न सदसच्छब्दनिर्देश्यम् ॥

Dayashatakam 16: The making and the unmaking of the universe thus reveal the redemptive mercy of Lord Srinivasa who gives a fresh oppurtunity for the soul to work out its destiny and get freed from bondage and enter Parama-pâdam.

आसृष्टिसन्ततानां अपराधानां निरोधिनीं जगतः ।

पद्मासहायकरुणे प्रतिसंचरकेळिमाचरति ॥

At the time of praLaya the condition would be such that there would hardly be any noticeable difference between the jivâtma-s on the one hand and the inert matter (*achid avishishhTân praLaye jantûn*) on the other. The Lord takes pity seeing the plight (*avalokya jâta nirvedâ*) and provides the âtmas with body and the senses (*karaNa kaLebara yogam vitarasi* –Daya.17).

The body and the senses are the evolutes of prakrti as discussed in VS 72 and in PNS: p263.

Vedânta is founded on the sentient B. Even the evolutes of prakrti take place with the implicit knowledge of and active participation (*sankalpa*) of B. It is B at the heart of all the agencies of creation. The agencies themselves are not aware of the presence of B who is their Inner Ruler. Shrutis which declare this truth are called Antaryami Brahmanam.

यः पृथिव्यां तिष्ठन् पृथिव्या अन्तरो यं पृथिवी

न वेद यस्य पृथिवी शरीरं यः पृथिवीमन्तरो

यमयति एष त आत्माऽन्तर्याम्यमृतः ॥

"He (B), who dwells in the earth, who is in the earth, whom the earth does not know, whose body the earth is and who rules the earth from within, He is thy âtman, the Inner Ruler (IR)."

The other agencies of creation under His control are: *ap, agni, antariksham, vayu, dyau, aditya, disha, chandra-tarakam, âkâsha, tama: teja: bhutas, prâNa: vak, chakshu:, shrotram, mana:, tvak, vijnyanam, reta:,buddhi:, ahankara, chittam, avyaktam, aksharam, vijnyanam and mrtyu.*

What was mentioned as vijnyanam in the above list of Kanva (a branch of Veda) is referred as âtma in Madyandina. It should be noted that the Lord attaches greater importance to âtma (*paramâtma sharîram adhikam*).

The above list will be found in Sri Bhâshyam (1.4.27), under the sutra: *pariNâmât.*

In VS 81a plethora of quotations from the lore are furnished in support of the Vedântic principle that the universe constitutes B's body (sarva shariram brahmam). A few are quoted below.

Shveta (I.12) A Vedântin should know that the three constitutes B –the experiencing subject (bhokta), the object of experience (bhogyam) and the IR who prompts from within (preritaram). This principle is explained in VS 129.

BG (10.20): "I'm the Atman, who dwells in the hearts of all".

BG (15.15): "I'm established in the hearts of all. From Me arise memory perception and its loss."

VP (1.20.38): All are Hari's body.

Sri Ramayana: "This whole world is your body" (*jagat sarvam shariram te*).

PNS: p 237. The author quotes the two riks of Antaryami Brahmana (Br 3.7.26 & 27) and concludes: "This mantra, as it were, the *maha vakya* of Visishtâdvaita in the sense that the universe has its meaning and motive only in B as the life of its life and the Lord of the lords of experience without the imperfections of the *sharira*."

VS 82: The best way to understand 'tattvamasi' is by applying the principle of '*sâmânâdhikaranya*'. Any other attempt will stultify its import.

इतरेषु पक्षेषु सामानाधिकरण्यहानिः

ब्रह्मणः सदोषा च स्यात्॥

Viewing from any other perspective will lead to two glaring errors – giving up the governing principle of coordination and ascribing defect to B itself.

PNS: p 597, "Ramanuja expounds *tattvamsi* as the relation of sharira and sharirin and affirms that B, the cosmic ground, is the inner self of the jîva as its sharirin. His interpretation reveals the meaning of the text in the light of the illustrations employed in the Upanishad, fits in with the context and satisfies the ends of synthetic philosophy.

"Overall, it is Visishtâdvaita, as Shariraka Shastra that presents a synthetic view, par excellence, of Vedânta, because, it is its avowed aim to harmonize the seeming contradictions of the shruti in the light of ghataka shruti-s by employing the samanvaya method, and it is the supreme merit of Bhashyakara to wind up the discussion with a note of harmony in the highest sense of the term: "Thus everything is satisfactorily explained (*iti sarvam samanjasam*).

B in effect becomes as *prakrti, purusha, mahat, ahankâra, tanmâtram, pancha bhuta*, senses, the cosmic sphere of Chatur Mukha Brahma consisting of fourteen worlds, the four types of living beings –gods, humans, animals and plants. The knowledge of B in the causal state leads to the knowledge of all (VS 87).

॥ एक विज्ञानेन सर्वविज्ञानं उपपन्नतरम्॥

According to BS (the sutra: *prakrtishcha pratijnya drshhTanuparodhat -* 1.4.23), B is the material cause, as made out in the opening declaration. Does it not follow that B itself transforms into prakrti? This view stands opposed since Upanishads declare that B is not subject to any modification in its substantive prestine nature. To resolve the issue the BS (the sutra: *nâtma shruternityatvat cha tabhya: --* 2 .3.18) should be kept in view. Here also it is denied the transformation of B into the infinite individual selves. The a/m sutra states that, "the individual selves are not originated at the time of *srishti* because the scriptual texts speak of the eternity of the individual selves." By the same token prakrti also is not originated (VS 89).

Riks from Shveta are quoted to show the unoriginated existence of purusha and prakrti. The purusha is bound in prakrti. Only prakrti suffers change (VS 90).

Shlokas in Gita reiterate the same point. The shloka (BG 13.19) state that prakrti and purusha are both beginningless (anadi). "*bhumi ...prakrti ashhTadhâ*" (BG 7.4). "*apareyam...jîvabhutam*" (BG 7.5) Verses from the 9th chapter, namely 8 & 10 are also cited: "*prakrtim svam ...puna: puna:*" & "*mayadhyaksheNa ... suyate sacharacharam*" (VS 91).

Shlokas in VP establish the same (VS 92):
Bhagavan Vishnu is both the causal reality (*avyaktam*) and the reality of effect (*vyaktam*). He is the Supreme Purusha and the Time is in His control (*kâla*). He plays the game of Creation like a child (*kriDato balakasyeva* --1.2.18). He is the Prime Mover (*kshobhaka:*) and the things that are moved (*kshobya*).

In VS 93, the terms praLaya and srshti are explained once again with the view to show that they are in conformity with the shloka VP (1.9.37): B is the cause of the effects, the unoriginated pradhana and purusha."

The terms Atma and Sharira are explained in VS 95. Simply put âtma is the one which has control over the body. The body is that which exists inseperably from âtma and exists entirely to serve the purpose of the âtma. In a similar manner, the Supreme Self (*Paramâtmana:*) has the world as His body (*sarva shariratvena*) and is therefore denoted by all words (*sarva shabda vachyatvam*). Just as the statement, 'all roads lead to Rome' here in Vedânta, all words in the Vedas are indicative of B. Krishna says, "It is I who has to known from all the Vedas" (BG 15.15).

॥ वेदैश्च सर्वैरहमेव वेद्यः ॥

In VS 98, the verse in Manusmrti (12.122) which deals with contemplation on B is explained. Seeing the Paramâtman vividly in contemplation is like dream coming true (*rukmâbham svapnadhîgamyam vidyâttu purushham param*).

<u>'Freedom from bondage'</u>
Point 1: The characteristics of the jivâtma: indivisible (*aparichchinna*); free from impurities (*nirmala*); by very nature it shines with knowledge (*Jnâna svarupa*);

177

Point 2: But the knowledge is covered by nescience which is in the form of karma (*karma rupa avidya veshhTita:*); the opacity caused depends on the karma (*tat tat karma anurupa Jnâna sangkocham apanna:*).

Point 3: This karma is wide ranging –from the highest Chatur Mukha Brahma to the lowest that of a blade of grass (*brahmadi stamba paryanta vividha vichitra deheshhu pravishhTa:*). This ignorance makes them think that 'body is âtma' (*tattad deha âtma manina:*) and make them engage in appropriate activities (*tat uchita karmaNi kurvaNa:*); suffer the travails of samsâra (*tad anuguNa sukha du:kha upabhoga rupa samsâra pravaham pratipadyante*).

Point 4: Only by surrendering to B (read Bhagavan) one can get freed from bondage (*eteshhâm samsâra mochanam bhagavat prapattim antareNa na upapadyate*).

Point 5: Spiritual science (Gita) teaches that differences exist only in the embodiment and not in the âtma (*devadi bheda rahita Jnâna eka akarataya sarveshham samyam pratipadya*).

Point 6: The individual âtma should also be aware of its subordinate relationship with B (*tasyapi svarupasya bhagavat sheshhata eka svarupa eka rasataya*) and the relationship is inseperable and everlasting (*bhagavat âtma katama api pratipadya*).

Point 7: The awareness of the auspicious nature of B (*bhagavat svarupam*) has a purifying effect on the one who contemplates on B (*heya pratyanika kalyaNaika tanataya ...sarvasya âtmabhutam pratipadya*).

Point 8: B's Absolute Power of holding everything under His control (*sva-sangkalpa pravrtta samasta chit achit vastu jatataya sarvasya âtmabhutam pratipadya*).

178

Point 9: Freedom from bondage (VS 99) is the attainment of B and the attainment is through devoted worship of B (*tadupâsanam sangam tatprâpakam pratipâdayanti*). See also the 19 verses of Gita (12-30 of BG 2) where the *âtma* is described in detail.

These points will be substantiated by quotes from standard texts (*shâstrâNi*). Shastra is a comprehensive term which includes shrutis, smrtis, itihasas and purânas. See also GBG 16.24.

VS 100: For Point 1 refer the defining verse in VP (6.7.22). The âtma is devoid of any inhibitions of the material world. It is out and out a spiritual substance (*nirvaNa maya eva ayam âtma*) possessing spiritual knowledge (*Jnâna maya:*). Suffering, ignorance and impurities are the properties of matter (*du:kha-aJnâna-mala dharma: prakete:*) and not contributed by the âtma (*te na cha âtmana:*) When in contact with matter such as a physical embodiment the âtma is subjected to the experiences of karma (*prakrti samsarga krta karma mulatvat*) or the travails of samsâra. The suffering is not due to âtma (*na âtma svarupa prayukta: dharma:*). The individual will be able to overcome suffering by developing discrimination between the âtma and prakrti (*prapta-aprapta vivekena "prakrte: eva dharma:" ityuktam*).

VS 101 & 102 are devoted to explaining several of the Points and Point 2. The one who has developed the a/m discriminative intelligence is glorified as 'The Pandit' (*svarupa vivechani buddhi: yeshham te panDita:*). Gitâchârya traces the profile of this pandit in verse (BG 5.18). He does not see variations in embodiments but sees the indwelling âtma as identical (*tatra tatra atyanta vishhama akare vartamanam samanakaram pashyanti iti sama darshina: ityuktam*). Such a pandit has the maturity to overcome bondage while living in this world itself (*iha eva = sâdhana anushhThana dashayam eva; tai: sargo jita: = samsaro jita: --BG 5.19*). Stainless (*nirdoshham*) means freed from the stain that consists in being associated with material embodiments –such as gods, humans, animals and plants.

VS 103: The âtma in its essential nature has only the nature of blissful spiritual knowledge and is therefore all the indwelling âtmas are alike. One should also be in the know that the âtma we have been talking about is wholly subservient to B (*âtmana: bhagavat sheshhataika-rasata*) controlled by B (*tanniyamyata*) and supported by B (*tad eka adharata*) in the respective bodies (*tat tat sharira tat tanu prabhrti bhish shabdai: tat samanadhi karaNyena cha*). The principle of grammatic coordination establishes the intimate relationship between âtma and B. This principle was Illustrative with copious texts taken from shruti, smrti, itihasa and PurâNa (*purvameva uktam*).

VS 104: Reference to Point 4 is the verse in Gita BG 7.14. Bhagavan Krishna says: "The matter having the three guNas (guNamayi) is under my control. I have used it for creation (*deivi he eshha*). The samsaris cannot cross this maya on their own accord (*mama maya duratyaya*). Only those who surrender to Me (*mameva ye prapadyante*) can cross and get freed from the strangle hold of maya (*etam mayam taranti*). GBG takes this oppurtunity to clarify that maya doesn't mean illusion as the Advaitins claim (*ato maya shabdo na mithyartha vachi*). The Pu 17 also states that there is no other way (nanya: pantha) to get moksha.

VS 105 More and more details of B are brought in to impress upon the reader the nature and power of B in the process of creation. Again, the quotation is from Gita (BG 9.4 & 5): "All this chit & achit is invisibly pervaded by Me (*idam sarvam maya avyakta murtina tatam*). All things are in Me (*sarva bhutani matsthani*) but I am not in them (*aham cha teshhu naavastita:*). We can understand this through an example. B's stand-off is like that of the tongue which tastes all kinds of foods but nothing sticks to it. So, to say the tongue doesn't need to be washed!

180

"I hold the whole world under my control with a fragment of my power" which means "I enter into this varied universe as its soul and hold it by my will. With innumerable attributes, I am a wonder to behold!" GBG 10.42 explains in terms of cosmic creation.

VS 106 B is one in many and many in one (*ekatve sati nanatvam nanatve sati cha ekata*); B's form is beyond comprehension (*achintyam brahmaNo rupam*); B being one controls all (*prashasitrtvena eka eva san*); B has entered the whole variety of sentient beings (*vichitra chit vastushhu antarâtmataya pravishya*) and exists in the variety of modes (*tattat rupeNa vichitra prakara:*); B is the engine for leading living beings into activity (*vichitra karma karayan nana rupatam bhajate*); and the wonder of wonders is that B has manifested from a small fraction (*svalpa amshena*) of His. The shrutis glorify each attribute of B with the following great names:

सर्वेश्वरेश्वरः परब्रह्मभूतः पुरुषोत्तमः

नारायणः निरतिशयाश्चर्य भूतः नीलतोयद

सङ्काशः पुण्डरीकदलामलायतेक्षणः सहस्रांशुः

सहस्र किरणः परमे ओयोम्नि - यो वेद निहितं

गुहायां परमे व्योमन् - तदक्षरे परमे व्योमन्॥

VS 107 The uniqueness of the Supreme Being is expounded. B has characteristics —such as diversity of nature (*svabhava:*), diversity of forms (*svarupa*) and manifoldness in activities (*karya shakti*) —not found in any being (*na ghaTate*). One single entity (*ekasya parasya brahmaNa:*) is endowed with an infinite variety of and attributes — all in one and one in all (*ekasyaiva vichitra ananta nana rupata cha punarapi ananta aparimita ashcharya yogena eka rupata*). Such mind boggling, opposing characteristics can only be found in B (*virodha chinta na yukta ityartha:*).

Varadaraja Panchasat (16). Seven special characteristics of the essential nature of B gets mentioned in this shloka (*sanchintayanti akila heya vipaksha bhutam*).

Vs 108 The observations made in the above paragraph are lyrically waxed in verses in VP. Take the diverse nature of two elements – fire and water –used as building blocks in creating the world. The property of heat in fire is not found in water. Such is the divergence in the property. Thus, Sage Parashara elaborates on the architectonics of B's creation.

The sage has devoted one full chapter (amsha V) for the narration of the biography (*janma and karma*) of Bhagavan Krishna. Akrura (a great bhakta of Krishna) expresses in raptures the vision he had: "O Krisna! What a wonderful vision you have given me. I got an insight into the Infinite Form of yours constituting the world of your creation (*jagad etat maha ashcharyam rupam* –VP V.19.7). Not all are favoured with this kind of vision. It is only for those whom B chooses!

VS 109 Several hymns in the Upanishads (*anekavidha: shrutayo vadanti*) speak about the creation / dissolution of the universe by B (*srshhTipraLayau brahmaNa:*). These texts can be brought under six groups.

VS 110 One group of texts describe B as "free from imperfections" (*niravadyam*), "free from evil" (*niranjanam*), "knowledge" (*viJnânam*), "bliss" (*anandam*), "partless" (*nishhkalam*), "free from activity" (*nishhkriyam*), "full of peace & tranquility" (*shantam*), "devoid of attributes" (*nirguNam*). Some texts add that apart from being "*nirguNam*" B is by nature "*Jnâna-svarupa*".

VS 111 (Group II) This group denies plurality: "*neha nanasti kinjchana*", "one who sees plurality, is not relieved from bondage".

PNS: p243, "The monistic texts deny not the pluralistic universe but only the pluralistic view of reality viz. B."

VS 112 (Group III) The texts in this group wax lyrical on the Absolute nature of B: "B who knows all, who cognizes all, and knowledge being His very penance" (*yassarvanyas sarva vit yasya njanamayam tapa:*). The familiar rik (Pu.16) is recalled: "sarvaNi rupaNi ...yadaste", "sarve nimeshha jagnyire vidyuta: purushhadadhi" (Maha), the famous guNastakam. These texts deny defect or imperfections to B (*heyata avagatam sarvam guNam nishhidya*", praise the infinite auspicious nature of B (*niratishaya kalyaNa guNa anantyam*), the all-knowing B (*sarvajnyatam*); B endowed with Absolute Power (*sarva shakti yogam*), all entities with names and forms embeded in B (*sarva nama rupa vyakaraNam*) and B, the support of all (*sarvasya adharatam*).

VS 113 (Group IV) "Everything indeed is B, for everything emerges, absorbed and has its being in B' (*sarvam khalvidam brahma tachjalan iti* –Chand 3.14.1); "all this is ensouled by B (*etdatmyamidam sarvam* – Chand 6.8.7); "all the discussions center around B" (*ekasmin bahudha vichara: --A VI.3*); The created world has all the multiplicity and variety but B is one (*brahma srshhTam jagat nanakaram pratipadya tadaikyam cha prati pâdayanti kashchana shrutaya:*).

VS 114 (Group V) Several riks are from Shveta to show that B is distinct from all and they emphasise the close relationship between B and the living beings.

VS 115 (Group VI) These riks relate to Antaryami Brahmanam dealt with earlier.

PNS: p 243, "The Antaryami Brahmana defines B as the Inner Self of the chetana and achetana… The interpretation of Vedântic texts in terms of Sharira-Shariri bhava has the advantage of reconciling

183

apparently contradictory texts without sacrifycing their primary and natural meaning or mukhyartha".

नानारूपाणां वाक्यानां अविरोधः

मुख्यार्थे अपरित्यागश्च यथा सम्भवति

तथैव वर्णनीयं वर्णितं च॥

VS 116 The texts discussed in Group I to VI are brought together and interpreted keeping in view the rationale and coherence of thought behind these texts. The shrutis which hold changelessness of B (*avikara shrutaya:*) stand unshaken since the form of B does not undergo change (*svarupa pariNama pariharadeva mukhyartha:*). B is nirguNa because B is free from defects of any kind (*nirguNa-vadashcha prakrta heya guNa nishhedha vishhayataya vyavasthita:*). The texts which deny plurality (*nanatva nishhdha vadashcha*) are not disregarded by us since all things other than B (sentients and non-sentients) constitute the body of B (*ekasyaiva brahmaNa: sharirataya prakarabhutam sarvam chetana-chetanam sarvasya âtmataya sarva prakaram brahmaiva avastitamiti surakshita:*).

Texts which declare several aspects —such as B is distinct and different from everything else (*sarva vilakshaNatva*); B is the Lord and Ruler (*pati & Ishwara*); B is the abode of all auspicious qualities etc.

PNS: p 243, "The absolutist as Jnâna-matra-vadin, who affirms the reality of pure-consciousness and denies its self-consciousness and concious nature, fails to explain the saguNa texts like B being the All-Self and the knower of all things (sarvajnya, sarvavit and Jnâna-maya) These texts define the nature of B as the cosmic ground (sarvadhara), the IR (*niyantr*) and Sarva Sheshin B is and has intelligence as its essential quality and from this definition (*svarupa-nirupaka-d*harma) flows an infinity of perfections. By denying predication (as in Advaita), knowledge itself is denied and stultified."

184

The fact that the nature of B is knowledge (*svarupamapi Jnânameva iti cha pratipâdanat anupalitam*) does not run counter to our view. The declaration of unity (*aeikyavadashcha*) stands very well established in our siddhanta thanks to the application of Coordinate Predication principle (*sharira âtma bhavena samanadhi karaNa mukhyartha upapâdanad eva susthita*).

VS 117 This paragraph is translated on page 245 of PNS:
"In a critical summary in the VS, Ramanuja concludes that this view is a reconciliation of the extremes of the Vedântic doctrines like the schools of *abheda*, *bhedabheda* and *bheda*. Abheda is established by the idea of B as the unity of sharira –sharirin relation in which the sharirin is the one without a second that sustains the manifold of chit and achit (*sarva sharirataya sarva prakaram brahmaiva avasthitamiti abheda: samarthita*); the view that the prakarin is the one that exists as the many prakaras supports the truth of *bhedabheda* (*ekameva brahma nana bhuta chit-achit-vastu-prakaram nanatvena avastitamiti bhedabhedau*); and bheda is proved by the fact of the eternal distinction between chit, achit and Ishwara in their nature and character (*achitvastunashcha chitvastunashcha ishvarasya cha svarupa-svabhava-vailakshaNyat asangkarat cha bheda: samarthita*)

PNS: p 273, "There is no confusion in the nature of chit, achit and B as non-sentient matter is everchanging, sentient souls are liable to suffering and B is ever pure and perfect."

VS 118 Is it not the knowledge of unity (*aeikya jnâna*) between B and jivâtma that is put forward in "tattvamasi, Shvetaketo!" & "yavadeva chiram" to secure liberation?

The above is not true (*naitadevam*). On the contrary, the exact opposite is what is recommended in the rik Shveta (I.12) which states that one should know that B is quite distinct and different from jivâtma, as given below.

॥ पृथगात्मानं प्रेरितारं च मत्वा जुष्टस्ततस्तेनामृतत्वमेति ॥

It is only through the grace of B that the jivâtma gets immortality (*tena paramâtmana jushhTa: amrtatvameti*). Thus, the direct means (*sakshat amrtatva prapti sâdhanam*) is knowing the difference between the individual jivâtma aspiring for liberation and the IR (*antaryâmi*) who acts as a prompter (*preritaram*) for the jivâtma to get moksha. This rik abundantly makes it clear that B is saguNa.

VS 119 The a/m rik from Shveta is not favourable to the Advaitin who considers SaguNa B as unreal. Why not the other way is true? We consider NirguNa B is unreal.

VS 120 Whenever there is a conflict between two riks (*dvayo: tulyayo: virodhe sati*) we should think of reconciling the two (*tayo: vishhaya: vivechaniya;*). The Advaitins committed a serious error by ignoring the great concept viz sharira- shariri- bhava which amounted to "throwing the baby out with the bath water"! The word 'tvam' should be viewed in the vedantic perspective. The individual âtma is a constituent of the body of B who is within the former as his IR and Director and therefore the word 'thou' (*tvam*) means B who has the individual self (*âtma*) as B's *prakâra* or mode. B the IR is free from all defects and imperfections and fit to be contemplated upon since He is the abode of all auspicious qualities (*kalyana guNa*).

अन्तर्यामिरूपेण अवस्तितस्य परस्य ब्रह्मणः

शरीरतया प्रकारत्वात् तत्प्रकारं ब्रह्मैव त्वम्

इति शब्देन अभिधीयते ॥

VS 121 Another rik in Shveta (I.12) lends support to Ramanuja's interpretation that B can only be saguNam.

The Vedântin should know three things –the experiencer (bhokta), the objects of experience (*bhogyam*) and the IR who prompts (*preritaram*). The objects of experience are the inanimate ones (achetanatvam) which are meant for others (*paramarthatvam*), and they are subject to continuous modification (*satata vikara-aspatatvam*). Such are the properties of matter (*ityadaya: svabhava:*).

The experiencer (*bhokta*) is the jivâtma. Its nature was mentioned earlier (VS 100): –*amala, aparichchhinna, Jnânananda svabhava:*. However, the jivâtma has a long history of karma attached to it (anadi karma rupa avidya krta:). This attachment enveloping âtma is nescience which attenuates knowledge in various degrees causing expansion and contraction (*nanavidha sankocha vikasau*). The main cause of karma is its association with matter, craving for experience (*bhogyabhuta achid vastu samsargashch*a). Nontheless, the jivâtma has the option to get freed from matter through devoted worship of B (*paramâtma upâsanat mokshashcha ityadaya: svabhava:*).

The third is that B is the IR of both –the experiencer as well as the objects of experience (*evambhuta bhoktr bhogyayo: antaryami rupe*Na *avastanam*). B's svabhava is that it is the repository of auspicious attributes. This rik of Shveta (I.12) inculcates discriminative of the three entities and the three forms in which B exists (*parasya* brahmaNa: trividhavastanam jnatavyam ityartha:).

VS 122 Acharyas earlier to Shankara, while dealing with Sadvidya, had interpreted tattvamasi only from the stand of saguNa B.

VS 123 Then a serious objection arises which should be sorted out. It was repeatedly said that IR as Antaryamin directs and controls all selves (*nanu cha sarvasya janto: paramâtma antaryamin tanniyamyam cha*

187

sarvam ityuktam). In that event, there won't be any person qualified (*adhikari na drshyate*) to follow the injunctions (*vidhi*) and prohibitions (*nishhedha*) as laid out in the scriptures (*shastranam*). Only he who acts using his own reason (*svabudyaiva*) can be given instructions such as 'do this' & 'don't do that' (*sa evam kuryat na kuryat iti*). How then can it be said that all actions get performed through the promptings of B (*sarvasya preraka: paramatma karayita*)? In addition, there is a shruti which states: "He whom B desires to raise, him B directs to do good things and conversely, he whom B wants to cast down, B directs him to do bad things." Can the all merciful B harbour ill will against some body? Is B partial? Cruel?

VS 124 The individual is free to do whatever he wants. B doesn't interfere. However, if an individual by himself is engaged in the pursuit of what agrees with the will of B and B being pleased with him confers upon him a holy disposition of will and intellect that would actuate him to come to Him (*kalyaNe pravartayati*). If on the other hand, a person has already begun to do evil deeds, B strengthns him in his evil nature ('stew in his own juice') and makes him do, of his own accord only cruel deeds thereafter (*tasya kruram buddhim vadan svayameva krureshhu eva karmasu prarayati bhagavan*).

VS 125 The observations are in perfect agreement with verses in Gita (BG X.10). Bhagavan Krishna: "To those who worship Me, I confer special intellect (*buddhi yogam dadami*) by which they attain Me (*yena mam upayanti te*). And I, dwelling in their hearts, am moved by compassion and destroy their darkness of ignorance by kindling the lamp of wisdom (*nashayami atma-bhavastha: Jnâna dipena bhasvata*)".

Regarding the evil-minded ones, refer the verse BG (XVI.19). Bhagavan Krishna: "But I throw the cruel ones who hate Me (*tanaham dvishhata: kruran*) into samsâra (*samsareshhu naradhaman*). Evil-minded are the asuric ones who begin their career of life from

188

being born in demoniac wombs (*kshipami ajasram asureshhu eva yonishhu*).

PNS: p184 / 5, "The true meaning of spiritual freedom ...consists in the knowledge that the real author of all our actions is the IR and in the dedication of every act of ours as the adoration of the highest Self or Parama Purusha (*patram ... bhaktya pratachchhati & yat karoshhi madarpanam* –BG 9.26 &27). The consciousness of Paramâtman is a revolution in life from the egocentric outlook to the theocentric." "The idea of the sheshin gives the highest meaning to moral and spiritual experience as He is the means as well as the end of conduct. This is the true meaning of kainkarya and the highest freedom of life lies in the selfless service to the Supreme who is the only Self without a second" VS 126. This paragraph outlines the attainment of B.

This B (*so ayam param brahma bhuta: purushottama:*) can be attained by devotion alone (*bhakti eka labhya:*). Bhakti is attainable by internal purity which consists in getting rid of sins (*niratishaya puNya sanchaya kshiNa asheshha janma upachita papa rashe:*). Purghing of sins can take place only when one turns one's attention towards God & surrender to His lotus feet (*parama- purusha- charaNaravinda- sharanagati janita tad abhimukasya*). Turning Godward essentially consists in owing allegiance to the Ideal Value System (IVS) as enshrined in the shastras and the shastras have to be known by coming under the influence of a good âchârya well versed in precept & practice view to acquire âtma guNas consisting of –control of mind (*shama*), control over the senses (*dama*), the practice of austerities and penances (*tapas*), purity of body (*shaucham*), patience (*kshama*), straight-forwardness or integrity (*arjava*), an intellect which discriminate between fear and fearlessness (*bhaya- abhayasthana viveka*), compassion (*daya*) and ahimsa.

The reader may refer to the first two verses of Nyasa Vimshati of Deshika where an âchârya and a disciple are defined.

Since the society consists of Brahmins, kshatrias etc.the IVS is enshrined in Varna Ashrama Dharma (VAD) applicable to the individual (refer GBG 18 verses 41 to 45). Worship of B consists in doing one's duty (*varna ashrama dharma uchita parama purushha aradha veshha nitya-naimittika karma upasamhati nishhiddha parihara nishhThasya*); performormed with the spirit of dedication to God (*parama purushha charaNarvinda yugala nyasta âtmatmiyasya*). Bhakti manifesting in every act (*tad bhakti karita anavarata*) – praise (*stuti*), remembrance (*smriti*), obeisance (*namaskrti*), service (*yatana*), recitation (*kirtana*), reflecting over God's attributes and giving vent to it through repeating and listening (*guNa shravana vachana*), contemplation(*dhyana*), offering beautiful, pleasant smelling flowers while doing archana, prostrations (*prâNama*) etc. The merciful Lord pleased with the devotion destroys the inner darkness of the devotee and prepares him to receive His grace (prita parama karunika purushottama prasada vidhvasta svanta dhvantasya). The devotee is blessed with a vision of the Lord during his contemplation (*dhyâna rupa bhakti eka labhya:*).

The *sine-qua-non* of Bhakti is illustrated in the following paras with quotes.

VS 127 Yamunacharya in his Siddhitraya made it clear that B can be attained by one who has got the mind purified by Karma Yoga & Jnâna Yoga and whose unalloyed devotion is wholly and solely directed towards B (*ekantika atyantika Bhakti Yoga labhya:*).

The term avidya in the rik Isa (11) as well as in the verse VP (6.6.12) refers onlyto the purificatory exercise through the performance of VAD. He who knows vidya and avidya is a vidvan and the knower secures immortality, and there is no other way (tamevam vidvan

190

amrta iha bhavati nanya: pantha ayanaya vidyate –Pu 17). "He who knows becomes immortal" (*ya enam vidu: amrtaste bhavanti –Maha*). "He who knows B attains B" –brahma vid apnoti param –Ananda-valli. "He who knows B attains B –*brahma veda brahmaiva bha*vati – Mund 3.2.9.

In all the quotes 'vedana' means 'meditation' (*vedena shabdena dhyanameva abhitam*). And 'nididhyasitavya' also has the same meaning (*aeikarthyat*).

VS 128 B is not attainable through intellectual exercise thinking or reflecting (*pravachana = manana, pravachana shabdena pravachana sâdhanam mananam lakshyate*). Even meditation or listening may not help (*na medhaya na bahuna shrutena*). B is attainable by him whom B chooses (*esha: paramâtma yam sadhakam prarthayate tena labhya:*). Love of God (*ananya bhakti*) on the part of upâsaka creates affection (*priti*) for the latter on the part of the former.

A pleased Krishna revealed Vishva Rupa Darshana to Arjuna.

VS 129 Ramanuja points out the one to one correspondence between the teachings of Parashara and Gitâchârya to buttress up his siddhanta. The sure way to please B is through the execution of ordained duties says VP (3.8.9).

Gitâchârya also in his teachings, first outlines VAD (BG 18 verses 41 to 45 and then the methodology to develop Bhakti is taught (*madbhaktim labhate param*).

VS 130 Ramanuja siddhanta is in aggreement with the teachings of preceptors –such as Bodhayana, Tanka (*Brahmanandin*), Dramida, Guhadeva, Kapardin and Bharuchi and not in aggreement with those of Charvaka, Sakya, Alukya, Akshapâda, Kshapanaka, Kapila and Patanjali.

Ramanuja highlights the role of Sriman Narayana as Chief Architect of Creation by taking quotations profusely from sources such as shrutis (*Shveta*) and from Pancha Suktas, itihâsas and massively from Vishnu PurâNa.

A few points may be noted. Creation and dissolution serve as entertainment sport to Him. Before creation He alone exists and during Creation He is all in all i.e. He is the material cause, the instrumental cause and the efficient cause. The three phases – Creation, Maintenance and dissolution –take place under His behest.

Ramanuja concludes by categorically stating that even Chatur-Mukha Brahma is an embodied soul just like us (VS 131 to 166).

शुभाश्रयत्वानहंत्वोपपादनात् क्षेत्रइं निश्चीयते ॥

Regarding the issue of apûrva, Ramanuja explains that the assumption of the apûrva is unnecessary, since Ishwara's pleasure or grace which has been secured by the activity of the sacrifice persists and can bring about the desired end. He substantiates his conclusions by a fund of hymns from the Upanishads, and copious verses from Gita and in addition verses from Vishnu PurâNa.

Ramanuja quotes the following from Gita: "I am the deity propitiated in all the sacrifices and, likewise, it is I who grant all the desires" (BG 9.24). Whatever be the body (tanu) that the devotee wishes to propitiate with earnestness and sincerity, I endow him with unshaken sincerity in that form of worship. Endowed with that sincere faith, the performs the worship (of that form of body of mine) Then does the devotee's desire gets fulfilled, whatever the desires may be, and these are granted by Me alone" (7.21, 22). In the verse (7.21) the term 'tanu' is used, meaning, "Deities such as Indira, Varuna and others are none other the bodies of Bhagavan who is within them as the Inner Ruler." "One attains peace by knowing that I am the enjoyer of sacrifices and austerities, the Lord of all the lords and a Friend of all" (5.29).

The nature is under His control: The Sun shines, the river flows and the sea is kept within the borders –all because of Him. The humans are controlled as per the commandments spelt out in the Vedas. Gitâchârya puts it succinctly. "But those who don't heed My teaching and who refuse to follow My faith, know them to be blind to all wisdom, and they would degenerate into lower and lower levels of consciousness (*nashta chetasah*)". The following observation made by Ramanuja is worth recalling (197).

इति स्वाज्ञानुवर्तिनः प्रशंस्य विपरीतान् विनिन्द्य पुनरपिस्वाज्ञानुपालनं अकुर्वतां आसुरप्रकृत्यन्तर्भावं

अभिधाय अधमा गतिश्च उक्ताः

It is not mere faith alone that is recommended as an option but it should be observed as a commandment of God. Bhagavan praises those who conform to His *ajnyâ* and reproves the contrary as under: "Those who always follow My commandment are released from samsâra but those who violate, I cast them, again and again, those worst of men, who hate Me, and who are hard hearted and who are unholy, into demoniac births. Having taken demoniac births and being deluded in birth after birth, they fail to attain Me and sink into lower and lower depths." (BG 16. 19-20) Those who follow His command are heirs to everlasting life (BG 18.56).

मत्प्रसादादवाप्नोति शाश्वतं पदमव्ययम् ॥

Freedom of will
The Kaushitaki Upanishad (3.9) states that the Lord raises the one whom He likes and casts one down whom He doesn't like. Is it not partiality, one may ask? It is answered thus: The Supreme Lord

193

endows all sentient beings with the power of thought and power of action. The individual thus equipped with all the requisite powers and capabilities, endowed with the power of initiative, engages in actions and abstinence from action by his own spontaneity of will (VS 124).

In this context, the illuminating pages of PNS (p146-9) should be gone through. A few leading lines for reference is given here: "The exact relationship between human and divine freedom may be determined by contrasting causality and free will...This idea of divine determinism and pre-destination is forcibly expounded in Kaushitaki Upanishad (vide VS 123; BS 2.3.40): "When the Lord elects to lead upwards from these worlds, He makes him do a good deed. When He elects to lead downward from these worlds, He makes him do a wicked deed." The two wills then co exist as one will, when the finite will is in tune with the Infinite and there is no contradiction in such coexistence or self communication."

All are free to do what they like- no restrictions whatever. If a person has already begun, of his own accord, to do things which are extremely pleasing to the Lord, eventually the Lord is pleased with his love and endows him with wisdom and inspires him to further deeds of merit. If, on the other hand, a person has already begun to do extremely evil deeds, the Lord strengthens in him his evil nature and makes him do, of his own accord, only cruel deeds thereafter.

Ramanuja resorts to verses from Gita in support of his Darshana: "To those who worship Me with loving devotion and who eagerly long for union with Me at all times, I graciously vouchsafe unto them the mental capacity to know Me."-*buddhiyogam dadâmi*. To enable them to attain my grace, I reveal My attributes within their minds and with shining lamp of wisdom concerning Me, I destroy all karma resulting from ignorance." (BG 10.10,11) Non-compliers are the âsurik, who get thrown into demonic wombs, as said before-dadâmi for the good and kshipâmi for the bad!

"I confer on men fruits good or bad, as that command of Mine is carried out or violated" (Sri Varadaraja Panchashat 13; See also Dayashatakam 78).

The Art of Living
A person has three types of activity to choose from. They are nishiddha karma or pratishiddha karma or what is forbidden by the Veda. *Kâmya* karma or what relates to a desire to be fulfilled. Nitya karma or what is compulsorily prescribed.

But the divine command is Nishkâma karma "which has an absolute claim upon our obedience and the violation of law is the repudiation of the divine will and the refusal to listen to the voice of God in the inner moral consciousness of mankind. Morality of an action depends upon the motive behind that action. The activity becomes divine when the motive stems from selflessness. The ethics of Karma Yoga strikes a middle path between activism in excess as it favors renunciation in action as opposed to renunciation of action as the ideal of conduct. The ethics of Nishkâma karma or action without the desire for the fruit thereof may now be expounded in the light of the Gita metaphysics of morals, which, for profundity and practical value, stands unmatched in the history of ethics in the East and the West...He (the sâdhaka) follows the middle course between the active and the contemplative life as it is more easy, natural, and conducive to spirituality than karman or karma sanyâsa... Nishkâma karma is really not an end in itself, but is a means to mukti through self purification and self knowledge...The practice of Nishkâma karma and ceaseless dhyâna lies in the recognition of shortcomings of human endeavor and the reliance on divine grace as the only means to mukti" (PNS p 335).

Coming back to Vedârtha Sangraha, the general discussion on Pûrva Mîmâmsaand 'apûrva' extends from VS 167 to 197.In SB it is clearly established that Pûrva and Uttara Mîmâmsatogether constitute one single Shâstra (vide. SB p9).

Existence of Sri Vaikundam

There are countless passages in the shrutis describing the enchanting form of Sriman Narayana, and His two Vibhuti(s)- Lîla and Nitya. The familiar Purusha Sûkta states that His complexion is of golden hue like the sun (*Aditya va*rna) and the Chandogya complements by saying that He is within the sun, golden in appearance. His eyes are like the red lotus which has blossomed with the first rays of the morning sun. (*kapyâsam pundarîkameva akshini*) He is golden (*hiranmayah*), residing in the heart, and can be grasped only by the mind pure and longing for Him-Mândûkya.

The God of the Upanishads has many varied hues not necessarily golden. He is "luminous like a streak of lightning enclosing a cloud"- Mahâ. It means that like a flame of fire burning within the small ether of the heart enclosing a dark water-bearing-cloud-like Bhagavan, ready to shower favor on the meditating person. The Supreme has a mind of His own, pure like the ether (*âkâsha*) has a delightful fragrance of His own, and with multifaceted tastes, sweet speech He permeates this universe (Chand 3.14.2). His raiment is saffron colored (Br 4.3.6).

The queen of the world (*asyeshânah jagatah*), Lakshmi is His consort. The Goddess of the earth and Goddess Lakshmi are His consorts-Purusha Sûkta. "The Sûris are always gazing at the Supreme Abode of Vishnu." "He lives beyond this universe of matter (rajas)" His celestial form is endless, incomprehensible, (*avyakta*), ancient, omnipresent, and beyond the region of tamas. (*vishvam purânam tamasah parastât*) "He who meditates on this Brahman residing in the cave of the heart, attains the supreme abode of Brahman." "He who

196

is the Lord of this is in the highest heaven." "He is the highest imperishable Parama Vyoma, i.e., Sri Vaikundam. He is indeed all this, past, present and future." Ramanuja thus asserts the existence of form of Sriman Narayana and His Nitya Vibhuti. For Ramanuja's own description in rolling phrases (as is his wont to express in the form of a gadya of his) refer to VS 198, and how he substantiates the tenets of his siddhanta through supporting texts from the Upanishads refer to VS 199-202.

तद्विष्णोः परमं पदं

सदा पश्यन्ति सूरयः ।

The meaning of the phrase '*sadâ pashyanti*' 'always gazing', is that there are certain great souls in the Nitya Vibhûti whose vision is eternal. In this sentence three things can be inferred: the suris are eternal, nitya; their vision and the Abode are also existing eternally. It can also be inferred that apart from nitya-suris, the mukta-âtmas who are the later entrants would be different from the eternally dwelling nitya suris. The mention of 'timeless seers', ipso facto, excludes individuals governed by karma.

Vedârtha Sangraha (contd)
Similarly, we can draw three inferences from the phrase 'Parama Pâdam': The highest abode is of course Parama Pâdam; the nature of the individual self freed from prakrti and the very nature of Bhagavan are also designated as Parama Pâdam. All these three are the supreme ideals to be attained. Ramanuja furnishes texts for its usage (VS 208, 9).

Again, in the passage, "He who lives beyond this rajas", inferential logic would facilitate drawing the conclusion that the Abode, (Parama Pâdam) is free from the properties of matter, i.e., free from the properties of mundane prakrti. For, matter consists of sattva,

197

rajas and tamas, and if any one only is mentioned we should take it that the other two are automatically included. Apply this logic also to 'tamasah parastât'. By the phrase 'imperishable highest heaven', *akshare parame vyoman* the imperishable character of that realm is affirmed and it cannot be any perishable region like the orb of the sun.

Referring to *gunâshtakam* (we have already made mention of it earlier), Brahman is free from the six heya guNas such as sin, old age, death, grief, hunger and thirst- all these are caused by the evil characteristics of prakrti with its three-fold properties. For, prakrti is the instrument of His cosmic play (*sva-lîlopakarana*). Satya kâma signifies that the objects and instruments of His experience are eternal whether in Nitya or lîla. For, eternity is of two kinds: these instruments while in play (lîla) are subjected to modification and hence unstable and changing, but still prakrti is anâdi and so eternal; however, in Parama pâda one experiences an opposite kind of nityatva which is unchanging stable and true (similar in principle as that of matter/antimatter concept of physics). The abiding nature is indicated by the term Satya. The term Satya Sankalpa enunciates the principle that these objects and instruments whether of the Nitya or of lîla, are all controlled by His will. God's will be done. By contemplating on Brahman, the sâdhaka gets totally influenced by Brahman; the sâdhaka becomes a soul not of this world; He becomes deserving to be an inhabitant of the Nitya Vibhûti and be with the Nitya Sûris. God's Satya Sankalpa enables the sâdhaka to get his true desire (*Satya kama*) fulfilled.

Then Ramanuja cites references to the Divine form of Lord / Parama Pâdam in Srimad Valmiki Ramayana and Vishnu PurâNa. Besides Mahabharata, the sage Veda Vyasa also establishes the fact that the Lord has a Divine Form in his BS 1.1.21. Taking up the cue and with the support of the Upanishads, Ramanuja gives a graphic portrayal of the magnificent form of Sriman Narayana, in rolling

198

phrases in gadya form. His famous description of the eyes (Ref VS 220) is as under:

गम्भीराम्भः समुद्भूत सुमृष्टनाल रविकर

विकसित पुण्डरीकदलामलायतेक्षणः ।

That the form of the Lord is perceptible to the inner eye is supported by Vâkyâkâra and Bhashyakara. The Shâstra verily speaks the truth. Remember what Nammâzhwar has said on this issue- *uLan*. Faith calls total belief in all that is said in the shrutis, including the form of God. And faith entails belief in the Vedas. The power of the words is eternal. It is true that very many words of the Vedas have found their way into common parlance and the same words convey different meaning than what was originally intended in the Vedas. It is not the fault of the Vedas. To retain the originality of the Vedas grammarians framed separate rules for them to protect the relationship between the Vedic word and its meaning that existed eternally. Great seers, prompted by the Lord, appear from time to time to compose the dharma Shâstra, Itihasas and purânas rooted in the vidhis, arthavadas and mantras for the welfare of the whole world (VS 232 & 233).

कल्पे कल्पे निखिलजगदुपकारार्थं वेदार्थं

स्मृत्वा विध्यर्थवादमन्त्रमूलानि धर्म

शास्त्राणि इतिहासपुराणानि च चक्रुः ।

A gist of metaphysics of Vishishtâdvaita is given in VS 234-237. The means for the attainment of Brahman is through *parâ-bhakti* and this para-Bhakti (Bhakti Yoga) is attained through the pathway of devotion, which in turn is promoted by the performance of the duties and rites prescribed for one in accordance with one's varna and ashrama (VS 238). A discussion on the nature of pleasure or pain such love is pleasing and joyful (239, 40). Entities other than Brahman can be a source of joy only to a finite extent. But the joy of Brahman is infinite (*ânando brahma*) (241).Contemplation on Brahman confers joy (VS 242) Brahman is an ocean of attributes. He is the sheshin. The individual self is subservient to Him. When the Supreme Brahman is meditated upon, He becomes an object of supreme love to the devotee, then He Himself effectuates the devotee's God-realization. Hence subservience to Brahman is most desirable (VS 243).

It may be argued that serving others is a dog's way of life and serving God would militate against the concept of liberation. The real relief from bondage could result only in independence i.e. freeing from the serving mentality (VS 244). The above argument stems from a non-comprehension of the self. In the state of embodiment like lion, tiger, human etc there is the mistake in identifying the body for the soul. We are so obsessed with the body that soul awareness hardly arises in the mind0 (VS 245). Now that, as a human, we have a rational mind we should correct ourselves and get equipped with the knowledge of the soul from the teachings of the Upanishads. According to VP (6.7.22) the soul which is in our heart is made of knowledge and is pure and this soul, according to shruti text (*Patim Vishvasya*) should serve the purpose for which it is created i.e. serve God and no one else (VS 246). For, several texts declare that Brahman alone is Bliss (VS 247). Anything other than Brahman, lacks the capacity to bring joy and Bliss. Bound by karma we suffer pain or pleasure depending upon the merit or demerit acquired earlier. There is no intrinsic pain or pleasure in the objects themselves. What was a source of pleasure at one point of time can well be a source of sorrow later. For example, sugar becomes loathsome after contacting diabetes and for another example, the same person who was a friend before turns later into an enemy (VP 2.6.44-47). Manu concurs with this view when he says that all dependence on others (animate or inanimate) causes sorrow.

Contact with the external world is sorrowful. Sorrow or pleasure is the property of matter and not the âtma. Unalloyed Bhakti alone, according to Gita (BG 14.26), is the key to overcome deleterious effect of prakrti (VS 250). Bhakti when in practice is service to God. The Purusha Sûkta (Rik 20) states that he who knows God becomes immortal here alone. "The chosen one gets it- *tena labhyah*." "Whom He selects" makes it clear that the seeker becoming the chosen one for Him. God obliges those who love Him. "I am very dear to the Jnâni and he is dear to Me" (Gita 7.17). That is, knowledge is of the nature of supreme devotion and it is the means for attaining Bhagavan (VS 251).

Bhakti is the hallmark of the grand epic Mahabharata, as highlighted at two important sections of the epic, namely in the section devoted to Moksha Dharma and in Bhagavad Gita. In the former section, Dvaipâyana presents the quintessence of the philosophy of the Upanishads and here also the aspirant for Moksha perceives the Supreme Brahman in the state of his Samadhi through the medium of Bhakti ripened through knowledge. Regarding the latter, refer to the Gitâchârya's verse BG 11.54: "I am attainable through the means of *ananya* Bhakti." Ramanuja himself has given a comprehensive description of "Bhakti" in Art126 in flowing epithets which keep ringing in the ears like his Gadya Traya (VS 252).

The Vedârtha Sangraha is addressed to those who have the power of discrimination, to those who have an absorbing mind and broadening intellect, to those who are free from swell-headedness and short-sightedness and above all to those who have a willingness to accept the authority of the ancient Sanskrit lore.

सारासारविवेकज्ञाः गरीयांसो विमत्सराः ।

प्रमाणतंत्राः सन्तीति कृतो वेदार्थसङ्ग्रहः ॥

Conclusion

It will be appropriate to end this section on "Vedântic Cosmology" with the words of PNS who concludes his massive soul-stirring treatment of Brahman (275 pages of Ref43):

"The full religious value of meditating on Brahman as the cosmic Highest is brought out in the tenth book of Bhagavata and the fifth chapter of Rahasya Traya Sara of Vedânta Deshika. The former extols Brahman as Satyâtmaka, Satyasya Satya and Trisatya (Bhag 10.1.27). That He is the soul and savior of the universe with chit-achit as His sharîra is expressed by Vedânta Deshika in his literal and symbolic description of the formless form (*purudan manivaramâga*). In that beatific form, the Jîva is the jewel Kaustubha, mûla-prakrti is Srivatsa and the five-weapons for preserving righteousness are mahat, ahamkâra and the indriyas. The idea of the Jîva abiding in the heart of Reality as Redeemer furnishes the raison d'être for universal salvation."

We would like to mention that there is a glaring omission in the passage quoted above. This is the paragraph occurring after the tenth chapter titled Cosmology. Grandson's Bhagavatam is referred to but no mention of the grand father or his work. If the verse in Vishnu PurâNa (1.22.67) is any indication, Parashara did not fail to mention his own grandfather from whom he had learnt the description of 'Bhûshhanastra- svarûpam of causal Brahman.' For, the basis of Swami's Tamil verse "Purudan manivaramâga" is the set of verses in VP 1.22. The following verse is the first one in that description.

आत्मानस्य जगतो निर्लेपमगुणामलम्।

बिभर्ति कौस्तुभमणिस्वरूपं भगवान् हरिः ॥

Sage Maitreya's verse requesting the Acharya to brief him on "The Astra Bhûshana Form" of Lord Almighty is the 66th verse for which, in response, Parashara begins the narration after paying obeisance to Lord Vishnu in the 67th and the comprehensive description extends up to the last verse 90. Incidentally this is also the last verse of the First Amsha of Vishnu PurâNa. The merit that accrues to the individual who knows the First Amsha is given in the last three verses. The 89th verse is as under:

कार्तिक्यां पुष्करस्नाने द्वादशाब्देन यत्फलम्।

तदस्य श्रवणात्सर्वं मैत्रेयाप्नोति मानवः ॥

7. Criticisms on Advaita

Some of the well known doctrinal tenets of Advaita criticized in SB are: B is the same as jivâtma, nirguNa B, the existence of two Bs, tattvamasi, neti neti and so on. The a/m topics will be discussed in brief under the respective headings.

I 'tattvamasi'

As Ramanuja himself says in Sri Bhashya, this Vedântic concept is very well explained in VS. (See 'Chatussûtrî ', p362). We have also discussed about it in the previous Chapter. For the present we will confine ourselves to its criticism. "Tattvamasi" is a simple sentence, which when read in the context where it occurs, conveys a very important principle in Vedânta. The interpretation of this sentence consisting of three words viz. tat, tvam & asi –is so important because it holds the master key to unravel the basic structure of Vedânta itself.

Why Ramanuja rejects the Advaita interpretation of 'tattvamasi' as untenable may be appraised here. "That would bring the principle of his interpretation into clearer relief. On the Advaita interpretation also, the term 'tat' stands initially for B the source of the universe characterised by all characteristics implied in being that. The word, 'tvam', stands initially for the individual self, subject to all imperfections characteristic of the finite individual. The identification of 'tat' and 'tvam' is certainly impossible as such.

Hence a drastic division of their connotations must be worked out to facilitate the identification. In the revised scheme, all that the word '*tat*' means by B's creatorship of the world gets abolished. Only the idea of B being infinite and non-dual remains. In the same way, all that is understood by the word, '*jīva*', its finitude, its subjection to evil, is to be rejected. Only its being the immediate and self-evident subject of knowledge is to be retained. The resulting import that emerges out of the identification is that the self signified by '*tvam*' is immediate and infinite.

The double pruning down of the connotation of the two terms costs a great deal. The entire thought that B is the creative source of the world is to be abandoned. The finiteness and evil associated with the individual self must be given up as just creations of misunderstanding and error. Ramanuja refutes this interpretation repeatedly, and most thoroughly in the Ananda-maya- adhikaraNa of SB as also in VS. The gist of the argument can be indicated.

The whole of the Sadvidyā upto the declaration '*tattvamasi*' builds up the concept of B as the source and sustaining soul of the cosmos. It is on that premise that '*tattvamasi*' is constructed. One cannot demolish the premise and enjoy the conclusion. The '*tat*' vanishes into nothingness, if every attribute distinguishing B is drastically cut out. The subjection to evil characterising the jīva cannot be abolished by the hypothesis that it is just a fabrication of error. The liability to such an error is itself a fundamental evil and if that is admitted, the identification of the jīva with the perfect *Sat* is an absurd proposition. The pruning proposed is utterly unworkable. Hence Ramanuja suggests that 'tvam' must not be mechanically understood as standing for the jīva but for the Supreme Self immanent in the jīva. B which is the ground of the world is identified with B, the ultimate self of all individual selves. This general thesis propounded in the sentences, "*aeitadatmyam idam sarvam tatsatyam sa âtmâ*", is particularized in conclusion, regarding Svetaketu, in 'tattvamasi'.

PNS: p90, "Visishtâdvaita does not favour these extreme views, and it provides both for religious adoration and for mystic intimacy by its idea of B as the Cosmic Ruler who is at the same time the Paramâtman in the jivâtman. The Chandogya text 'Thou art That' does not posit the identity of Iśwara and jîva by removing their self-contradictions in the light of *jahat-ajahal-lakshana* according to which the jîva and Iśwara become identical by the sublation of the self-contradictions of nescience. It intimates the truth that Iśwara, the cosmic Lord, is the Inner Self of the jîva and guarantees the bliss of spiritual communion between the two. The infinite that transcends the starry heavens is the same that is immanent in the finite self. Thus the 'I' of the subject philosophy or the Self that illumines the jîva within is the 'Thou' that is the Iśwara of the object philosophy. This view frees the subject philosophy from the charges of subjectivism and atheism and the object philosophy from the charges of deism and divine determinism. And it is the philosophy of truth, as it defines B as not only what is, but also what is self – revealing.

II. B is the same as jivâtma

To prove this fallacy of Shankara's interpretation four sutras of BS are brough forward for discussion. The first one is 4.1.2; the second 3.2.23; the third 4.4.4 & the fourth 1.4.22.

The first one (4.1.2) reads as *"atmeti tupagachchhanti cha"*. The meaning of the sutra is plain. The sadhaka should direct his contemplation on one's own self. It appears to indicate the identity of jivâtma & B, but there is a catch to it that should be resolved keeping the following sutra in view.

The second sutra (3.2.23) for consideration reads: "*api samradhane praktyaksha anumanabhyam*". The most important term is '*samradhana*' which literally means worship. If instead of B, the contemplation is on the 'âtma' then would mean worshipping one's own self –an absurd inference. "Shankara understands it to signify meditation, loving devotion and reverential attention (*dhyana, bhakti, pranidhana*). The peak level contemplation spoken of in these two sutras is one and the same and the interpretation is forced upon us that the contemplation on B should be one's own soul or âtman but it should also be of inward worship or adoration. Shankara attempts to annul the dualistic implication –self & B –of samradhana.

The third one for consideration is –avibhagena drstatvat (BS 4.4.4). The point is whether jivâtman in the state of perfection or moksha divides itself from B? The sutra asserts that it does not so divide but indivisibly one with it. "The said sutra makes the position unambiguous. The treatise does not conclude with this sutra. It goes on to declare in a subsequent adhikaraNa (4.4.6 –*jagad vyapara varjam*) that the jîva though one with B, as asserted in the second adhikaraNa, does not discharge the cosmic functions of B affirmed in the very second sutra of the work (*janma-adyasya yata:*) purporting to define the Supreme. Hence here again we come across a hurdle, a great one at that, against the thesis of utter oneness."

The fourth one is the sutra (1.4.22). "There is one adhikaraNa in the whole treatise which on Shankara's interpretation states the final monistic position unambiguously without any qualification whatsoever."

In the following topic, titled Vakya-anvaya-adhikaraNa (33), the subject matter discussed pertains to the famous dialogue between Sage Yagnyavalkya and his wife Maitreyi. The sutras in the topic are 19 – 22. The point at issue is whether word âtma in the rik pertains to jivâtma or B?

207

॥ आत्मा वा अरे द्रष्टव्यः ॥

Three Sages Asmarathya, Audulomi and Kashakrtsna explain it in three different ways and they respectively correspond to sutras 20, 21 & 22.

For Asmarathya, âtma includes B but according to Shankara, Sutrakara rejects the explanation of Asmarthya since causal process cannot be accepted as real. Audulomi has explained that jîva attains oneness with B in his final state of perfection. There is an anticipatory identification in the discourse. Shankara derives support from Audulomi but holds on to his view that limiting conditions unreal. The final view is that of Kashakrtsna:

॥ अवस्थितेरिति काशकृत्स्नः ॥

The above sutra means that Yagnavalkya identifies the two âtmans –jivâtman and B –on the ground of avasthiti. Shankara interprets the word "avasthiti" to mean that it is B that exists as jîva and according to him this view is accepted by Sutrakara also. The word avasthiti can hardly mean 'existing as'. Sutrakara uses it, according to Shankara himself, thrice in the sense of 'existing in' (vide sutras 1.2.18; 2.3.25 & 3.3.32). In all these cases, it means 'dwelling in' or 'location in' or simply 'existing in'. The idea of Kashakrtsna is simple immanence. Avasthiti meaning dwelling does not call up the question 'as what?' but does call up the question 'where?'. The Antaryami Brahmanam of the same Upanishad answers the question 'where' by pointing out that B dwells in the âtma. But Shankara would not entertain any of these explanations and what is worse is that he drags Sutrakara supports his erroneous viewpoints.

SSR: The reader may refer to p62 for a full account of the Yagnavalkya Maitreyi dialogue and the view of Shankara: "The

208

present adhikaraNa adds the all important doctrine (of Advaita) that B and the individual (âtma) are one integrally.

III. World is illusory

The second sutra of Chatus Sutri, viz. *janmadyasya yata:*, declares in massive terms that B is the architect of the cosmos and the main burden of the two adhyâyas of BS is to establish this truth. The first adhyâya brings forward many upanishadic passages to signify that B is the ultimate principle explanatory of the cosmos. The second adhyâya is devoted to the justification of this position. It is within this general background that the problem of the reality or otherwise of the world must be viewed. We can take a cross section of the BS for finding out whether Shankara's *'jagan mithya'* holds good or not.

To begin with we find that the term maya occurs in BS 3.2.3 (1). Here the Sutra-kara considers only the dream world as maya but Shankara hastens to add that the world is no different in the waking state also as he has already prepared the ground in an earlier context (arambhana-adhikaraNam BS 2.1(6). The first sutra of this adhikaraNam reads as under.

॥ तदन्यत्वमारम्भणशब्दादिभ्यः ॥

We have already discussed in VS regarding cosmology –the effect is not something newly originated but simply the unfoldment of the potentials pregnant in the cause. This is known as satkarya-vada. It is at this juncture the above sutra is framed. It simply means that there is non-difference between the cosmos and its cause. We have repeatedly stressed that what was subtle in the state of cause became gross in the state of effect and there is continuity throughout. But Shankara would have none of it as he is not satisfied with the position that the effect is continuous substantively with the cause but asserts that whatever is found in the effect not found in the cause is unreal.

209

Shankara shattered the cogent philosophy of Sutrakara by breaking the system of BS into two fragments —one propounding the theory of B as the complete cause of the world and the other dismissing the world as illusory because B cannot be the cause at all.

PNS: p65, "The Advaitic acceptance of parnama vâda or the theory that B evolves into the universe with a view to its later rejection in terms of vivarta or phenomenal or illusory development is a typical example of the self-contradiction implied in its philosophy of two standpoints."

PNS: p256, "Causality is nowhere condemned to be self contradictory or illusory but is employed as the fundamental category to expound the origin of the universe. The terms sad eva and arambhana bring out the fact of causality as parinama or transformation (SB 2.1.15) and not of illusoriness or *vivarta*. If, as the illusionist urges, the cause is real and the effect is false, this falsity will infect the integrity of the cause itself, and then Veda and the mumukshu who relies on it will be false.

Visishtâdvaita is opposed to the Advaita theory of Maya-vâda and identity philosophy, as it affirms the reality of jagat and recognizes only visishta-aeikya and not svarupa aeikya."

Ref 59 p72/73: "This adhikaraNa 2.1(6) is of great importance and consists of seven sutras. Of them the first is the heart of the second adhyâya and we may say it is the heart of the philosophy taught by Badarayana, according to Shankara...The first sutra effects a revolutionary change of perspective in Shankara's interpretation. According to it the world effect of B is unreal in so far as it is different from B." In the adhikaraNa-wise analysis of Shankara's interpretation, the author pauses for a brief review (p78).

There are three propositions to choose from:

(1) B becomes the world.

(2) A part of B transforms itself into the world.

(3) There is no evolving of B into the world. The world is a mistaken view of B, which is transcendent and integral altogether.

The first two possibilities are rejected by the Sutrakara, according to Shankara, and the last is adopted along with the hypothesis that the world and its conjectured origination in B are fabrications (*ashruta kalpana*) of mere 'avidya', the principle that conceals the real and shows up the unreal. The compositeness of B required by the second alternative can very well be the figment of the same avidya".

It was shown in VS that Ramanuja goes with the first possibility while he rejects the second and third possibilities and strongly establishes his viewpoint resting squarely on the solid pillars of BS. Shankara's claim is suspect as it will appear hallow and void when viewed against the sophisticated siddhanta of Ramanuja.

IV. NirguNa B

The two concepts of B, according to Shankara are the NirguNa (attributeless) and the SaguNa (with attributes) and likewise the pairs, Nirvishesha –Savishesha, Nirvikalpa –Savikalpa & Nirdharmaka –Sadharmaka are all the respective equivalents of NirguNa & SaguNa B. The two issues discussed earlier –identity of B with jivâtma & illusoriness of Jagat –hinge upon the third issue whether B is Nirvishesha or Savishesha? Hence it becomes necessary to scan the whole of BS to decide one way or the other the third issue from the stand point of Shankara. Chatus Sutri gets excluded from the scan since B is undoubtedly SaguNa and hence Shankara does not make a whisper of a mention about it!

While introducing the sixth adhikaraNa Shankara puts the thin end of the wedge by positing his pet theory of two B's: the higher NirguNa B and the lower avidya ridden SaguNa B. He does not find a single adhikaraNa in the first pâda in support of his theory. All the Upanishads considered for all the adhikaraNas prove that B is undoubtedly the ground of the universe and hence SaguNam only.

The second pâda abounds in guNas. To start with, the Sandilya-Vidya of Chandogya refers to B as the repository of great guNas BS 1.2(2).

॥ विवक्षितगुणोपपत्तेश्च ॥

The third - BS (1.2. (3) - identifies the person in the eye (vide Chand. 4.15.1) as B, for He is said to be the Visishta or qualified by Supreme Bliss —sukha visishta abhidhanadeva cha. The next BS 1.2. (4) identifies the attributes of B as that of B of Antaryamin [Brhad. (3.7.42)]. BS 1.2. (5) talks about the imperishable principle Akshara (vide Mundaka). Sutrakara concludes that Akshara is B with attributes.

॥ अदृश्यत्वादिगुणको धर्मोक्तेः ॥

The reader may note that the above sutra has both the terms —guNa & dharma —abundantly emphasizing that B can be only SaguNa. The last topic Vaishvanara 1.2(6) can hardly be disputed if one remembers Gita (BG 15.14).

The elucidation of B as SaguNa B is continued in the third pâda. The 2nd adhikaraNa 1.3(2) relates to Bhuman of Chand. B is with dharma-upapatteshcha -1.3.8.

These illustrations drawn from the first chapter explicitly associte B with defining terms —such as dharma, guNa and visheshana. In all the references to the scriptures we come across B described with sensuous attributes and distinguishing characteristics affirming that B is SaguNam.

Now we shall move on to scan the second adhyâya of BS to find the elusive NirguNa B of Shankara.

The first pâda (2.1.10) is concluded thus: sarva dharma upapattesh cha. If this sutra is any indication it shows unmistakably the conviction of Sutrakara of SaguNa B and he does not give any room for entertaining the idea of NirguNa B. The whole of pâda 2 (BS 2.2) is devoted to the criticism of the rival systems (those that don't belong to Upanishads) and rejects their theory of cosmos as the entities posited for the purpose are qualitatively deficient. The third and fourth pâdas detail the process of world formation in relation to the several elements and the sensory equipment of creatures. All these flow from the abundance of perfection in B.

Let us bypass the third adhyâya for a moment and proceed to the fourth and the last adhyâya. The adhyâya deals with jivâtma's ascent to liberation conceived as union with B (avibhaga –BS 4.4.4). For a detailed discussion see PNS: p 483 /4.

For Shankara, a votary of NirguNa, may take it to mean 'merger' with B in which case the jivâtma loses its individual identity. But the sutrakara does not go with Shankara as he maintains in another sutra (4.4.17) that the liberated soul shares bliss of equal measure with B sans B's cosmic activities –jagatvyaparavarjam. It is possible that the Sutrakara has two ideas of moksha –the higher one of total identity and the lower one of union. But he gives no hint of two level and if at all it must be admitted, it should spring from two conceptions of B.

In fact, the adhikaraNa 4.4.(3) raises this question: does the liberated âtma atain to the qualitative perfections such as the one referred to in Dahara vidya or does the âtma simply abide as mere substantative and non-relative consciousness, which the NirguNa B is held to be? Jaimini holds the former view and Audulomi the latter. Sutrakara gives his decision (sutra 7) to the effect that the two views are to be combined as they involve no contradiction. Shankara explains that the non-contradiction is due to Audulomi being correct from the higher point of view and Jaimini from the lower SaguNa mode of thinking. The NirguNa point of view, Shankara asserts, has been established in the adhikaraNa 3.2.(5).

Before going to that vital adhikaraNa, let us take note of one important point: The 4th Adhyâya concludes with an adhikaraNa which Shankara cannot but concede. It pertains to the destination of the aspirant of SaguNa B and the Sutrakara states that once reaching the goal there is no more return to this mundane world of samsâra. Shankara hastens to add that the knower of NirguNa B attains higher.

Continuing the scan, we must find where in the third adhyâya, the NirguNa B of Shankara is hiding, assuming for a moment that such a B at all exists, certainly not in the third pâda since this pâda abounds in brahma-vidyas involving meditation on the auspicious form of SaguNa B. Searching for NirguNa B here would be like searching for a desert within a dense rain forest!

The pâda (BS 3.1) deals with transmigration and maintains that on death the âtma carries the elements of the body it leaves behind and carries with it the load of its karma to the new embodyment. The second pâda (BS 3.2) analyses in the beginning the self in the state of dream and points to the creation of the dream world in which it wallows with its powers curtailed by ignorance and as the consequence of bondage. Then the state of deep sleep is analysed.

214

In this state, the self withdraws into rest in B and is temporarily seperated from the external worlds of waking and dream. Nothing happens to the self-identity of the jîva at the time of its stop-over in B during deep sleep. For, that consummation devoutly wished by the self can come about only through the final vedantic enlightenment by way of sâdhana. There is a third state discussed, which may be termed as swooning or coma. An account of the three states is given, according to Shankara, for purposes of generating vairagya or detachment towards the mundane life of bondage.

Then follows the crucial adhikaraNa based on which Shankara is said to have propounded his NirguNa Brahmam. A part of the sutra itself would serve as the appropriate heading for discussion.

V. Ubhaya-Lingam
The important sutra which is of paramount significance to Shankara, namely, BS 3.2.11, is as under.

॥ न स्थानतोऽपि परस्योभयलिङ्गं सर्वत्र हि ॥

First, let us explain its import appropriate to its present context. Having described the despicable state of Jivâtma in the previous four adhikaraNas, the Sutrakara propounds in this adhikaraNa that the Paramâtman, inspite of His dwelling in all states of the individual, which is a source of suffering and misery, He is not affected by it (*na sthanatopi parasya*), because of the two special characteristics which are ever natural to Him: *ubhayam lingam sarvatra hi*) viz. being devoid of all imperfections and being endowed with auspicious qualities. This is the normal understanding of the sutra.

However, according to Shankara, this sutra poses and resolves the idea of the Supreme B based on the Upanishads. We have Upanishads speaking of B with attributes and statements that B is without any such determination thus representing it as NirguNa or

215

Nirvikalpa or Nirvisesha. B cannot have both these characteristics for they are self contradictory. One of them must be the truth and the other must be rejected as false. This is denoted by *'na ubhaya lingam'*. But it may be argued that one way holds good regarding the intrinsic nature of B and the other represents it as conditioned by its cosmic location. The Sutrakara, according to Shankara, asserts that the intrinsic nature is the reality and what is conditioned by external and adventitious factors can only be a distorted representation and therefore false. So, despite immanence in the phenomenal world, B cannot be both Nirvishesha and Savishesha. This point is conveyed by the words, *'na sthanatopi ubhaya-lingam'*.

Of these two ways of taking B, which is the well based one and which is not? Shankara understands the Sutrakara to be answering this question by the words 'sarvatra hi'. It means that everywhere in the Upanishadic, B declared as undetermined by guNas or vishesha or vikalpa. It is pure subject not brought under any predication. Hence B is to be understood as NirguNa only.

We have given a brief account of Shankara's elucidation.

Let us determine whether Shankara's interpretation is legitimately borne out by the original sutra as conceived by Sutrakara.

1. The para in the sutra is Paramâtman as distinguished from jivâtma whose transmigratory existence is brought out in the preceding adhikaraNas. That distinction can be made only within the framework of the concept of SaguNa B.

2. The sutra concedes that the Paramâtman dwells in cosmic positions (what could be termed as *antaryâmin*) as it clearly mentions sthanas of Him. That sthana means upadhi and upadhi is just a false imposition of Avidya or Nescience is not conveyed in the sutra. A genuine immanance in the

216

world order is the very pres-upposition of the sutra. That the upadhi is set up by avidya is stated by Shankara in two other contexts viz. sutras 11 & 15. Precisely the point is whether immanence in the world would nullify the nature of B. If there is nothing in which it is to be immanent, there is no reason to argue out of the undesirable implication of immanence. Moreover, the sutrakara has concurred with Kashakrtsna's contention that B dwells in or as the jivâtma "avasthiti" is the word (1.4.22).

3. The '*ubhaya lingatvam*' means the two characterisations of B. The sutra does not put the tag as SaguNa and NirguNa. The identification is conceptualisation by Shankara. There is no basis or hint in the original text to vindicate the two-fold conceptualisation.

4. The words of '*sarvatra hi*' of the sutra signify for Shankara that the Vedântic revelation proclaims everywhere and all thought that B is NirguNam. There is no specific mentioning of NirguNa vidya or NirguNa B or nirvikalpa or nirvisesha or nishprapancha any where in the Upanishads. It does indeed occur once in Shvetashvatara but it occurs in a passage that is profoundly theistic.

The texts in the Upanishads adduced by Shankara in support of his NirguNa B are the following ones:

"*astulam ananva hrasvam adirgam*" –Br 3.8.8
"*ashabdam asparsham arupam avyayam*" –Katha 3.15
"*adreshyam agrahyam*" etc.—Mundaka 1.1.6

The Sutrakara has already declared under BS1.2.22, that B enjoys possession of qualities like invisibility etc., as in the text, because they belong to Him as His natural." "*adrshyatvadi guNaka:*

dharmokte:". The author here identifies openly as guNa what Shankara would not! Similarly, Brha. Up 3.8.8 (as quoted above) is also decided by him at BS 1.3.9 as describing B with the attributes of 'not being gross, not subtle, not short, not long', as such physical measurements apply to material world of prakrti and not Him. There are repeated references to B earlier as possessing 'dharmas' (e.g. 1.1.21).

We may sum up the findings:

Firstly, in this crucial sutra Paramâtman is discussed. Secondly, the *sutrakâra* is denying that the ultimate principle is in joint possession of two alternative sets of characteristics which are not further specified. Thirdly, Shankara fills the gap and identifies them as representing the NirguNa and SaguNa modes of conceiving. He further rejects the possibility of SaguNa characterization being true. He has gone so far to eliminate SaguNa B from the reckoning. Fourthly, this rejection is also the exegetical decision of his own. Lastly, he adduces scriptural evidences on behalf of Sutrakara and that evidence fails in proving the point at issue. He seems to have breached the intellectual property rights of *sutrakâra*, so to speak, by overburdening the sutra with his own doctrines thereby bringing in a contradiction into the otherwise coherent philosophy of Badarayana's BS.

It is patently clever on the part of Shankara in retaining the terminologies SaguNa and NirguNa, while ascribing to them meanings mutually contradictory to serve his purpose of wrecking the idea of SaguNa even as the Sutrakara was bent upon maintaining and upholding the SaguNa B throughout the BS.

NirguNa B, in short, is a figment of imagination and a brain-child of Shankara!

In the preface, SSR writes: "The BS is a derivative classic and its fountainhead is the Upanishads. If Shankara did full justice to the Upanishads, his deviation from the import of the BS is no major error. This line of thinking is put forward by the great commentator of Shankara, Vachaspati Misra. The trend receives powerful expression from Madhusudana Sarasvati in his refusal to revere Vyasa, the author of BS. The question is whether the Upanishads propound the notion of B as an impersonal abstraction or as the Supreme and concrete divinity in which the individual finds its enrichment. Ramanuja sets forth an interpretation of the Upanishads, in his SB & VS which establishes a concrete and theistic view of the upanishadic B without the abstraction of NirguNa B and the drastic reductionism concerning the individual and the cosmos. His interpretation of the Upanishads confirms his understanding of the BS. There is no disowning of the Upanishads in the interests of loyalty to the BS."

PNS: p230, "The Advaitic view of NirguNa B as *nirvisesha-chinmatra* or indeterminate consciousness is mainly a philosophy of negation, as its interest lies in affirming the reality of SaguNa B as a religious necessity with a view to demolishing it dialectically by subsequent Jnâna and declaring its philosophic futility. But Visishtâdvaita is a 'yes' philosophy as it affirms everything and denies nothing, owing to its insistence on self-revelation of B in the universe as its all sustaining soul...

"The Buddhist view of qualities without substance is countered by the monistic view of substance without qualities and these extremes find their reconciliation in the Visishtadvaitic theory of the world as the viseshana of B."

VI. 'Neti, neti'

Sutras 11 to 29 of BS 3.2 comprises of, according to Ramanuja, of two adhikaraNas –*ubhaya-linga* (sutras 11 to 25) & ahikundala (sutras

26 to 29). This partitioning of the sutras agrees with Shankara as far as the general trend is concerned though he has broken up into some more adhikaraNas. The entire range of sutras should be analysed for a proper perspective and sutra 21 (ibid) is of great importance. The sutra is reproduced below:

प्रकृतैतावत्त्वं हि प्रतिषेधति ततो ब्रवीति च भूयः।

The two versions of interpretation are as follows:

Ramanuja: "The context denies "so much only of B" because, further the up.text declares repeatedly the abundance of B's attributes."

Shankara: "(the text) denies the suchness of B and then declares something more (than the characterisable B)."

Which of these two is correct?
Titbaut, a British pundit, gives his judgement: "I decidedly prefer Ramanuja's interpretation of the sutra (quoted above). As far as the sense of the entire sutra is concerned and more especially with the regard to the term 'prakrta etavatvam' whose proper force is brought out by Ramanuja's explanation only."

Let us turn our attention to the issue, 'neti-neti'- occurring in Brha -Up (2.3).

The concerned sutra is understood as refuting a prima-facie view and framing the right explanation of the negative declaration of the Upanishad. What the words 'neti neti' mean is brought out in the siddhanta. The concerned passage of the Upanishad in question outlines a few profiles of B and hastens to add that it is only illustrative and not exhaustive. Who can fathom the Infinite B!

A few illustrations are specified.

B is said to have pairs of forms (dve rupe) of polar contrast: concrete / non-concrete (*murtam / amurtam*), mortal / non-mortal (*martyam / amrtam*), static / dynamic (*sthitam / sachcha*), the here and the beyond ones (*yat / tyat*).

Next, the Upanishad proceeds with the substantiation of such forms.

The essence of concrete form is the B who shines radiantly in the orb of the Sun. The non-concrete one is the same Purusha who shines in the Sun's disc. The vital breath (*prâNa*) and space (*âkâsha*) constitute the non-concrete, and the essence is what one sees as the Person in one's right eye (*dakshine akshan purushah*).

Then the Upanishad states that B is not that much alone, 'neti neti'. The text further glorifies B in more positive descriptions with which this section of the Upanishad is concluded –there is no one above B (*na hi etasmaditi paramasti*); B is the Ultimate Reality (*satyasya satyam*).

The Advaitins shoot off at a tangent and read many things in the negation not intended or anticipated by the author of BS.

According to Shankara, the concerned Upanishad passage teaches the attributes of B first only to negate it later. This diabolical nerve of Shankara is condemned severely in Bhagavad Guna Darpana:

"If the qualities of B are to be negated is the purpose of these poor vedic texts describing B as having qualities? If the reply is that there is necessity to mention the existence of qualities for negating them, why mention them at all and then negate them? Is it written on its pate that the shastras should speak about an irrelevent thing and then say it is irrelevent? This reminds us a saying in Mahabharata: "Why touch mud and clean your hand? Better keep away and not touch it at all.""

॥ प्रक्षालनात् हि पङ्कस्य दूरादस्पर्शनं वरम् ॥

Why should Shankara venture to write a commentary on Vishnu Sahasranama which is after all about SaguNa B. He should have abstained from writing and kept himself 'clean' by not writing? —asks Parashara Bhattar.

Let us project Shankara's philosophy of negation and sublation. The stupid world conceives all sorts of B and this stupidity is sought to be cleared here. This obsession to all conceivable forms of B involving the attributes of B is the condition of bondage. In other words, "a form is that by which the formless is brought into figuration by ignorance and false impositions. Such forms are likely to delude the world (*vyâmohâspâdam*) and are of the nature of mirage (*mrga trshnika*) or magical hallucination (*indrajala*) or at the least like mere painted figures on walls and cloth (*pata bhitti chitrava*) and mere illusion.

To clear the mind the Upanishad adopts this negation procedure likea formula, as *'neti neti'*, occurs five times. All the positive attributes previously described stand cancelled. Shankara hastens to add that the assertion of the negative culminates in 'Being' and not in 'Non-Being'. The statement in question is not 'abhava-vasana' but 'brahma-vasana'. In other words, negation does not apply to B but only to the super-imposed forms. That residual affirmation stands undiminished. In fact, it is on the strength of positivity that negations have meaning. There is no way of indicating B other than this mode of negation, as expressed in 'neti'.

But unfortunately for Shankara 'neti' is not the last word on the subject in the text. The Upanishad makes a further remark that B is the 'Real of reals' (*satyasya satyam*). That remark would be absurd if the previous negation were total and final. Ramanuja attacks the raw deal meted out by Shankara to our holy Upanishads and proves that the whole of his mis-interpretation is nothing but nonsense. Let us keep the criticism aside for a moment and experience the soul-stirring account he has given on the import of 'Satyasya Satyam'.

PNS: p 106 provides a brilliant account of the explanation providedby Ramanuja based on his commentary of sutra SB 3.2.21.

Refer also to Yatiraja Saptati 38. "Ramanuja extended a helping hand to B to rescue B from the hands of maya-vadins."

कुदृष्टिकुहनामुखे निपततः परब्रह्मणः

करग्रहविचक्षणो जयति लक्ष्मणोऽयं मुनिः ॥

Now we will show that Advaita is indeed a hodge-podge of religions of non-believers in God. Examples of such religions are: Charvaka, Buddhism, Sankyam and the idealism of the monists.

Charvaka's philosophy is that the self is the body and everyone should eat, drink and be merry and feed on pleasures by fair means or foul. According to him, the veda is false and of no validity. There is no heaven or hell, and mukti or release cannot mean anything but death. He identifies the body with the âtma. Virochana, king of the asuras (vide Chand. Up. 8.8) is one such example.

A confirmed materialist but a shallow optimist and a down right hedonist that he is, a Charuvakan feels that he alone possesses the happy-go lucky frame of mind. It is an appeal to common sense and sensibility and though it may seem repugnant to reason, is yet ineradicable, as the foundations of this philosophy are deeply laid in human nature and animal faith. The modern-day moderate hedonist would utilize reason as the ally of passion and think of happiness as the end and aim of life. The altruist pursues the logic of hedonism still further, and defines the end of conduct as the attainment of the greatest happiness of the greatest number. This is schematically represented by a pyramid or a triagle known as "Maslows Hierarchy of Human Needs". For details see author's book: "Yoga in Visishtâdvaita".

Then there are philosophers wedded to world negation, who in their extreme zeal for asceticism, hold the view that spirit alone is real and not matter. The three schools viz. Buddhism, Advaita and Samkya fall in this category. Buddhism would negate even spirit (âtma) as unreal as it grants no substantiality to anything in its grand scheme of Nihilism, while Advaita would admit the spirit but prohibit all predications to it. It should be borne in mind, to negate all else beside B is neither the intention of the shruti text and the context where it occurs, nor that of the Sutrakara and even otherwise Advaita leads to Nihilism as nothing remains other than Vacuous Absolute.

On the principle of sublation or *apaccheda nyâya*, it follows that what cannot be subsequently sublated is alone real and according to Shankara, NirguNa B alone is *'sat'* without a second as it defies further sublation. Ramanuja sees no reason why apaccheda should not be extended futher upto its logical end viz. Universal Void? Nihillism and Universal Void are the two sides of the same coin.

The words used by Shankara are typically those of the nihillists: The world form of God described in the Upanishads is meant to delude (*vyamohâspâdam*) the world. And are the nature of mirage (mrgatrshnika) or magical hallucination (*indrajâla*). Like painted figures on walls and on the canvas (*pata bhitti chitravat*) and are illusions (*mâyâ*). He would dub the theists as pseudo vedantins (*upanishadam manyamanah*)!

Ref 56 p132, "Because of double combination of world negation and negation of all predicationsfor B, Shankara arrives at a grand

Nihilism, no less 'impressive' than Buddhists', and richly deserves the following criticism of Aurobindo:

"Therefore, we arrive at the escape of an illusory non-existent soul from an illusory non-existent bondage in an illusory non-existent world as the supreme good which the non-existent soul has to pursue! For, this is the last word of the knowledge: there is none bound, none freed, none seeking to be free! Vidya turns out to be as much a part of the phenomenal as avidya. Maya meets us even in our escape and laughs at the triumphant logic which seemed to cut the knot of her mystery" (p47)!

Aurobindo here seems to be almost translating Ramanuja's sum up of Advaita in the opening paragraphs of VS (3)! Few Advaitins have ever realizedthat 'neti neti' misinterpreted the Shankara way, leads only to the Buddhist Nihilism."

A gist of the passage in VS (3) will be found in PNS: p59.

The criticism of Advaita as Buddhism in disguise (pracchanna bauddha) is met by modern expounders by the counter argument that Buddhism itself is Advaita in a negative aspect. Thus, Advaita has two faces: one a happy face as a Hindu and the sad face as a Buddhist! If it accepts Ishwara it is the former but if it denies Ishwara it follows the devasting dialectic of a Buddhist and ends up in *sunyavâda*.

After all Buddha, according to Bhagavad Guna Darpana, is an avatar of Vishnu. Refer to the nâmâvalis in Vishnu Sahasranama beginning with Durârihâ (787).

Regarding this aspect there is an interesting verse (32 of Ref 35). It appears that the fun-loving Lord (*narma lilam vidhitso: vibho:*) takes up different avatars appropriate to the prevailing dharma and the conducive environment. He rises to the occasion to fulfill the needs of the times and the aspirations of the people.

The secret Behind Ramanuja's Avatar

If the king commits an error and is not in any mood to listen to the advice of His ministers, a loyal and faithful minister will try to wipe out the effect of the error though he may find himself unable to prevent the commission of the error. That is precisely what Vishvaksena is said to do. He incarnates as Ramanuja and tells people not to pay heed to the Lord's own words which were uttered purely in a sporting and flippant mood. Like a teacher who uses whip or the police the lathi, to check the waywardly conduct, Ramanuja uses argument as powerful weapon to deal with questionable non-Vedic faiths. Incidentally the two verses (12 of Ref 18 & 33 of Ref 16) deal with this secret role of Ramanuja.

It is the Divine secret and the Vaishnavite belief that teaching descends from the Divine Couple to the humans in an unbroken line of Acharyas through the good offices of Vishvaksena. Note this aspect is alluded to in 3 of Ref 18 and the word Shiksha occurring in the 5th shloka of Daya Shatakam.

Disappearance of Buddhism in India

We find an interesting account of it in the book Raghavan: Sanskrit p 94. A galaxy of Buddhist metaphysicians and logicians, Nagarjuna, Dinnaga, Dharmakirti, Dharmapala illumined the history of Indian philosophy with their brilliant contributions. Mādhyamika metaphysic developed as one of the high-water marks of the Indian mind. But Buddhism suffered a setback with the advent of Shankara who strode over the whole field of philosophy like a colossus; his epoch saw not only the other other orthodox systems vanishing into silhouttes in the background but the decline of the major rival, Buddhism, the giant sister Banyan whose main trunk disappeared but whose offshoots took root over a wide world all round India.

226

However, the succession of Buddhist logicians continued beyond the period of Shankara & Kumarila continued to the times of Udhayana, after which at about the time of the Muslim invasions, Buddhism disappeared. Whether it was because of the triumph of the three luninaries on the side of the orthodox systems, Kumarila, Shankara and Udhayana or because of the destruction of the great monastic centres by Muslim invasions, Buddhism bowed out, after making for about 15 centuries magnificent contribution to Indian philosophy.

The story of the spread of Buddhism to central Asia, China, Japan and to Korea, and nearer home over Tibet has been studied far better as its materials are ample (p87 of Ref 90).

We may mention here the prodigious output from another great lady Madame Blavatsky (1831 -91). This Russian lady retired to Tibet and studied under Buddhist monks and wrote several volumes. She founded what is called Theodophy which is a combination of the tenets of all religions. Known as the Theosophical Society it was also founded in US.

Though Buddhism is not virulent in India, it is very much kept alive by the continuing efforts of the Nobel laureate Dalai Lama and the people of Tibet.

8. Chatussûtrî

अखिलभुवनजन्मस्थेमभङ्गादिलीले विनतविविधभूतव्रातरक्षैकदीक्षे।

श्रुतिशिरसि विदीप्ते ब्रह्मणि श्रीनिवासे भवतु मम परस्मिन् शेमुषी भक्तिरूपा॥

Sri Ramanuja begins his Sri Bhashya (SB) with the above shloka dedicated to the Lord of the Seven-Hills. While in the next verse, by mentioning 'Pârâcharya vachah' (which means, 'words of Parashara's son') Ramanuja has revealed, though indirectly, his reverance not only for Veda Vyasa the son but also for the Maharishi Parashara, the father as well, who is the renouned author of Sri Vishnu PurâNa. For a standard book for references to SB, we have chosen the Srirangam Srimad Andavan Ashnamam edition (now available with them) consisting of about 902 pages (Ref 63). Cross references to page numbers in SB will be only with regard to this book which is in two volumes.

The two verses though seemingly simple and sweet to recite have enormous depth since they convey the sum and substance of the entire Brahma Sutras (BS). The meaning of the two verses is beautifully expounded in 'Sukhabhodini' (Ref 64).

On SB p 6, Ramanuja defines Brahman (B): "B is the Reality of Realities, 'Satyasya satyam'. It transcends matter and the finite selves.

228

It is pure and far from any imperfection or evil. It is perfection par excellence by the infinite and boundless perfections of attributes. For the definition of B given by Deshika see p71 of Ref 65.

In SB the criticism of Advaita takes place in the first 160 pages though it extends from sutra 1 to the last sutra, if we follow the observations made by Swami Deshika in Adhikarana Saravali. However, in the main, the criticism is conducted in three divisions, namely, the laghu (minor or rudimentary level), maha (major or advanced level) and in the section devoted to an appraisal of the error in the concept of avidya as in Advaita Siddhanta. By no means are the criticisms simple to deal with. They have exercised the mind of scholars who have published thesis after thesis in these areas of criticisms and it is aimed to bring them to focus at the appropriate contexts during the course of this book. The following sequence of topics occupy the a/m 160 pages (SB p1-160).

1 लघुपूर्वपक्षः। 2 लघु सिद्धान्तः। 3 महा पूर्वपक्षः। 4 महासिद्धान्तः। 5 श्रुतिघट्टः।

6 स्मृतिपुराणघट्टः। 7 अविद्याविषयसप्तविधानुपपत्ति। 8 संग्रहेण सिद्धान्तोपन्यासः।

9 महासिद्धान्तोपसंहारः॥

BS shapes the teachings of the Upanishads into a unified and coherent body of philosophy in terms of a rationale. This involves an interpretation of the major passages of the ancient texts according to a standard logic of interpretation. The interpretation should stand rigorous scrutiny throughout. For it can fail through the weakest link. In the process of such a fool-proof exercise we have a reasoned and integrated doctrine supported by a reasoned elucidation of connected texts. The reasoning is at its philosophical best and has withstood the test of time thanks to Ramanuja's SB. But for the light of Ramanuja the world would have remained in abysmal darkness, with questionable religions holding the people to ransom (56 of Ref 18)!

निरालोके लोके निरुपधिपरस्नेहपरितः यतिक्ष्माभृद्दीपो यदि न किल जाज्वल्यत

इह।

अहंकारध्वान्तं विजहति कथंकारमनघाः कुतर्कव्याळौघं

कुमतिमतपाताळकुहरम्॥

The spirit of reasoning is further employed to answer rationalistic objections to the philosophy propounded thereby. BS contains a dialectical part of considerable strength seeking to demonstrate in terms of reasons the unsatisfactory character of the anti-Vedântic systems of philosophy evolved through the ages. Thus, the work constitutes a logical reconstruction and vindication of the philosophical inspirations of the Upanishads. It is an intellectualist rendering of the basic Vedântic intuitions.

Almost every sutra and every passage is subjected to a critical examination, possible prima facie views are refuted and the final lucid import is established like the proofs of the theorems in Euclid geometry- QED i.e., Question Ended without Doubt! The process of elucidation has a built-in procedure of *samsaya* (doubt), *pûrva paksha* (opposite wrong view) and *siddhanta* (correct view established). The process involves upholding the Vedânta because it is flawless while at the same time pointing out the defects in non-Vedic systems and rejecting them.

The BS has several other alternative names such as *Uttara-MîmâmsaSutra*, *Vedânta Sutra* and *Shârîraka Sutra*. The last mentioned one is a hoary title adopted even by Shankara and more ancient writers such as Upavarsha mentioned by Shankara and Bodhayana who is revered by Ramanuja.

The first chapter (*adhyâya*) of BS accomplishes the amazing feat of compressing the decisive elucidation of all the central, crucial and doubtful passages of the major Upanishads and the demonstration of their signification of Brahman. This exegesis leading to the building up a single thesis is a major asset for Vedânta.

While this is the objective, set forth for the first adhyâya, some special observations are necessary regarding the first four sutras which are extremely important since they set up the orientation for the study of the entire treatise. The four sutras (which go by the appellation *Chatus Sûtrî*) serve as an introduction to BS itself. Some distinguished commentaries such as *Panchapadika* confine themselves only to these four and don't go beyond the four. The importance attached to *Chatussûtrî* can also be gauged from the fact that in the two volumes of Ref 63 nearly half of first volume is occupied by Chatussûtrî alone. The book (Ref 98) of 600 pages with Tamil translation is a recent addition on Chatussûtrî .

Ramanuja undertook the task of putting Shankara's Bhâshya on BS under the scanner and showed that it is flawed. In an overbearing manner Shankara launched his own doctrine known as Advaita casting aside the theme on which Veda Vyasa labored hard to establish in BS. Under the pretext of a commentary Shankara threw the baby out with the bath water! Ramanuja's task of reviewing Shankara's commentary (with the concern for retriving the baby!) did not confine with that of Shankara's alone but his criticism extended over a host of Advaitins belonging to Shankara's school, such as Mandana, Sureshwara, Padmapâda, Vimuktâtman, Vachaspati Mishra and Prakashâtman, all of whom had contributed to restore the faulty Advaita of Shankara. The obsession with Shankara's Advaita was so great that a Vachaspati Mishra would even wink at Shankara's manipulation of the original text of BS. Madhusudana Saraswati, for example in his 'Siddhanta Bindu' would

231

adore Shankara and Sureshwara but would even refuse to revere Vyasa, the very author of BS. The bile of bias did not allow them to relish the milk of BS. The Brahman had to be virtually rescued from the hands of the Shankarite-s (38 of Ref 18)!

|| करग्रहविचक्षणो जयति लक्ष्मणोऽयं मुनिः ||

Hence a sizable portion of Sri Bhâshya is devoted to the refutation of the tenets of Advaita which are classified as minor (*laghu*) and major (*mahâ*) *pūrvapaksha*. The broadside of the attack is especially directed on those seven kinds of *avidya*. After providing the correct interpretation as intended by the author (namely Veda Vyasa), Ramanuja provided the necessary corrections to restore the central theme (*siddhanta*) in all its glory and grandeur. Hence a clear understanding of BS is possible only with recourse to Sri Bhâshya (61of Ref 18).

सिद्धान्ता न समिन्धते यतिपतिग्रन्थानुसंधायिनि।

Chatus Sûtrî
The first Sutra is worded as '*atha atah brahma jijnyâsa*'

|| अथातो ब्रह्म जिज्ञासा ||

The first word '*athâ*' means 'then' and it clearly indicates that the enquirer on Brahman should start the study of BS only after examining (or completing) the study of the preceding Karma Kânda. Broadly, the subject matter of Vedic study has two parts: (1) Karma Kânda and (2) Brahma Kânda.

In the Vedic jargon the term Mîmâmsais specially used for the study of Vedas. The study of Karma Kânda is denoted by Pûrva Mîmâmsawhile the subsequent study of Brahma Kânda (what is the same as BS) as Uttara Mîmâmsâ.

The next word in the sutra '*atah*' means 'therefore': the motivating cause for undertaking the present enquiry. It means the realization on the part of the enquirer of the impossibility of securing the highest good life by means other than the knowledge of Brahman.

The first sutra instructs that as the Pûrva Mîmâmsa is productive of only petty and short-lived fruits and as the Uttara Mîmâmsaholds the promise of imperishable and immeasurably superior fruit, the enquirer should get the inspiration for the study of BS after duly equipping himself with the study of Pûrva Mîmâmsawhich instructs the duties and responsibilities of an individual.

It is like studying a bachelor's degree course before taking up the masters. The BS can be compared to the wave equation of Quantum Physics. Only a developed mind well verse in the intricacies of particle physics and mastery over the language of mathematics will be able to understand and appreciate the nuances in the interpretation of the wave equation. Similarly, the coded aphorisms of BS can be understood only by a mind developed and nurtured in the system of Vedic learning and Vedântic thought.

The syllabus for the whole course of Vedic learning would thus include the study of the entire Mîmâmsa Shâstra –starting with the first sutra of Pûrva Mîmâmsato the last sutra of Uttara Mîmâmsâ.

मीमांसाशास्त्रम् "अथातो धर्मजिज्ञासा" इत्यारभ्य

"अनावृत्तिःशब्दादनावृत्तिःशब्दात्"

इत्येवमन्तं सङ्गति विशिष्टक्रमम्॥

The approach philosophy of Ramanuja is lucidly expounded in the following passages (p135 of Ref 43): "The Vedic imperative of dharma, which is the subject matter of the Pûrva Mîmâmsa (*karma vichâra*), therefore, requires reorientation in the light of the Vedântic

233

philosophy of Brahman. The end of moral endeavor is the realization of Brahman and the attainment of eternal bliss. The ethics of the Pûrva Mîmâmsa has its value only when it is related to the Vedântic good as revealed in the Uttara Mîmâmsa; but there is no contradiction between the two. The two Mimâmsa's are integral parts of one systematic whole, and their object is to lead the seeker after truth step by step till he ascends to his home in the Absolute. Ramanuja following Bodhayana, therefore thinks that the entire Mîmâmsa Shâstra with its twenty chapters beginning with the sutra 'Now therefore the enquiry into dharma", and ending with the sutra 'from there, there is no return' has a definite spiritual meaning and value."

Thus, equipped the seeker should engage himself in 'jijnyâsa' meaning inquiry. The sutra announces the exact nature of BS. It embodies intellectual and critical pursuit of knowledge. BS is addressed to philosophical understanding and aims at the promotion of knowledge. The style of the entire work carries out the spirit of enquiry. What is the subject matter of enquiry? The sutra answers that it is Brahman. The word Brahman, according to Vedic etymologist Yâska, is one who is "immense or infinite in every way-*paribridam sarvathah*" "Brahman is not only immense but also imparts immensity on those who meditate on Him":

॥ बृहति बृंहयति तस्मादुच्यते परं ब्रह्म ॥

Brahman is Paramâtma (BG 15.17) or Purushottama (BG 15.18), who is free from every imperfection and who is the seat of hosts of auspicious qualities the excellences of which has no limit. Brahman should be approached for release by those who are caught up in bondage known as samsâra. A prisoner in fetters is not approached for help by those similarly placed. That means to say that the word Brahman cannot apply to a Chaturmukha Brahma or a Shiva or anybody else since they are all fettered by karma.

எருத்துக்கொடியுடையானும் பிரமனும் இந்திரனும் மற்றும்
ஒருத்தரும் இப்பிறவியென்னும்நோய்க்கு மர்ந்தறிவாருமில்லை
மருத்துவனாய்நின்றமாமணிவண்ணா மறுபிறவிதவிரத்
திருத்தி உங்கோயிற்கடைப்புகப்பெய்
திருமாலிருஞ்சோலையெந்தாய்.

The second sutra and incidentally the second adhikaraNa define the Brahman as the ground of origin, continuance and dissolution of the universe. This definition (*lakshaNa*) of Brahman is found only in the Vedânta (for a representative sample, reference is made to Bruguvalli of Taittiriopanishad). By specifying the Vedic source the sutra rules out the prakrti of Sankhya and the atomic theory of Nyâya Vaiseshika, which are non-Vedic systems. All these are brought out in the exhaustive arguments advanced in support of Vedânta. The sutra BS 1.1.2 is quoted below.

॥ जन्माद्यस्य यतः ॥

yatah= out of which; *janmâdi* = Birth, Existence and Death; *asya*= of this universe.

Varuna replies to his son Brugu who had enquired about Brahman: "From which are born these beings, by which these beings live and into which at the time of dissolution they dissolve into, know that as Brahman."

By providing an apt quotation for the enquirer the Vedânta has stolen a march over the Sankhya and Vaiseshika systems. The latter two have no god in their philosophies and that does not mean that they have no merit at all in them. However, for the sake of arguments to highlight the par excellence of Vedânta, the views of the two philosophies are repeatedly brought in for a rigorous scrutiny and they get thrown into the shade. Why at all the two should be brought in the first place for discussion is another matter that would be explained at the appropriate context.

The third sutra and the third adhikaraNa is BS I.1.3:

॥ शास्त्रयोनित्वात्॥

The enquiry should be guided in the direction of Vedânta because the Shâstra is the only source of our knowledge of Brahman. The Shâstra contains a body of instructions, do's and don'ts which have cause and effect relationship between them and by following the instructions some fruit is gained in the process. How can this be true in the case of Brahman who can only be inferred? This objection from the opponent is countered in this 3rd sutra. The cause and effect issue in relation to Brahman is also the subject matter of afore mentioned Upanishad viz. Bruguvalli. In other words, the sutra affirms that the Brahman is conjoint with Vedânta which also falls within the definition of Shâstra. The cause and effect principle runs the gamut of the whole Vedas from the beginning to the end. The sutra provides a proper link to the rich discussion brought forward while explaining the next sutra.

The opponent interjects and argues: "I hold that Brahman can be known only by inference. Admitting that Vedânta is a Shâstra, what benefit accrues from a knowledge of Brahman? In the absence of tangible benefits, how is it possible to conduct an enquiry into Brahman? Will it not be an exercise in futility and a waste?" The opposition is countered by '*tu*' in the following sutra BS I.1.4.

॥ तत्तु समन्वयात्॥

All the Vedic Shâstra is beneficial and a knowledge of Brahman is supremely beneficial since it secures release from bondage. What greater benefit can there be than the direct means to ultimate Bliss? The issue is broached elegantly in the Upanishads as under:

1. A *mumukshu* (seeker of liberation from bondage) must get a true knowledge of *Âtma* and *Paramâtma* (*Tattva*)

2. He must engage himself in meditation, worship and adore the Supreme, Sriman Narayana (*Hita*)
3. This knowledge with devotion (*Bhakti*) leads to the realization of the Supreme (vide the opening para of Vedârtha Sangraha)

॥ अत्यर्थप्रियः तत्प्राप्ति फलः ॥

Incidentally the title for the first adhyâya of BS is named after the fourth sutra of Chatussûtrî viz. Samanvaya. Thus, the Chatussûtrî sums up the wisdom of the Upanishads by establishing the reality of Brahman as the ultimate reason of the universe and by connecting such knowledge by the *samanvaya* method or method of coordination with the supreme value of life consisting in the realization of Brahman (SB p216).

॥ इति श्री भाष्ये चतुः सूत्री। श्रीरस्तु॥

In the brief presentation of ours, though it is very much desirable, it will not be possible to deal with the *laghu* and *maha-purva paksha* seperately and hence the two sections are omited. The laghu siddhanta was presented in Ref 44. Hence we have fast forwarded to the next segment, Maha-siddhanta.

Weak Foundation of Advaita

Dr.K.C. Varadachari, in his doctoral thesis, on "The Theory of Knowledge" (Ref2) makes the following observation: "The major fault of Maya vâda and Advaita has been due to such facile universal propositions derived from a few fragmentory experiences. To build on such frail foundations a grand superstructure needs a profound optimism, and that optimism manifests itself in the great but misunderstood doctrine *of so'hamasmi*..What is not possible to the soul when it is indeed God? Even the illusion cannot serve itself, and thus we are left alone when all intelligibility, the one criterion of logical and philosophical thought, is thwarted and denied its rightful place in the scheme of metaphysics, not to speak of epistemology. Epistemology cannot have a place in that kind of idealistic thought that finally culminates in the affirmation of the mere self, albeit a universal self. A dualistic epistemology can perhaps go with monistic metaphysics but there cannot be a monistic epistemology."

The continuous docturing on Advaita can be compared to the Leaning Tower of Pisa's nearly 800 year long chequered history. During the first stage of construction of the tower (1173-1178 AD), it had developed a tilt towards the north due to differential settlemrnt of the foundation. Plans for further construction were modified to correct the tilt and accordingly the second stage (1273-78 AD) saw the completion of seven stories of the tower. Instead of correcting the tilt, it only resulted in the shift of the tilt, from north to the south. The modified 8th story and the bell chamber were added during 1360-70 AD raising the height to 55 metres. But the tilting only continued unabated and has reached an abominable value of 5.227 metres of tilt off centre markedly endangering its stability. What with periodical correction the tower has become banana shaped or is it a question mark? This ancient landmark is now closed for visitors since a cathedral (of Pavia) in the neighbourhood collapsed suddenly in 1989. The tower is now under constant vigil and it is hoped that the efforts taken to keep the tower standing would make it stand in the current century. Advaita shares the same fate as Pisa Tower!

But what a pleasant contrast in the other camp! It was Vedânta Deshika, the Ghantâvatara of Tirumalai, who enriched and strengthened the Grand Edifice of Visishtâdvaita or to put it in other words Vedânta Deshika has acted as a strong fence to the garden containing the flowers and fruits of Ramanuja's teachings. The Grand Edifice of Ramanuja is founded more on the philosophy of religius experience, metaphysics and ethics than on epistemology, since physics is rationally related to metaphysics and metaphysics

238

has its basis in religion. "The self is not God, but belongs to God who is the Supreme Subject of knowledge and the Object of love. In mukti, the self regains its universal knowledge and attains fulness and freedom. Dr. K.C.Varadachari has thus clearly brought out the central truths of Epistemology of Visishtâdvaita and shown its integral relation to metaphysics and religion." The matter given within quotes is from the reviewer P.N.Srinivasachari and the book reviewed is titled "Ramanuja's Theory of Knowledge", the thesis of KCV for which he was awarded the Doctor of Philosophy by the University of Madras in 1932 (Ref 2).

Before entering into the criticism of Advaita both the above mentioned pandits broach the subject by introducing the Philosophy of Advaita. As the subject matter discussed by the two authors complement each other we will give below a composite presentation.

Any siddhanta gets enriched by a criticism of its rival system, a knowledge of the outlines of Advaita is presupposed in understanding Visishtâdvaita; and a brief summary of the former may serve as a critical introduction to the latter. Brahma-Jnâna in Advaita is Jnâna that is Brahman and not of Brahman, and is therefore pure consciousness (*nirvisesha chin-mâtra*) which simply is and cannot be described, as it transcends or sublates relational thought. But as a philosophy, it has to establish this truth, and it does so in a negative way, by denying false knowledge or aJnâna. Owing to avidya, the âtman, which is pure consciousness, mistakes itself for anâtman, as the shell is mistaken for silver, and this leads to *adhyâsa* or super-imposition of *anâtman* on âtman. Owing to maya which is avidya in its objective or cosmic aspect, the world of *nâma-rûpa* is superposed on Brahman, and therefore appears to be real. How the real coexists with the unreal and is conjoined with it is the crux of monistic metaphysics (SB p 117).

तस्यैवावस्थाविशेषेण अध्यासरुपे जगति ज्ञानबाध्यसर्परजतादिवस्तु तत्तज्ज्ञानरूप

अध्यासोऽपि जायते। कृत्स्नस्य मिथ्यारूपस्य तदुपादानत्वं च मिथ्याभूतस्यार्थस्य मिथ्याभूतमेव कारणं भवितुमर्हतीति हेतुबलादवगम्यते॥

The problem is admitted, but the solution is that it somehow exists there, indeterminable philosophically. But the problem is dissolved when *ajnâna* is sublated by *jnâna* in the state of Brahma-Nirvana or pure consciousness, the Ultimate Substance, just as one thorn is used to remove another and both are thrown away afterwards. Pure consciousness is eternal or timeless, effulgent, beyond the subject-object consciousness and thus absolutely transcends the relation of the enjoyer or *bhoktr* and the object enjoyed or *bhogya*. It is *sat, chit, ânanda* not in the adjectival sense but as absolute experience realized in *jîvanmukti*.

For Advaita, the Ultimate Substance is Consciousness which alone is Truth, Intelligence and Eternal and One only, *Satyam, Jnânam, Anantam, Brahma*, which all mean the same thing. This Brahman is mere experience or *anubhûti* or *Samvid*. The primal substance is neither the individual nor the objects of cognition, but an all-embracing consciousness, which is never absent, for its absence we can predicate nothing, nor of its non-existence can we speak with any sense of intelligibility, as it is consciousness alone that make such a judgement which it cannot do it if it was not. *Samvid* is thus One all-embracing consciousness which is the same throughout, whatever be its content, either illusions or objects, or dreams or real knowledge itself. Indeed we may say that it is absolute consciousness or experience where subject and object have no meaning; it is unrelationed and all relations between subject and object are unreal and do not pertain to the Ultimate Substance.

In yoga there is a fourth or *turīya* state of consciousness, in which there is said to be the realization of the unchanging Self. Gaudapâda, one of the most profound thinkers, in his karika on Mandukya Upanishad has stated that in this *turia* state, the subject-object relation stands dissolved in an all embracing consciousness (*ajâti vâda*). There is every reason to believe that Gaudapâda was influenced by Buddhistic Yogachara school. However it should be mentioned that Buddhistic thought does not accept permanent self, though it might accept an *âlaya-vijnâna*, a store-house of impressions which is also a momentary thing.

In Advaita, the Ultimate Substance, as Dr.KCV puts it, the realm of the objective, is a huge categorical make-up. Thus to Shankara, it would mean that the emperically real, which we shall call the Actual, is unreal though it is a manifestation or phenomenon of the noumenal and the real is never the actual; in the sense of only ideally present is it actual in any sense. In which case Truth or Satya is ideal and real, the actual is unreal because it is actual...It is due to an eternal *ajnânam* (darkness) overlaying itself on the shining and self luminous background Brahman, which is the passive intelligent spectator of the whole thing, where the various apparent manifold creation of objects and things and egos arise. The clouding or overlaying is to Maya, a mysterious power, not describable as real or as unreal. The real is thus experience which is not 'involved' in the unreal manifold, yet really appearing as manifold. That Absolute Experience, which is known only by those who give up this multiplicity, is best described as Truth (Satyam); meaning by that not-false, Jnânam because it is not ignorance and matter; Anantam (Eternal) meaning by that not perishing and timeless. All positive predication it refutes, because every qualification means reduction of quality, and reduction of it to the level of the definite and the differenced. This Unknowable, however speciously concealed under the name of the attainable, transcends all limiting categories of

241

thought, but does not such a thing thus standing undefined, equally give itself to non-being because we never come across such an entity and cannot speak about it? Does not such an attitude perilously descend to Sûnya vâda against which Sri Shankara so ably lifted his banner of revolt?

On page 269, Dr KCV goes on to show that the roots of Advaita indeed lie in Buddhism and Samkhya. "Shankara availed himself of all the battery of dialectic of the Buddhistic thought and utilized it to save the Self that transcends all change and movement and dialectic. The result was something similar to Kant's philosophy but more vital and self revealing. He built up his system of Advaita on the Non-dual reality on the experience of the Atman or Atta. This atta or âtman is the magnus or Brahman not the individual egoistic soul formed out of samskara and vasana. Buddhistic psychology and Samkhyan psychology had helped the discovery, comprising of the four-fold nature of ego-buddhi, ahamkara, chitta and manas. The ego is the unreal reflection of the infinite Self and parades as jîva or individual soul. However Shankara refuted Nagarjuna and Yogachara doctrines.

Vedânta Deshika's well known epigram in Nyaya Siddhanjana that the system of Nirvisesha Advaita is a commixture of the systems of Samkhya, Saugata (Buddhism), and Charvaka (Lokayata) stands substantiated in Shatadushani.

साङ्ख्य सौगत चार्वाक सङ्करात् शङ्करोदयः ॥

That the epistemology and logic of Nirvisesha advaitins is substantially drawn from the Buddhistic system has been shown in many works of Vedânta Deshika and Meghanadari Suri in Nyaya Prâkâsha. It has been stated in Tattvatika at the beginning of Mahasiddhanta that while Buddhists have taken the juice, Nirvisesha Advaitins have taken the dross (kalka) of tarka and have reared them on their advaita system. The logic of Madhyamika logic is inexorable in that when once it is adopted one cannot escape concluding in nihilism. Its starting scheme starts in *kshana-bhanga* and terminates in *sarva sunya* and the brute force of such a logic is intolerant of partial adoption or rejection.

Dr KCV conducts his criticism of Advaita in the two domains- "The Metaphysics of Sri Ramanuja's Sri Bhashya" and "The Epistemology of Visishtâdvaita". Let us refer to page 76 of the former work to continue his discussion. He considers that the metaphysics of Advaita is wrong at the core. "Ramanuja refutes the conception of substance of Advaita categorically in his Mahasiddhanta of Sri Bhashya. The theory of consciousness as Substance is a very faulty conception, because the subject of experience is not consciousness but a conscious subject –a subject who possesses consciousness as an instrument of functioning in the act of cognising or knowing. Consciousness does not subsist in all states (avasthas). Consciousness is not eternal and so on. Owing to the influence of karma it becomes of a contracted nature. (SB p75)

क्षेत्रज्ञावस्थायां कर्मणा संकुचितस्वरूपं तत्तत्कर्मानुगुण तरतमभावेन वर्तते।

"The Philosophy of Sri Ramanuja like most other systems of thought in India is based more on Religious experience, metaphysics and ethics rather than on epistemology. Epistemology came in to substantiate the conclusions of metaphysics arrived at through psychology. It is undoubted that at a later critical period as evidenced in Buddhistic schools and Advaita the psychological approach had more and more yielded ground to transcendental *apriori* thought construction (*a priori* reasoning involves using a known principle to work out facts or effects). This transcendental approach is considered by some to be well grounded, and it is claimed that our experience must yield its place to the transcendental deductions of *a priori* philosophers. That logic should legislate our experience is certainly an important thing and cannot be denied. But logic itself find its feet on the ground and cannot and should not soar in the sky without any let or hindrance or control of fact. Thus the viciousness of the *a priori* usually consists in its consistent rebuttal of the evidence of experience (the revelational *a priori* is different from Kantian *a priori*). Nor could experience be considered to be of a particular kind. Experience is manifold, and the truth about experience must embrace all facts falling within experience. The doctrine of nihilism will result if any particular segment of experience alone is accepted and the rest denied. Universal propositions founded on the basis of partial applications will find logical collapse. The critical method is all for the best, but with the best of intentions the critical methods of early Buddhists and of Kant have floundered hopelessly in the ocean of fact. There is no other alternative to the critical except to end in that wonderful night wherein all cows are black or else simulate a phantom dialectic and claim reality to a non-existent spirit...

"All metaphysical search, then, is after the concept of the Real, the total. Knowledge of Real is possible, and this total reality is not self contradictory and discrete. It is a comprehensive explanation of this Reality that is being sought. Knowledge about reality turns out to be a real knowledge of itself. Reality is the source and substance. The causal teleological and cosmological factors about it have been examined in the earlier work. There are several theories of knowledge. Epistemology deals with the how, that is, as to how we apprehend the real. It investigates the apparatus of knowing and the structure of thought. It is psychological in approach as well as logical. The criterion of reality has to be formulated. The nature of the subject and the nature of the object, the nature of their compresence have to be understood... Thus usually epistemology which is said to be the creator of metaphysics, is really a hand-maid finding reasons for the system adopted... Likewise there is another kind of epistemological idealism which claims that One undifferentiated Consciousness (Experience) under the stress of illusion of diversity fulgurates or differentiates, or appears to do so in an unreal manner, into subjects and objects. This is epistemology that has ascended to metaphysical status. This also therefore is what we have to criticize if we would save true metaphysics. Sri Ramanuja undertakes to point out the defects of the epistemological absolutists...

"Sri Ramanuja starts from a metaphysical view and seeks to make out that his is metaphysics that reconciles all conflicts according to every pramana (source of knowledge)." A few points of his are noted.

A sentence is incapable of denoting any object devoid of attributes or it cannot convey an abstract non entity. Any word comes either under a noun or a verb, *suptingantham pâdam*.

प्रकृतिप्रत्यययोगेन हि पदत्वम्॥

That is according to the Panini's Sutra (1.4.14) a word should consists of a root and a termination which differ. Sentences are formed from words which convey different meanings (SB p50).

Next Ramanuja begins his argument on perception as the first source of right knowledge. Advaita borrowed from the Nyaaya Vaisheshika school the two stages (or two kinds) of perception, the nirvikalpaka, indeterminate, and the savikalpaka, determinate perceptions keeping in view the theory of kalpana which is a term used for modification. Modification can pass for either falcification or illusification. Ramanuja's task was to show that Naiyayic nirvikalpaka has nothing in common with the Shankarite version except the name. Ramanuja elucidates the theory of perception by analysing the three possibilities: nirvikalpa pratyaksha (the naiyâyika view) is not definite knowledge and as such it is neither true nor false. Secondly, the term does not convey *anubhûti* as the Shankarites

245

claim. Thirdly, cognition is always with respect to an object (p30 Ref 60a). Ramanuja accepts the two classification of pratyaksha, but both the types comprehend only *savishesha vastu* (see bottom of SB p51).

अतः प्रत्यक्षस्य कदाचिदपि न निर्विशेष विषयत्वम्॥

For matters regarding the specific points discussed in Mahasiddhanta the reader may also consult several books such as Ref 68 and Ref 15. In the former book Swami Vireshwarananda has brought the areas of difference under thirteen headings and in the latter book also Narasimhan discusses the specific points of difference with respect to specific passages quoted from Sri Bhashya. By no means even the two books taken together is exhaustive since the whole field of criticism is vast like an ocean. As we peruse the pages a few points are noted and a sanskrit line occuring in the particula page of Sri Bhashya is also given in paranthesis to serve as milestones covered. In the Sri Bhashya, Maha Siddhanta occupies the lion's share and the subject matter extends from page 48 to 160.

No inference can be drawn from a matter devoid of attributes. Inference is a *pramana* next in operation after *pratyaksha*. There is first the knowledge of the hetu in the *paksha* through pratyaksha from which the presence of a possibility is inferred. If Brahman has no attributes then a hetu in Brahman should be furnished to prove that Brahman is nirvisesha. That is how inference works. But the moment the hetu is cited it ceases to be nirvisesha. "As Ramanuja puts it , the assertion that something is nirvisesha because it is of special nature, is similar to the one that one's own mother is barren" (top of SB p53).

॥ जननीवन्ध्यात्वप्रतिज्ञायामिव ॥

In Defence of Difference: According to Ramanuja, it is not only that there is no pramana in regard to undifferentiated Brahman, but also that difference as an entity, cannot be dismissed as illusory... His view is that difference is not of the nature of the object (*svarûpa*) it is its dharma...His view is that the postulation of a separate principle as jati (a borrowed term from Nyaya vaisheshikas) is superfluous; its equivalent word *samsthana* is better suited (SB p54). The reader can benefit by turning to page 265 of Ref 64.

॥ संस्थानमेव जातिः ॥

The notion of commonness that arises among several objects of the same kind has led Nyaya Vaisheshikas to postulate a separate entity called jati which is seen as a unifying concept (like lion belonging to cat family). As each object is seen to be distinct, it was argued that there should be some aspect called *bheda* which is responsible for the notion of difference. But according to Ramanuja, it is *samsthana*, or the specific configuration which does the function of both. That is, in as much as it produces the notion of commonness, its serves as *jati* and as it distinguishes the object, it serves as *bheda*.

When one reflects on the nature of the world, the Advaitins contend, it cannot be treated to be real or absolute nothing, but should be treated as illusory. For, according to them, whichever is variable (*vyâvartamâna*) and sublated (*bâdhita*) is not real and that which is unchanging (*anuvartamana*) and unsublated is real. But according to Ramanuja, the concept of bâdha and nivrtti are thoroughly misinterpreted by the Advaitin. Some more misconceptions are added to the list, such as, existence (*sat*) itself is knowledge (*anubhuti*) and so on.

Dharmabhûtajnâna

In this world of matter, every experience makes the object come into existence in consciousness and therefore it becomes possessed by consciusness. This possession, in other words makes the object an adjective of that consciousness. An adjective cannot exist without a substrate. The stream of consciousness is possessed of objects and their impressions as images reveal the transitoriness of worldly existence. The continuity of consciousness as a stream grants it the quality of being the substrate of these experiences of objects. Consciousness becomes an eternal and universal background of all phenomenal experience.

"Against such views as these, Ramanuja holds that the seeming absoluteness of consciousness, or rather its universal presence has been misunderstood and misinterpreted for the sake of a false metaphysics. It is based on false psychology. A correct epistemological undestanding of the nature of consciousness would require a more detailed study of consciousness and its processes." The quote is that of KCV who makes a brilliant exposition of it in the third chapter, "Nature of Consciousness- p241". According to Ramanuja, five fundamental features make up consciousness:

1. Consciousness is an attribute belonging to a permanent subject and is not the pure 'that' or existence which is observed in nirvikalpaka pratyaksha.
2. Consciousness is not a permanent but a transitory function, or rather it is present whenever the subject cognizes...
3. Consciousness is aware of its absence...
4. Consciousness is neither agent nor subject but the act of cognition of a subject to whom it is specially related as a function...
5. Consciousness is not the Absolute Brahman nor yet the âtman the individual soul. Because even though one might seek to dissolve all souls or subjects into objects of the Divine Lord or dependent on the absolute existence the effort will not entail the granting the nature of being a substance to consciousness.

These five -fold objections against the monistic idealistic theory of consciousness are serious enough. Ramanuja shows that on grounds of actual experience and discriminate criticism there is no ground at all for asserting that consciousness is a substance or a witness or pure experience without subject or object."

Such a thing is termed sky-flower: "The self without self consciousness is as inconceivable as self consciousness without the self. The self has *dharmabhuta-Jnâna* as attributive consciousness as its *sine qua non*. 'Consciousness is either proved or not proved. If it is proved, it follows that it possesses attributes; if it is not, it is something absolutely nugatory like a 'sky-flower'(SB p57&65)! Refer also to page 380 of Ref 64.

॥ गगनकुसुमादिवत्॥

Consciousness is the attribute of a permanent conscious self. In the judgment 'I know', the thinker is different from the thought and the dharmin and the dharma are inseperable like light and its luminosity" (page 111 of Ref 43).

To be conscious is to be conscious of something. In other words, *jnâna* reveals itself only when it reveals some object. At other times it remains only as a potency of the self to apprehend objects and is not svaprâkâsha at that time. Hence, knowledge is that which manifests itself to its substratum, as and when it is present or that which manifests its objects to its substratum (SB p57).

अनुभूतित्वं नाम वर्तमानदशायां स्वसत्तयैव स्वाश्रयं प्रति

प्रकाशमानत्वं स्वसत्तयैव स्वविषयसाधनत्वं वा॥

It is observed only in the case of pratyaksha which operates through sense organs that it grasps objects that are present at the time of its functioning. But this rule cannot be applied in the case of Jnâna as a whole; for it is observed in the case of recollection, inference or yogi-pratyaksha that objects of different times are apprehended (SB p58, p387 of Ref 64).

॥ कलान्तरवर्तिनोऽपि ग्रहण दर्शनात् ॥

These issues are discussed on page 66 of "Gleanings from SB". The Advaitic view of eternity of consciousness is untenable...If avidya is not accepted to be really different from Brahman, then it will tantamount to Brahman itself is avidya (SB p64).

॥ वस्तुतोऽविद्यैव स्यादात्मा ॥

Sadhana /Sadhaka
In Ramanuja Darshana the sadhaka, the finite self is a real entity and never a fictitious construction. Sadhana is possible and even significant in this school as the reality of the sadhaka and the sadhya is well established. The author Dr NSA in his doctoral thesis "The Philosophy of Sâdhana in Visishtâdvaita", has devoted three chapters respectively to the Sâdhaka, the Sâdhya and the Sâdhana spanning over 150 pages. Simply put the sadhaka is one who strives hard to attain the state of liberation. The process is termed *mukti sâdhana*. Swami Deshika steers clear the confusion created by the Advaitins relating to the understanding of the soul in his work Nyaya Siddhanjana and the author NSA has explained on the basis of the views of Swami Deshika. Incidentally, this books abounds in quotations from SB I.1.1 (SB p 66).

More and More *vs* Less and Less
After exposing the defects inherent in Advaita, Dr KCV makes the following observation (p254): "There is one objection that might with success be brought against the theistic and common-sense position of Ramanuja namely, all these are perhaps true of the ordinary human consciousness. This we also admit but they are not true of the absolute consciousness. Illusion makes all the difference... Knowledge becomes just approximation towards more or less unreality. In the Buddhist schools these

approximations are dynamically construed, in Advaita they are practically construed. In neither case, is reality possible within experience as we can know it. Further in these theories the constructive dynamism of thought is fundamentally of the vitiating character. Less and less of thought means more and more of Reality. Ramanuja standing on the bed-rock of scriptural experience declares that more and more knowledge it is that leads to perfection of consciousness and not less and less...

We thus find that if it is admitted that consciousness is more of the subject than of the object, then "knowledge like pleasure manifests itself to that conscious person who is substrate and not to anybody else." The self thus owns consciousness just as it does all experiences as manifested in the judgements "I know this", "I enjoy this". Consciousness thus is not the absolute but the personal attribute of a self, invariably associated as its function, dharma. Therefore is it known as *dharma-bhuta-Jnâna* as distinguished from *svayam prâkâshatvam* of jîva or *kshetrajna*. It is creative in its perfect state of expansion(*vikâsa*) and contraction in its lesser stages of perfection (*sankocha*). For a more detailed study the reader should consult Deshika's Nyaya Parishuddhi. "Swami Deshika makes a distinction between the self which is the nature of knowledge (*svarupa Jnâna* also known as *dharmi Jnâna*) and knowledge which is the attribute of the self (*dharmabhuta-Jnâna*). The self is the substrate (*dharmin*) and knowledge is its attribute (*dharma*) The two are distinct but inseperable (*aprtak-siddha*) (vide Ref 69). See also "The Nature of *dharmabhuta Jnâna*"(p27 of Ref 43).

KCV proves that Ramanuja's views are quite compatible with the views of modern scholars. He quotes from Lossky (see foot-note on p82): "Every fact of consciousness is made up of atleast three moments; every such fact depends for its existence upon the presence of an ego (read *ahamartha*) of a content of consciousness, of a relation between these two... Every fact in reality with which I

251

am acquainted is not merely a fact, it is also owing to relation of 'having in consciousness' a content of consciousness, in other words, the Ego exercises towards it the function of becoming conscious", Again after quoting profusely from Lossky, KCV concludes his chapter on "The Nature of Consciousness" thus: "The above extracts are called from Professor Nicola Lossky's important contribution on intuitive Logic entitled "Transformation of the Concept of Consciousness in Modern Epistemology and its bearing on Logic" to the Encyclopedia of Philosophical Sciences Vol.I. They serve to illustrate the modernity of Sri Ramanuja's views on the subject of Consciousness".

'I' Cognition

The reason why Ramanuja launches a scathing attack on the subject is because of the confusion in the Advaitin's interpretation of *ahamartha*. The whole idea is wrongly conceived, per se (SB p68).

अहमर्थो न चेदात्मा प्रत्यक्त्वं नात्मनो भवेत्॥

It is improper to say that the I is not the self as it amounts to saying that the self is not the self. It is the nature of the self to know itself as I. If release means the self free from the notion of I, then that would be nothing short of destroying the self itself, in which case moksha will cease to be a desired end. One assiduously pursues all that is prescribed in scriptures with a view to attain release under the hope, "I will get removed of all the traces of pain and enjoy Infinite Bliss in moksha". But if the I itself is destroyed in moksha, then it will no longer be a cherished end at all. Moreover consciousness cannot exist without this self and with the destruction of I, consciousness also ceases to exist even as the act of cutting cannot exist when the wood-cutter and the tools are absent.

That self is a knower is taught in sutras 18 and 19 of BS II.3 and the self is *Kshetrajna*, as taught by Gitâchârya (BG 13.1).

252

A flame of the lamp is itself luminous, manifests itself, and with its rays illumines objects. The ray is made of the same substance as the flame, yet the ray is called the attribute of the flame, because it is always found in the flame , surrounding the flame and depends on it. Like the flame, the self has the consciousness as its attribute. With this attribute, the self knows itself as well as others. This is the view found in all the scriptures (see page SB p71 for a list of quotations from the Upanishads). A few are translated and given below.

"Atma has no inside or outside like a lump of salt- *prajnânaghanâ*", "the capacity of the knower to know is not lost as it is imperishable", "it is this purusha (self) who is in the midst of the indriyas, who is the light within the heart and who is characterised by *vijnâna* or attributive consciousness" etc.

॥ ज्ञोऽत एव ॥

While dealing with the above sutra (BS II.3.18) at the place where it occurs (SB p538) Ramanuja quotes the very same texts as in the aforementioned context (SB p71). The reader may glance through the two pages and get convinced about Ramanuja's effective and efficient method of teaching. Parrot-like repetition is perhaps the art of teaching young minds! And the inescapable flow of logic by associating the same set of ideas as is evident when we study Sri Bhâshyam and Vedârtha Sangraha together.

Advaitins do not agree that the âtman is the content of I-cognition and their contention centers around three arguments (p66 Ref 15): If the self knows itself as I, then it would give rise to the error of the self itself becoming the subject or object of knowledge of I, which, however is an impossibility. I-cognition involves the larger question of knowership itself, and according to Advaita, knowership is an acquired feature and not the essential nature of the self. It is contended that I-cognition is the foremost of all *adhyasa-s* and it does not belong to the self.

But according to Ramanuja, the content of I-cognition is the self, which is a whole and does not consist in analyzable constituents. The self represented by I is not illusory, but a real and a separate entity in itself.

The second argument is that if the self knows itself, then it will become a knower, and knowership essentially involves change which cannot be the function of the unchanging âtma. Hence *jnâtrtva* which is illusory rightly belongs to *antahkarana*. Ramanuja does not agree with this. *Jnâtrtva* is the property of a sentient being and to postulate it to an insentient *antahkarana* defies all logic. Just as knowership cannot be of the body so also *antahkarana* which is similar to the body in many respects, cannot be a knower (SB p74).

एवमन्तःकरणरूपाहङ्कारोऽपि तद्द्रव्यत्वादेव तैरेव हेतुभिः तस्माद्विविच्यते ॥

In the state of embodiment of a being, the *dharmabhûtajnâna* is subject to contraction and expansion because of karma and it operates through the limited scope of the sense organs which are instruments of knowledge for the indwelling self. During such cribbed, cabined and confined bound-states the knowledge suffers rise or fall causing expansion or contraction and hence *jnâtrtva* involves change. Since shrutis declare that self remains changeless, only the *dharmabhûtajnâna* is subjected to change but the *dharmin*, remains changeless (SB p75).

अतः क्षेत्रज्ञावस्थायां कर्मणा संकुचितस्वरूपं तत्तत्कर्मानुगुण तरतमभावेन वर्तते ॥

At the state of release, however, the *dharmabhutaJnâna* expands to the maximum such that its intensity attains the same intensity and kind as that of the Supreme and the consciousness of the self attains infinite range equivalent (*parama sâmyam*) to that of the Supreme Lord.

But some Advaitins contend that *jnatrtva* is not possible either to the changeless Atman or to the inanimate *antahkarana*. But a unity brings about it. Ramanuja strongly opposes this unjustifiable claim since it does not fit in with their theory. It cannot be argued that due to association of self with *antahkarana* the latter acquires *jnatrtva* just as in the case of an iron rod which burns when in association with fire. When the fire is put out all get reduced to ashes but the iron remains. What is present in fire, namely heat could be transferred to iron, but jnatrtva not present in the self cannot be transferred to the *antahkarana* (SB p76).

अहंकारस्य त्वचेतनस्य ज्ञातृत्वासंभवादेव सुतरां

तत्संपर्कात् संविदि ज्ञातृत्वं तदुपलब्धिर्वा ॥

The third argument is that I-cognition is not found in deep sleep. Advaitins contend that during sound-sleep there is the feeling of pure bliss devoid of the notion of I, "I slept happily unaware of myself". Ramanuja proves for precisely the same reason the self remains ever cognized as I. The recollection of the form '*sukham aham asvaptam*' goes only to prove that the âtman by nature is blissful and an experiencer. As it is impossible for the self to recall something it had not experienced earlier, the recollection only proves the continued existence of *ahampratyaya* during sleep. Sleep is caused by tamoguNa, there is no experience of any external objects as all the sense organs do not function, and the *dharmabhutaJnâna* lies highly contracted with its potency to know dorment (SB p79).

॥ सुषुप्तावपि नाहंभावविगमः ॥

Knowledge as well as ignorance reside in the self and ahankara is not the knower. I-cognizance exists even in the state of release otherwise release would mean the destruction of I and the entire shastra on liberation would be meaningless and redundant. *Ahamartha* never ceases to exist since the self is eternal.

When the self is freed from the limitations of karma, the mukti brings about infinite intelligence and omniscience to the finite self. Its *visishta-aeikya* is then apprehended in non-difference from Brahman. (Please note that *visishta-aeikya* is quite different from *svarûpa aeikya*- p231 of Ref 43). Rishi Vamedeva, Bhakta Prahlada and Nammazhwar realized the truth of *aham* in Brahman. The Supreme Being is also spoken of by the scriptures as having the consciousness of the I. For example, the Chandokhya (6.2.3) states: The *sat* deliberated 'May I become many; may I be born' In this context the verses uttered in first person by Bhagavan Krishna are quoted in support of 'Aham' (vide SB p83). "As I transcend the perishable and am above even the imperishable, I am celebrated as Purushottama among the people of the world and in the vedas" (BG 15.18).

यस्मात्क्षरमतीतोऽहमक्षरादपि चोत्तमः ।

अतोऽस्मि लोके वेदे च प्रथितः पुरुषोत्तमः ॥

Ramanuja hastens to add that *ahankara* is quite different from *aham*. This *ahankara* is one of the 24 prakrti tattva (BG 13.5) and is the cause for delusion by mistaking the body for the soul (VP 6.7.10).

॥ अविद्यायाः स्वरूपं अनात्मन्यात्मबुद्धिः ॥

"The moral philosopher, who knows the psychology of the emperical 'me' or ahankara as the result of the conjunction of the âtman with prakrti, concludes that karman is due to the action and reaction of the guNas, is not influenced by the conceit "I am the doer", and seeks to renounce the egocentric mentality of ahankara" (p328 of Ref 43).

अहङ्कारविमूढात्मा कर्ताहमिति मन्यते ॥

The Shruti Ghatta (p 89 to 96 of SB)

In this section belonging to Mahasiddhanta, Ramanuja unequivocally establishes that all the Upanishads in one voice proclaim that the Brahman is savisesha (with attributes) and a Brahmam without attributes (nirvisesha) is not only inconceivable but an impossible myth that does not exist. At best nirguNam can only mean absence of any defect and not absence of guNa.

Among the Upanishads, Chandogya and Taittiriya are the most important ones. Any misinterpretation and / or misconception would render the meaning wrong, the message lost and the study, a waste. Hence Ramanuja takes care to clarify the crucial passages and rebuts Advaitin's erroneous interpretations.

To begin with, Tattvamasi does not represent a nirvishesha Brahman as the Advaitins claim, but a savisesha Brahman as Ramanuja expounds its meaning. Tattvamasi is a supreme statement (*mahâvâkya*) when read in the context where the expression occurs, and Ramanuja shows the awe inspiring nature of Brahman displayed during the process of creation from conception to execution- Brahman forming the material cause as well as the instrumental cause, an all-knower, wielding unimaginable power, all pervasive, very subtle and a myriad other attributes-all of which only the Para Brahman can have. The father (teacher) pours out in ecstacy; "What a wonder Shvetaketu, the self same God who created this world is residing in you as Antaryamin!" Can there be anything more precious than God who is residing in one's own heart (SB p89)?

कल्याणगुणविशिष्टतां कृत्स्नस्य जगतः तदात्मकतां च प्रतिपाद्य एवंभूत

ब्रह्मात्मकस्त्वमसीति श्वेतकेतुं प्रति उपदेशाय प्रवृत्तत्वात् प्रकरणस्य।

Mund 1.1.5/6 : "That which is not perceived, not grasped, without origin, colourless, without eyes or ears or hands and feet –that which is eternal yet of manifold expressions, all pervading, extremely subtle and undecaying, the source of all creation –the wise behold every where". In the first part of this rik, all the evil qualities of prakrti in B are denied and the later half ascribes to B all auspicious qualities. The words such as *nirguNam, niranjanam* mean only the absence of *prâkrtic* qualities. Being His own creation, the matter cannot have a corrupting influence over Him. The NirguNa texts do not as such contradict the possibility of determination, but deny only the predication of evil or imperfection to Brahman as otherwise negation would lead to nihilism or sunyavada. A few hymns from the Upanishads recalled here (SB p91) establish B as a sentient principle with attributes and not nirvisesha B as Advaitins claim.

Shveta 6,7: Brahman is the Ruler of rulers, God of gods, Master of masters and the one incomparable Absolute.

॥ विदाम देवं भुवषमीड्यम्॥

Katha (5.13): Eternal peace results for those sadhakas who see the Brahman as the one Eternal sentient being who accomplishes the desires of the many eternal jîvas as He is the indweller of the jîvas. A jîva endowed with such a vision should no longer be called a jîva but a *dhîra* (recall the line *'pashyanti dhîrâ: parijânanti yonim'* of Purusha Sukta). The first two lines of the following hymn is common to Shveta (6.13) also. The Vedântins insist that only by meditating on saguNa Brahman, a bound soul can get freed.

नित्यो नित्यानां चेतनश्चेतनानां एको बहूनां यो विदधाति कामान्।

तमात्मस्थं येऽनुपश्यन्ति धीराः तेषां शान्तिः शाश्वती नेतरेषाम्॥

Shveta (6.19): The aspirant who is keen on bringing an end to sorrow should meditate on Brahman who is partless, who has done what has to be done, who is without any defect, who is the bridge

258

to the attainment of liberation and who is self effulgent like the glowing flame which has consumed the last remnants of firewood.

एष आत्माऽपहतपाप्मा विजरो विमृत्युर्विशोको विजिघत्सोऽपिपासः सत्यकामः

सत्यसङ्कल्पः ॥

एष सर्वभूतन्तरात्माऽपहतपाप्मा दिव्यो देव एको नारायणः ॥

Chand. 8.1.5: By the former epithets in the above hymn, the Brahman is free from six heya guNas- devoid of sin, free from old age, free from death, free from sorrow, free from hunger, and free from thirst. The saguNas are the two kalyana guNas viz. *satyakâma* and *satya sankalpa*. These 6+2=8 qualities are called 'guNâshtakam' and Ramanuja attaches great significance to it (148 of Ref 60a). The sadhaka who contemplates on Brahman with the above guNas would naturally be able to get rid of the *heya guNas* afflicting him and also acquire the kalyana guNas leading to his release. A career in God realisation calls for cultivation of the a/m qualities. Turn to SB p256 where '*apahatapâpma*' is explained and the entity, according to Subâla (7), is none other than Narayana.

This page and the succeeding two pages SB p257 & 258 are important for the wealth of quotations they contain. The verses quoted when read together with Ramanuja's brief comments on them, highlight the nature of the Supreme Lord (that He is not of the prâkrtic substance) and that He is more concerned with sadhakas who are devoutly attached to Him (*sâdhu paritrâNa*) than punishing the wicked. A set of verses describing Him as Antaryamin is appended under the sutra-*bhedavyapadeshâcchânyah*.

The hymn given below is oft quoted by the Advaitins in support of NirguNa B.

निष्कलं निष्क्रियं शान्तं निरवद्यं निरञ्जनम्।

259

अमृतस्य परं सेतुं दग्धेन्धनमिवानलम्॥

Ramanuja does not agree with the Advaitins. According to him, texts that expressly negate all guNa-s like nirguNam, niranjanam, nishkalam, nishkriam, santam, etc., are incapable of establishing an attributeless B. This is because it is simply not possible that there could exist a thing without properties and the proposition goes counter to many other passages which extol the glories of B stating them to be natural to it (p99 Ref 15):

पराऽस्य शक्तिर्विविधैव श्रूयते स्वाभाविकी ज्ञानबलक्रिया च॥

It appears as if there is contradiction between the nirguNa and saguNa texts and it is this contradiction that leads us, according to Advaita, to uphold those texts that deny qualities as more powerful and the others as less powerful, thus being over-ruled by the former. The saguNa shruti-s refer to B with qualities and they are intended for meditative worship, while the nirguNa texts have no function other than negating all characteristics. Further, the nirguNa shruti-s in order to negate qualities in B necessarily stand in need of saguNa shruti-s, as they alone provide qualities in respect of B. Hence the saguNa shruti-s operate prior to the nirguNa shruti-s. The latter being subsequent (para) are powerful on the basis of *apaccheda-nyāya*. According to Ramanuja, however, there is absolutely no conflict between the two types of texts, as the content of each one is different. While the nirguNa shruti-s negate all those that are inauspicious and imperfect in the case of B, the saguNa shruti-s speak of all the auspicious and perfect qualities in It and as such there is no conflict between them. This type of reconciliation is shown by the text, "*apahatapapma vijaro... satyakamah satyasankalpah*", which negates all empirical qualities and specifies the presence of extra-empirical qualities like *satyakāma* and *satyasankalpa* with respect to B.

Further there is the maxim that general rule becomes inapplicable when there is a specific one; and this is known as the *utsarga-apavâda-nyâya*. The unkindest cut of theirs is yet to be mentioned.

Ramanuja further clarifies (by way of rebutting the view of the Advaitin) that mere Jnâna alone does not secure liberation but must be accompanied with worship, *Jnânam cha upâasanâtmakam*, and one can worship only a Brahman with attributes (SB p93).

उपास्यं च ब्रह्म सगुणमित्युक्तम्।

Shruti Segment: *Anandavalli*
Ramanuja considers the Taittiriya upanishad and in particular the Anandavalli part of it as expressing the essence of the whole Upanishads. It is so important that he has recommended its recitation along with Purusha Sukta during the aradhana in temple worship. Anandavalli, as the very name indicates, is melodious and soul filling to listen during its oral rendition, easy to remember and runs the gamut of the entire *tattva- hita-purushârtha* in a nut-shell. No wonder Veda Vyasa has devoted one full adhikaraNa (Anandamaya Adhikarana, the sixth in the series) for describing Para Brahmam as Anandamaya and Ramanuja's discussion for it extends over 25 pages. (SB p229-243). Besides , for expounding his siddhanta, he repeatedly recalls Anandavalli. For example, refer to SB p92 (*Shruti ghatta* of *Mahasiddanta*) and the penultimate adhikaraNa of the first adhyâya (SB p434). Name of the adhikaraNa and the particular sutras where references to Anandavalli occur are furnished below for quick reference SB 1.4.7.

॥ प्रकृत्यधिकरणम्॥

। आत्मकृतेः। परिणामात्।

Anandavalli begins with the assersion that the one who contemplates on Brahman, i.e., Brahmavit, attains the highest and

261

verily Anandavalli is all about that Brahman. The statement "*brahmavidâpnoti param*" distinguishes between the self that attains Bliss and the Brahman that is attained. The Brahman possesses three mighty powers, Satya , Jnâna and Ananta and He resides within the cave of the heart of the one who contemplates. Though the powers of the Brahman are many these three are His defining or determining qualities- *svarûpa nirûpaka dharmas* (p248 Ref 43): "These are distinguishing marks of Brahman. These are systole and the diastole of the all-sustaining and pulsating life of Paramâtman which is to be intuited rather than logically explained." The Brahman is referred as vipashcit to distinguish Him from the rest of all the sentients which include the bound souls, muktas and the nityasuris. Attaining the highest means, attaining the Abode of the Supreme (*Parama Vyoman*) which is *Parama Pâda* or *Sri Vaikunta*.

In Brguvalli it is made clear that Anandamaya is the Brahman. All living beings are born in Ananda. Having been born they live, move and have their being in Ananda. Like the stability of the atom is explained due to the pull of the nucles, the stability and sustenance of living beings is due to the presence of Antaryamin (indweller) or Anandamaya.

This Anandamayi is also conceptualised as a bird. This beautiful bird has *priyam* (love) as the head; happiness (*moda*) forming the right wing; enjoyment (*promoda*) as the left wing; The soul of this bird is Ananda or Bliss; and the stabilising tail is of course the Brahman.
The reader may pause here to reflect over the unitary teachings of the Upanishads by comparing the teachings as in the Anandavalli and as in the Chandogya which was discussed earlier: *kâmayata* of the former is the equivalent of *aeikshata* of the latter. The sport loving God was bored to be alone. He decided to become many (Taittiriopanishad. 2.6).

॥ सोकामयत। बहु स्यां प्रजायेयेति ॥

The Brahman willed: "May I become many! May I be born!" He made a deliberation and created all this and entered them. Thus, a host of embodied sentient beings (that forms the ground of non-sentient) and the inanimate matter (that are created to serve the sentient embodied beings) came into visible manifestation. In the transition process, the un-manifested Brahman came into manifestation- the subtle transformed into gross. The changeover occurred from subtle *sûkshma kâranâvasta* to the gross *sthûla kâryâvasta*. As per the principle of *Sâmânâdhikaranya* the parity between the two states of Brahman as between the various epochs always remain conserved, like mass-energy conservation in physics. After creation of the life support system which includes bringing into existence the solar system also, the Brahman undertakes the task of governance. The rise of the sun, the blowing of the wind and the functions of Indra, Agni and the god of Death —all phenomenal happenings take place out of fear for Him. The universe is like a modern-day manufacturing concern with portfolios fixed and the selection of the candidates made according to the merit of the individual. Anandavalli outlines the levels in the hierarchy. The lowest is the highest in the world of homo sapiens. The unit is that of a human of exemplary character who is strong in body and mind and who can rule the whole world single-handedly. In other words, the unit is that of an Emperor. The powers and pleasures that an emperor enjoys constituting the fundamental *manushya* Ananda. A hundred times the pleasure of emperor constitute the pleasure of a Gandharva and so on.

"The shruti employs a calculus of pleasures in an ascending scale of values, and ends with the highest bliss of Brahman. It is supreme and not to be surpassed and can not be adequately described or defined. The pleasures of the finite self ranging from earthly paradise to the perennial delights of Brahmâ (as distinguished from Brahman) are tinged with pain and pale into nothingness when compared to Brahmânanda." Brahma may be enjoying the privileges of a high post but even he is burdened with heavy responsibilities-bound with shackles of gold but nonetheless a high-ranking karma-bound prisoner all the same, observes Swami Deshika (Varadaraja Panchashat 29).

We have mentioned how God governs using fear as the key. "Uneasy lies the head that bears the crown": Damocles' sword hangs over the head waiting to descend and severe the head of the person sitting in the chair when he commits an error. It is as difficult to gain the post as it is difficult to retain it. For example, a hundred Ashvamedha Yaga must be performed to secure the post of Indra. But the case of a sâdhaka aspiring for moksha is quite different from those aspiring for various posts in the hierarchy mentioned earlier. The unsullied mind of this sâdhaka (*dhîra*) is such that he is of the firm conviction that the Lord on whom he is meditating upon is different from *banda* Jîva(s), and mukta(s). When all the unwanted thoughts get eliminated, his meditation gets stabilized. He gets freed from fear of mistaken identity.

प्रतिष्ठां विन्दते। अत सोऽभयं भवति॥

As the concentration develops further and further, the sâdhaka gets established in Brahman enjoying tranquility and bliss. The extreme desirability of this state of mind is such that, according to Anandavalli, the sâdhaka becomes restive and gets overpowered with fear when he loses the vision of the Lord (in his mental arena) even for a moment.

In this section, there occurs a clash between the two. Refer the passage 8 of Anandavalli —*yadâ hi eva eshha etasminudaram antaram kurute, atha tasya bhayambhavati.* The Advaitins interpret the underlined word as *bhedam* i.e., one who sees things other than B, he gets the fear of samsâra. This they say conforms to their standard refrain –*sarvam khalu idam brahma tat jalan iti shanta upasita* –Chand 3.14.1.

The advaitin's version of antaram as bheda is not acceptable. According to Ramanuja antaram means 'a break' or 'an interval' which fits very well with the context. For the upâsaka, to fix the mind on the abstract B is difficult since the B is unperceivable (*adrshye*), bodiless (*anâtmye*), inexpressible (*anirukte*) and groundless for gaining fearlessness (*abhayam pratishhTham vindate*). After struggle, he gains B and acquires fearlessness. When there is even a slight break in his contemplation on B, he gets gripped with fear –fear of losing Him. Ramanuja highlights the super sensitivity of the sadhaka with a popular verse from Garuda PurâNa.

यन्मुहूर्तं क्षणंवाऽपि वासुदेवो न चिन्त्यते।

सा हानिः तन्महच्छिद्रं सा भ्रान्तिः सा च विक्रिया॥

The shruti ghatta of Maha Siddhanta ends with the above verse.

The 'Unkindest Cut
We must sort out the text '*satyam Jnânam anantam brahmâ*'. This is interpreted by the Advaitin in a secondary sense, involving a negative way of interpretation. Accordingly, the terms satyam etc., convey what B is not, rather than what it is. It is satya. not because it is constant, but because it is changeless; Jnâna, not because it is sensient but because it is not inert (*jada*) and is infinite (*ananta*) not because it is so but because it is not finite. The advantage of interpreting this way is that B is portrayed only in a negative way, thus avoiding the possibility of being viewed as being associated with any positive attributes. Another advantage is that B is spoken of and yet its unspeakability is maintained. It is spoken of what it is not and not spoken of as what it is" (p 96 of Ref 15).

Moreover, the stripping of attributes to make B nirguNam is the norm: "The Advaitins deny all atributes of B and establish It as homogeneous; they argue that, on the principle that texts of different branches of the Upanishads have the same purport, all the texts dealing with causality of B should be taken as teaching a non-dual B. This B which is indirectly described or defined by the causality texts is directly defined by the Taittiriya as 'Existence, Knowledge, Bliss is B' and so this text also defines It as non-dual, especially as otherwise these would militate against those texts which describe it as without attributes. All this is not a sound view, says Ramanuja" (p51 of BS).

॥ सर्व शाखा प्रत्ययन्यायश्च अत्र भवतो विपरीत फलः ॥

Shankara adopts these devices to set the vedic sentences against each other and applies the Occam's Razor to get rid of them from the purview of discussion or for reconsideration. Take for example the principle of the Purva Mimamsa known as Apaccheda nyâya (SB p31 Mahapurva-paksha).

अपच्छेदन्यायेन निर्गुणवाक्यानां गुणापेक्षत्वेन

परत्वात् बलीयस्त्वमिति न किंचिदपहीनम् ॥

Apachchheda- nyâya is supposed to be applied when there is a direct conflict between two scriptural texts. According to the principle, the later texts should prevail over the earlier ones; i.e., the later (para) is more powerful than the former (purva). Let us illustrate the danger inherent in the application of this line of reasoning.

When one shruti text reads "the world exists", the Advaitin on the authority of the later text would contend that "It does not exist, only Brahman exists" as according to them the denial of the world being later prevails. If we take their conclusion as granted, then using the same line of reasoning, the Sunyavadin's statement that "There is nothing at all that is real" would have to be considered as true because there could be no more denial or contradiction of it at all. Hence to deny reality is to embrace void!

The major fault in these futile exercises has been due to facile universal propositions derived from a few fragmentary and isolated instances torn out of context –trying to skate hopefully on a hopelessly thin veneer of ice. The brute force negation finds fulfillment in Shûnya as it is free from subsequent sublation.

A few more instances of their mind-set may be cited (see page 216 of Ref 43). "The Advaitin also follows the same line of reasoning and comes to the same conclusion, but his pet theory of Maya-vâda overpowers his aesthetic inclinations; and he suddenly arrests with his destructive dialectics the free flow of aesthetic intuition. He concludes the adhikaraNa (Ananda-maya) by saying that the self consisting of bliss is the highest self and then brings a surprise by contradicting it." The 'myat' acts like the 'nyat'- the veto power of the Russians!

Turn to page 160 (ibid): "The monists who explains avatara as the incarnation of the maya-ridden Ishwara and finally reduces Him to the status of the avidya ridden jîva follows the God-destroying logic of subjectivism and does not respond to the logic of the heart."

The grammar principle of samanadhikaranya establishes the identity of one object associated with several aspects. The principle emphasises satya Jnâna etc., as positive aspects of B and establishes B as the one that possesses these qualities. Extracts from Ref 43:

The first three words Satyam, Jnânam and Anantam qualify the noun Brahman and the three define the attributes (*kalyana guNas* or determining qualities) of Brahman. Ramanuja shows the far reaching impact of coordinate predication principle at several places

267

in his works (SB p90; SB p237; 24Ref 60a) and accordingly the author expains its significance and the ramifications of this principle in the various pages of his work: "The true meaning of samanadhikaranya is not identity, non-duality or unity, but is the inseperable relation between a thing and its attributes or dharmin and dharma…prakâra and prakârin…Visishtâdvaita alone takes the dilemma by the horns" (p71 ibid). "Samanadhikaranya, which says that words having different meanings may denote only one thing. A term connoting the effect state of Brahman, including its modal self, connotes also the same Brahman in the causal state. "The unity of manifestation" is "the unity of composition" owing to the non-difference of cause and effect and the self identity of Brahman" (p85 ibid). Visishtadvaitin's samanadhikaranya pitted against Advaitin's apaccheda nyâya. (p87 ibid) "While coordination enriches the meaning, sublation destroys it" (p229). "The mantra which defines Brahman as satya, Jnâna and ananta also defines it as abounding in bliss and in the light of the rule of coordinate predication, the term 'anandamaya' connotes Brahman and not the jîva. The Upanishadic, "He who knows Brahman attains the highest" distinguishes between the self that attains bliss and Brahman that is attained. Brahman the cosmic self, is also the inner self (Antaryamin) of jîva and It finally imparts Its bliss and Brahmanizes it (the jîva)" (p215 ibid).

ब्रह्मविदाप्नोति परम्। तदेषाभ्युक्ता॥

"The cosmological truth that Brahman as upâdâna-karana is also Brahman as upadeya falls into line with the law of coordination and there is no self discrepancy between the two states, just as there is no self discrepancy between the childhood of a person and his youth" (p230 ibid). "The rule of samanadhikaranya as the grammar of Vedântic thought enables us to understand the epistemological exposition that the world of matter and souls is the aprthak-siddha-visheshhana of Brahman" (p230).

Smrti (Bhagavad Gita) / PurâNa (Vishnu PurâNa) Segmant (*ghatta*)
This section begins with a plethora of quotations from the above
two books. While the former has been adequately discussed, we may
take note of a few points pertaining to the latter.

Alavandar, in his Stotra Ratna (4), has expressed the quint essence
of VP as containing elaborate teachings on Tattva Traya and the
methodology of liberation, the Ashtanga Yoga. And even in those
teachings, the Isvara tattva as Bhagavan is the crest jewel of the
entire work. The context in which the word 'Bhagavan' is defined:

One aspiring for moksha should meditate on Brahman and more
importantly the meditation should be on the Brahman with
auspicious qualities. The byword for such a Brahman is Bhagavan.
Ramanuja has selected verses from this section of VP (6.5.68 up to
the concluding verse 87) and has quoted them in his SB.

In view of its paramount importance Ramanuja has quoted these
verses on "Bhagavan" in his other works as well. The reader should
refer Vedârtha Sangraha para48 (containing verses from Gita) and
para 49 (verses from VP defining Bhagavan), wherein the *samanvaya*
principle is in evidence to remind us the equivalence of Krishna with
Bhagavan. In the light of Vishnu PurâNa, Lord Krishna is Bhagavan
Krishna and the Lord's utterances are '*bhagavânuvâchâ*'. Again,
observe the opening words "*bhagavannârâyaNâ*" in Sharanagati
Gadya: How else can one bring home the Truth of the great
significance of the word Bhagavan as highlighted by Parashara to
his disciple Maitreya: (6.5.76) Ramanuja, for his part, has done it par
excellence.

॥ एवमेष महाशब्दो मैत्रेय भगवानिति ॥

269

A clarificatory note may be added here regarding Ramanuja's style of approach. The primary concern of Ramanuja in the three works- Vedârtha Sangraha, Sri Bhâshya and Gita Bhâshya –is to expound his religious philosophy while critically examining the rival religious systems and philosophies. In the first two and to some extent in the third, he assumes the role of a controversialist engaging in powerful logical reasoning to refute rival philosophical systems to establish the soundness of Vishishtâdvaita system. But in Gadya Traya the controversy is completely set aside and the devotional part alone is stressed. Even in SB, considerable length of the text is devoted to an appraisal of VP as a source of devotional literature of the highest value. The singularly important significance of "Bhagavan" is included in the three gadyas, in an awe-inspiring manner, with choicest epithets and rolling phrases that are music to the ears. In their commentaries on Gadya Traya, Sudarshana Sûri and Peria-Vâcchân-Pillai, have brought forward all the relevant verses of Vishnu PurâNa and Bhagavad Gita which Ramanuja had in mind while composing the Gadyas.

As we have said earlier, the word "Bhagavan" etymologically represents the universal set of six attributes and this set finds a place in all the three *gadyas* as well.

॥ ज्ञानबलैश्वर्यवीर्यशक्तितेजः ॥

"The Vishishtâdvaita school is an effort to restate the Tantric position in a new manner which is synthetic. This vision of the Seers of the Vedas and Pancharatra school as also the mystic utterances of the Azhwars are sought to be reconciled (*Samanvayât*). Ramanuja's acceptance of the Pancharatra literature is more known through the rhapsodies in prose. (gadya) which are only three in number-viz., (1) on Sharanagati (self surrender), (2) on Vaikunta (the celestial abode of Brahman) and lastly on Sri Ranganatha (the God of Sri Rangam

270

or the Divine Theatre), than in his Sri Bhâshya." – from 'Complete Works of Dr K.C.Varadachari', volume 7 page 390.

The tattva-traya is taught in VP through dialogues between Sage Ribhu and his disciple Nidhaga and the dialogue between Jada Bharata and the king Raghuvana. The sentient principle (*chit*) is taught by Ribhu:

Strangely enough the teacher while revealing his identity says that he has come to teach Advaita! "Stop indulging in external perception of beings such as king, elephant, crowd, you and I. The souls (*âtma-svarûpam*) that dwell in these entities are identical. Don't be enamored of the outer embodiments. I came here to convey this Advaita-thought that the physical embodiments vary, but there is no difference in the respective indwelling souls." How do you account for differences in embodiments (VP 2.16.23 & 2.13.98)?

पुमान्न देवो न नरो न पशुर्न पादपः ।   शरीराकृतिभेदास्तु भूपैते कर्मयोनयः ॥

सोऽहं स च त्वं स च सर्वमेतदात्मस्वरूपं त्यजमोहम् ॥

Ramanuja commenting on the above verse emphatically denies that the above line conveys that all the souls are one and the same. Souls are identical in form but all are different and independent. Ramanuja makes it abundantly clear by showing numerous passages from the Upanishads (vide SBp108 &109). The two-bird analogy, clearly makes the distinction between the âtma and B. The object of the sutras (BS 1.2.21, 22 & BS 2.1.22) is to convey unambiguously the above idea of difference or Bheda. Even at the stage of liberation there is no question of merging or becoming one (SB p109).

नापि साधनानुष्ठानेन निर्मुक्त अविद्यस्य परेण स्वरूपैक्यसंभवः ।

As we said earlier, teachings on adhyâtma shastra in general and VP in particular fall under three headings viz. tattva, hita and

271

purushârtha. And tattva consists of three-*chit, achit* and *Isvara.* The teachings of *tattvatraya* is essentially from Jada Bharata and as far as teaching on hita is concerned it is the step by step description of Ashtanga Yoga as given by Kesi dwaja to Khandikya (VP 6.7.27 to 96).

योगस्वरूपं खाण्डिक्य श्रूयतां गदतो मम।

यत्र स्थितो न च्यवते प्राप्य ब्रह्मलयं मुनिः ॥

The Ashtanga Yoga is discussed on SB p100 mainly to emphasise the auspicious form for contemplation known as Shubhashrayatva (chapter 8 of Ref 44).

Jadabharata's teachings to the king Sauvīra
VP gives a vivid description of nature. The reader would be put up with an enquiry as to why such an elaborate description of nature? The nature is God's creation and as it forms the body of Vishnu, the nature consisting of the vital oxygen constituting the air, the generation of oxygen through the process of photosynthesis, the mountains, the seas, the rivers —all this eco-system form the life supporting system. They are there for us to see, enjoy. Worshipping nature constitute worship of Lord Vishnu.

Ramanuja takes this opportunity to have a dig at the Advaitins. He posits their *âtmaikya* tenet and advances a stout denial, as mentioned below (SB p141):

ज्ञानस्वरूपस्य ब्रह्मण एव सत्यत्वं नान्यस्य। अन्यस्य चासत्यमेव। तस्य भुवनादेः

सत्यत्वं

व्यावहारिकमिति तत्त्वं तवोपदिष्टम् इतिह्युपदेशो दृश्यते॥ नैतदेवम्। अत्र भुवनकोशस्य विस्तीर्णं स्वरूपमुक्त्वा पूर्वमनूक्तं रूपान्तरं संक्षेपः श्रूयताम् इत्यारभ्याभिधीयते॥

Towards the end of 12th chapter (VP 2.12) the teacher is keen on imparting a very important lesson on metaphysics and these teachings are elaborately explained, verse for verse in SB. The main hero of second amsha is of course the emperor Bharata whose biography extends over three lives, as king, as a hermit in the forest tending to an orphaned deer, extreme attachment to the deer giving rise to the king taking the life of a deer in the next birth, and the third life of Bharata as a Brahmin of immortal fame as Jada Bharata. It is said that the secret teachings on metaphysics acquired in his previous lives helped him to be a born spiritualist and his eccentric soul-centered behavior earned him the prefix 'Jada' attached to his name Bharata. Irony indeed that a highly-advanced spiritualist (*Brahmajnâni*) should appear 'Jada' (which means inert) in the eyes of the ordinary mortals (2.13.44)!

हिरण्यगर्भवचनं विचिन्त्येत्थं महामतिः। आत्मानं दर्शयामास जडोन्मत्ताकृतिं जने॥

The light, rivers, mountains, seas- all these form the body of Vishnu. (*vaishnavah kâyah*) From a macrocosmic description of matter constituting nature, the teacher turns his attention to the more important microcosmic soul which forms an essential part of Vishnu. The soul exists in its various embodiments such as a deva, a human, an animal or a plant. An embodied soul is called a 'Jîva' (living being). There is a vital difference between the two constituents of a Jîva viz. the soul (*âtma*) and the physical embodiment (*sharîra*). Âtma in its intrinsic content can not undergo

273

any change and it has no beginning, there was never a time when it did not exist and is indestructible. That is, âtma has neither beginning nor middle (2.12.41). In all the jîvas, the âtma is present and the âtma has identical characteristics (recall BG 5.18). But the differences in physical embodiment are due to karma and unlike âtma the body composing matter is subjected to continuous change. What comes to exist gets destroyed in a moment. That means to say, matter has a beginning and an end. The teacher explains with a concrete example. A lump of clay can be formed into a pot and the pot can be broken to pieces and powdered and can be further & further divided and even to an atom or a molecule. But the âtma cannot be subjected to such a process of division by any means. The perishable matter is associated with the word 'nâsti' and the imperishable âtma is referred to as '*asti*' (2.14.24). When the karma responsible for conditioning the soul is exhausted, the soul is restored to its pristine state of pure conscious entity (*jnânam vishuddham*) devoid of all impurities –free from taints (*nirmalam*), free from worries (*vishokam*) and free from all kinds of defects such as greed etc. which come because of contact with the material world (2.12.44). *Chit* (*asti*) and *achit* (*nâsti*) together form a part of the body of Vasudeva. The three constitute what is known as *Tattva Traya* – the three fundamental realities.

Man is not aware that he is a victim of his own contending passions and that he is losing his precious trust for a mess of pottage. The delusion (*moha*) does not allow him to become aware of the precious soul which he possesses. Knowledge of '*Tattvatraya*' would make him realize this truth and motivate him to get out of samsâra. Ramanuja expounds the import of the verses beginning from 37 to the last verse 47 (of VP 2.12) in the pages SB p141-143.

जगद्याथात्म्यज्ञानप्रयोजनं मोक्षोपाययतनमित्याह यच्चैतिति ॥

The 'Yes-Philosophy' Of Ramanuja

Ramanuja's theory of truth and knowledge relies more upon the organic and common-sense position than on any other system of thought. "The illusion of the double moon, of the white conch seen as yellow, of the fire brand seen as a continuous circle of light when whirled round are respectively traceable to the distorting medium, natural disorder and the law of persistence of vision" (p43 Ref 43). KCV in his book 'Theory of Knowledge' necessarily deals with the same subject in Chapter IV: 'The Cognitive Relation', albeit in an elaborate manner since it formed his doctoral dessertation. For the context in question refer to p294: "Jaundice is an organic defect; mirage is due to perceptible illusion (the modern day student of physics would explain it as the phenomenon of refraction of light)… In this sense all experiences of states of consciousness are real in so far they have a beginning in real causes and produce actual effects. The reflection of the face in the mirror is due to the fact of rapid movement of light from the face to the mirror and back again and this interval is perceived by us." –the reader may recall that this is exactly the principle behind Michelson and Morley experiment (SB p136).

॥ दर्पणादिषु निजमुखादिप्रतीतिरपि यथार्थो ॥

"The thing appears in a particular form to sense or sensation and it is not a fragment of the object at all. The inference as to the nature of the thing as in itself is a real inference based on the whole series of observations and disinterested discriminations made of it. The perception of silver in shell and snake in rope are merely instances of fragmentary appearances which are not unreal but on the other hand fully real and articulate in the real thing. They however claim to be the whole thing. In other words, "we seem to emerge with the result however we may feel baulked by the problems of hallucination, illusions and error, that the real is not a few selected appearances only, that everything that appears at all is real so far as

275

the foregoing considerations teach. The real means all that is and what is, includes all that it seems to be. In a word, all appearances that ever are, are real" –KCV p287 & SB p132 to138.

॥ सर्वं विज्ञानजातं यथार्थम्॥

Then follow 13 verses explaining the theory of *Trivrt-karana* of the vedic view regarding science of Cosmology (see also p265 of Ref 43for the explanation of the verses which also include a supportive verse from VP 1.2.52).

Our tradition is based on scientific thinking (buddhi) and KCV explains it in his brilliant thesis (p400): "This is what is meant by saying that it belongs to the physical order of continnuum or in one word Nature, despite what may be apprehended of it by the individuals. This is the central principle also of the Yathârtha Khyâti of Ramanuja, of Nathamuni before him,and of Sri Vedânta Deshika and other writers of Visishtâdvaita School of thought that all knowledge is of the real is a general tenet of Prabhakara and this includes perceptual knowledge too. This is what Ramanuja points out as the view espoused by the knowers of Veda. Yamunâchârya in the Atma Siddhi writes that Nathamuni, the first amongst the Acharyas of the Vaishnava school held the Yathartha Khyati view. In Nyaya Parishuddhi, Vedânta Deshika affirms that Nathamuni and others held this view. That this view is held and expounded by Nathamuni (vide Nyâya Tattva) is specifically get mentioned in a verse of Deshika's poem Tattva Muktâ Kalâpa (TMK for short):

४ बुद्धिसरः १० यथार्थख्यातिसिद्धान्ते औचित्यम्

॥नाथैरुक्ता यथार्था विमतमतिरपि न्यायतत्त्वे॥ २३५

Tattva Muktâ Kalâpa

The numbers mentioned above should be explained to get an understanding of the content of TMK. There are five main topics of which the fourth one is Buddhi Sara (the others are, Jada dravya, Jîva, Nayaka, and Adravya). The number ten indicates that this is the tenth sub-topic in Buddhi sara. There are 70 sub-topics in Jada dravya, 75 in Jîva, 79 in Nayaka, 134 in Buddhisâra and 139 in Adravya. Almost every topic is headed with a leading verse and the above quote is the 235th of the total of 500 verses. Each verse is followed by an explanation in prose known as Sarvârtha Siddhi.

From the 'Introduction' of Ref 65: "Sri Bhâshya of Ramanuja and Shrutaprakâshika of Sudarshana Sûri no doubt contain most of the doctrines of Visishishtâdvaita including criticisms of theories opposed to Vishishtâdvaita. But these texts intended primarily as an exposition of the Vedânta Sûtras were devoted mainly to the interpretation of the sutras and the connected scriptural texts. Thus, there was need for an independent treatise presenting in a consolidated and logical way the epistemological, ontological, cosmological and eschatological doctrines of Vishishtâdvaita more based on logic than on scriptural evidence. This need came to be fulfilled with Vedânta Deshika's independent and comprehensive philosophic treatise titled Tattva-Muktâ-Kalâpa followed by a scholarly commentary thereon known as Sarvârtha-siddhi."

The author makes a clear distinction between the two of his works. "In the textual light of Tattva-Mukta-Kalâpa, the notion that Vishishtâdvaita is a theological system is dispelled and its philosophic core is established beyond doubt...Shata-Dûshani is an important polemical work devoted mainly to the refutation of the doctrines of Shankara's Advaita Vedânta by adopting dialectical arguments. It is designated as a *Vâda-Grantham*, the aim of which is to refute the doctrines of the Advaita Vedânta with a view to establishing the Vishishtâdvaita Vedânta on a logical basis. In view

277

of this, it is compared to a sword (*shastra*) used to destroy the opponents in contrast to the purely constructive work Sarvârtha-siddhi which is compared to a shield (*kheta*) that is used to defend oneself" (vide Saptati-Ratnamâlika 48).

सर्वार्थसिद्धिः शतदूषणी च द्वे खेटशस्त्रे कथकाग्रगानाम्।

आद्येन तत्र क्रियते स्वरक्षा प्रत्यर्थिभङ्गः कलहेऽन्यतःस्यात्॥

A Brief Summary of Ramunuja Siddhanta
Ramanuja delivers a severe blow to Shankara's audacious interpretation for the verse BG 13.2. The verse is quoted:

क्षेत्रज्ञं चापि मां विद्धि सर्वक्षेत्रेषु भारत।

क्षेत्रक्षेत्रज्ञयोर्ज्ञानं यत्तज्ज्ञानं मतं मम॥

Shankara's interpretation runs like this: "The identity between B & jîva, affirmed in the (above) Gita verse, may be accepted in a straight manner. The supreme principle appears as the individual owing to the force of ignorance. This teaching of identity is for removing that ignorance. Just as the teaching 'this is no snake, it is just a rope' puts an end to the illusion of snake, even so the teaching of the benevolent Lord, puts an end to the illusion of individuality that sets up the kshetrajna as a reality other than Ishwara."

Ramanuja rejects the a/m interpretation of Shankara and asks sarcastically, "Does the great God Vasudeva, know the ultimate reality and is he competent to teach Arjuna? If he has not realized the absolute unity, being himself ignorant, he is not qualified to be a teacher of that truth. Gita tells that only seers of Truth should teach (BG 4.34). This dilemma is enough of a counter blast to the interpretation of Shankara."

The message conveyed by Gitâchârya can be put thus – sarvakshetreshhu = in all embodiments, *kshetrajnam chapi mam viddhi*= know that I am also present in the âtma. *kshetra + kshetragnyayor yat Jnânam*= That knowledge which is of the body & the âtma, *Tat Jnânam mama matam* = is indeed knowledge according to My siddhanta (Gitâchârya explains the body and âtma in defining terms in the verses that follow 13.2 ibid).

Ramanuja's criticism is two fold: There is the textual criticism emphasizing the significance of 'api'. The other is the criticism reducing to absurdity the possibility of any preceptor imparting to his disciple the tenets of Advaita.

After the criticism, Ramanuja expounds his siddhanta which runs the gamut of all the shrutis and smrtis that trace the contour of his siddhanta-which include bheda shruti-s, abheda shruti-s and ghataka shruti-s. Broadly the shrutis are brought nine categories of fundamental propositions. The first category for example, culled out from the principal Upanishads and Gita sharply distinguish the âtma from physical reality and distinguish both from Ishwara (the nine categories are expained in p145 of Ref 48).

Ramanuja's entire set of Sanskrit texts is appended at the close of Jignyasa- adhikaranya under the title 'SamgraheNa siddhanta upanyasah' (SB p 153 – 157) Thus Gita Bhashya is brought in line with SB.

Avidya: "Avidya according to Advaita, is the innate obscuration of pure consciousness which somehow divides the absolute and distorts it into the world of difference. It is an innate error which is beginningless, positive and indeterminable, though it can be removed by Jnâna. Ramanuja subjects this theory to severe criticism and his classical refutation of it is known as *saptavidha anupapatti* or the seven-fold inadmissibility. The seven charges are: *âshraya-*

279

tirodhâna- svarûpa-anirvachanīya-pramâNa-nivartaka-nivrtti / anupapatti.
The author explains them briefly (p55 Ref 43).

Regarding the last 7th one: *"Brahmajnâna* is not, according to Advaitins, the Jnâna of B but it is Jnâna that is B. It is said that Jnâna stultifies aJnâna and then stultifies itself; if so, Jnâna is an act of spiritual suicide. With vanishing of avidya, jagat and Ishvara also perish and Advaita is nihilistic."

This segment on '7 types of Avidya' extends from SB p 113 to 160. Ramanuja concludes his arguments on avidya by stating that it is enough of flogging a dead body.

॥ इत्यलमनेन दिष्टहतमुद्रराभिघातेन ॥

However undaunted by defeat after defeat, Advaita would raise its head again and again masquerading as Brahmâdvaita, Sivâdvaita, Vasudevadvaita, Sphotadvaita, Samvidadvaida or Sadadvaita – all of which, according to Vedânta Deshika, have not the slightest bit of premeya (support) in their favour (the chapter on Prachchanna Baudha of Ref 66). The sutras of BS from first to last are absolutely against them, as they are wholly untenable. Of the a/m advaita-s only Samvid-advaita-bhanga vâda (Ref 67) and *sutra-svârasya-bhanga-vâda* are alone available now. That Shatadushani was the earlier work of Swami Deshika can be inferred from the concluding lines found in Para-mata Bhanga.

9. Comparing Advaita & Visishtâdvaita

The subject matter of this chapter pertains to the famous work of Deshika known as Shatadushani. For the material of this chapter we have drawn extensively from the popular book of SMS Chari (Ref 70). "In the portion of Sri Bhashya called *jignyâsâdhikarana* , Ramanuja states briefly the essential teachings of the Advaita Vedânta and subjects them to a critical examination. The arguments given in Sri Bhashya were further elaborated by Vedânta Deshika who wrote an independent work setting forth in detail and in a systematic way the criticism against the Advaitins". The criticism of Advaita has a long history.

"Earlier to Yamuna, Bhaskara who is believed to have flourished in the early part of the 9th century had attacked vigourously the Mâyâ Vâda of Advaita Vedânta which he regarded as a version of nihilism of Mahâyânika Buddhism. After Ramanuja, Sri Madhva figured as an uncompromising critic of Advaita Vedânta. The Upâdhikhandana ... are independent treatises which are mainly devoted to the criticism of Advaita. Based on these works, Jayatîrta, the greatest among the disciples of Madhva, wrote a small independent work called Vâdâvalî, wherein he criticised the Advaitin's doctrine of the illusoriness of the universe and the theory of mâyâ. Based on Vâdâvalî, Vyâsarâya wrote his famous polemic work, Nyâyâmrtam which was later criticised by Madhusûdana Saraswati in his dialectical work Advaita-siddhi which has become a well known classic of Advaita Vedânta. The latter work has been criticised by Râmâchârya in his Tarangini, which again has been attacked in defence of Advaita-siddhi by Brahmânanda in his *Gaudha-brahmânandîyam*, also known as *Lagu-chandrika*. There are many other dialectical works belonging to these three schools of Vedânta either in defence of their own systems of Vedânta or in criticism of the rival schools of thought.

"It is therefore no use in either condemning a system of philosophy or upholding another as a sound one. The function of criticism, in my opinion, is not to refute the opponent out of existence but only to define and distinguish one's own position from that of others with a view to establishing the soundness of one's own position – *paramata nirâkaraNa* and *svamata sthâpana* (from the Preface section of Ref 70).

It also brings out fully the philosophical implications of the basic theories or issues. Herein lies the philosophic value of a polemical work (p180 ibid).

Though the issues discussed in Shatadushani are many, each discussing a specific problem, they are focussed on one central doctrine of Advaita,that Brahman alone is the sole reality and everything else is illusory. The same is expressed in the famous and oft quoted couplet:

ब्रह्म सत्यं जगन्मिथ्या। जीव ब्रह्मैव न परः ॥

This is the main theme of the Advaita System, and its other associated doctrines, particularly the doctrine of Mâyâ which is unique to the Advaita, emerge from this. Ramanuja also has the same thesis in view when he states the position of Advaita as *Mahâ-pûrvapaksha* in the opening section of his Sri Bhashya...All the criticisms that he levels against Advaita, are mainly directed to

282

disprove this central doctrine of Advaita. Vedânta Deshika, who follows the same line of argument as set forth in Sri Bhashya concentrates his attention on the same. The several vâdas of Shatadûshani are ultimately directed to set aside this central doctrine of Advaita.

The second question is with regard to '*anubhuti*' or consciousness about which we have discussed at length in the chapter 'Chatussûtrî'. "The third question which the critic of Advaita raises is whether the universe is illusory. This theory of universe is the main edifice of the philosophy of absolute Monism. The doctrine of Maya is its necessary corrolary. Vedânta Deshika has examined in detail all the important arguments that are advanced to prove the illusoriness of the universe and shown that they do not establish the theory. He has also subjected the doctrine of Maya to a searching logical analysis following the seven-fold criticisms by Ramanuja and has shown how it is riddled with contradictions" (p175).

We will come to the vadas where these questions are discussed.

Literature survey on Shatadushani:
The afore mentioned book of SMS: "Advaita & Visishtâdvaita" had its first edition published in the year 1961and it was the outcome of the doctoral thesis submitted by him during 1941-43. There is another book (published in 1974, but now out of print) on the same subject titled 'Shatadushani' written by two authors, namely, Keshava Aiyangar and Srivatsangachar- the former contributing a brief rendering in english of each of the 66 vadas, apart from a fairly long introduction on the subject and the latter, a great scholar in Sanskrit, furnishing the sanskrit versions of the original texts.

There is a recent publication (the second edition in 1995, a Chowkamba publication) which gives a gloss in Hindi as well in addition to the Sanskrit texts. This book gives a measure of the length of the vadas (Ref 72).

In addition, Shatadushani has three classical commentaries in Sanskrit. One is by Mahâchârya popularly known as Doddayâchârya. It is called 'Chandamaruta' (according to Yatindramatadipika, Mahâchârya has to his credit more than seven works). The second is by Nrsimharaja. It is called 'Prâkâsha'. The third is by Srinivasâchârya. It is called 'Sahasrakirani' There is a translation in Tamil for the first 55 vadas by Sri Mahamahopadyaya Chetlur Narasimhâchârya.

Knowing the significance of a polemical work

The word 'dialectic' is derived from two Greek words which mean "to speak between", fairly corresponding to the sanskrit word *'vâdâ*. Dialectics has accordingly come to signify that branch of logic which expounds the laws and modes of sound reasoning. The process of thought dialectical. Thought is the very life of man and dialectics is the very breath of that life. The value of dialectics is as much intellectual as spiritual. Hence its excellence and nobility... Shatadushani is a model classic of dialectics and a stately product of reasoning in refutation of nirvisesha-advaita and is vindication of visishta-advaita philosophy. The object of vâda is not to decry others but to save wavering and immature minds from the allurements of the various rival systems.

"If a system is right it has to be fought for; if wrong it has to be cast off. Neither needs an apology. It is not adequately realised that vâda is really a process of diamond-cutting-diamond very often into lovely forms and luminous facets. Diamond experts detect the flaws in a diamond because it is a diamond. The cutting and detection go to emphasise the value of the thing as diamond. The analogy applies with greater force to vada" (Ref 71).

When this work 'Shatadûshhani' came into existence
A sort of diary of life and works of Swami Deshika can be gathered from two sources of records viz., Guruparampara Prabhava and Vaibhava Prakashika. Apart from these records the Swami's srisuktis themselves throw light on the time of production of his works. We shall presently indicate through an illustrative example. There seems to have been an extensive debate in Sri Rangam (extending over seven days) between the Swami and the pandits of the Advaita philosophy. The proceedings of the debate were written down by somebody and handed over to the Swamy who revised it after putting them down in a proper order and gave the caption 'Shatadushani' to it (Vaibhava Prakashika stanza 47). The scrambled nature of the vadas in Shatadushani indicate that the work is based on the arguments advanced in the debate. Hence the order of arrangement of vadas show the trend of the debate rather than the topics debated.

A time later to the above event, there occurred another long debate between the Swami and the followers of other faiths at the venue, Tiruvahindirapuram which is incidentally one of the two pilgrimage centres known as Nadu Nattu Tirupatis, among the 108 tirupatis. Unlike Shatadushani, the debate is crystallised into a well ordered book, titled, Paramatabhangam, containing 24 chapters. At the end of the book Swami's couplet proclaim the venue of the debate in no uncertain terms.

பொன் அயிந்தை நகரில் முன்னாள் புணராத
பரமதப்போர்பூரித்தோமே,

It is said, "The intensive depth of Shatadushani is matched by the extensive sweep of Paramata Bhanga." The first four chapters of Paramata Bhanga establish the soundness of Visishitadvaita system and it is practically the epitome of the 22 chapters of Rahasya traya sâra (RTS). In chapter 5 the Swami focusses the defects in all the other systems taken together collectively. And in the following 15 chapters each faith is taken up one after another for a detailed analysis and the defect in that particular system is lucidly highlighted. Of particular interest for us now is the 11th chapter which is devoted to the criticism of the doctrine of Advaita. This chapter in itself is sufficient to know the defect in Advaita. For a far more detailed analysis, the Swami says, one should refer to his earlier work on the subject. The concluding words of the 11th chapter, in Swami's own words:

வேதாந்த ஸூத்திரங்கள் ஆமூல சூடம் இவர்களுக்கு
விரித்தங்கள் என்னுமிடமும் சததூரஷணீ ப்ரப்ருதிகளிலே
பரக்கச்சொன்னோம்.

As mentioned earlier Swami's Sri Suktis themselves serve the purpose of fixing that which are earlier or later of his work. From now on we will proceed with a brief discussion on the contents of Shatadushani.

Shatadushani as the very name indicates should contain a hundred criticisms, "why only 66?" one would ask. There is every reason that suggest the remaining 34 vadas are lost (page ix of Preface Ref 71). If the passage in Paramatabhanga is any indication, vadas relating to Brahmadvaita, Sivadvaita, Vasudevadvaita, Sphotadvaita, Sadadvaita are lost. The existing vadas themselves (*jîvanmukti-bhanga vâda* 31 & *jîvagnana-bhangavâda* 40) make cross- reference to vadas *Sharirâdi-mithyatva-bhanga-vâda* and *antahkarana-pratibimba-vâda* respectively and the vadas referred to are all lost.

"It has been explained" writes Keshava Aiyangar, "by Mahâchârya the commentator of Shatadushani that though in each vâda several refutations are made still in view of the (one hundred) main topics which were taken up for refutation the work is named 'One-hundred Refutations' (Shatadushani) is therefore quite proper. That Shatadushani did consist of one hundred vadas of which sixty six alone are available now is therefore incontrovertible.

286

"Every vâda in Shatadushani opens with a shloka extolling the glory of Para Brahmam (Lord Sri Hayagriva) and mention is made of the particular topic of disputation. What is poetically experienced is dialectically demonstrated... We have in Vedânta Deshika's works the unique combination of the ineffable charm of poetry and the irrefragable power of reason. Hence the universal acclamation of Vedânta Deshika as Kavi Tarkika Simha (lion among poets and logicians). The myth that poets cannot be logician-philosophers and vice versa stands exploded thereby. We have also the sublime example of Vyasa the author of Mahabharata and Brahma Sutra."

Mention Kavitârkika Simha, we are reminded of Swamy's own verse in Paramata-bhanga.

आशामतङ्गजगणानविषह्यवेगान् पादे यतिक्षितिभृतः प्रसभं निरुन्धन्।

कार्यः कथाहवकुतूहलिभिः परेषां कर्णे स एष कवितार्किकसिंहनादः ॥

Obviously the addressee in the above verse is a follower of Ramanuja. "Don't allow your desires to take the better of you. Don't allow the passions go out of conrol like the intoxicated wild elephants. To arrest them, bring them under the benign influence of Ramanuja Darshana. For a list of benefits that accrue see 94th of Ref 16. To free yourself from the corrupting influence of the rival religions utter loudly the compositions of Kavitârkika Simha and see how they run in panic-similar to the sound of Pancha-janya that broke the hearts of Kauravas; or like the roar of a lion that sends a hoard of elephants running for cover!"

In order to keep the rival religions at bay, the pâsurams of Paramata-bhanga are included in Deshika Prababdam which contains 18 poems of 405 verses. It is to be noted that the larger ones are the poems Paramata-bhanga and Adhikâra Sangraham containing respectively 54 and 56 verses.

287

<u>Auspicious Start</u>
Sri Hayagriva is considered as the first of the avatars of Maha-Vishnu since the Lord as Hayagriva redeemed the Vedas from the asuras, namely, Madhu and Kaitabha and got the Vedas restored to the rightful authorized owner viz., Chatur Mukha Brahma. Only Brahma holds the intellectual property rights over the Vedas and no one else (*yo brahmâNam vidadhâti pûrvam*—Sveta). For having imparted the knowledge of Vedas to Brahma, Lord Hayagriva became the first and foremost Acharya in the Guru-Parampara line of Acharyas. Added to this is the fact that Vedânta Deshika got blessed with the gift of an icon of Hayagriva from Garuda as a fulfillment of his Garuda Mantra japa. This was singularly the most important event in the Swamy's life and he had commemorated it by his first poetic composition, Hayagriva Stotram. Verses from this panegeric on Hayagriva have been chosen by the Swamy himself as the auspicious opening verse (Mangala Shloka) of his other works. For example, the verse '*samâhâra sâmnâm*' is the mangala shloka of Shatadushani while the verse '*prâchî sandhyâ*' is the mangala shloka of the ten act play, 'Sankalpa Suryodayam'.

There is a similarity of purpose of His avatar as Hayagriva and that of a verbal warfare. Vedas were redeemed from the hands of the asuras in the former while in the latter, Vedas have to be reclaimed from the usurpers and destroyers of Vedic tradition. For the Kavi-tarkika-simha, the lord fights seated on the tip of the tongue (*jihvagra simhasana*).

वादाहवेषु निर्भेत्तुम् वेदमार्गं विदूषकान्।

प्रयुज्यतां शरश्रेणी निशिता शतदूशणी ॥

<u>Advaitin's Starting trouble!</u>
The very first vâda of Shatadushani concerns with the inapplicability of the thought provoking definition of Brahman to the philosophy

288

of Nirvisesha Advaita. The definition, per se, has zero impact on the psyche of a Monistic thinker who looks the other way and prefers to get lost in the thoughtless void! For one who prefers to revel in nothing, is there anything like "growing or causing to grow' which is what the Brahman is all about. "There can be no desire to know a bare being Brahman in all the emptiness of husk and in all the jejuneness of vacuity", as Keshava Aiyangar puts it.

न हि निर्विशेषतयाऽभिमते शुद्धे बृहति

बृह्मयति इति श्रुत्युक्त निमित्तमस्ति ॥

The gist of the second vâda is that the desire to know would be wholly inappropriate to the Nirvisesha Advaitins. The third also follows suit. "The first three disputations (vadas) show at the very outset, that the very opening sutra (aphorism) of BS is against the Nirvisheshha Advaita system. The first sutra is in these terms:-"Hereafter, therefore, the desire to know Brahman". In this sutra we have, first the Brahman whose knowledge is desired. Secondly, we have the desire to know Brahman (*Jignyâsa*). Thirdly, we have the desire to know Brahman as a sequence (*athah*) and as a consequence (*atah*) of an antecedent concurrence. This opening declaration of BS is, according to Vedânta Deshika, incompatible with the system of Nirvishesha Advaita and the first three disputations are accordingly in the nature of a preliminary objection which means that Nirvishesha Advaitins have no right of entry into BS... In the third vâda the Visistadvaita view of the unity and the continuity of the science of Mîmâmsa comprising Karma (Jaimini's sutra) (earlier) and Brahman (Vyasa's sutra) (later) parts and hence the sequence and consequence of the desire to know and the investigation and acquisition of the knowledge of Brahman as declared in the first aphorism was established... The fourth vâda is a refutation of their theory that a mere knowledge of the word-meaning of the Vedânta texts declaring the bare oneness of Brahman effects soul's

289

liberation... The fifth vâda is a sequel to and amplication of the fourth...

"The sixth vâda refutes Advaitin's view that karma (action enjoined in the Vedas) aides the generation, not of true knowledge (Jnâna) but of the desire to know (vividisha). Action (karma) has its roots in the reality of difference and therefore, according to Nirvishesha Advaitins, it cannot aid the generation of true knowledge which, according to them negates the reality of difference. Hence their theory. According to Visishtadvaitins, differences are real and therefore there is no repugnancy between karma (action) and Jnâna (knowledge). Karma imparts purity to the mind and hence its need for a proper function of the mind. Accordingly enjoined action, aids, not desideration but deliberation in contemplative serenity.

"The seventh vâda refutes their view that verbal knowledge is immediate. This question has already been adverted to above... According to them, words (Vedânta) would not be *pramanas* (knowledge generators) but mere *anuvâdas* (repeaters of what perception generates). According to Visishtadvaitins verbal knowledge is mediate and, not per se, intuitive. Its authority is supreme in the supersenuous and transcendental intuition... Hence the importance of this vâda (seventh) which refutes the immediacy of mere verbal knowledge and the elaborate investigation of the topic."

The eighth vâda is a refutation of Advaitins view that sâdhana chathushhtaya- the discrimination between eternal and ephemeral objects, the achievement of mind equipoise and sense control, the desirelessness of fruit enjoyment here and hereafter, and the desire to attain liberation- is the antecedent occurrence contemplated in the first aphorism of BS (Ref 73). According to Visishtadvaitins they are not the intended antecedents to a desire to know and to a study and acquisition of a knowledge of Brahman (Vedânta). If it preceded there would be no need and no desire to study Vedânta and know Brahman because a knowledge of what is eternal and what is ephemeral has, ex hypothesi, been already acquired and therefore nothing more to acquire by a study of Vedânta...This view of the Advaitins is like the case of putting the cart before the horse. Liberation is a serious matter. It is not a mere verbal knowledge of a few vedanta texts in their isolation from the rest, but whole hearted devotion to and loving contemplation of the Supreme Brahman as enjoined in the Brahma vidya.

Regarding the order of the vadas in Shatadushani (page 12 of Ref 70): "The vadas as such do not appear in a logical order. The only order in which the vadas are presented is that found in the Laghu Siddhanta and Maha Siddhanta of the Sri Bhashya. But even that order is not strictly adhered to by Vedânta Deshika. Thus, the first eight vadas which deals with the discussion of the issues arising out of the interpretation of the first aphorism of the Vedânta Sutras-the import of the term, 'Brahman', the enquiry into the nature of Brahman, the preliminaries required for the purpose, the place of karma in the philosophic discipline and its relation to Jnâna and other allied doctrines- closely follow the arguments contained in the Laghu-purvapaksha and Laghu Siddhanta of Sri Bhashya. Vada 9, which is concerned with demonstrating the intelligibility of the Advaitin to be a party to philosophical debate is based on the opening sentence of the Maha siddhanta of Sri Bhashya. Responding to his formulation of Advaita in purvapaksha, Ramanuja begins his reply with a jibe that those who have no devotion in their hearts have no right, per se, to approach BS which is devotion in essence –a warped mind spoiled by beginningless sin:

तदिदं औपनिषद् परम पुरुष वरणीयता

हेतुगुण विषेष विरहिणां अनादिपाप वासना

दूषित अशेष शेमुषीकानाम्

291

Vadas 10 to 30 which are devoted to the discussion of the nature of the perception and difference, the Advaitin's theory of the illusoriness of the universe, the nature of consciousness (anubhuti), the relative validity of scripture and perception and other allied doctrines closely follow, with the exception of two vadas (18 and 19), the order of the arguments found in the Sri Bhashya commencing from the Maha siddhanta upto the topic known as the 'Shruti ghatta'. The 31st vâda which relates to the discussion of the doctrine of Jîvan-mukti follows, while this doctrine is discussed in the Sri Bhashya in the SamanvayadhikaraNa. Vedânta Deshika himself seems to be aware of this fact as he attempts to give an explanation at the outset of the 31st vâda for changing the order of the topics (see below). The vadas that follow subsequently do not strictly adhere to the same order as that of the Sri Bhashya though most of the vadas are based upon the arguments presented briefly in the Sri Bhashya."

समन्वयाधिकरणभाष्ये परेषां सयूध्यकलहमुपक्षिप्य

जीवन्मुक्तपक्षः प्रतिक्षिप्तः तदेवात्र पूर्वापरसङ्गतेव्याकुर्मः ॥

From the foregoing analysis of the contents of Shatadushani it is clear that the subject matter needs classification and reordering and accordingly SMS has outlined his plan of dealing with the arguments. The 66 vadas are brought under 8 headings: 1. Pramanas 2. Perception and Difference 3. The nature of conciousness (anubhuti) 4. The Individual self and the Absolute 5. The NirguNa Brahman 6. Universe 7. The doctrine of Avidya and 8. Sadhana and Mukti.

"1. Pramanas: The discussion regarding the 'Pramanas' is confined to the controversial issue whether the pramanas that are not absolutely real could be an evidence of what is real (vâda 30). The Advaitins view is that pramanas, even though illusory in character, can reveal what is ultimately real. The main argument adduced in support of it is that such a thing is found possible in our ordinary experience when a rope, for instance, which is mistaken for a snake, causes fear. This view is critically examined in all its aspects and the conclusion reached is that what is not real can never reveal what is real. It is also pointed out that if the pramanas do not have a real existence, the metaphysical discussion cannot be carried on (vâda 9). On the same ground, it is also held that scripture too cannot be claimed as the ultimate authority in spiritual matters in so far as there is nothing to distinguish it from the so called non-authoritative sacred texts of the Buddhists (vâda 14). Nor is it possible to claim a superior validity to scripture over perception in case a conflict arises between the two, as scripture, like perception, has for its source avidya- a defect (vâda 29). It should be mentioned that the 3rd a d 4th vadas are ontological issues and refer to the question whether the individual self is one and whether it is identical with the Absolute.

Vada 30 can be gone through some what in greater detail as explained by Keshava Aiyangar, who, beside being a great legal luminary of his times, was also a very popular man of letters and a poet. " The 30th vâda is a refutation of the Nirvisesha Advaitin's view of the "emergence of truth from untruth", (asatyât satya-siddhi). According to Nirvisesha Advaitins, satya (true) Brahman can be established by asatya or mithya (untrue) vedas. Vedas are, according to Nirvisesha Advaitins, illusory. Brahman is however true- the only truth and Reality. The objection raised to that view is how could (knowledgs of) Truth (Paramartha)-Brahman-emerge from or issue out of untruth (mithya)-Veda? Nirvisesha Advaitins meet it by pointing out instances where such results occur: e.g. untrue silver in the shell silver produces true joy, and untrue serpent in rope-serpant illusion produces true fear in the persons who are respectively subject to the illusions. Similarly also untrue Veda produces knowledge of true Brahman, which according to them is nirvisesha. This view has been elaborately refuted in this vâda and it is

293

established that Veda is satya (true) and the sole pramana with respect to supersenuous and transcendental truths; that Brahman is established by that truth, pramana. Brahman is therefore Prameya and true. The truth of the Prameya (Brahman) rests on the truth of the Pramana (Veda). Hence the untenability of the view of Nirvisesha advaitins. It has also been pointed out by Vedânta Deshika in Tattva Tika that on the view of the Nirvisesha advaitins that truth can emerge from untruth they have to concede that out of untrue subtratum illusion can emerge and therefore their refutation of nihilists (mâdyamikas) on the ground that without a true substratum there can be no illusion is self contradictory."

The second chapter (Ref 70) deals with the second group of vadas of Shatadushani relating to 'Perception and Difference' as mentioned earlier. This topic "centres around the epistemological issue, viz., whether perception reveals pure 'Being' or difference. The prima facie view that comes up for criticism here is that perception is of the one real, difference being subsequently super imposed thereon. The nerve of the argument put forth in support of this claim is that difference being a relative notion is dependent for its cognition on the knowledge of its counter-correlate and substrate while 'Being' is not so. Secondly the concept of difference when subjected to logical examination does not stand the test and as such it is not real. Both the aspects of the problem are discussed at great length with particular reference to the examination of the dialectic on difference. The conclusion reached is that difference is real and is logically intelligible and is also revealed in perception (vâdas 12 & 13). In this connection, the theory of determinate and indeterminate perception is also discussed (vâda 11) and the correct definition of the nirvikalpa and savikalpa perception as understood by the Visishtadvaitin school of thought is pointed out.

"The discussion on the 'Nature of Consciousness' (3rd chapter Ref 70) is mainly confined   to an examination of the Advaitin's

294

contentions that consciousness is identical with Reality, that it is indeterminate in character, that it is self-luminous, homogeneous whole which is neither produced nor destroyed, and lastly that it is identical with the very self in us. The arguments mostly in the form of inferences, that are put forth in support of these contentions are critically examined and refuted by showing the logical fallacies involved in them and also their opposition to the ordinary experience on the one hand and scriptural texts on the other. The criticism is mainly based on the theory that consciousness is that which involves the duality of the subject and the object and, as such, it is the characteristic feature of the self. It is determinate in character. Although it is self luminous, it is not absolutely unknowable. It is not one but many and is subject to change in the form of contraction and expansion (vâda 10, 20-25)."

Ahamartha

For the above topic refer 'Nature of the individual self' (chapter 4 Ref 70: "The nature of the individual self". He broaches the topic with the following remarks: "With the refutation of the theory that consciousness is identical with the self, we are presented with the problem as to what the self is? According to Visishtâdvaita Vedânta, the individual self or the jivâtman as it is called, is an eternal spiritual entity. It is the very Ego or the entity denoted by the notion of 'I' (ahamartha). Thus it is not mere knowledge, but a knowing subject (*jnâta*). All jîvas have their own individuality. It is also a separate entity distinct from Brahman, 'a spiritual monad' (*amsha*) of Brahman. The Advaitin holds a different view which is in direct conflict with the above doctrine...Thus there are four issues involved in the doctrine of the individual self. The first one which is psychological in character refers to the question whether the 'Ego' is the self? The second issue, which is epistemological in nature, relates to the question whether the self is a knower. The third and the fourth are ontological issues and refer to the questions whether the individual seif is one and whether it is identical with the

295

Absolute. Vedânta Deshika discusses each one of these issues at great length and refutes the Advaitin's views with a view to defending Visishtadvaitin's doctrine (vide vadas 26, 27, 36 and 37). The entity denoted by I (ahamartha) is the self (26); the notion of the self as cognizer is not illusory; the self is the knower (27); the supposition that the self is one but appears to be many owing to the difference of the adjuncts does not stand (36); the finite self cannot be identical with Iswara (37).

"The individual selves are subject to karma, possess unfulfilled desires and are tortured by the three-fold misery. They are, therefore, seeking some means of overcoming the bondage. Thus, it is evident through perception that the individual selves are not identical with Iswara"-the subtantative part of vâda 37.

There are numerous scriptural texts which explicitly point out the difference of the individual self from the Absolute. In other contexts the texts also refer to the *sambanda* or the relationship between the self and the Absolute which accounts for the difference. All these texts bearing on the subject are quoted as foot notes on page 75 & 76 of Ref 70.

NirguNa Brahman

The chapter five Ref 70 is captioned as "The Doctrine of NirguNa Brahman". The author brings to focus several of the vadas of Shatadushani bearing on the subject.

"The most distinguishing feature of Advaita Vedânta on its metaphysical side is the advocacy of the doctrine of NirguNa Brahman. The one and the only reality admitted is the pure Brahman devoid of all determinations (*nirvishesha*). In view of this Advaita is designated as Nirvisheshha Brahma Vada (the opening sentence of vâda 1) This doctrine is established mainly on the strength of the scriptural texts...

"Shruti is the final authority in spiritual matters and hence the question whether Brahman is saguNa or nirguNa in character will have to be ultimately decided on the strength of the scriptural texts. But here we are faced with a difficulty. There are scriptural texts which speak of Brahman as devoid of qualities, while there are also texts which openly declare Brahman to be qualified by numerous attributes (refer to bottom of the page 78 for a listing of the relevent texts). How are we to overcome such a conflict? There are two ways of resolving it. One way is to accept the validity of both the texts and interpret them in such a way that the apparent conflict does not rise at all. This is the method adopted by the Visishtadvaitin. The other way of solving the difficulty is to ascribe a superior validity to one of the two conflicting texts and deny the other as non-authoritative. The Advaitin who does not agree with the former method adopts the latter…

The Theory of *Akandârtha*

"We now come to the second issue (p80 ibid), namely, whether any of the scriptural texts can convey an impartite and non-relational sense (*akândartha*). This question arises particularly in connection with the interpretation of the Upanishadic text, satyam, Jnânam, anantam, brahma, which gives the definition of Brahman as 'Truth, Knowledge and Infinitude'. The main issue is whether in this text the terms in question denote the very svarûpa of Brahman or its characteristics. The Advaitin maintains the former view while the Visishtadvaitin holds the latter…(vâda 38).

"Brahman as advitîya (p87 ibid): Vedânta Deshika also examines the meaning of the scriptural text which refers to Brahman as one only without a second (*ekameva advitîyam*) and points out that the term *advitîya* in the text does not imply a Nirvisesha Brahman (vâda 59).

Upabrumhanas and Brahman

"It was shown in the previous section that the scriptual texts in general do not support the theory of Brahman advocated by the Advaitin. We now come to the question whether Smrti texts and the Vedânta Sutras do teach such a doctrine. Vedânta Deshika examines this issue and comes to the conclusion that neither the smrti texts nor the Vedânta sutras are in consonance with the Advaitin's theory of Reality…

"Vedânta Deshika, therefore, argues that it is not possible to uphold Smrtis and PurâNas as *upabrhmanas* unless it were admitted that Brahman taught in the scripture is endowed with infinite attributes and vibhûtis. The attributes and vibhûtis of Brahman which are not ordinarily known through scripture are revealed by Smrtis and PurâNas and as such the latter could rightly be called upabrhmanas in the true sense of the term viz., manifestation in elucidation of what has been said in scripture" (vâda 48).

Vedânta sutras and NirguNa Brahman

The discussion on the question whether the doctrine of Reality advocated by Advaita Vedânta is in consonance with the teachings of Vedântra sutras is rather elaborate. The various topics or Adhikaranas of Vedânta sutras bearing on Brahman are examined briefly and shown to be in direct conflict with Advaita (vâda 66). We will enumerate here the main points of the criticisms without entering into a detailed discussion of the interpretation of the sutras by the two schools of Vedânta. The relevant sutras are listed on the bottom of the pages 97 & 98 of Ref 70.

Nature of the Universe

The above issue is the subject matter of chapter 6 Ref 70. The author begins his discussion by presenting a broad view of the Advaitins: "The theory of reality as advocated by the Advaita Vedânta presents a problem which every monistic system has to face. If the self or

298

Brahman alone be real, how the plurality of the universe, which we perceive, is to be accounted for? This is the vexed problem of the one and the many--the hard rock on which most of the monistic systems break. A solution is offered to this problem in the Advaita system by maintaining the theory that the universe is illusory (mithya) How far does the theory solve the problem.

Universe is illusion because it is perceptible. Whatever is perceptible is illusion: as for instance, shell-silver. So also the universe. Therefore so illusion. This syllogism has been subjected to a very critical examination in this vâda and the theory of illusion is refuted under seven alternatives and it is shown that the process of reasoning abounds in falacies.

We may mention here the foot note (p100 Ref 70): "The theory of the phenomenality of the worldly existence is first propounded by the Vijnâna vâdins and Madhyamikas. This has been adopted by Gaudapâda who establishes the illusory nature of the world of experience on four grounds:
1. It is similar to dream states;
2. It is presented;
3. The relations that organise it are unintelligible and
4. It does not persist for all times (vide "Indian Philosophy" Vol 2 p.458).

Except the first all the other views are examined by Deshika... "Deshika subjects this syllogism, "Whatever is cognised is illusory, *mithya*" to a critical examination. He first examines the meaning of the term mithya. It is resolved into seven alternatives keeping in view the different interpretations of the Advaitins:
1. Unreality (*tucchatva*);
2. Being the content of apprehension otherwise (*anyatha-khyâti vishhayatvam*);

3. Being different from the real as well as the unreal (*sadâsad-vilakshanatvam*);
4. Being the counter-correlate of the negation of what is found in a particular locus (*pratipanna-upâdhau nishhedha pratiyogitvam*);
5. Being cognized in the same locus as its own absolute non-existence (*svâtyantâ-bhâva samanâdhi-karaNyatayâ pratîyamânatvam*);
6. Being different from the real Brahman (*satyabrahma vilakshanatvam*);
7. Something else.

All the aforementioned alternatives except the last one, namely the seventh, have been stated by Chitsukha in his Tattvapradîpika as a purvapaksha.

"The first two alternatives are not of importance as the Advaitin himself does not admit them. By illusoriness he does not mean either that which is totally unreal (*tuccha*) or that which is the content of apprehension otherwise." The other alternatives will be found discussed in the book. It will be clear that one's philosophy is as good as the alternative one chooses. Having made the choice he cannot go back and change from his chosen position. This will be demonstratively illustrated with one such argument connected with the illusion theory itself. Turn to page 111 of Ref 70. "The material causality of Brahman may be understood in three ways.

1. Brahman itself may transform into the universe just as a lump of clay undergoes the transformation into pot etc. This is the view of Yadava Prâkâsha known as *Brahma-parinama-vada*.

2. Brahman associated with chit and achit in their subtle form (*sukshma chid-achit-visishta*) is the material cause of the world. This is the view of the Visishtadvaitins.

300

3. Brahman is the basis of the illusory appearance of the universe. This is the view of the Advaitins, known as *vivartha-vada*. The Advaitins reject the first two views and uphold the last one as the only possible explanation. Regarding the untenability of Yadava Prâkâsha's view refer to vâda 53 (also para77 Ref 60a).

Brahman itself appears as the universe. This is explained on the analogy of the rope appearing as a snake. The rope does not transform itself into a snake. On the contrary, it only appears as a snake due to *ajnâna*. The rope is regarded as the cause of the appearance of the snake in so far as it is the basis or substrate of the illusory snake. In the same way, Brahman which is the basis or the substrate of the world-appearance is said to be the material cause of the universe. Such a view accounts for the material causality of Brahman in conformity with the illustration cited in the Upanishads, without at the same time contradicting the scriptural text referring to the immutable nature of Brahman" (vâda 53).

The "theory of illusion" is contested in several vadas such as 15,53, 54 and 55 and by far the vâda 15 is the longest vâda in the entire Shatadushani.

Maya as the material cause of the universe
The meaning of *mâyâ* is analysed under the above heading (p116 Ref 70). "Some Advaitins who do not subscribe to the view that Brahman is the material cause maintain that maya is the material cause of the universe. This view is maintained on the strength of the Upanishadic text *mâyâm tu prakrtim vidyât*. The meaning of the text according to the Advaitin is that maya is the material cause, the word prakrti being understood as material cause. The term maya is current in the sense of illusoriness. Hence, it follows that the material cause of the universe is illusory in character. If the cause be

301

illusory then its effect must be of the same nature. Accordingly, the universe which is the product of maya is also illusory.

Vedânta Deshika criticizes the above view… "The scriptural text preceding the one in question is as under:

अस्मान्मायी सृजते विश्वमेतत् तस्मिंश्चान्यो मायया संनिरुध्दः ॥

In this passage both the terms *mayin* and *maya* are used but their meaning is not pointed out. Obviously the subsequent text is intended to explain the meaning of these terms. Thus, it is stated "know maya to be the prakrti and the wielder of maya (mayin) to be the supreme Lord". Hence the word maya refers to the prakrti which is well known in the Upanishads as the material cause of the universe, while the word mayin means the supreme Lord who is the basis or *adhishhtâta* of prakrti and the individual selves constituting the universe" (vâda 54).

In Paramata Bhanga the meaning of the word maya is explored (vide chapter 'Achit-tattva Adhikâra –p 237 of Ref 66). If maya stands for illusion (mithya) then its usage in such contexts- "*deva mayena nirmita*", "*tena maya sahasram tat*" etc-would be unintelligible. We may compare maya with the word 'amazing' which invariably passes for a thing of wonder.

Vâda(s) on Avidya
This issue is broached in the 7th chapter: The Doctrine of Avidya Ref 70. "What is avidya? According to Advaita Vedânta, it is the name given to the cosmic principle which gives rise to the world-illusion… Does their theory satisfactorily solve the problem? According to the critics of Advaita, it does not. It explains away the problem instead of giving any satisfactory account of the universe. The critics , therefore, have subjected the doctrine to a severe criticism. In fact, no other doctrine has been so vehemently attacked

as that of avidya... This is the seven-fold criticism (*sapta-vidha-anupapattih*) levelled against the Advaitin's doctrine of avidya by Ramanuja. Vedânta Deshika adopts these criticisms and elaborates them further in his Shatadushani, devoting a separate vâda for each of these issues (vâda numbers 19,35, 39 to 44).

The last topic of Shatadushani is concerned with 'Sadhana and Mukti' Ch8 Ref 70. As regards Sadhana, there is a polar contrast in the way the two systems interpret the upanishadic text (given below). The text occurs in Brhadaranyaka Upanishad 4.5.4.

आत्मा वा अरे द्रष्टव्यः श्रोतव्यो

मन्तव्यो निदिध्यासितव्यः ॥

According to the Advaitins, "Darshana here stands for the self realisation, the final goal and as such it is not enjoined. In other words it is only a restatement (*anuvâda*), while shravana, manana and nididhyasana are enjoined as auxiliaries to darshana. These three subserve darshana by removing the cognition of difference which is a hindrance to the onset of the knowledge of the meaning of the scriptural text. With the onset of Brahman knowledge avidya which is bondage is also removed. In examining the above theory, Vedânta Deshika points out that knowledge as derived from the hearing of the sacred texts (*vâkyârthajnâna*) will not by itself serve as a means to moksha... Thus for instance, defects like cataract and jaundice are also illusory in character but they are removed by means other than knowledge. Similarly we have to admit, contends Deshika, something else besides the mere knowledge generated by the hearing of the Upanishadic texts as the means (*sâdhana*) to moksha" (vâda 4).

For a comprehensive understanding of the discussion on the above aspect of sâdhana, refer p364 of Ref 43: "Equipped with these disciplines, the upâsaka enters on the life of meditation, and cultivates the love of God. Upasana is a divine command like the performance of dharma, but while the vedic 'ought' is of the form 'Do your duty without caring for the consequences' the vedantic 'ought' is of the form 'Know the deity that is your self'. Of the three Upanishadic injunctions of shravana, or hearing, manana or reflection and nididhyasana or medittion, the first two naturally lead to the third, and dhyâna is the only divine command; shravana and manana as the aperception of scriptural terms and the assimilation thereof by reflection have no value unless they deepen into *dhyâna*." The theory of jîvanmukti is an Advaitin's concept of release p 465 Ref 43: "Mukti is the destruction of avidya and the consequent release from embodiment. Hence the idea of jîvanmukti or freedom in embodiment, which involves the continuance of the body even after release is a manifest self contradiction. It is sought to be explained by the Advaitin by the analogies of the whirling of the potter's wheel even after the potter has stopped turning it (the momentum gathered makes it move for a while), of the perception of the double moon even after dissolutionment and of the velocity of the flying arrow after it is discharged."

This is the theory of Badhita-anuvrtti and in the case of a jîvanmukta "Even after the onset of knowledge, embodiment is possible because of the persistence of the trace of avidya... The self is released even when it is embodied. The body which persists has no power to cause bondage, just as the burnt cloth is not useful for wearing purposes. Vedânta Deshika argues that the conception of *jîvanmukti* is a self contradiction (vâda 31).

The state of Moksha

SMS continues his thesis of highlighting the sharp difference in the concept of Moksha between 'Advaita & Visishtâdvaita' (p172 Ref 70). "We have to discuss the Advaitic theory of Moksha or the final release. There is no seperate vâda in the Shatadushani devoted mainly to the discussion of this topic. The vâda (51) devoted to the discussion of the nature of the individual self in the state of release contains some arguments relating to the nature of moksha and these may be noted down here, as the subject matter is of great importance.

"The issue under dispute is whether the individual self in the state of release becomes identical with the Absolute or does it remain different from the Absolute without losing its individuality. The former is the view held by the Advaitin while the latter is the view of the Visishtadvaitin. The Advaitin takes his stand on the scriptural text viz., *brahma veda brahmaiva bhavati* (Mund. 3.2.9). This text which is understood literally is interpreted to mean that the Brahman-knower becomes Brahman, which implies the identity of the individual self and the Absolute. Vedânta Deshika, on the contrary, urges that the text in question does not so much refer to *tâdâtmya* or identity as to *sâdharmya* or equality (refer to Gita '*mama sâdharmyam âgatâh*'). The chief argument in favour of this issue is that brahman itself becoming brahman cannot constitute the goal as it has already been accomplished. Nor is it possible for one different from brahman to become brahman itself as it would result in an apasiddhanta. Two different entities cannot be identical. It is therefore logical to hold that the individual self attains the status of Brahman (*sâdharmya*) This interpretation is also in consonance with other texts openly declaring sâmya of the self with Brahman (*paramam sâmyamupaiti*- Mund. 3.1.3).

"The individual self not only retains its individuality in the state of release but it also enjoys the vibhutis of Brahman as is evident from the scriptural text (*so'shnute sarvân kâmân saha*-Tait.up 1.1.2). The Upanishadic passages wherein the text appears (popularly known as Anandavalli) is very significant. The passage begins with the text "*Brahmavid apnoti param*" etc. referring to the nature of Brahman, the contemplation thereupon, the attainment of it and ends with the texts *so'shnute* etc., referring to the fruit of contemplation. The word

305

saha indicates that Brahman together with His vibhutis is experienced by the individual self.

"That the self becomes omniscient in the state of release is evident from the scriptural text *"sarvam ha pashyah pashyati"*. This omniscience is not something that is newly produced in the self. The self by its very nature is omniscient, but its omniscience was not manifest in the state of bondage owing to karma with which it was overlaid. With the removal of karma the true nature of the self becomes manifested. This is compared to the nature of the gem which is hidden by dirt and which is made manifest by merely removing the dirt. Similarly, the self becomes omniscient like the Lord after its impurities in the form of karma are removed. The self then becomes almost equal to Brahman in every respect except in the matter of the creation, sustenance and destruction of the world (*jagat vyapara varjam*-BS 4.4.17; *bhogamatra samya lingaccha*-BS 4.4.21)."

We have dealt with all the eight main topics of Shatadushani. By no means we can claim that we have done any justice to a vâda grantha except that we have noted down some points here and there. Now we may take up other vadas which deal with some minor topics. A passing mention may be made that the 62 vâda to 65th deal with matters pertaining to achara-s and rituals.

Vada 62

This vâda relates to *'apashûdra-adhikaraNa'* pertaining to Brahma Sutra 1.3.(9) Ramanuja himself conducts a lengthy discourse in this section and Swami Deshika advances additional arguments against Advaita. The purpose of this adhikaraNa as envisaged by Badarayana is to highlight the eligibility criterion for teaching knowledge of Brahman and as the heading of the adhikaraNa indicates, a shudra is not eligible. In the varna-ashrama tradition only a trivarnika is eligible. This requirement is explicitly specified in Manusmrti (4.80; 10.126) and Gautama Dharma (12.3) This criteria is not maintainable with the kind of doctrine the Advaitins have. To prove the flaw in their theory Ramanuja shows how the concept of Moksha as developed in the BS is at variance with the theory of Advaita. He begins by outlining the concept of Moksha as per Advaita.

"Brahman is nirvisesha and mere *chit*. He alone is real, everything else is unreal. Bondage is not real; and it is to be removed by the mere knowledge of Brahman generated by a sentence; and its removal alone is release."

निर्विशेषचिन्मात्रं ब्रह्मैव परमार्थः । अन्यत् सर्वं मिथ्याभूतम् । बन्धश्चापारमार्थिकः ।

स च वाक्य जन्यवस्तु याथात्म्य ज्ञानमात्र निवर्त्यः । तन्निवृत्तिरेव मोक्षः ॥

According to the Advaitin illusion disappears when the true nature of things becomes known. For example when one mistakes a piece of shell-silver for real silver, a friend's statement, "it is not silver" removes his illusion. By comprehending the truth, doubt/ illusion gets cleared. Similarly anyone seeking freedom from bondage has to get rid of his illusion, because illusion is avidya, a stumbling block to God realisation. This illusion persists in the ignorance of perceiving difference between âtma and Brahman and one can get rid of the difference through lisening to enlightening discourse on the upanishnishadic text 'Tattvamasi'. This can happen to anyone irrespective of caste consideration. But varna-ashrama dharma prohibits imparting vedic knowledge to a person belonging to the fourth varna. This prohibition is not maintainable with the kind of prescription for bondage advocated by Advaita. There is much more to it than meets the eye, contends Ramanuja and seizes this oppurtunity to recall (refer to SB p378) what was said in laghu siddhanta and elucidates on the true philosophy of liberation as contemplated in BS.

The 66th and the final vâda needs special mentioning as it is devoted to a demonstration of the Nirvisesha Advaita system being a contradiction of BS. It is shown that their theory is incomparible with every one of the 156 adhikaraNa-s. This last vâda commences thus:

॥ अथ परमते सूत्रस्वारस्यभङ्ग वादः ॥ ६६

नमोऽस्तु ब्रह्मणे तस्मै बादरायणरूपिणे।

यस्यैव ब्रह्मसूत्राणां रचना सगुणायते॥

अद्वैतमतनिष्ठामनुष्ठानमपाकृतम्।

ब्रह्मसूत्रार्थवैरूप्यं तेषामथ निरूप्यते॥

Before proceeding to First Adhyâya of SB, we may mention a few more points on the subject of criticism. Swamy also conducts a debate on the drama stage itself to delight the audience.

<u>Criticism of Advaita in Sankalpa Suryodaya</u>

Sankalpa Suryodaya (SS) is a ten act play and in Act II Swami Deshika adorns the role of a disciple of Ramanuja and crosses swords with an array of disputants from the enemy camp. Several verses from Yatiraja Saptati will be found here in this act during the debate to establish the invincibility and supremacy of Ramanuja Darshana. Swami Deshika sorts out the NirguNa Vâda through an interesting comparison with an episode occurring in Ramayana viz. the fight between Indrajit and Lakshmana. What with weapons secured through boons from Rudra, Indrajit appeared invincible. Lakshmana (brother of Rama or Ramanuja), for that matter even Rama, stood baffled before the onslaught of Indrajit. It appeared, indeed like a war between God and Mammon! The NirguNa concept of Shankara has a similar effect of frustrating the coordinate-predication principle of Ramanuja (Sankalpa Suryodaya 2.90). But Lakshmana banked his faith on dharma and finally defeated Indrajit. Ultimate victory is for dharma. Similarly, it is SaguNa Brahmam who ultimately wins since He the Lord rests four squares on pramana(s). The NirguNa Brahman would land the adherent in the universe of dreadful Sûnyam or void. A *moha Shastram* calculated to please the *tâmasik* oriented ones, as observed by Deshika (also 'tvam hi...' vide Rahasya Traya Sara):

तथा च कुम्भकर्ण एव विजयेत शाप एव तस्य अनुग्रहः स्यात्।

Even some western scholars tremble before these concepts! "Advaita is a philosophy of stagnation favoring a life of inertia and void and that it is an empty intellectual abstraction devoid of spirituality and virility of western thought", observes Gough. And according to Thibaut, "Advaita is too little in sympathy with the wants of the human heart; and the system of Ramanuja influenced by the Bhagavata school and the Bhagavad Gita alone satisfies the needs of love."

"This dual standpoint is admittedly a learned error or true lie and it freezes the heart, misses the delights of devotion and dries up the springs of sympathy and love. But Visishtâdvaita meets the demands of metaphysics and satisfies the supreme call of love by its theory of bhakti-rupapanna-Jnâna or Jnâna turned bhakti" (p 361 of Ref 43).

Advaita: '*learned error*'
Keeping in view the several criticisms, the philosopher statesman Dr. S Radhakrishnan had to openly admit the inadmissibility of Advaita: "Philosophy has his roots in man's practical needs. If a system of thought cannot justify fundamental human instincts and interpret the deeper spirit of religion, it cannot meet with general acceptance. The speculation of philosophers which do not comfort us in our stress and suffering, are merely intellectual diversion, and serious thinking... The absolute remains indifferent to the fear and

love of the worshippers and for all those who regard the goal of religion as the goal of philosophy- to know God is to know the Real- Shankara's view seems to be a finished example of learned error. They feel that it is as unsatisfactory to natural instincts as to trained intelligence... Shankara does not deal justly with the living sense of companionship which the devotees have in their difficult lives" (vide pp 225-26 of his book titled "The Vedânta According to Shankara and Ramanuja").

An additional point is that the Sanskrit Thesaurus (Yatindramatadipika –Ref 74) throws light on the grand fool-proof structure of Visishtâdvaita.

For the triumph of Ramanuja refer to the verse 21 of Yatiraja Saptati: Ramanuja and his faithful and adorable followers have achieved an almost impossible task of fathoming the unfathomable ocean of Vedânta. They have in fact touched the floor, a consummation devoutly wished for and achieved. By the force of their very breath they have swept away the rival disputants. They are pure-enough to confer bliss:

श्वसितावधूतपरवादिवैभवाः निगमान्तनीतिजलधेस्तलस्पृशः ।

प्रतिपादयन्ति गतिमापवर्गिकीं यतिसार्वभौमपदसात्कृताशयाः ॥

Doing poetic justice is a fine art of the Swamy's compositions. Contrastingly what is unfathommable is Daya of Srinivasa (Daya Shatakam 103)! One other interesting comparison can be made between *yatipati-daya* (Saptati 60) and Amudanar's pâsuram 25.

காரேய் கருணை இராமானுச இக்கடலிடத்தில்
ஆரேயறிபவர் நின்னனருளின் தன்மை, அல்லலுக்கு
நேறேயுறைவிடம் நான்; வந்து நீ என்னையுற்றபின் உன்
சீரேய் உயிர்க்குயிராய் அடியேற்கு இன்று தித்திக்குமே.

This chapter can be concluded with the observations made at the end of the book (p601 of Ref 43): "Shankara the practical Vedântin, who accepts the Bhagavata way of devotion and worships Govinda (vide the famous poem "*Bhajagovindam*") and works for world welfare, is more helpful to humanity than Shankara the dialectician, who destroys the world with the all-devouring weapon of sublation. The pure Visishtadvaitin as a theistic monist and mystic must accept the non-dualistic implications of the terms *aprthaksiddha-viseshana*, *visishta aeikya*, non-difference in the causal relation, and *avibhâga*, and practically recognize the points of rapprochement between his system and that of Advaita in the vyavaharika state, which alone provides a basis for inter-Vedântic understanding. What is beyond Veda and thought is beyond experience and is not a subject of enquiry. Dvaita rightly stresses the eternal distinction between Brahman, the Jîva and the universe and the way of Bhakti to mukti; but it does not bring out the omnipotence of love and the loss not of, but in, personality which the mystic experience in the ecstasy of communion. There is no sinner as such in the religion of love, and sin destroys itself by contacting divine love.

"The theory of Brahman as the All-Self or Sharîrin of all beings who is immanent in all jîvas and in all religions with a view to Brahmanising the self-furnishes the most inspiring motive for spirituality and service. All philosophies and religions meet in Vedânta and work hand in hand for the elevation of humanity and the establishment of the spiritual kinship of all jîvas, including the sub-human species. The Vedântin is not a conservative who adores the past, nor a progressivist who looks forward, but is a religious philosopher who seeks the Eternal One in and beyond the temporal, sees Him directly and works for universal salvation. Even the lowest of the low and the worst sinner can attain God if he but trusts Him."

For the believer, the truth of His existence shines brilliantly in his mind, says the Upanishad.

॥ अस्तीत्येवोपलब्धस्य तत्त्वभावः प्रसीदति ॥

10. Sri Bhâshyam First Adhyâya:
samanvayâdhyâyah

Shârîraka Shâstram

The accompanying chart titled Shariraka Shastram shows at a glance the whole content of BS. The word '*Sharîram*' means body and since the world consisting of sentient beings (*chetana*) and insentient matter (*achetana*) forms the body of Brahman, BS is named Shârîraka Shâstram. Ramanuja establishes this name in Sri Bhashya in *Ananda mayâdhikarana*. Reference in Taittiriyam: *eshha shârîra âtma yah pûurvasya*. In Adhikarana Saravali Swami Deshika has show-cased it as 'nikhila tanu taya syad asangkocha vrttih'. Sevaral authors in their works have adopted this concept. For example, Kumarila Bhattar, in his 'grha ekatva adhikaraNa' has maintained that Âkâsha, Veda, yagnya etc. are Sharira of Bhagavan. Udayana in his Kusumanjali (Fifth Sthapaka) has referred to *paramaNu-s* as the body of Ishwara. Ramanuja has again established this concept in VS 81 and in vilakshana adhikaraNa [2.1.(3)]. This concept is enshrined as foundational principle –Visishtâdvaita Prati Tantra as showcased in Rahasya Traya Sara.

यद्येतं यतिसार्वभौमकथितं विद्यादविद्यातमः प्रत्यूषं प्रतितन्त्रम्

The BS has a magnificent architecture of its own. Its structure is brilliantly conceived from the point of thorough going analysis, ordered sequence in the arrangement of the aphorisms and the conclusions arrived at (Siddhanta) expressed in crystal clear terms.

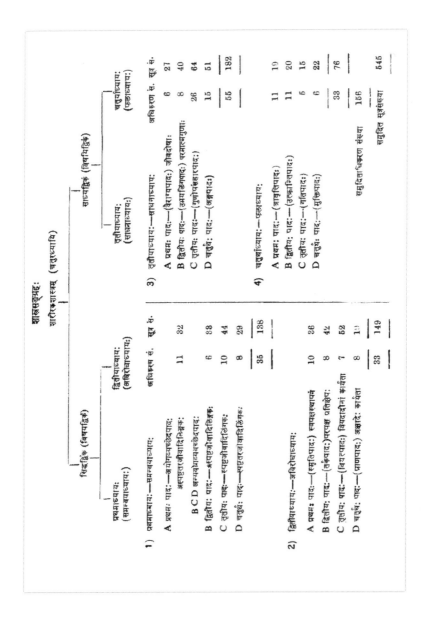

The BS is divided into four chapters (*adhyâyas*) and each adhyâya consists of four quarters (*pâdas*). Each pâda contains several groups of sutras called *adhikaraNa(s)*. Each adhikaraNa deals with a topic and the topics are arranged in a flowing sequence, the succeeding adhikaraNa logically linked with the preceding one. This link is

314

known as sangati. Within the adhikaraNa also there is sangati between the sutras arranged in a sequence. By and large, the adhikaraNa(s) contain several sutras and some do have only one. While this is the structure of BS, the homogenous theme of the four adhyâyas shows philosophical design of the highest order. Each adhyâya has set for itself a definitive function of the theme.

Adhikarana Sârâvali

Adhikarana Sârâvali (AS for short) is a poem composed by Swamy Deshika. This poem of 562 verses (in sragdhara metre) is a treatise expounding the rational essence of each adhikaraNa of Brahma Sutra based on Ramanuja's Sri Bhâshyam. "The Tattva-muktâ-kalâpah (another poem of Vedânta Deshika composed also in sragdhara metre, consisting of 500 verses) discusses comprehensively all the theories of Visistadvaita-epistemological, ontological, cosmological and eschatological- and establishes their soundness by examining critically the corresponding theories of rival schools of thought including Advaita Vedânta. The Adhikarana Saravali, on the other hand, is confined to the study of the Brahma Sutra Bhashya of Ramanuja and it presents the essential teachings of each adhikaraNa or section dealing with specific topics of Brahma Sutra, as interpreted by Ramanuja. In the Tattva-mukta-kalapa, Vedânta Deshika does not enter into the discussion of the Scriptural texts for the obvious reason that he wanted to prove the soundness of the Visishtâdvaita theory more on a logical basis than on the Scriptural authority. But in AS which directly deals with Sri Bhâshyam, he attempts to establish that the doctrines of Visishtâdvaita are in full accord with the Upanishadic teachings and the Vedânta Sutras. These two classics are complementary and are comparable, in the words of Vedânta Deshika, to the two hands, each complementing the other while clapping (*anyonyahastapradam* – AS 559). A study of both these works is considered essential for a fuller understanding of Visishtâdvaita Vedânta in all the miriad aspects" (preface of Ref 75).

315

Auspicious start: Swami refers to '*yatipati*' in the first and the last (562) shloka of AS. The Poem begins with the auspicious word '*svasti*' and ends in *Tarkshyah* who is Garuda, the very embodiment of Vedas. Another noteworthy feature is that he begins AS by reverently recalling the award of the title 'Vedântâchârya' bestowed on him by the Lord Sri Ranganatha (Ref 76 & Ref 77).

॥ तेन देवेन दत्तां वेदान्ताचार्यसंज्ञाम्॥

The metrical melody of the poem (the whole poem of 562 verses is set in sragdhara meter) is such that it is meant to be enjoyed by listening to it and the listener should grasp the brilliance of sound echoing the sense. In the second verse the Swamy also recalls the blessings he had received from his âchâryas such as Nadâdûr Ammâl and Atreya Ramanuja. Swamy compares the brilliance of this work to the Sun (*dinakarakirana shrenikeva*) as it will dispel the inner darkness of the reader in very many ways. It will sharpen and stabilize the intellect. Is the work devoid of any blemish as such? The Swamy counters it by saying that pearls, secured at considerable risk, are not thrown back into the sea just because they have some small defect in them . The precious pearl may even occupy the place of the pendent.

The commentary on the Veda and Vedânta is known as Mîmâmsashâstra and it contains twenty adhyâyas or chapters. Swamy affirms (AS11) that the entire twenty constitute one single book, *Vidyâ Sthâna*.The twenty fall under three broad divisions: the first 12 adhyâyas constitute Karma Kânda and is authored by Maharishi Jaimini. The next four adhyâyas comprise Devatâ Kânda (also called Samkarsha Kânda and it is authored by Kâshakrtsna-AS 15) and the last four adhyâyas constitute the Brahma Kânda or Jnâna Kânda (the book is titled as Vrtti Granta, authored by Maharishi Bodayana). In AS 5 the Swamy has given the gist of the

12 adhyâyas of Karma Kânda in 12 epithets and also briefly indicates the characteristics of the deities of Devata Kânda and the benefits that one can derive by worshipping them. The Swamy has shown the transitory gains (*alpa asthira artha*) of such worship in AS 6, and the need for enquiring into Karma Kânda before taking up Brahma Kânda is stressed from different stand points.

We can compare the twenty kândas to a Grand Edifice or Structure having twenty levels or floors. For a person who wants to enjoy infinite bliss he should climb to the 20th level and reach the terrace at the top (*pragnyâ prâsâda*). It is impossible for a novice to do it. For, it is not easy for a person to get himself freed from the clutches of karma since every one is born with three kinds of debt and it is his bounden duty to clear the debts before embarking on Brahma Prâpti. (For a profile of the sadhaka see NSA's volume on "The Philosophy on Sadhana") Hence there are mandatory duties (*iti kartavyata*) which are specified in the Karma Kânda. A knowledge of the specific duties has to be known from the shastras.

शास्त्रज्ञानं बहुक्लेशं बुद्धेश्चलन कारणम्।

उपदेशाद्धरि बुध्वा विरमेत् सर्वकर्मसु॥

Thus a person is caught up in the web of karmas and duties and hence he needs councelling and that reminds us of the hymn in the Mundakopanishad (1.2.12) : "Only a reflection on the transitory and sorrow ridden nature of life can make one turn away from the mundane world and prompt him to go in search of an âchârya who is well established in Brahmam."

समित्पाणिः श्रोत्रियं ब्रह्मनिष्ठम्॥

The Gurukulam thus served as an institution for the sadhaka to gain the necessary and sufficient knowledge so that he can get rid of karma or samsâra. The Guru functions like a lift, as it were, to climb the Grand Edifice, and the arduous task of climbing is common to

317

both the student as well as the teacher since both of them have to work out their destiny to gain mukti. The very name âchârya conveys that he is one who follows the precepts (*svayam âcharate*) and it is impossible for the disciple or the student to adequately reward the âchârya for the services rendered by him (for the exact quotations regarding âchârya refer to the Swamy's 'Rahasya Ratnavali Hrdayam- VS 28). By surrendering the fruits of karma, the sadhaka gets an easy lift from Brahman (as a quid pro quo for the renunciation) who is overall in charge of the lift of the Grand Edifice. Adopting a Brahma Vidya, the sadhaka finally reaches the terrace where a launch-pad is located. The Swamy has depicted the advanced stage of Vishnu Bhakti (climax) reached by the sadhaka in the tenth act of the play Sankalpa Suryodhaya. It is Brahman who arranges for the transport (a flying palanquin!) of the sadhaka from the launch-pad to Sri Vaikuntam through the route popularly known as *archirâdi mârga*.

An appropriate verse for the present context is the verse in Sri Rangaraja Stava (II.19) of Sri Parashara Bhattar:

आदौ वेदाः प्रमाणं स्मृतिरुपकुरुते सेतिहासैः पुराणैः

न्यायैः सार्धं त्वदर्चाविधिमुपरि परिक्षीयते पूर्वभागः।

ऊर्ध्वो भागस्त्वदीहागुणविभवपरिज्ञापनैस्त्वत्पदाप्तौ

वेद्यो वेदैश्च सर्वैरहमिति भगवन् स्वेन च व्याचकर्थ॥

A cursory meaning of the above verse is as follows:
"O Bhagavan! The first and the foremost support for your existence is the extant Vedas. The smrtis (Manusmrti and such other smrtis which are extant), the great epics, the purânas and the two-part mimamsa (the purva and the uttara) are the books which have come later to expatiate the Vedas. Of the two mimamsas, the purva serves as a manual for your worship (archa vidhi) and the uttara provides

318

knowledge of your glorious history, attributes, and your great vibhutis, the knowledge of which enables one to attain your Lotus Feet. You came down as Gitâchârya taught and confirmed that you alone are to be known from the Vedas."

For an in-depth understanding of the verse quoted above, refer Tani Shloki (p44 of part 3). Let us proceed with the discussion on Adhikarana Saravali (AS).

In AS 9, several tenets of Advaita are criticized. The entire Mimamsa of 20 is one shastra. The objections raised against this view are not sustainable (AS 10-14). Some doubts regarding the authorship of the two sub-sections of Karma Kânda are clarified in AS 15.

AS 16 codifies the entire content of Brahma Sutra in terms of mnemonics. The verse number 16 itself is indicative of the 16 pâdas. The total number of aphorisms of BS is expressed uniquely as shubhashi 545, the total number of adhikaraNas is chinmayi 156. The adhikaraNas in the first pâda is aksha (number of sensory organs, indriyas) 11, urmi=6, asa=10 and ahi=8. Thus the first adhyâya of four pâdas adds upto 35 adhikaraNas and so on.

The eight kinds of link (sangati) provide structural stability to the BS. They are as under:

शास्त्र। काण्ड। द्विक। अध्याय। पाद। पेटिका। अधिकरण। सूत्र॥

Verses in AS are specially devoted to highlight the above links thus fortifying the BS as a whole. The verse AS 17 is one such exercise to start with. The four chapters are Samanvaya, Avirodha, Upâya and Prâpti. The four adhyâyas form two dvikas (pairs). The first pair consisting of the first two adhyâyas is siddha dvika and the latter pair is sâdhya dvika. The first pair unequivocally establishes the existence of Brahman on the strength of the shastras. And the very

319

same Brahman is the means to attain Him. Thus the whole BS is one monolithic shastra. AS 18 outlines the plan of the whole BS in general and the first adhyâya in particular. The polar contrast that exists between the Shariraka Shastra of Sutrakara and Sankyan Philosophy of Kapila can be appreciated by considering the fact that the former is at pains to prove the existence of Brahman while the latter denies the existence of Brahman. The former has three, prakrti, purusha and Brahman while the latter has only two, prakrti and purusha. In their attempt to deny Brahman, Sankya goes hammer and tongs to make the existence of Brahman null and void by equating purusha of Sankya with Brahman of Upanishads, thus playing foul with the belief system of God-centric Vedânta. They employ the familiar technique of reductio-ad-absordom which means reducing a proposition to an absurdity. The strategy adopted to combat the Sankhyan is to arrange the texts of the Upanishads in four grades constituting the four pâdas of the first adhyâya. The first concerns with texts which are vague, the second with texts which are clear, the third with texts which are clearer and in the fourth pâda the texts which lucidly and unequivocally expound the supremacy and glory of Brahman, ad majorem dei glorium! A fight tooth and nail to prove the imitation and bring out the merit of the real.

Then a doubt is likely to rise: Is the BS a medley of pâdas, blowing hot and cold? Is it a haphazard heap of assertions and denials? This issue is addressed in AS 19. This verse provides a grand perspective of the teaching of BS providing a close link that exists in the 16 pâdas. Swamy has summarised each pâda in a single phrase and sixteen phrases for the sixteen pâdas. The oft quoted verse is given below.

स्रष्टा देही स्वनिष्ठो निरवधिमहिमाऽपास्तपाधःश्रितास्नः

खात्मादेरिन्द्रियादेरुचित जननकृत् संसृतौ तन्त्रवाही।

निर्दोषत्वादिरम्यो बहुजननपदं स्वाहंकर्म प्रसाद्यः

320

पापच्छिद् ब्रह्मनाडीगतिकृदतिवहन् साम्यदश्चात्र वेद्यः ॥

The Brahman is:
1. The Creator.
2. The Possessor of the Universe as His body.
3. Self Supporter (no outside support from anyone else)
4. Splendid with boundless glory. (All pervading)
5. His existence cannot be denied.
6. Genial friend who can be approached by all.
7. Creator of life support system and the jîvas.
8. Provider of senses and prâNas.
9. Controller of beings caught up in the web of samsâra
10. Beauty personified, untouched by any blemish and full of kalyana guNas.
11. Object of devotion and meditation.
12. Who can be pleased with the performance of one's duties.
13. Destroyer of sins when approached.
14. Provider of guidance for the sadhaka's âtma to make the final exit through the Brahma nâdî.
15. Provider of further assistance or guidance so that the jîva takes the final journey through the auspicious route, Archiradi marga.
16. He who grants the jîva, a status equal to His own (the reader may also refer to the Swamy's poem Maiviratamanmiyam (verse 19) wherein the four adhyâyas of Brahma Sutras are summarized in lilting Tamil).

The Swamy clarifies a point mentioned earlier. If it is stipulated that the study of Karma Kânda is mandatory, then it would be well nigh impossible to take up the enquiry into Brahman. It should be noted that study does not include knowing the meaning of the vedas since to known the meaning one should be well versed in the six limbs (angas) such as rules of vedic grammar, science of phonetics etc.

321

Study means adhyâyana (memorising the hymns) during the period of boyhood when it is easy to do it. Hence gifted people (krtinah), out of fear of the appalling effects of Kaliyug, take up directly the study of enquiry into Brahman skipping the study of Karma Kânda (AS 20).

Can one do away with the guidance of an âchârya altogether and take up the study independently from the books? Self study will not be as effective as being taught by a teacher (Chand.4.9.3).

आचार्याद्धैव विद्या विदिता साधिष्ठं प्रापत्॥

A significant feature of AS is that the Swami has listed and given the essence of the Adhikarana in each pâda invariably in a single verse and the summing up verse will be found at the end of the respective pâda. For example, the four pâdas of the first adhyâya are summed up respectively in AS verse numbers 78, 98, 129 and 151. Many of the authors on Sri Bhâshya restrict their reference to these summing up verses of AS (See Ref 80) adopt such an approach. The reader can also enjoy listening to the six CDs based on AS (Ref 81). Now we shall proceed with the few remaining verses left in Shâstrâvatâra section of AS.

Can we know the existence of God (Brahman) through any other source of knowledge other than the Shâstra? No other ancient lore gives a presentation of the cause and birth of the universe so rationally and with so many details as that of the Shâstra. Hence other sources lack the merit of the Upanishads and they cannot be entertained or countenanced. But even in the Upanishads three entities get mentioned. How can we decisively say that they all point to one and the same entity? There is what is called 'vyutpatti' which means an exact relationship between the word and its meaning. We are not quite certain about this aspect also? Then the question of 'vidhi': certain things (actions) are specified to get certain results. The Upanishads doesn't seem to stipulate any action as such in clear terms. These doubts are dispelled by the first four adhikaraNa(s) (aphorisms, sutras) known as Chatus Sûtrî. The first two Adhikarana(s) form one set (petika) and the latter two form another petika. The first Adhikarana runs the gamut of the entire Upanishads in general and the second concerns with the characteristic feature of Brahman alone. Thus, the lofty ideal of Brahman and why we should aspire for Him is graphically portrayed in the *Chatussûtrî* itself. The modern-day organizations proudly present their Statement of Objective' in laudable terms. Similarly, the *Chatussûtrî* is the Statement of Objective', viewed from the standpoint of the Upanishads, which is God's own work, *apaurusheyam*. There can't be any doubt about the purport and utility of that 'Objective'.

In the ultimate analysis, the aim of the Upanishads is to make the aspirant desiring moksha to become deserving by knowing the munificent God who must confer that mukti (AS 22).

The Swamy uses the word *ruju* (AS 23) while complementing the Sutrakara. Ruju is one who is firm in thought, word and deed and who does not swerve from his position. He would be open minded while considering the merits (if any) of the oppositions' view points but rebut the oppositions' claim with support from the Upanishads, thus establishing the pre-eminent status of the ancient lore.

The marvelous approach through Chatussûtrî of Veda Vyasa has come for appraisal. According to Gitâchârya's verse (BG 13.6), the Brahma Sutra existed even prior to Gita and because Vyasa was a contemporary of Bhagavan Krishna, the Sanâtana Dharma of BS is as old as the period to which the two authors belonged i.e., five millenniums old! It withstood the test of time simply because the Chatus-Sûtrî rests on the bed rock of Vedânta (AS 24).

The mighty minds of old have accepted Chatus-Sûtrî as serving the purpose of providing a grand introduction to BS. The Swamy also pays tribute to his own preceptor, Vâdi Hamsambuvaha, besides mentioning Seneshwara and Vishnuchitta (AS 25).

There is rhyme and reason in the order of the four sutras. This order is of a piece with Bruguvalli. Any attempt to change the order would not be welcome to the scholars (AS 26).

With that we come to the end of the section known as Shâstrâvatâra. The first adhyâya of BS is called *Samanvaya Adhyâya* and as the name indicates this adhyâya coordinates and integrates all the passages of the major Upanishads while proclaiming Brahman as the ground of the cosmos. The four pâdas of the first adhyâya take up for analysis four distinctive type of Upanishadic passages selected based on their degree of obscurity in determining Brahman as the supreme reality. Conversely, they pertain to statements in the Upanishads which are vague in the extreme (*aspashtatara* vide A in the chart) whether they teach about jivâtman. Statements which are not so clear (*asphashta*) belong to the Second Pâda. The Third Pâda deals with statements which appear to speak clearly (*spashta*) about jivâtman. And the Fourth Pâda deals with statements which appear more clearly (*spashtatara*) about either jivâtman or prakrti. The names of the 4 pâdas are as under.

अयोगव्यवच्छेद पादः अस्पष्टजीवादिलिङ्गक पादः

स्पष्टजीवादिलिङ्गक पादः स्पष्टतरजीवादिलिङ्गक पादः

The term *ayoga vyavaccheda* which is an alternative name of the First Pâda is explained a little later. Regarding the classification in Ramanuja's own words refer to the passage (given below) occurring at the completion of the commentary on the First Pâda (p 277 of

SB). The passage provides the rationale and link between the First Pâda and the rest of the three pâdas of the First Adhyâya.

सार्वज्ञयसत्यसङ्कल्पत्वाद्यपरिमितोदार गुणसागरतया

स्वेतरसमस्तवस्तुविलक्षणः परंब्रह्म पुरुषोत्तमो नारायण

एव वेदान्तवेद्य इत्युक्तम्। अतः परं द्वितीयतृतीयचतुर्थेषु पादेषु

यद्यपि वेदान्तवेद्यं ब्रह्म एव तथापि कानिचिद्वेदान्तवाक्यानि

प्रधानक्षेत्रज्ञान्तर्भूतवस्तुविशेषस्वरूपप्रतिपादनपराण्येव

इत्याशङ्क्य तन्निरसनमुखेन तत्तद्वाक्योदितकल्याणगुणाकरत्वं ब्रह्मणः

प्रतिपाद्यते। तत्रास्पष्टजीवादिलिङ्गकानि वाक्यानि द्वितीये पादे विचार्यन्ते

स्पष्टलिङ्गकानितृतीये तत्तत्प्रतिपादनच्छायानुसारिणि चतुर्थे॥

The strategy or scheme of arrangement of the four pâdas of the first adhyâya is explained in the above passage of Sri Bhâshya. Consider the statement *"shankah pândara eve"* (conch is white only). If an opponent, a skeptic, contends that whiteness and conch don't go together (*ayoga*), then proving that his contention is false and establishing the whiteness of conch in unequivocal terms is a logic known in Sanskrit as '*ayogavyavachchheda Nyâya*'.

To put it in another way, the opponent objects to B being the cause of creation since B does not exist at all –it is like a picture without a canvas! This objection is taken as the prima facie view and the same is refuted. *Ayogah = IskshaNa asambhavah, tat vyavacchedah.* The first pâda based on this principle of logic proclaims that Brahman is incontrovertibly the cause of creation of the universe.

Then in the next three pâdas the opponent assumes a new role, and contends that one text or the other of the Upanishad does not refer to Brahman. If he should succeed he would stake his claim that all other texts would conform to his conclusion. It is like finding a loophole in the argument between two contending parties in a court case.

Consider the statement: *"pârtha eva dhanurdharaḥ"* (Pârtha is the only archer). There are the terms dharma and *dharmi*. Archery is dharma and the archer is *dharmi*. Archer, in the true sense of the term applies to the one and only Pârtha. The word 'eva' (only) is intended to provide the needed emphasis. The uniqueness of the term Brahman is established by enquiring into in the pâdas 2, 3 & 4. The whole Upanishads speak in one voice about the existence of the one and only B. Any attempt to posit any other entity (*anya yoga*) is refuted (*vyavacchedaḥ*).

Thus, the four pâdas are brought under two groups- the first pâda is one group and the next three pâdas form the second group. For this reason, the second group goes by the name *Tripâdi*.

The application of both the *nyâyas —ayoga-vyavaccheda nyâya & anya yoga vyavaccheda nyâya —* it is unequivocally established that the Upanishads extol B who is none other than Sriman Narayana.

By way of references to excellent books on Sri Bhashya we shall indicate the broad outline of BS.

First pâda (BS I.1)
This pâda is known as *ayogavyavachcheda* pâda and why it is so worded was explained before. This pâda is the largest as it begins in page number 1and ends in 275 of Sri Bhâshya (Ref 63). The first pâda consists of eleven adhikaraNa(s). The first four form one petika (set), the *Chatussûtrî* and the remaining seven adhikaraNa(s) are as under.

ईक्षति। आनन्दमय। अन्तर। आकाश। प्राण।ज्योतिः। इन्द्र प्राण।

Adhikarana Saravali verses 1to 78 deal with the eleven adhikaraNas of BS I.1. We have mentioned that *Chatus Sutri* serves the purpose of introduction (*upodhghata*) to Brahma Sutra (AS 26) See also Ref 82.

Swami has devoted eight verses (AS 27-34) for the first adhikaraNa, six verses (AS 35-40) for the second adhikaraNa, five verses (AS 41-45) for the third and seven verses (AS 46-52) for the fourth adhikaraNa. In the first two it was shown that enquiry into Brahman is not an impossible task after all and in the latter two it was shown that it is a mandatory exercise most beneficial and nothing stops one to undertake the study. Since the four provide the motivation for study, the *Chatus Sutri* constitute one *petika*. The Brahman on whom the study is taken up is one who created the universe (vide 31 *Kâranatvâdhikarana*) and the one confers nothing but Bliss as He is a personification of Infinite Bliss. (vide 78 *Ubhayalingâdhikarana*). Thus the Swami underscores the importance of the enquiry in AS 53. Swami gives another verse to highlight the essence of it so that the student is motivated to take up the study enthusiastically. The student is pre-empted to prepare for a frontal attack on the adherants of Sankhyan Philosophy who will start pulling his legs from the fifth adhikaraNa (BS I.1.5) onwards and drag on till the close of the first adhyâya (AS 54).

BS I.1.(1), *athâto brahma jignyâsâ,* establishes that *Brahma jignyâsâ* is to be undertaken after completing the study of *Pûrva mîmâmsâ* and realization of the futility of the fruits of the ritualistic deeds and the permanency of the spiritual value to be achieved by the study of Vedânta.

BS I.1.(2), *janmâdyadhikaraNam*, establishes that the wholesome teachings offered by the Upanishads provide the knowledge of Brahman directly.

BS I.1.(3), *shâstrayonitvâdhikaranam*, proves that shastra is the only basal text for knowing the existence of Brahman.

BS I.1.(4) *samanvayâdhikaranam*, establishes that the teachings of the Upanishads are purposeful and ennobling since by knowing Brahman, the embodyment of Infinite Bliss, the supreme goal of mukti is attained.

BS I.1.(5), *îkshatyadhikaraNam* , AS 55-57. In Sri Bhashya it occupies 12 pages (from SB p217 to 228) Chandogya dealing with Sadvidya, *sat* is identified with *âtman*. The Sankyan identifies sat with pradhana which is insentient. If sat were pradhana, tvam referring to jivâtma should be one with pradhana, a non-sentient entity. Again, if *sat* were *pradhana*, its anupravesha (entering into) along with *jîva* is not a possibility at all. Hence Sankhyan theory stands rejected. Swamy affirms (AS 56 & 57) that this addhikarana traces an important profile of Brahman- He is the cause of the universe through the operation of His free will.

BS I.1.(6), *ânandamayâdhikaranam*, AS 58-61. Ramanuja expounds the greatness of Anandavalli in 24 pages (SB p229-252). For all intents and purposes, Anandavalli is the anchor upanishad of Visishtâdvaita. "The major objection is that what is described as anandamaya is jivâtma svarupa. This is based on the assumption (purvapaksha) that jîva and Brahman are not different. Ramanuja devotes special attention to refute this primafacie view" (p33 of SMS book).

BS I.1.(7) *antaradhikaraNa*, AS 62-65; SB p253 to 258 (six pages). The view that the shining self in the Sun with a golden complexion

328

and eyes like the lotus mentioned in Chandogya (I.6.7) is the jîva stands rejected. The quality of being devoid of sin can only pertain to Brahman and not to Sun-god, Aditya. See Dr. NSA's volume on Chandogya p29.

BS I.1.(8) *âkâshâdhikarana*, AS 66-69; SB p258 to 263 (six pages). The term âkâsha occuring in Chandogya (1.9.1) Sage Salavatya wanted to know the ultimate goal and he got the reply: "It is âkâsha. All these beings moving and non-moving originate from âkâsha. It is verily âkâsha alone that is greater than all these. Âkâsha is the Supreme Goal." What is discussed in this section of the upanishad is not the elemental ether but the Brahman. Brahman in the sense that He illumines everything else (*âkâshayati*) and He also shines everywhere.

BS I.1.(9) *prânâdhikarana*, AS 70; SB p263. The issue is *prâna* occuring in Chand (1.11.5): Does it stand for vital air or Brahman? Refer to Dr NSA's volume for the context. *Prâna* should be treated on a par with âkâsha. The Taittiriya states that no one other than Brahman can provide life sustaining *prâNa* to all.

BS I.1.(10) *JyotiradhikaraNa*; SB p264-268. AS71-73. In the statements "*âkâshât vâyuh vâyoragnih*" it was clarified that these words which normally represent the respective elements, when read in the context of Upanishads they denote Brahman. In a similar manner the word *jyotis* occuring in Chand. (3.13.7) also represent Brahman. "Now that light which shines above this heaven, higher than everything, in the highest worlds beyond which there are no other worlds, that is the same light which is within man."

The word '*charana*' occuring in the sutra is the equivalent of pâda in Chand (3.12.6) and Ramanuja seizes this oppurtunity to expound the significance by referring to hymns of Purusha Sukta.

BS I.1.(11) *Indrapranâdhikarana*; SB p269-275. AS 74-77. A passage occuring in Kaushitaki Up, refers to Indra. The doubt is whether the name refers to the chief of the celestial deities or the Brahman? "The criteria adopted in interpreting the general terms such as *âkâsha, prâNa, jyotis, indra-prâNa* etc. in favour of Brahman is not uniformly the same and it differs in accordance with the subject matter in which the Upanishadic statements are made" (p47 Ref 75). The Sutra occurring in this adhikaraNa (BS 1.1.31) needs special attention.The said sutra reads as: *"shâstra drshhTyâ tûpadesho vâmadevavat"* The reader may turn to p82 of SB where also Vamadeva rishi gets mentioned. PNS explains its special significance (p487 Ref 43):

"Self illumination in the state of mukti brings out the infinite intelligence and omniscience of the finite or monadic self, when it is freed from the limitations of karman. Its visishta-aeikya is then apprehended in non-difference from B. The Vedântic seer intuits B as his very self when he says: "I am Thou, Holy Divinity and Thou art myself." 'What He is, that am I.' Prahlada, like Vamadeva, in his ecstasy, thus describes the onset of cosmic consciousness and All-Selfness: "As the infinite is all pervading, He is myself, all things proceed from me, I am all things, all things are in me who am eternal." (VP I.19.85) The âtman is non different from the Supreme Self by attaining the being of its being. Nammazhwar also affirms the truth of this cosmic experience when he, in the excess of his love, imitates and mirrors forth the glory of God and claims in his Tiruvâi Mozhi (V.6), the two vibhutis of the cosmic and ultra-cosmic functions as his own."

The adhikaraNas of BS 1.1 are discussed in chapter two of Ref 75 and pages (416 – 419) of Ref 43. In AS 78, all the adhikaraNas barring Chatussûtrî are summarised.

The second pâda is known as *aspashhtajîvadilingaka pâda-* BS I.2. By giving the arrangement of the four pâdas of the first adhyâya in verse AS 79, the link (*sangati*) between the first pâda and the three pâdas is established and the same with respect to the respective nomenclature is expressed in clear terms (*vishadam prakâshayan*) AS80.

2. pâda (*aspashta jîvâdilingaka pâda*)

The six adhikaraNas of this pâda (12 to 17) are as follows:

सर्वप्रसिद्धिः। अत्र। अन्तर। अन्तर्यामि।

अद्दइयत्वादिगुणक। वैश्वानर।

BS I.2.(1) *sarvaprasiddhyadhikaraNa*, SB p276-286 (eleven pages); AS85.

Prasiddhi shows that the teachings of the Upanishads are popular since they are the time-honoured ones. The famous passage in Shandilya vidya occuring in Chand. (3.14.1). "A person is characterised by his calm disposition which has come as a result of meditation. As one meditates upon Brahman here in this world, so he becomes after departing from this world. Hence one should meditate with conviction."

Subsequent hymn (ibid 3.14.2) states that meditation should be observed on that which is *mano-maya*, *prâNa-sharira* and *bhârûpa*. It would appear as if these terms refer to jîva. This view will get thrown into the shade with an indepth understanding. *Prana sharira* means that Brahman is the supporter and ruler of Prana. Refer to similar words occuring in Mundaka and Kena Upanishads where these words relate to the dharmas of Brahman.The reader should go through the rest of this section3 &4 of Chand (3.14) to know more of the attributes of Brahman.

BS I.2.(2) *atradhikaraNa*, SB p286- 291 (five pages); AS 86,7. Refer to Kathopanishad 2.25. An entity swallows all the movables and immovables in one go and for whom the god of Death, *mrtyu* serves as pickles! It is common knowledge that gluttony is associated with a karma-bound embodied being. Is the entity a jîva or Brahman?

Ramanuja explains the whole Upanishads for a full appraisal before answering this question. There are six chapters (also called vallis) in this upanishad and concerns with the famous dialogue between the *wunderkid* Nachiketas and the Lord of Death Yama. The latter gets wonderstruck at the maturity of the boy and imparts secret knowledge for attaining immortality. Obviously, Yama should have been in the know of the secret teachings since he decides the fate of individuals. Ramanuja shows that Paramâtma is the one who swallows.

BS I.2.(3) *antaradhikaraNam*, SB p292-298 (seven pages); AS 88-90. The purusha seen in the eye of the Yogins (vide Chand. 4.15) is Brahman or some other being? Brahman, 'akshi-purusha' resides in the yogins who are highly purified. They become the starry-eyed Yogins. This conclusion is corroborated in *"yashchakshushhi tishtan"* (Brahad.3.7.22).

BS I.2.(4) *antaryamyadhikaraNam*, SB p299-304 (five pages); AS 91,2. In the same section of Brahad.(3.7), a plethora of examples are cited where the Brahman resides as the Indweller- Antaryamin.
BS I.2.(5) *adrshyatvâdiguNakâdhikaranam*, SB p304-310 (sixpages); AS 93. The passage which needs clarification occurs in Mundaka (1.1.5,6).The question is whether 'akshara' pertains to Brahman or prakrti or jîva. The teacher of this upanishad is sage Angiras and the addressee is Saunaka. Undoubtedly Akshara refers to Brahman.

BS I.2.(6) *vaishvânarâdhikarana*, SB p311-320 (ten pages); AS 94 & 95. Refer Chand. (5.11) Five great householders along with Uddalaka approached the king Aswapati of Kekaya contry and asked the king to enlighten them about Vysvanara. The humble king welcomes them with these words, which reflect the great ambience prevailing in those times: "O venerable sirs, in my country there is no thief, no drunkard...I propose to perform a sacrifice shortly. I shall give you the fees for taking part in the sacrifice." They declined the offer: "Please teach us only the Vysvara Atman."

Vysvanara is personified as possessing different parts- aditya as its eyes, vayu as its *prâNa, âkâsha* as its body etc. This kind of personification can apply only to Brahman and not to any jivâtma. AS 96 clarifies terms such as Brahma, purusha and âtma. AS 97 defends Sutrakara's strategy to put down the opponents and AS 98 summarises the six adhikaraNas of BS I.2.

SMS has discussed the six adhikaraNa-s of this pâda BS 1.2 in his book, pages 53 -74 of Ref 75, Chapter Three, titled "The Distinguishing Characteristics of Brahman".

PNS (p419 of Ref 43) begins discussion of BS 1.2: The second pâda of the First Adhyâya consists of six adhikaraNa-s and it establishes the supremacy of B as the sharīrin or Inner Self of all by ruling out the claims of the finite self." The description of the second pâda ends on p421 ibid with his observation: "This section has deep religious significance and shows that the infite Lord in His boundless tenderness is unable to bear the separationof His other self and therefore stations Himself in the heart of the jîva with a view to leading him back to His highest abode. The aim of Vedânta is to reveal the divinity that lies concealed in the heart of all jīva-s."

3rd pâda, spashtajîvâdilingaka pâda

BS I.3. SB p321 to 386 (sixty six pages). The ten adhikaraNas (18 - 27) are as follows:

द्युभ्वादि। भूमा। अक्षर। ईक्षधिकर्म। दहर।

प्रमित। देवता। मधु। अपशूद्र। अर्थान्तरत्व॥

The link between the pâdas made clear in AS 99. Out of the ten adhikaraNas, 7 are directly linked and 3 are incidental.

BS I.3.(1) *dyubhvâdyadhikaraNam*, SB p321- 326 (six pages); AS 101-3. The issue is concerned with Mundaka (2.2.5): "Heaven, earth, mind, vital forces and the sense organs- all these are connected by the unique âtman. Know this as the bridge to immortality (*amrtasya esha setuh*)". The doubt is whether the hymn pertains to jîva or Brahman? The word *âyatana* (which means support) in the sutra BS I.3.1 clarifies that it is Brahman who is the warp and woof of the universe, the mind and vital airs are woven to form the life support system. This upanishad abounds in passages showing clear demarkation between jîva and Brahman. The oft quoted *'dvâ suparnâ'* occurs in Mundaka 3.1.1. "The Upanishadic analogy of the two birds on the same tree, of the shining one above and the suffering one below, becoming united in the end is more sublime and more appropriate than that of the fowl and the two halves. The Infinite is in the finite self with a view to infinitizing the content" (vide page 425 of PNS).

BS I.3.(2) *bhûmâdhikaranam*, SB p 326-32 (six pages); AS 104-7. Before stating the point at issue, let us refer to the particular section of the upanishad where the word Bhûma occurs. Refer to Chand (7.1) Sage Narada approached Sanatkumara for enlightenment and after giving an exhaustive list of all that he knew, Narada said, "Revered Sir! I know only the words of the mantras but I have not

334

known the Supreme Atman. I have heard from respectable persons like you, that a knower of the Atman will cross over sorrow. Enlighten me" (7.1.3). In response, Sanatkumara suggested meditation on a series of subjects- nama, vak, ...prâNa (fifteen of them, AS 107). A doubt occurs whether Prana is Bhuman. This view is rejected. Bhuma does not refer to jivâtma denoted by the word prâNa but to Brahman.

"The finite self connotes Brahman as its true self and the meditation on the Bhuman leads to the attainment of Brahmananda. Thus the philosophic knowledge of Bhuma-vidya leads to the mystic experience of the bliss of Bhuman" (PNS).

BS I.3.(3) *aksharâdhikarana* , SB p333-337; AS 108. Earlier 'akshara' was discussed in BS I.2.(5) with respect to the Mundaka where Brahman was described in terms of negative attributes such as *adrshyatva* but the basis was Brahman as *sarvajnya* and *sarvavit*. Presently the same word, akshara occurs in Brhadaranyaka (3.8.7) in the context of Yajnyavalkya's teachings to Gargi. Here also the Brahman is associated with negative qualities such as asthula, ananu etc It is used in the sense that Brahman is adhara or supporter of the universe by virtue of His absolute power to command (*prashâsana*). By akshara, the sage was not referring to prakrti or purusha. "From the point of view of spiritual experience or anubhava, this Akshara-vidya inculcates the worship of Brahman as the cosmic ruler or the father of all jîvas...The father of all is not only in heaven, but is the Inner Ruler, and His redemptive will is self-revealed on earth and in heaven."

BS I.3.(4) *îkshatikarmâdhikaranam*, SB p337-340 (three pages) AS 109,10. The point at issue is a passage in Prashnopanishad (5.5). This upanishad (six sections) is in the form of questions and answers. Six aspirants after Brahman approach Pippalada for instruction. The first question is about the creation of the universe.

Coming to the issue: 5.5 (ibid) relates to meditation on the Supreme Self by means of practicing Pranava mantra as a means for mukti, maintaining the stipulated three matras. Ramanuja has explained the significance of matras. The aspirant attains Brahmalokam. The issue is whether Brahma refers to Four-faced Brahma or the Brahman? If the upâsaka meditates on the Supreme Brahman he should attain the same Brahman and not Hiranyagarbha as Shankara contends. The characteristics mentioned in this upanishad do not apply to Hiranyagarbha. (vide AS 109) Brahma loka cannot be the perishable world of the four faced one. This issue crops up again in karyadhikaraNam, BS IV.3.(5). There are two facts to help to decide: The meditator is released from all sins and travels to Brahma loka on the way leading through the Sun. Secondly, *sadâ pashyanti* signifies that the place reached by the sadhaka is Sri Vaikundam where nitya-suris feast their eyes looking at the Supreme Being. What is seen by them is the world of Vishnu as taught by other Upanishads. There is no denying the fact that Brahman is the object of attainment of the muktas (*muktabhogya svabhâvah*- AS 129).

BS I.3.(5) *daharâdhikarana*, SB p341 to 351(eleven pages); AS 111-115. Dahara vidya, Chand. (8.1.1) enjoins meditation on ether of the heart. Human heart is figuratively described as lotus-like abode of Brahman. Within this heart, there is a subtle space known as 'Dahara-âkâsha' (Dahara means small). The description of Dahara Âkâsha conforms to Brahman. The opponent refuses to accept that it is Brahman? The adhikaraNa by a process of elimination excludes two alternatives of the elemental ether and establishes the ether in the heart is Brahman. Further Dahara Âkâsha is stated to be the support of the entire universe (*viswa-eka-adharata* -AS 114) and this special feature is not applicable to jivâtma. The *alpatva* of Para Brahmam cribbed, cabinned and confined within the inner recess of one's heart is for the sake of meditation of the upâsaka. It is not therefore His natural form (*svabhavika*). Hence dharâkâsha cannot be jivâtma.

Further, the hymn Chand (8.1.5) ascribes to the Brahman with eight perfections (*gunâshtakam*) which imply freedom from evil in its physical, moral and metaphysical aspects: free from the following six negative characteristics such as evil (*apahatapapma*), oldage, grief, hunger, thirst, and death and two positive attributes i.e., true desire and true will. That these eight cannot pertain to jivâtma would become clear from the teachings of the three hymns of Mundaka (3.1.1, 2 & 3). When the karma bound bird representing jîva realises its folly and sees the luster in the other bird only then jîva gets freed from sorrow. Only after the *bhagavad-darshana* the ignorance representing karma vanishes, pâpa and punya gets shaken off and the wise jîva thenceforth becomes worthy of being called a vidvan. An upâsaka of Dahara-vidya gets blessed with Gunashtaka after attaining mukti (refer to the shloka *'vitamasi pade lakshmî-kântam'*- RTS 22).

BS I.3.(6) *pramitâdhikaranam*, SB p351-3 (three pages) ; AS 116. Ramanuja brings to focus the three places in Kathavalli (4.12,13) & (6.17) where mention is made of a thumb-sized purusha- the point at issue is whether it refers to the Brahman or a jivâtma? "The thumb-sized entity ever resides in the hearts of humans (*janânâm hrdaye sannivishjtah*). Its power is so great that it is called *Ishânah* which means one who controls and rules as the Inner Ruler over mighty forces of nature. Out of fear for Him fire burns, sun shines and so on. He holds the thunder-bolt ready to unleash destruction comparable to the sword of Democles. He is the Lord who is ever present- past, present and future. He is Jyotis- powerful light without smoke. This kind of description of a thumb-sized entity cannot apply to jîva.

The human heart is conceived as the size of thumb of a human being only for the purpose of meditation. Since the Para Brahmam resides in the heart, the size of Brahmam is that of the thumb. However there is reason for the rise of the doubt as in Shveta 5.8 *angushta* (thumb) refers to jîva though not the whole of the thumb but somewhere in the cave of the heart. But the size of jivâtma is clearly specified (5.9 ibid): "one hundredth part of one hundredth part of the size of human hair." Hence while arriving at the meaning we should keep the context in view and not jump to conclusions. Relatively speaking, thumb is infinitely greater than the microscopic part of the hair example.

BS I.3 (7, 8 & 9) *devatâdhikaranam, madhvadhikaraNam and apashûdrâdhikaranam*, SB p353 to 380 (twenty six pages); AS 118 to 127.

If the thumb-sized Brahman stays at the heart of humans, then the question arises whether the devas (who are formless) are eligible for meditation for eventual Brahma *prâpti?* The discussion on these lines extend in the seventh, eighth and ninth adhikaraNa and the following conclusions are arrived at: The devas are eligible. "The Madhu-vidya is also Brahmopanishad, as it explains the nectar of the sun extracted by the devas in a vedic way (Chand.3.1.1) as the bliss of Brahman that is the Light of lights and the Inner Self of the sun. The self within the eye is Brahman, the beautiful and the blissful. (Chand.4.15.1). He is called *vaminîh* (ibid 4.15.3) for He bestows all blessings, *bhâminîh* (ibid 4.15.4) for He is the Jyotis or splendour that shines in all the worlds. He is ka or pleasure and kha, the all pervading infinite. In the exposition of Bhuma-vidya, Ramanuja, following the author of the sutras (BS I.3.7 & 8) concludes that Bhûman or Infinite Bliss" (PNS p215). As regards the fourth varna is concerned they are not eligible as brahma-vidya is open to the trivarnikas only.

BS I.3.(10) *arthântaratvâdhikaranam*, SB p382-6 (five pages); AS 128. As the explanation provided by PNS is brief it is given here: "The last topic of the section is the Chand.8.14.1 that speaks of the ether as the evolver of names and forms. This ether is not the elemental ether or âkâsha or the jîva but is Brahman. This is clear from the description given that He is the Lord of lords who rules the self even in the state of deep sleep."

Incidentally, this section is also the end of the teachings of Chandogya Upanishad. The aspirant is sanguine about the Brahma prapti and makes the following fervent appeal. "May I attain the self of Brahman, the self of all living beings. May I attain the Paramâtman who is effulgent, the form of yashas. May I never enter into the womb of a woman."

References: The ten adhikaraNas of BS 1.3 are discussed in pages (424 – 430) of Ref 43 and between pages 74 & 97 of Ref 75.

Dr. NSA concludes his volume on Chandogya (8.15.1) as under: "A person who devotes himself to the study of the veda, to the propagation of vedic learning, to the performance of obligatory duties as accessory to the meditation upon Brahman attains Brahman and never more returns to this world of samsâra as typyfied in the statement '*na cha punarâvartate*' as he will have attained the highest goal of life."

4 spashtatarajîvâdilingaka pâda
SB p387 to p438: As the title of the pâda indicates, such of those upanishadic statements which appear as if echoing Sankhyan views are examined and proved that they pertain to Paramâtman of Upanishads and does not favour Sankhya. Out of the eight adhikaraNas, six meet the objections raised by Sankhya and two that of Yoga school. Hence the two sets form two petikas. Some

âchâryas are of the view that the eighth adhikaraNa is the summary of the four pâdas of first adhyâya (AS 130).

In AS 131, a more detailed view of the eight adhikaraNas are lucidly presented. "It has become necessary to confirm what was expressed in *janmâdhyadhikaraNa* (BS I.1.(2)), that Brahman is the primary cause of Creation, Sustenance and Dissolution of the universe. This need arises because there are a few important passages in the Upanishads, particularly in the Katha, Brhadaranyaka, Svetashvatara and Kaushitaki which convey the idea in more unambiguous terms (*spashtatara*) that either the prakrti (*avyakta*) or *purusha*, a sentient principle higher than non-sentient prakriti is the cause of the universe. These passages, prima facie reflect the theories of Sankhya and Yoga, the two schools of thought which were predominant during the time of Badarayana. Badarayana therefore devotes special attention to the examination of these passages and shows that even the statements referring to the prakrti and purusha in these Upanishads support the vedanta theory of Brahman as the sole cause of the universe" (p101 0f Ref 75).

The eight adhikaraNas (28 to 35) of BS I.4 are as under:

आनुमानिक। चमस।साङ्ख्योपसंग्रह। कारणत्व।

जगत्वाचित्व। वाक्यान्वय । प्रकृति। सर्वव्याख्यान॥

BS I.4.(1) *ânumânâdhikaranam*, SB p387-394 (eight pages); AS 131-3. The third valli of Katha outlines the profile of a sadhaka aspiring for mukti. An allegorical comparison is made to a chariot. The sadhaka is the master of the chariot and the body is the chariot itself. His intellect is the charioteer while the mind is representative of the reins. The senses are the horses and their respective objects as the paths on which they tread. The âtma of the sadhaka associated with the body, senses and the mind is the enjoyer. If the horses are good (which means well tamed) the chariot can be directed to fullfil the

340

purpose of sadhaka and on the other hand if they are wild and uncontrollable the sadhaka will be confined in samsâra.

Coming to the point at issue of this adhikaraNa, the term *avyakta* mentioned in Katha (3.11) does not denote the pradhana of Sankhya but the physical body of the sadhaka in the allegorical example provided by the upanishad.

The final ideal of life and state of attainment is conveyed in unequivocal terms in Katha since the defining expression –"tad vishnoh paramam pâdam" –is used. The Purusha of the Upanishad is the ultimate Vishnu of Rig Veda and *para gatih* signifies the highest goal and sole refuge.

॥ पुरुषान्न परं किंचित् सा काष्ठा सा परा गतिः ॥

BS I.4.(2) *chamasâdhikarana*, SB p395-401 (seven pages); AS 134. Shvetashvatara Upanishad has 113 mantras spread over six chapters. Dr NSA in his introduction to this upanishad says, "The 'Bheda' shrutis of this upanishad are clear and decisive and Bhagavan Ramanuja quotes from this upanishad to point out the difference between jivâtman and Paramâtman... The fact of the Lord being the 'Antaryamin' in all is expounded in this upanishad very clearly."

The controversy is with regard to '*ajâ*' occurring in 4.5 (ibid): "*ajâmekâm*". It is clarified that '*ajâ*' as prakrti cannot be the cause of the universe independently without the involvement of Brahman. The Taittiriya, as per AS 134, makes it even more clear.

BS I.4.(3) *sânkhyopasangrahâdhikarana*, SB p402-4 (three pages); AS 135,6. The point at issue is with regard to Brhad. Up (4.4.17). The term *pancha-pancha-jana* has nothing to do with the Sankhyan theory of prakrti, but should be taken as a technical word suggestive of any five entities similar to *sapta-sapta rishayah* or *sapta-rishis*.

BS I.4.(4) *kâranatvâdhikarana*, SB p405-8 (four pages); AS 137,8. Here it is discussed that the concepts of *avyâkrta* and *asat* used in Brhad and Taitiriya respectively does not support Sankhyan theory. BS I.4.(5) *jagadvâchitvâdhikarana*, SB p408-417 (eight pages); AS 139, 40. The point at issue is whether 'purusha' mentioned in Kaushîtaki Upanishad dealing with Bâlâkî Vidya is jivâtma or Brahman? The relevant sutra reads *'jagatvâchitvâ'* which means 'it is Brahman because of the mention of the universe created by Him'. Almost the same passage gets mentioned in Brhadaranyaka (2nd chapter) where Ajâtashatru teaches about Brahman to Balaki.

When the word karma is associated with Brahman it is with regard to creation of *jagat*. See Chintamani for AS 139.

BS I.4.(6) *vâkyânvayâdhikaranam*, SB p417- 426 (nine pages); AS 141-3. The subject for discussion is the famous Maitreyi Brahmanm where a soul searching dialogue takes place between sage Yajnyavalkya and his wife Maitreyi (Ref 78). For further details the reader may refer to Brhadaranyaka Upanishad (p118 Ref 79): "Maitreyi sought to become immortal and Yajnyavalkya teaches that the âtman alone is to be seen, reflected upon and meditated upon for attaining immortality. So the âtman here signifies Paramâtman."
BS I.4.(7) *prakrtyadhikaraNam*, SB p426-437 (eleven pages); AS 144-8. There is an attempt by the opponent to separate- Brahman as the *nimitta karana* and prakrti as *upâdana karana*. Badarayana disaggrees with this view and clarifies both the karanas are attributed to Brahman on the basis of the various Upanishads. Ramanuja arranges all the upanishadic texts in a logical sequence and sketches the construction of his Grand Edifice.

BS I.4.(8) *sarvavyâkhyânâdhikaranam*, SB p437-8 (one page); AS 149-50. Thus the first chapter closes with a resounding note that everything is satisfactorily explained and the rationality established on a firm footing.

The fourth pâda (BS I.4) is summed up in AS 151. The two religions, namely, the god-less religion of Sankhya and Seshvara Sankhya (Yoga) which admits Iswara as the nimitta karana of the universe- these two have heen refuted in this pâda and the doctrine of vedanta is upheld.

For detailed treatment of all the eight adhikaraNas see pages (p102 -121of Ref 75).

The Second Adhyâya deals with two types of opponents, the outsiders and insiders of Vedic religion (AS 152). There are shruti texts which appear to be in favour of arguments put up by the opponents who oppose the causal Brahman. That this contention of the opponent is ill-founded is proved in BS II.1. There is another class of opponents who claim that their theory is in aggreement with shrutis and this claim of theirs is refuted in BS II.2. The apparent contradictions within the shruti texts themselves are sorted out in pâdas 3 & 4 of BS II. That BS does not support Mâyâvâdins (Advaitins) is made abundantly clear in AS 153. With these observations the First Adhyâya stands concluded and the link between the First and Second Adhyâya established.

11. Sri Bhâshyam Second Adhyâya: *avirodhâdhyâyah*

The second adhyâya of BS offers defensive reasoning and further affirms the conclusion arrived at in the first Samanvaya Adhyâya. Hence the second one is appropriately named as Avirodha Adhyâya meaning that all the contradictions that could be raised against the position are thoroughly discussed and eliminated and the Brahman of the Upanishads is established on a firm footing. The first pâda (*smrti pâda*) raises a series of objections to the thesis that Brahman is the cause of the world-process and answers them in progressive depths. Some of the finest arguments are contained in this pâda. The second pâda (*tarka pâda*) undertakes to examine the philosophical alternatives to the position advanced and concludes that they are untenable in the extreme, thus reinforcing the thesis of the *Samanvaya Adhyâya*. The third *pâda* (*viyat pâda*) and the fourth (*prâna pâda*) engage themselves in determining the exact mode of Brahman's causality in relation to the varied factors that constitutes the realm of effects, such as the elements, space, air, fire, water and earth and the 11 senses inclusive of mind, the life principle designated prâna and the individual self or Jîva. The causal process gets highlighted in its subtle details by this explication. In the third pâda especially there is a revealing elucidation of the uncreated nature of the finite self and the sense in which it is an effect. In this context, the nature of the finite self (Âtma) is revealed and its relation to the Supreme Spirit (Paramâtma) in the status of a part (amsha) is given. Thus, the second adhyâya fulfils the role of justification, defensive elaboration and the demonstration of philosophical inconsistencies of other philosophical systems. The first and second adhyâyas jointly serve to present the metaphysical thesis of the BS.

The second adhyâya addresses the quession, "Where is the need for the second adhyâya?" Persons with weak intellect (*mrdu dhiyâm*) are likely to get unsettled with opposing faiths. The bamboo posts which hold the pandal have to be well shaken and tested for their firmness (*sthûnâkhâtakramena*). Hence an exercise is undertaken here to subject other philosophical systems to rigorous scrutiny and by contrast prove that the philosophy of the Upanishads is unassailable (AS 154). The contents of the first two pâdas and the later two pâdas are explained in AS 155. The link between the last pâda (BS I.4) of the previous adhyâya and the first pâda of the current adhyâya (BS II.1) is outlined in AS 156. The pressing need for second adhyâya is underscored in AS 157.

Chapter Five of Ref 75: SMS begins the chapter highlighting the link between BS 1.4 and BS 2.1: "The *prakrt-adhikaraNa* to which we have referred earlier mainly deals with the subject'. Several objections are raised against this theory by the Sankhyans. These are dealt with in the adhikaraNas of the First Pâda of Second Adhyâya. The first pâda (BS II.1) consists of two petikas. The first two adhikaraNas form the first petika dealing with the objections raised by the smrtis. In the other petika (consisting of 8 adhikaraNas) objections raised by tarka are countered (AS158).

5. Smrti pâda, (BS II.1) SB p 439- 504 (sixty six pages)
The ten adhikaraNas of this pâda (36 to 45) are as under:

स्मृति। योगप्रयुक्ति। विलक्षणत्व। शिष्टापरिग्रह।

345

भोक्त्रापत्ति। आरम्भण। इतरव्यपदेश। उपसंहार।

कृत्स्नप्रसक्ति। प्रयोजनवत्व॥

BS II.1.(1) *smrtyadhikaraNam*, SB p439-44 (six pages); AS 159. From the stronghold of vedanta doctrine of Brahman being the cause of the world, the smrti of Kapila will have no scope. There are other more authoritative smrtis such as Manusmrti and these would be rendered unauthoritative if we depend upon Kapila-smrti for ascertaining the meaning of the upanishadic texts. Elucidation can occur only when the smrti in question clarifies (*upa-brahmanam*) the shruti. Kapila whose teachings are opposed to the scripture have to be discarded. Just because Kapila was a born sage as eulogised in Shveta. Up (V.2) can we accept his system as authoritative? The reply given is rhetorical: can we accept the teachings of Brihaspati who is spoken of in all scriptures? He is also discorded because he preached materialism. Ramanuja shows that Manu's view on creation are of a piece with that of VP & BG.

BS II.1.(2) *yogaprayuktyadhikaraNam*, SB p444 (one page); AS 160. This Yoga smrti founded by Hiranyagarbha is also discarded as unauthoritative just as Kapila smrti.

BS II.1.(3) *vilakshanatvâdhikaranam*, SB p 445-62 (eighteen pages); AS 161, 2. The Sankhyans oppose the claim that Brahman cannot be the cause of the universe since the two, causal Brahman and the universe as its effect (*kârya*) are not of the same nature. Badarayana opposes: the two need not be of the same nature. For example, there is a causal relationship between cow dung and the scorpion but we do not notice any common feature between the two. "As explained earlier, Brahman does not transform itself into the universe in which case its nature would be affected. But on the contrary, the achit or the cosmic matter which constitutes the sharira of Brahman undergoes modification. The change in the cosmic matter does not affect Brahman which is *âdhâra*, in the same way as the changes taking place in the body of a person do not affect the self within." This is Shârîraka Shâstra which was explained in Grand Edifice.

BS II.1.(4) *shishtâparigrahâdhikaranam*, SB p 462 (half a paragraph); AS 163. Sankhyan System has been rejected from the following considerations- it does not stand to reasoning, it keeps changing its stand i.e., unstable and that it is opposed to the views of vedanta. Similarly all other religions such as Buddhism, Jainism etc. which solely rely on arguments and which are opposed to vedanta, cannot be countenanced and are therefore deemed, mutadis mutandis, as refuted. Mere arguments alone, cannot establish a religion. It should be based on a time honoured supporting document like Vedânta.

BS II.1.(5) *bhoktrâpatyadhikaraNam*, SB p462-4 (two pages); AS 164. Sankhyans raise the objection that if the universe of sentients and non-sentients form the body of Brahman would it not experience sufferings (*duhkha*) even as the jîva experiences pleasures and pains? This objection is refuted on the basis of a plethora of Upanishads which talk about the polar contrast that exist between the jîva and Brahman. Pleasure and pain is caused by one's karma. Consider the example of a ruler and the ruled. Those who comply with the command of the ruler enjoy whereas those who disobey are punished. Brahman the Ruler is not bound by karma.

BS II.1.(6) *ârambhanâdhikaranam*, SB p465-90 (twenty six pages); AS 165-7. The Vaiseshikas maintain that cause and effect are absolutely different and as such Brahman cannot be regarded as material and instrumental cause of the universe? This view is refuted and the causal relationship is explained interms of non-difference (*ananyatva*). The discussion can be compared to the conservation laws of physics. We may illustrate the relation between cause and effect through a simple example. A palm-leaf and an ear-ring made out of it. When the leaf is flat it is called a scroll but when rolled it is called 'ear-ring'. For a detailed treatment on the subject the reader should refer to chapter X: 'Cosmology' of PNS's book.

BS II.1.(7) *itaravyapadeshâdhikarana*, SB p491-5 (five pages); AS 168. If Brahman is stated to be non-different from jîva, then it would follow that a Brahman with full of defects, creates a universe not beneficial to it?

This objection is countered by the fact that Brahman and jîva are absolutely different - *"adhikam tu bheda nirdeshât"*. Ramanuja does not agree that Brahman and jîva are essentially one (*svarupa- aikhya*) but are regarded as non-distinct (*ananya*) in the sense that Brahman abides in jîva as *antaryâmin*. Brahman and jîva are inseparably connected hence the two are one but by virtue of *svarupa* the two are absolutely different. Hence the defects found in the universe do not affect Brahman, even though it is the creator of the universe. The tongue tastes many kinds of foods but none stick to it. In this way the Brahman is like the tongue.

BS II.1.(8) *upasamhârâdhikarana*, SB p495,6 (two pages); AS 169. Admitting that Brahman functions in the capacity of material as well as instrumental cause, but still it does not have the accessories for the creation of the variegated world. This objection is countered by examples: what accessory does a spider use to construct its own web? Milk turns into curd by itself. Brahman creates this world out of His sankalpa.

BS II.1.(9) *krtsnaprasaktyadhikaraNa*, SB p497-502 (six pages); AS 170,1. If Brahman itself becomes the universe then a question arises whether Brahman as a whole is transformed into the universe or only a part of it is transformed?

Answers to these type of questions must be gathered from the Upanishads. Brahman cannot be seperated into its constituent parts.

348

Brahman alone existed prior to creation- *âtmâ vâ idameka evâgra âsît.* The creation is the manifestation of the subtle into the gross. Brahman did not have any organs- *nir-avayava.* (Shveta VI.8). Though the Brahman has no sensory organs He can still see, hear etc. and go without a pair of feet and grab things without hands (ibid III.9). Just as the fire has the property to burn and water remains cool and so on, even so Brahman has the power to Create a universe. Parashara Maharishi gives a glimpse of Brahman in the third chapter of the first amsha (VP 1.3.2). Ramanuja fills in details as he steers clear objections. They all go up in the construction of the Grand Edifice.

BS II.1.(10) *na prayojanatvâdhikaranam,* SB p502-4; AS 172-4. Is there any purpose in creating this universe? It cannot be for the benefit of Brahman since He, left to Himself, does not have any desire which are yet to be fulfilled (*avâptasamastakâmah*). Neither it is for the benefit of others since no body would prefer to be in a suffering-laden world. Then it follows that Brahman, as the cause of creation of this world, is not maintainable?

This objection is not well founded. Creation is indulged as a mere sport. It can be explained with the analogy of a king. Though the king has no specific objective to achieve he indulges in sports like gambling etc. purely for self entertainment. This point is elucidated in PNS's chapter on 'Cosmology' (page 269): "The Sutrakara takes his stand on Vedic authority and denies the sceptic view that there is caprice and cruelty in the divine nature. He admits inequalities of life but traces them to karma. Refer VP1.4.51, 52."

It is worth noting Swamy's brilliant observations made in the verses corresponding to the beginning and end of BS II.1 In AS 159, that is at the commencement of the pâda, there is reference to Sage Kapila who is an amsha of Vasudeva, and whose awesome feat as described in Valmiki Ramayana, gets mentioned. And in AS 173 (at

349

the close of the pâda), mention is made of *asamanja* known for his gruesome murder of children of Ayodhya who were thrown into the flood waters of the river Sarayu. Citing of these incidences clearly shows that the Swamy has Ramayana in mind. To say that God is not merciful would be unfair in the extreme. Did not the heartless Kaikeyi compare Rama, known popularly as Karuna Kakutsa to Asamanja? For us the Lord Almighty is All Merciful- Lord Srinivasa is *Daya Svarûpi*!

All the ten adhikaraNas of BS II.1 are summarized in AS 175.

6. Tarka pâda, BS II.2, SB p505-561(fifty seven pages)

The need for this pâda will be found forcefully expressed by Sri R. Keshava Aiyangar in his book, Shatadûshani: "Vedânta Deshika with a view to explain the necessity for, and the propriety and utility of, Tarka pâda has in his AS, first raised the objection by way of *pûrvapaksha* (prima facie view) to the relevancy and propriety of Tarka pâda. The objection is to the following effect: The validity of Brahmic causality having in the preceding chapter and quarter been declared established on the strength of unshakable Veda in harmony with other pramanas, why should Badarayana who is detached and free from ill-will to anybody disparage others once again? To put it in other words: let Badarayana by all means affirm the validity of Brahmic causality rooted as it is on the rock of Veda. But why should he, instead of stopping there, go further and refute the systems of others who affirm the contrary? Vedânta Deshika answers the objection thus: Badarayana is not out to disparage anybody. He is too noble and dispassionate to do it. What he really does is to clear the doubts that might be created in uncritical and immature minds on account of the impact of many systems of celebrity and antiquity which propound the contrary view with equal confidence. On account of the conflict of such renowned systems, each with others and all with Vedânta, it might be regarded by immature minds that they may all be of equal validity with Vedânta.

350

It is that many-sided dubitancy that had to be removed. A demonstration of the invalidity of the counter systems and the consequent removal of the doubt engendered by their impact could be effected only in a pâda devoted to rational disputation (*tarka*). Doubt should be removed so that the faith in the teachings of vedanta might not be shaken and the summum bonum of vedantic life might not be lost to them. The process is essentially protective. Badarayana's purpose is therefore not to decry anti-vedantins but to save doubting and immature minds from being decoyed by the alluring fallacies of the various counter systems, which according to him do not explain truth, do not answer the purpose of truth and are opposed to truth. Hence the necessity for the common platform of rational disputation in which alone the validity of rival systems could be tested and the invulnerability of Brahmic causality could be conclusively demonstrated and maintained. Disparagement is no part of vâda and in truth is repugnant to it. Knowledge should not be left in a dubious state. All doubts must be cleared by the generation of correct knowledge of truth. Doubt is one impediment to fulfilment. The doubting man effects his own frustration- is the Lord's declaration in Gita."

The eight adhikaraNas of BS II.2 are as follows:-

रचनानुपपत्ति। महद्दीर्घ। समुदाय।

उपलब्धि। सर्वथानुपपत्ति। असम्भव।

पशुपति। उत्पत्यसम्भव॥

BS II.2.(1) *rachânanupapatyadhikaraNam*, SB p505- 520 (sixteen pages); AS 176-82. Prakrti cannot be the cause of the universe because of the untenability (*anupapatti*) of cosmic creation without an intelligent being guiding the process of creation. The examples given by Sankhya are unacceptable to a vedantin. Ramanuja explains the Sankhyan view before rejecting it. The concept of adhyasa employed by Sankhya (to explain mukti) is severely criticised.The

351

subject matter discussed in the remaining seven adhikaraNas may be briefly mentioned.

In the second adhikaraNa Vaiseshika's contend that though the existence of Ishvara is acceptable to them, they are of the view that *paramanus* or atoms constitute the creation of the universe. Since they are unable to explain how two atoms combine, their atomic theory stands rejected.

Three adhikaraNas, 3,4 &5 deal with the four schools of Buddhism. The Vaibhasika and Sauntrantika schools trace the origin of the universe to the *paramanus* which is regarded as momentary (*kshanika*) in nature (*samudayadhikaraNa*). This theory is rejected on the ground that cognition would become impossible if buddhi itself is unstable and transitory.

The fourth is *upalabdhyadhikaraNa* dealing with Yogachara Buddhism which denies even the existence of external world of objects. The criticism of this theory is directed towards two impossibilities. It is not possible to deny the existence of external objects because our experience shows that knowledge is always related to a subject and an object. (*na abhâva upalabdheh*). Secondly, external objects experienced when we are awake are not similar to the experience as in the state of dream. See TMK 4.27.

The fifth, *sarvathânupapatyadhikaraNa*, deals with Madhyamika theory of Buddhism. In their view everything in the universe is indeterminable (*sarva-shunya*). Since this is purely a speculative theory, it is totally untenable as it is lacking textual basis and therefore unacceptable. It is as indeterminable as sky flower (*gagana kusuma*- AS 199).

The sixth-*ekasminasambhavâdhikarana*- refutes Jainas. The main argument concerns with the logical untenability of sapta-bhangi of

Jainism. The seven types of 'may be' (*'syâ*) is explained on page 166 of Ref 78 (AS 202-4 & TMK 3.28).

The seventh adhikaraNa is directed towards the refutation of Pâshupata. According to Ramanuja this religion is riddled with inconsistencies. Their code of conduct is suspect as they don't stand scrutiny when viewed in the light of Vedânta (AS 205-9).

The eighth adhikaraNa forms a petika by itself and it concerns with a stray statement found in Pancharatra Agama- viz. the origin (*utpatti*) of jîva. It suited Shankara, a staunch sublationist, to apply the Occam's razor to axe Pancharatra completely and dump it on the flimsy ground that origin of jîva cannot be accepted. It was the most unkindest cut of all! Badarayana contends that *utpatti* has nothing to do with the origination of jîva. The merits of Pancharatra are highlighted in eighteen verses AS 210-17. PNS has devoted several pages (vide index) in highlighting the greatness of Pancharatra.

While concluding the second pâda of second adhyâya of BS, Ramanuja highlights the greatness of Pancharatra Agama Shâstra consisting of one and half a crore of shlokas spread over 210 samhitas. PNS covers this in page 246 of his book "The Philosophy of Vishishtâdvaita."

"In summing up and estimating the philosophy of the *Shârîraka Sûtras* in the first two chapters relating to ontology and cosmology, Ramanuja reveals his synthetic insight into the soul of Vedântic thought by his attitude to the other systems of Vedic and *âstika* philosophy and the method of interpreting their inner connection. In solving the problem raised in Mahabharata composed by the same Rishi Veda Vyasa, the question whether the Sankhya, the Yoga. the Veda, the Pashupata and the Pancharatra systems have a common philosophic foundation, Ramanuja adopts the *samanvaya* method by his acceptance of the essentials only (*svarûpa mâtra*) of these schools in so far as they do not contradict the central truth of the *Shârîraka Shâstra*. While Sânkhyan cosmology of the twenty-five categories has its meaning in the basic idea that the twenty-five *tattvas* have Brahman the twenty sixth Tattva or Truth as their source or sustaining self, the scheme of Yoga discipline has its end in the meditation on Brahman. The Vedic insistence on the performance of karma has its consummation in the Vedântic view of regarding work as the worship of the Supreme Self (*ârâdhana*). It also recognizes Pashupata variety in so far as it accepts the immanence of the *Antaryâmin* and its ethics (the religion of Pashupata is rejected by Vishishtâdvaita since that religion recommends unsound rituals and practices which run counter to the teachings of Veda). Refer to Tamil verses 91 and 99 of the Hundred on Ramanuja. The Pancharatra as revealed by the Lord Sriman Narayana Himself contains the essentials of all the afore mentioned acceptable systems and is their very soul (Sri Bhâshya 2.2.8 and Agamaprâmânya, a work of Alavandar).

एतदेव परेण ब्रह्मणा नारायणेन स्वयमेव

पञ्चरात्रतन्त्रे विशदीकृतम् ॥

Thus, the *Shârîraka Shâstra* as a synthetic view of Vedânta accepts whatever is true, good and beautiful in other systems owing to its criterion of comprehensiveness which means that what is true works as opposed to the pragmatic view that what works is true. It is also to be distinguished from eclecticism which pieces together what is good in all systems without proving their vital relations. The truth of Brahman as the *sharîrin* of all beings is clearly intuited by the Azhwars and summed up in the Tamil Veda (*udalmisai uyir*- TM 1.1.7).

Ramanuja thus shows that the foundational truth of Brahman as *sharîrin* furnishes the key to the understanding of all philosophic systems. In the highest sense of the term, the Sri Bhâshya concludes with the Shârîraka Mimamsa's very significant note *Sarvam Samanjasam* (everything is satisfactorily explained). This includes philosophical satisfactoriness as well as spiritual satisfying-ness which is traceable to the infinite suggestiveness of the synthetic insight afforded by the *sharîra-sharîri-bhâva* called the differentia and raison d'être of Ramanuja's Darshana" (page 247).

It merits to mention two companion volumes written by the 40th Pontiff of Ahobila Mutt: "Sri Bhashyartha Manipravala Dipika" and the 44th Pontiff's "Sûtrârtha Padya Mâlika" Both these works are rendered into easy tamil by Dr. S.V.Narasimhachari and published in 1989. The reader may refer to pages of the above books wherein Swamy's verse occuring in TMK 2.75 is quoted and explained. This verse sums up succinctly the concept of mukti in the various systems such as Pashupata, Advaita etc. In the same context Dr. S.V.N also quotes and explains the verse AS 219, the summing up verse of pâda BS II.2.

7. Viyat pâda, BS II.3, SB p 562-598 (thirty seven pages)
Pâda sangati AS 220; Adhikarana sangati AS 221.This pâda has seven adhikaraNas (54 to 60).

वियत्। तेजः। आत्मा। ज्ञा।

कर्ता। परायत्त। अंश॥

BS II.3.(1) viyadadhikaraNa, SB p562-567 (seven pages); AS 222,3. In the previous pâda jîva-*utpatti* was refuted on the ground that the word '*utpatti*' was not used in the sense of origination but as a formal expletive (*aupacharikam*). Now the question is whether origination of *viyat* also follows suit? Passages from Chand. (6.2.3), Taitt (*âkâshah sambhutah*), Mund. (*jayate prânah*) are examined. *Avyakta* refers to evolution of matter such as *mahat, ahankara, tanmâtras* and the senses. All these are modifications and the *tanmâtras* are the stages immediately preceding the evolution of the great elements- ether, air, fire, water and earth (the order and stage of creation is clarified in the next pâda). Put simply matter is in a state of continuous flux. Gitacharta has called it *anitya* (BG 9.33).

BS II.3.(2) tejodhikaranam, SB p567-73 (six pages) AS 224.
Is the evolution of matter from one form to the next takes place by itself? It is not so. For example *'tejo aeikshata'* which means *'tejas* willed'. The question of willing cannot be that of inert tejas. And similarly *'vayu aeikshata'* etc. In all these statements of the Upanishads it is implied that a sentient principle Brahman is the Antaryamin of Tejas and the Super Intelligent Scientist creates this universe by His mere will or sankalpa.

BS II.3.(3) *atmâdhikarana*, SB p573-6 (three pages) AS 225-8.
Is âtma also a product of the evolutes? Has the Brahman created the âtma at the beginning of creation? The answer for both these questions is an emphatic no. The âtma is nitya since it existed prior to creation as declared in the scriptures- *ajo nityah* (Katha), *nityo nityanam chetanah chetananam eko bahunam vidhadhati kaman.* And so on.

BS II.3.(4) *jnâdhikaranam*, SB p576-84 (eight pages) AS 229-32.
The innert matter does not possess knowledge where as Atma is all knowledge, 'Jnâna svarupa' or 'viJnâna svarupa'. Due to its association with antahkarana or internal organ, it is regarded as *jnâta* or knower.

BS II.3.(5) *kartradhikaraNam*, SB p 584-588 (four pages) AS 233-5.
Here it is discussed whether or not jîva is a karta or the agent of action. The Katha tells that the self is not the killer and Gita also ascribes the act of agency (kartrtva) to the three guNas of prakrti

356

(BG 3.27). So it appears that the jivâtma is not the karta. Badarayana sets aside these views and affirms jîva is the karta. Swamy points out that the admission of jnatrtva, kartrtva, bhoktrtva for the self (âtma) does not affect its immutable character. By being the substratum of jnâna which is subject to modification, the svarupa of the jîva does not undergo a change. Take the computer architecture. It remains unaffected not withstanding whatever that is taking place in the domain of the memory.

BS II.3.(6) *parayattadhikaraNa*, SB p589-90 (two pages) AS 236-243. This adhikaraNa deals with the dependence of jivâtman on Paramâtman and the matters related to free will. The doubt arises because of the fact if jîva is not free to act (*svatantra*) and is dependent on the paramâtman, it cannot be regarded as a karta. In the absence of freedom, scriptural injunctions commanding to do good deeds and not to do what is prohibited would not be of any use.

PNS sorts out the issue brilliantly in the chapter on "The Psychology of the Jîva" (p291). "If activity were determined by the divine will, the self would only be an automation or a conduit pipe of the cosmic purpose which would then appear capricious and cruel and freedom of the will would be an illusory fiction... Freedom is a skill or capacity as well as an activity and the jîva has moral freedom even if it does not exercise it actively just as a carpenter is a workman whether he uses his tools or not (BS II.3.39). 'Ought' implies 'can' and the moral self can attain self-sovereignty or svarajya by subduing his animal inclinations consisting of instincts like 'self assertion, anger, jealousy, and fear and choosing the ways of the mumukshu including bhakti (devotion) and prapatti (self surrender) or sink into animality by choosing the way of sensuality and becoming its slave." It would also be appropriate to mention here that Ramanuja employs the same logical reasoning as in his Vedârtha Sangraha 123, 4 & 5.4.

357

BS II.3.(7) *amshâdhikarana*, SB p591-8 (eight pages) AS 244-52.
Is jîva different from Brahman or is it non-different from Brahman?
Several Upanishads talk about the simultaneous existence of two
entities. Though this issue was broached in ArambanadhikaraNa,
the issue is taken up once again to remove the doubts stemming
from conflicting views advanced by different schools of vedanta
(*bahu kumati mata kshiptaye*-AS 244). The following authors have
explained brilliantly in their respective works.

SMS: "According to Ramanuja, amsha is an essential attribute of a
qualified substance. The essential attribute which is inseperably
connected to the substance is an *amsha* of that substance. Such a
relationship between the two is known as *amsha-amshi bhâva* or
visheshana-visheshya bhâva. In the ontological sense it is called as
sharira-shariri bhava or the relation between the body to the soul. In
the same way jîva is related to Brahman as *amsha* to *amshi* (Brahman).
This explains both difference (*nânâ vyapadesha*) and non-difference
(*anyathâ cha*) between jîva and Brahman."

PNS: "The term *sharîrin* as applied to the âtman should satisfy the
three conditions of modality, dependence and serviceability. Firstly
as a mode it derives its being from Brahman as the very life of its
life (*svarûpâshrita*) and is sustained by its immanence (*âtmaika-
prakâratva*). Secondly it is controlled by its will (*sankalpâshrita*) and
absolutely depends on it (*âtmaikâshrayatva*). Finally the self subsists
as a means to the realization of the divine purpose
(*âtmaikaprayojanatva*). Thus the jîva derives its substantiality from the
Brahman as the *adhara*, depends on His redemptive will as the *niyantr*
and exists as a means to the satisfaction of the *sheshin*. Brahman as
the source, sustenance and satisfaction of the finite self is called its
sharîrin. Every term connoting the sharira connotes the sharirin and
the jîva connotes also Brahman, its sharirin. There is a plurality of
jîvas each having its own distinct character, although all jîvas are

358

alike in so far as they have intelligence for their essential nature" (BS II.3.48).

|| असंततेश्चाव्यतिकरः ||

KCV: "The finite existences have undoubtedly a reality of their own, not as pure parts amshas in the materialistic and fragmentory sense, but in the sense of being related as bodies of the Supreme. This conception entails the view of direct relationship with the Supreme Person. It means that the world consists of souls which are individually bodies of the Supreme, in the sense they are sustained, supported, governed and led to the fullest experience of Himself through Himself...The individual farms an integral significant amsha, portion of the Divine. The truest definition of an amsha is the definition which keeps the soul neither aloof nor isolated but keeps it inseparably and inalienably integrated with the whole, without making it lose its individual character and emotion. The character of the part might undergo modification in so far as it becomes conscious of its dependence on the central self of its existence, and almost wear even a diaphanous coat or body which makes one see it as if it is indistinguishable from the whole. It may even perceive its own unity to be firm and thorough, so that it cannot see itself as existent apart from it. But the germs of its particularity and amshatva remain" (vide 'Brahman The Highest Unity'-vol six, Complete Works of Dr.K.C.Varadachari).

8. *Prâna pâda*, BS II.4, SB p 599-618 (twenty pages)
In the previous *viyat pâda* it was categorically stated that transformation in the effected state takes place only for prakrti and its evolutes while no transformation for the jivâtma. Besides the svarupa of jivâtma was determined from the texts of the Upanishads. In this pâda the accessories of âtma, as taught in the Upanishads are enquired into. Among the eight adhikaraNas in this

pâda, the first and the last are directly linked while the intervening six are coincidental (AS 253,4).

The eight adhikaraNas (61-8):

प्राणोत्पत्ति। सप्तगति। प्राणाणुत्व।

वायुक्रिया। श्रेष्ठाणुत्व। ज्योतिराद्यधिष्ठान।

इन्द्रिय। संज्ञामूर्तिक्लृप्ति॥

BS II.4.(1) *pranotpatyadhikaraNam*, SB p599-601 (three pages) AS 255. A passage occurs in Satapata Brahmana: "Before creation this was asat. Then they asked, "what existed then?" "Before creation rishis existed." They asked, "Who are meant by rishis?" "Pranas were the rishis." With the mention of prâNa the scenario that was emerging at the epoch of creation is brought into purview for appraisal. Before evolution commenced there was no differenciation, and there was no object with a form and a name. Speech and other senses did not exist then, as they had no function to perform. The word prâNa should denote the only thing that existed, viz., Brahman.

BS II.4.(2) *saptagatyadhikaraNam*, SB p602-4 (three pages); AS 256,7. Mund.(2.1.8): "*sapta prânâh... sapta saptâ*" Are the *indriyas* only seven? Sensory organs and motor organs- all are jîva's instruments. When a higher number is stated in the upanishad we should take it to include different functions of the mind and when a lower number is stated, only the particular functions are contemplated. For example, Brhad (3.9.4) gives the number 11 to include five jnânendrias and five karmendrias and the mind. See also VP (1.2.47), Gita (BG 13.5).

BS II.4.(3) *prânânutvâdhikaranam*, SB p605-606 (one page) AS 258. Two sections of Brhada. (1.5.13 & 4.4.2) seem to blow hot and cold. But it is not. The first is for purposes of meditation and the later refers to exit of prâNa out of the body. Since no one can see the exit of prâNa, it must be very subtle, the size of an atom.

BS II.4.(4) *vâyukriyâdhikarana*, SB p606-8 (three pages); AS 259. Can prâNa be equated to the second element vayu of the pancha bhutas? It is contended that it is not like the air which has free movement. Prana is a functional element as a life support system for the jîva. When Prana-vayu takes the functional role (*kriya*) it assumes different names such as prâNa, apana, samana, vyana and udana, the five collectively known as marut panchakam. We should bear in mind that prâNa is distinct frm the eleven indriyas mentioned in the second adhikaraNa of this pâda.

BS II.4.(5) *shreshtânutvâdhikarana*, SB p608 (half a page) AS 260.Prana is of atomic size since prâNa exits along with âtma when the jîva breathes its last. Prashnopanishad (2.6): "*ara...prane sarve pratishtitam.*"

BS II.4.(6) *jyotiradyadhishtânâdhikarana*, SB p609-10 (two pages) AS 261.So far the discussion centered around matters- such as the generation (*utpatti*) of sensory organs, prâNa, the size and number of sensory organs, the distinct characteristics of prâNa and its size. The enjoyership of jîva through its instruments (*bhogopakarana*) as typified in Brhad (2.1.18): "Just like a great emperor moves about as he likes in his own domain, so also a dreaming person at that time takes his sense organs and moves about as he pleases in his own body." The thing to be known is whether all this is self effort (*svayattam*) or it is that of *Paramayattam?*

The function of the indriyas and prâNa is controlled by jîva but the power is endowed to jîva by Paramâtman. Similarly the devas like Agni who are the presiding deities of the sense organs including mind are controlled by Brahman as the Inner Ruler of all bodies as stated in Antaryami Brahmanam.

361

BS II.4.(7) IndriyadhikaraNam, SB p611 (one page) AS 262. The term prâNa denotes the senses and the prâNa. BG 13.5 states indriyas are ten and in BG 15.7 indriyas with the mind as the sixth. In deep sleep prâNa continues to work while the sensory organs are at rest. Prana supports the body and the senses. Because of this fact, the senses are denoted by the term prâNa. In support of the pre-eminence of prâNa the hymn of Brhadaranyaka (1.5.21) is quoted- *"ta etasyaiva...prânâ iti"*

BS II.4.(8) *samjnâmûrtiklrptyadhikaraNam*, SB p612-8 (seven pages); AS 263-8. From the beginning of viyat pâda (BS II.3) to the end of the last adhikaraNa, BS II.4.(7) the teachings belonged to the domain of *samashti srshti* and hence they form one set or petika. This eighth adhikaraNa alone is concerned with *vyashti srshti* and it forms a petika by itself. Evolution of elements constituting jîva's instruments evolved from Brahman. Does the authorship of making names and forms belong to Chatur Mukha Brahma or Para Brahmam? There are three sutras in this adhikaraNa. The first sutra attributes the making of names and forms to Him who is also the author of the emergence of life supporting evolutes (BS II.4.17). It was stated that Agni is the ruling deity of indriyas. Please refer to Chandogyopanishad sixth chapter. "The Para Brahmam made each one of the three elements three fold and three fold. The three, *tejas, ap* and *anna* were mixed up. From each one of these three deities were made" (Chand. 6.3.4). A colour is assigned for each of these elements. Red for *agni*, white for water and black for *anna*. This is known as *trivrtkaranam* or tri-partition. Mixing of these colours is similar to cromo-modulation employed in TV technology.

The next sutra BS II .4.18 refers to the continuation of teachings in the very same upanishad (6.5 ibid). The food, water and tejas- each of these give rise to three sets of products: faeces,flesh and mind from food; urine, blood and vital air from water; and bone, marrow

362

and speech from tejas. An objection is raised: it would be more appropriate to assign the solid stuff like bone to earth rather than tejas? This objection is replied in the next sutra.

BS II.4.19 *vaisheshhyâttu tadvâdastadvâdah* . This denotation is due to the predominance of an element in each compound. The tri-partition also implies quintuplication. Each of the 5 elements- earth, water, fire, air, and ether- is divided into two parts and one half of each is combined with one eighth of the remaining elements. It is only by such quintuplication that things with specific names and forms are created. It is quite rational when we consider the different combinations of carbon, hydrogen and oxygen producing millions of products of Organic Chemistry. To give an example, water is associated with the property of the land. We call it mineral water. So, earth element is present in water. Humid air has water content in it and so on.

Swamy says in TMK (*"dvedhâ bhûtânî"*-I.17) that *trivrtkarana* is not different from *Panchîkarana*.

Prâna pâda (BS II.4) is summed in AS 266. In the Second Adhyâya, pâdas 3 & 4 attack the opponents view (AS 267) while Mrshâ vadins are out maneuvered in AS 268.

12. Sri Bhâshyam Third Adhyâya: *sâdhanâdhyâyah*

The third and fourth adhyâyas move on to a different type of consideration. They relate to the plane of realization as contrasted to the theme of reality which has been dealt with in the first pair of adhyâyas. Thus, the four adhyâyas can also be divided into *dvikas* (couples or pairs). The first two adhyâyas forming the first *dvika* is termed *as Siddha Dvika*. The *adhyâyas* 3 and 4 forming the second pair is known as *Sâdhya Dvika*. *Siddha Dvika* deals with Brahman as the cause of the world and *Sâdhya Dvika* deals with means for liberation and nature of liberation. As mentioned earlier, the etymology of Brahman expresses the two-fold excellence of Brahman viz. *brhatva* (glory of exaltedness) and *brahmanatvah* (exalting glory). The former pertains to causation and the latter to liberation. In the former sense, Brahman is the abode of auspicious qualities- *kalyânaika tânatva* and the latter as the destroyer of sin and grief- *heyapratyanikatva* in transcendental infinity. They constitute the two-fold characteristics of Brahman as explained in the *Ubhayalinga-adhikaraNa* (this central principle of Brahman occupies almost the central position, the 79th adhikaraNa of the total 156). The first two adhyâyas expound the *brhatva* and the last two expound the *brahmanatva* of Brahman.

A verse in Harita Samhita recaptures the five important elements (Artha Panchakam) that one should know seeking release from bondage, *samsâra*. They are: the nature of Brahman (the target to be attained), the nature of the individual-self seeking attainment, knowledge about the means, knowledge about the fruit and the hindrances to the attainment of Brahman.

प्राप्यस्य ब्रह्मणो रूपं प्राप्तुश्च प्रत्यगात्मनः।

प्राप्त्युपाय फलं चैव तथा प्राप्ति विरोधि च।

वदन्ति सकला वेदाः सेतिहास पुरणकाः॥

Compare the above verse with Vishnu PurâNa 6.7.93 quoted earlier. Swami establishes, in Adhikara Sangraha, that Shri plays a vital role in each aspect of Artha-Panchaka.

The third adhyâya devoted to the account of the path way in the realization of the Divine, analyses the various states of human experience inclusive of transmigration and rebirth and points to the transcendent glory of Brahman, culminating in the formulation of the human endeavor, Sâdhana, for the attainment of the supreme goal of life in Brahman. The first two pâdas of third adhyâya (*vairâgya* pâda and *Ubhayalinga pâda*) bring out the fact of human bondage, in all states of existence and consciousness, and the perfection and blessedness that lie in Brahman. The two sides of the treatment are devised to produce discontent about actual life and longing and aspiration towards the attainment of Brahman.

"A psychological insight into the imperfections of the karma-ridden jîva is essential to the practice of *vairâgya* or self renunciation as a preparation for Vedântic life and the Sutrakara therfore devotes a special section called the Vairagya Pâda to its study" (p306 of Ref 43).

The third pâda (*gunopasamhâra pâda*) covers the entire ground of the Upanishadic literature and distinguishes the several types of meditation and the special attributes of Brahman that should go into every meditation and special attributes that characterize the theme of varied meditations. In this long pâda, almost all the principal modes of contemplation enjoined in the major Upanishads are discussed with a view to find out their identities and differences in terms of the attributes of Brahman selected in them for devout attention. Much in the Upanishads that have been left out in the longer interpretative consideration of the Samanvaya Adhyâya is taken up here and decisive exegesis is offered. The last pâda (anga pâda) discusses the claims of jnâna and karma to be the means of perfection and concludes that the former is the final means, the ultimate sâdhana. Its accessories are finely analyzed and set down in proper perspective, indicating the relative order of significant and mutual inter-relation. In this connection, the role of karma as an accessory to jnâna is recognized in the spirit of the Gita. All the requisite details are filled in. The outcome of this entire pâda of the third adhyâya is that a full picture of the life of meditation on Brahman gets drawn up.

9. *Vairâgya pâda*, SB p619-641 (twenty-three pages)

The reality of Brahman and His Vibhutis were established (*Siddha vishaya nirûpanam*) in the previous two adhyâyas. Hence the title 'Siddha Dvika' is appended to the first pair of adhyâyas. What can be achieved by a sâdhaka will be established (*Sâdhya vishaya nirûpanam*) in the remaining third and fourth adhyâya-*Sâdhya Dvika*. If it is said that liberation is not brought about by self effort on the part of the individual then the existence of the Third Chapter would become purposeless. On the contrary if one's effort alone can secure it then it becomes perishable, not worth aspiring for. Then how can it be said that once liberation is attained there is no return from the most desirable state of Mukti. The reply is that it is not so: for, the enjoyment of Brahman did not exist in the bonded state, and the *ânanda* is brought about by the meditation on Brahman. In mukti the constraint that contracts knowledge is removed once and for all and there is no upper limit for the expansion of knowledge. It doesn't terminate at any point of time (AS 269).

SMS provides a recap of the First & Second Adhyâya and broaches the Third Adhyâya. (see Chapter Seven of Ref 75): "In the Third Adhyâya dealing with Sadhana or means of attainment of B, Badarayana discusses the theory of transmigration of the jîva and its condition in the states of waking, dream, deep sleep (*sushupti*) and swoon (*mûrcha*). Six adhikaraNas of Pâda 1 and four adhikaraNas of Pâda two- (BS III.1 & BS III.2) – cover these subjects. In the Fourth Adhyâya which deals mainly with the Supreme Goal to be attained by the jîva, he examines the status of the jîva in the state of moksha in the six adhikaraNas. We shall discuss all these matters in the present chapter. The nature of jîva in the state of mukti will be considered in the chapter on the Supreme Goal."

The four pâdas of BS III are divided into two pairs: Motivation for Brahma Vidyâ in the first pair of pâdas and details of different types of Brahma Vidyâ with accessories (angas) in the later two pâdas. In the first pâda a strong will on the part of the *sâdhaka* to dissociate from the materialistic world is brought to focus. In the second it is taught that the *sâdhaka* should develop a strong desire for *Parama Purusha*. The different approaches (*vidyas*) available for the fulfillment of the desire are delineated in the third pâda and in the fourth the accessories that go with the performance of a *vidyâ* are outlined (AS 270).

The six adhikaraNa(s) (69 to 74) of BS III.1 are:

तदन्तरप्रतिपत्ति ।कृतात्यया। अनिष्टादिकार्य।

तत्स्वाभाव्यापत्ति। नातिचिरा। अन्याधिष्ठित॥

BS III.1.(1) *tadantarapratipatyadhikaraNam*, SB p619-25 (seven pages); AS 272-4.

Even at the very beginning itself, the need for spiritualism was stressed. Why broach the same topic again in this pâda? One needs a greater determination to practice what was preached. In order to develop that kind of force of conviction, one should become fully aware of the causes for the sorrows that are associated unavoidably with the various phases of day to day life as in the wakeful state (*jâgrata*), as in dream (*svapnâvasta*), as in deep sleep (*shushhûpti*) and the oweful state of unconsciousness (*mûrchâ*) or coma.

The Upanishads do teach *vairâgya*. For example the teachings to Svtaketu does not confine to chapter six of Chandogya alone where his father taught him the principles of cosmology but in chapter five he gets lessons on *vairagya* not from his father but from somebody else. Since the matter concerns with how a jîva is conceived in the womb (known as *panchagni vidya*) neither the father was aware of this vidya nor he could have discussed this sensitive issue which concerns with the issue!

BS III.1.(2) *krtâtyayâdhikaranam*, SB p626-29 (three and half pages); AS 275-8. Gitâchârya has also said that stay in heaven lasts only so long as the credit of *punya* lasts and the jivâtma has to return to earth to experience the karma. Shrutis and smrtis declare that souls take rebirth in the different wombs according to the nature of deeds. (virtuous or sinful) Chand (5.10.7): "Those whose conduct has been good take birth in a virtuous family. Bad conduct would result in landing in the womb of a dog or a pig or a chandâLa."

BS III.1.(3) *anishtâdikâryâdhikaranam*, SB p629-34 (five and half pages) AS 279-80.

Like the Indian Penal Code which specifies particular punishment for a certain crime, here in vedanta a wide ranging discussion is conducted on sin/merit and the allotment of hell / heaven. The rise or fall takes place according to *punya* or *papa* (sutra 13). The arbiter

368

of justice is Lord Yama (sutra 14). All come under Yama's regime (VP 3.7.5&6). There are some who do not come under his regime (VP 3.7.14). Seven types of hell such as raurava etc., are intended as torture cells (like jail or prison, with simple/rigorous imprisonment) for the punishment of various types of sinners (*"api saptā"* sutra15). Yama's regime includes those hells (sutra 16). But those who perform meritorious deeds go to moon. Besides there are two paths for good souls- *Archiradi mârga* for those who have practiced *vidya* and *Dhûmâdi mârga* for those who have done meritorious *punya karma (vidya karmanoh iti tu prakrtatvât-* sutra 17). There is a doubt concerning the soul's ascent to and descent from the moon and the categories who get embodiment through fifth oblation.Chand 5.9.1: "Thus waters oblated in the fifth fire like this assume the name of purusha. That foetus enclosed in the membrane remains ten or nine months within until it is time to be born." Remember five questions that were put to Svetaketu for which he (and his father) drew a blank (Chand. 5.3. 2&3). The answers to those questions stand completed in 5.9.1 (ibid) "Of the five oblations viz., *shraddha, soma, vrishti, anna* and *rethas,* the subtle elements embracing the jivâtma called by the name waters, assume the name of Purusha. Here the fifth question stands answered."

In sutra 19, it is clarified that people with extraordinary merit, such as Draupati and Drshtadyumna, do not necessarily go through the fifth oblation. Draupati was born from the fire-altar of a sacrifice and Drshtadyumna from the fire itself.

What are the categories which go through the fifth oblation? The answer is in Chand (6.3.1): "Living beings have three origins: egg born like birds, snakes etc; womb born like humans, animals like cows, sheep etc; and sprouting from seeds such as creepers, plants, herbs and trees. Beings born from sweat and heat are included in the seed category. (sutra 21) According to Kaushitaki (1.12) even insects and worms undergo the phase of *panchamâhuti.*

369

BS III.1.(4) (5) these two adhikaraNas deal with minor issues relating to Chand 5.10. 5 and 6 respectively; AS 281, 2.

BS III.1.(6), *anyadhishtitâdhikaranam*, SB p637-41(five pages); AS 282-7. Chand (5.10.5&6) The jivâtma gets into the water-bearing clouds and reaches the earth through rains. He is born as paddy and other food grains." The word 'born' is an expletive. The harvested paddy is subjected to drying, husking, pouring of water, cleansing, cooking and eating and all these can affect paddy and not the jivâtma that is attached to it.

Ashuddhamiti chet na shahdât (BS III.1.25) This sutra, according to our purvâchâryas, is aimed at refuting the Sankhyans who want to catch the adherents of the vedantic faith on the wrong foot. The Sankhyans in particular claimed that observance of yagas such as Jyotistoma or Vajapeya results in cruelty to sacrificial pashu (four-legged animal) and this sin of cruelty gets attached to the individual who had performed the yaga either with some end in view or merely because it is prescribed as a daily mandatory/ compulsory ritual.

The rebuttal calls for a hair-splitting discussion which can be known from the book such as *"Yajnyasamrakshini"* written in Tamil, published in the year 1945. The following forward from A.V. Gopalâchârya explains the purpose of the book: "the very text of the Brahma Sutras make it quite clear that the Vedic view is that Agnihotram and Yagnas are compulsory rites; that the Vedântic *mumukshu* is also bound to perform them though with renunciation of fruits. This renunciation is the general rule in his case regarding all Nitya karma, *Shrouta* and *Smarta*. The Kapila Sankhya view that there is a small proportion of sin in the performance of Vedic sacrifice because *Pashu-himsa* and that yagas, though obligatory and substantially good and necessary and indispensable, are *ashuddha* in a way because the *himsa*, is refuted by Badarayana in the last

370

Adhikarana of BS III.1.in which it is emphatically denied that there is any *ashuddhi* at all and that the immolated *Pashu* is blessed with higher life. All the Bhâshya are agreed about this interpretation of BS. The Gita states clearly that the settled view of the Divine singer is "that *Yajnya(s)* must be performed and not omitted". The Bhâshya(s) of the Gita justify the killing of opponents in war as involving no sin on the analogy of *Pashu* sacrifice in compulsorily prescribed *Yajnyas*. Both are prescribed as Dharma and could not therefore be *Ashuddha*.

"The author (Agnihotram Sri Gopaladesikâchâryar) has canvassed all passages in the works of Ramanuja and his followers bearing on this matter. The book is a model of lucidity and thoroughness." Of interest for us, the verses of Swami Deshika AS 284, 285 and TMK 5.78 are explained by the author in the body of the text.

The Sutras BS III.1. 26 &27 traces the further stages of getting into the male through food and ejected as semen and lodged into the womb of the female.

The author of Sukhabodini (English), Srinivasaraghavachariar has included a separate annexure at the conclusion of BS III.1. He outlines the purpose of the 'annexe' as follows (page 53).

"The various sufferings the jîva has to experience in this wakeful state are being given in detail here so that a spirit of detachment for the wordly pleasures may arise in his mind. Though Bhashyakara, Ramanuja, has not described all of them, we are writing here what is declared in the Upanishads and other religious works." The subject matter is described under the following sub-headings elaborately in ten long pages: Jîvas return to the world- The entry of the individual soul in the body of the father- The Jîva in the digestive fire in the body of the father along with the food- The passing of

Jîva from marrow state to semen state- The way of work of the unwholesome lust. It is concluded with an "Important Note".

Manu's prescription for developing the spirit of detachment: How does a sin get committed and what are the consequences? Manusmrti (12.9) explains it thus: "There are three ways in which sins are being committed- by thought, word and deed. By uttering sinful words the man attains the state of an animal in future births. By sinful thoughts he attains the state of an outcaste. By sinful acts committed by the body he attains the state of plant life. There are five places in the house where cruel acts get perpetrated (Manu3.68): "When he burns a twig or a piece of wood, the insects in the fuel are burnt. Similarly, during grinding, sweeping with a broom stick, killing waterborn insects etc. House-holder's life is bedevilled with causing harm (*himsa*) and even torture and death to living species. Even in the course of the performance of obligatory rituals there is crulty which has been prohibited. AS 186 discusses this issue and states that if we accept the maxim of general rule with its exception then only it will be possible to perform the obligatory rites. The cruelty is not based on the desire of the person.

A number of verses in Manusmrti stresses the greatness of the sanyasa dharma: "The life-style of a mendicant does not permit doing any harm to any one. He does not cause an iota of fear to the dumb creatures living in the forest. Thus leading a sinless life he is freed from fear and death (6.40). For fear that he may step over an ant or an insect, he looks with watchful eyes on the ground while walking in the day-time and totally avoids movement in the night time (46 & 68 ibid). Again, Manu compares the body to the structure of a house: "with bones as pillars, sinews as cords and flesh as cement and mortar and skin as roof. Obnoxious smell fills the house what with sweat, urine and stools. The house gets dilapidated with oldage, illness and what not. You should find ways and means to get rid of- *bhutâvâsamimam tyajet.* 66,7. Tirumangai Azhwar has adapted the same simile (Peria Tirumozhi 1.6.9 *–ûnidai chuvar vaiththu* …). The vairâgya pâda is summed up in the verse AS 288.

10. *Ubhaya-linga* pâda, SB p642 to 672 (thirty-one pages). In this pâda the auspicious nature of Para Brahmam is discussed. The question is why again this topic which was discussed elaborately in the first and second adhyâya? (AS 289) The bull, *mrshâvadins*, are taken by the horns in AS 290,1. Pâda sangati in AS 292; the unacceptable view point in AS 293. The eight adhikaraNa(s) (75-82) of this pâda are as under:

सन्ध्या। तदभाव। कर्मानुस्मृति। मुग्ध।

उभयलिङ्ग ।अहिकुण्डल। पर।फल॥

BS III.2.(1), *sandhyâdhikaranam*, SB p642-7 (five and half pages) AS 294-8.

The Adhikarana concerns with Brhada (4.3.10). Paramâtman is the creator of objects in dreams and the dreamer experiences individual-specific dreams according to his karma. For an in-depth treatment of this adhikaraNa refer to Dr.K.C. Varadachari dissertation, "Dreams in the Philosophy of Ramanuja." This is how he commences the discussion: "We shall see in the following pages that Sri Ramanuja holds the view that dream state is a state intermediate, that it is the period of experiencing moral deserts, that the creations are by the Supreme Lord for the enjoyment of the individual soul as reward for such activities as are of minor importance, that it is that which leads to the deep sleep state. The prophetic quality of dreams such as are mentioned in the Chandokhyopanishad is due to the characteristic activity of the Supreme."

The intermediate state is described by the Brhadaranyaka (4.3.10) thus: "There are no chariots in that state, no horses, no roads; then

He creates chariots, horses and roads. There are no blessings, happiness, joys and so on. For He is the Creator."

To whom does this power to create belong? BS III.2.2 states the *pūrvapaksha* that the individual soul is the creator. The next sutra (3 ibid) refutes it and says that the dreams are due to Maya- are created by the Lord through His Maya. The Supreme Person and not the individual soul, is the creator for the individual is a creature and not a creator" (page 424).

"The more the dreamer becomes moral, receptive and capable of self control, the truer would his dreams become, that is, and the more would it conform to the prophetic type of communion with the Divine. One's dreams get realized in a truer sense than one's wishes get realized in the doctrine of *sankalpa siddhi*" (page 449).

PNS makes a passing mention of dreams on page 51 and explains the sutras of BS III.2 in the pages 295 to 297 and his concluding note is worth noting down: "The Jîva having a record of wickedness is hurled into hell, suffer from pains proportionate to its evil deeds and is reborn in the world with a fresh opportunity to undo the past. The self has thus freedom to grow into *sâttvik* goodness or lapse into *tâmasik* wickedness (recall the Gita verse BG 14.18). It subjects itself to the adventure of numberless births and deaths, and is caught up in the seesaw of samsâra. While destiny drags the Jîva down and subjects it to sorrow, the inner divinity in each Jîva urges it to choose the way of blessedness, and it drifts between destiny and divinity till it decides on *mukti* and becomes a *mumukshu*."

BS III.2.(2) *tadabhâvâdhikaranam*, SB p647-9; AS 299.
Chand. (8.6.3): "The Jîva during deep sleep does not see any dream as he enters into these veins. Untouched by evil he is with Brahman."

Brhada. (2.1.19): "The Jîva moves through 72,000 nerves that extend from heart towards pericardium (*purîtat*) enters the heart and relaxes there. Jîva thus remains in the heart with Paramâtman."

BS III.2.(3) *karmânusmrti-sabda-vidhi-adhikaraNam*, SB p649-50. AS 300-1. Several verses from Chandogya are quoted to show that Jivâtma rests with Brahman during dreamless sleep also. It can be compared to a person who takes off the load for a while before resuming the journey. Resting with Brahman is only a halt and not the destination.

BS III.2.(4) *mugdhâdhikaranam*, SB p650 (half a page); AS 302. Coma is a state different from death. In death, the vital air completely stops while in coma the body is still having the vital air in a subtle form.

A short summary of the matters discussed so far is given by SSR: "The first quarter (of third chapter) gives in some detail the eschatology of transmigration culminating in the certainty that the individual obtaining in the mundane world of birth, life and death has arrived at the scene loaded with karma of the past, working itself out through its inevitable fructifications…This descriptive survey of the states of individual life is not conducted arbitrarily but keeps close to the Upanishadic data on them. The controlling purpose of the survey is to generate a critical and enlightened aversion to the states. It is for '*vairâgyodaya*'." A note on the two petikas (AS 303).

BS III.2. (5) *ubhayalingâdhikaranam*, SB p651-62 (twelve pages); AS 304-9. It is common knowledge that Shankara established his Advaita based on his own reading of certain sections of BS pertaining to *sad vidyâ*, *anandamaya*, *ubhaya-linga* and *kârya* Brahman. SSR in his thesis pin-points the sections where he has deviated and here we invite the reader's attention to the section concerning the present Adhikarana. "The Ubhaya-Lingatvam means the two characterizations of Brahman. The sutra does not identify them in

375

terms of SaguNa and NirguNa. The identification is the contribution of the commentator (Shankara). There is hardly any basis or hint of a basis in the original text to indicate this version of the two-fold characterization." (The quoted passage occurs on page 200. However, this criticism begins from page 198 onwards. Dr NSA also joins issue: "The explanation of Adwaitic philosophers given to the term 'Ubhaya linga' as relating to SaguNa and NirguNa Brahman is not compatible with the context" (Refer to page 77 of his book "The Philosophy of Sâdhana").

The above reference is necessary in view of the polar contrast in Ramanuja's interpretation. Before giving his version the important sutra (BS III.2.11) needs to be mentioned and explained.

न स्थानतोऽपि परस्योभयलिङ्गं सर्वत्र हि।

'na sthânatah' means in the context of the preceding adhikaraNa(s) dealing with the four states of Jîva, that Para (Paramâtman) is not touched by the defects found in the bodies of jîvas and other things as Antaryâmin. The rationale for this is provided in the following two words 'Ubhaya lingam sarvatra hi' which means that in all shrutis and smrtis (sarvatra) Brahman is popularly described as possessing two-fold character (Ubhaya lingam), that is, as essentially free from all defects (nirasta- nikila doshah) and endowed with countless attributes (samasta kalyana gunâtmaka). Ramanuja substantiates by quoting abundantly from the Upanishads and smrtis, particularly from Vishnu PurâNa.

SMS: "Vedânta Deshika concludes that Brahman is Ubhaya Linga, that is, it is free from all defects and filled with all the auspicious attributes and that this is the well established theory of Vedânta" AS 309.

तस्मात् ब्रह्म द्विलिङ्गं द्विविधविभवमित्येव

वेदान्त पक्षः ॥

A Special Note Ref 83: In this great treatise of Veda Vyasa if one asks 'Which is uppermost section of BS?', the answer undoubtedly is '*ubhaya linga pâda*'. Of the two most distinguishing features (*ubhaya linga*) of Paramâtman is that He is opposed to the slightest trace of imperfection on the one hand and on the other He is the repository of infinite auspicious attributes. The two pet phrases of Ramanuja is as under:

॥ अखिलहेय प्रत्यनीक कल्याणैक तान ॥

But for these two paramount attributes, we cannot derive any benefit from B. If He is also like any one of us subject to human frailities —such as anger frustration etc., in what way he could influence us and transform us into perfect beings? He is free from defects —'*kuRai onRum illatha Govinda*' —as Andal puts it. Every one of His auspicious attributes is vast like a fathomless sea, infinite! Hence we approach Him to cross the sea of samsâra. He is not merely free from defects (*heyarahitan*) but acts as an antidote to defects in us (*pretyanikan*). Even the liberated souls and the Nitya Suris are free from defects but they are not capable of removing our defects. Those who are pure are purified by His sankalpa. His very nature act as a deterrent by way of removing defects in those who meditate on Him. Read further Ref 83.

BS III.2.(6) *ahikundalâdhikaranam*, SB p663-5 (two and half pages); AS 310,11. In the previous Adhikarana it was stated that Brahman is free from defect. Is non-sentient matter a form of Brahman? "*dve vâva brahma rupe*" and such other texts would suggest that the two forms of Brahman can be compared to the two postures of a snake-coiled up in the state of rest or straight while moving. Or, as suggested in the next sutra 27, like a source of light and its rays-

377

though the source remains static the rays spread by moving. Both the examples are rejected and the one acceptable is as established in BS II.3.7. If jîvas form inseparable part of Brahman, even matter can form part (*amsha*). The Brahman is logically and metaphysically the true abode of all things while He Himself is neither composed of nor made up of parts. Nonetheless He is distinct from them. He expresses through the parts. Achit and chit form the sharîra but the changing character of achit does not touch Brahman. Brahman is essentially the sentient principle as borne out in Brhada. (4.4.25): "That infinite, birth-less, un-decaying, indestructible, immortal and fearless self, Paramâtman is the Supreme Brahman" Chand. (8.1.5). "This Brahman does not become old." These kinds of perfections are predominantly that of a sentient principle and not inert matter. It is also mentioned that he who knows the Supreme Brahman thus, becomes the fearless Parabrahman.

SMS lucidly expounds the great significance attached to these two adhikaraNas –ubhaya lingam (79) and ahikundalam (80). "Badarayana provides two additional reasons for establishing that B is the worthy object of meditation and attainment (*prâpya*). These are:

1. B is the Supreme Reality (para tattva) which implies that there is no higher reality than B.
2. B bestows all desired goals (purushârtha) including moksha to those who worship Him. Both these points are important to justify the need of seeking B only as the object of meditation." (p225 Ref 75)

BS III.2.(7) *parâdhikaram*, SB p665-9 (four pages); AS 312-4.

॥ परमतः सेतून्मानसंबन्धभेदव्यपदेशेभ्यः ॥

The above sutra refers to "a few stray spiritual texts which describe Brahman in terms of such as *setu* or bridge, *unmâna* or having a dimension, *sambanda* or connection to something else to be attained and *Bheda* or existence of a different higher entity. Badarayana mentions the points, as prima-facie view in the sutra." Refer to page 225 of SMS's book for the lucid explanation of this Adhikarana.

BS III.2. (8) *phalâdhikaranam*, SB p669-72 (three and half pages); AS 315-8. In the next pâda 'Upâsana', the means of meditation is going to be dealt with. In this last Adhikarana of this pâda it is stated that the fruits of meditation are obtained only from Paramâtman (refer to Sukhabodini for a detailed treatment of the present Adhikarana). Further, it should be noted that the discussion is essentially the same as in Vedârtha Sangraha VS 167-185. Ramanuja has referred to it at the end of *Jijnyâsâdhikarana* itself in Sri Bhâshya (page 172).

The purport of the *Ubhayalinga* pâda is highlighted in AS 319 and the summary in AS 320. For more details on 'paradhikaraNam' (81) and 'phaladhikaraNam' (82) see pages 225 -227 of Ref 75.

11. *Gunopasamhara* pâda, BS III.3
This is the largest pâda in BS consisting of twenty-six adhikaraNa(s) (83-108) and occupies ninety-two pages (SB p673-764). An over view of this pâda is given in AS 321.

BS III.3.(1) *sarva-vedânta-pratyayâdhikaranam*, SB p673-678 (five and half pages). It was declared in the previous Adhikarana that the giver of all fruits is Para Brahman and the Brahma Vidyâ is essentially meditation on Brahman. Now the topic is introduced whether the vidyas are one or several; afterwards it must be decided whether the attributes of Brahman in those meditations are to be included in one act of meditation or not? First, we must consider whether the meditations such as Vaishvanara Vidyâ constitute one meditation or manifold? The meditations are several, the opponent avers. But the same type of meditation is repeated in several *shâkas* (branches of Vedas) without any difference under a different topic. This view is rejected by the sutra.

Sometimes the same vidyâ is prescribed in two Upanishads: For example, take the same Vaishvanara, for instance. It is found in Agnirahasya as well as Chandogya. For a second instance, Dahara Vidyâ is taught in Chandogya and Taittiriya and so on and the instances are not many though (the oft quoted hymn 'daharam vipapmam' is explained in Sukhabodini BS III.3. (19) '*lingabhûyastvâdhikaranam*'). Swami's verse (16) of Nyasa Tilakam may be recalled here- terms such as vedânta, dhyâna, Upâsana and Darshana all mean the same.

"There are thirty-two varieties of Brahma vidyâ described in the Upanishads for securing moksha...Owing to the differences in the psychological dispositions of the adhikarin and the ultimate unity of the result, the Upanishads provide options to each upâsaka to choose his own vidyâ" (*vikalpah-avishishtaphalatvat* - page 367 of Ref 43).

"The entire Third Adhyâya of BS which is titled Sadhanadhyâya is devoted to the discussion of Sadhana. Nearly 55 adhikaraNas included in the four pâdas of this adhyâya and six adhikaraNas of the First Pâda of the Fourth Adhyâya deal with different aspects of sâdhana" ("Doctrine of Sadhana" chapter Eight Ref 75).

SMS: "The commentators on the BS have acknowledged 32 such vidyas which are taught in different Upanishads for attaining Brahman. Hence these are called Brahma Vidyas. A list of these as acknowledged by Deshika in AS is given in appendix II along with the references to the respective passages of the Upanishads and the names of the adhikaraNas in which these are dealt with" (p229 Ref 75).

12.*anga pâda*, BS III.4, SB p765- 807 (forty-three pages).

There are fifteen adhikaraNa(s) (109 to 123):

पुरुषार्थ। स्मृतिमात्र। परिप्लव। अग्नीन्धन।

सर्वापेक्ष। शमदमादि। सर्वान्नानुमति। विहितत्व।

विधुर। तद्भूत।स्वामि। सहकारि। अनाविष्कार।

ऐहिक। मुक्तिफल॥

BS III.4.(1) *purushârthâdhikaranam*, SB p765-780 (sixteen pages); AS 395-9. There are 20 sutras in this Adhikarana. The six sutras commencing from the second are of the opponents view while the rest are view point of Badarayana. His view is stated in the first sutra itself:

॥ पुरुषार्थोऽतः शब्दादिति बादरायणः ॥

The opponent's view is that the karmas are of paramount importance (this view is held by Maharishi Jaimini himself, who is a devout deciple of Badarayana) whereas the vidyas are auxiliary to karmas. But Badarayana contents that karma cannot be the direct sâdhana to moksha but it is vidya aided by karma. That is karma is an anga (limb) of vidya.

How are the doing of karma by some and abstention from it by others to be reconciled? Ans: When karma is done without an eye on its fruits, it serves meditation and its performance is justified. This will be pointed out in sutra 26. But karma done with an eye on fruit obstructs meditation on Brahman and the only fruit of meditation is release from bondage of karma and its abandonment is hence equally appropriate (*tulyam tu darshanam*-sutra 9).

Sutra 13 answers sutra 7: Gitâchârya has sung in praise of Janaka, (referred to in sutra 3) a model karma yogin. But the point is that

Janaka observed meditation till his last breath though he was physically incapacitated to observe karma.

Sutra 14: Isâvâsya states that one should keep doing karma throughout one's hundred years of life (*kurven eva karmani*). Read what the second verse states: "If you live thus, and not otherwise (like Yayati, for example), you who find no pleasure in worldly matters, will not be stained by karma."

Sutra 15: Certain branches in vedanta go to the extent of preaching that one may at pleasure give up the life of a grahasta.

Sutra 16: Destruction of karma (the root of all evil) takes place by the divine grace during meditatation (Mund 2.2.9).

Sutra 17: Supervailing injunction to be followed is celibacy (*urdhvaretas*). Some rare noble souls unmindful of the discomforts of forest life retire to penetential woods for meditation. Such persons who have abandoned the life of a grahasta cannot do Agnihotra, darsha, pûrnamâsya and such routine rituals. Where is the question of karma for them?

These examples no doubt emphasise the importance of karma that one should observe karma in parallelly along with vidya till the objective is achieved but the greatness of vidya is that the observance of karma becomes redundant in due course of time "*na karma lipyate nare.*" Karma which is responsible for sorrow comes to an end- *kshîyante châsya karmâni.* Agnihotram, for example, is prescribed only to those who have not developed an aversion for mundane life.

Sutra 18: Jaimini is still not convinced that one can give up the karma. But Badarayana thinks that mandatory provisions stands

382

waived for sanyasins and brahmacharins if the statement of praise: "*trayo dharmas skandhâh*", is any indication.

Sutra 19: Ramanuja explains the above rik of Chand. (2.23.1). "There are three facets of dharma. Sacrifice, study of vedas and giving of gifts form the first facet; austerity (tapas) is the second; exhausting one's life in the household of a preceptor practising continence is the third facet of dharma. All these lead to the attainment of virtuous worlds. He who is steadfast in Brahman attains immortality. The first facet refers to the householder's dharma. The word tapah relates to *vaikanasa, parivrâja* oriented upâsaka. The way of life consists in subjecting the body to torture in the form of denial of food and exposure to cold, heat and wind. They attain the world of Brahma samsthanam. Parashara Maharishi highlights the merit in each walk of life. (VP 1.6.34-39) A sublime warrior, for example goes to the world of Indra. A meditator on Brahman goes to the highest domain viz., Sri Vaikuntam- *teshâm paramam sthânam yadvai pashyanti sûrayah.*

Sutra 20: According to Jâbâlopanishad, one need not necessarily wait for the completion of life in any particular asrama to take up the life of renunciation.

We have completed the first adhikaraNa of anga pâda (BS III.4) Of the forty three pages, the first adhikaraNa alone occupies sixteen pages, and the remaining twenty seven pages deal with fourteen adhikaraNas. They are all minor ones compared with the first and they trace the contour of the necessary equipment expected of a sâdhaka of Brahma vidya. Hence a brief description of the remaining 14 adhikaraNas are given below to complete the treatment of Anga Pâda. The verses in AS pertaining to these 14 adhikaraNas are from AS 400 to AS 423.

Chand. (1.1.3) The Omkara is termed Udgita. The Rik is not meant as a mere praise but as a vidhi enjoining the upâsana (2 *stutimâtrâdhikarana*). A question arises whether biographies of *Pratardana* and *Shvetaketu* rendered with svara, are to be treated as stories or vidya? They have to be treated as vidhi enjoining vidya (3 *pari-plavadhikaraNam*). Those who pursue meditation on Brahman are required to do the prescribed karma. However it is not mandatory for sanyasins to perform rituals which involve litting of sacrificial fire (4 *Agni-indhanadhikaraNam*).

"Exceptional conditions do not apply to grahasthas who are eligible to perform rites…A horse which is intended for the purpose of going from one place to another is to be used along with requisite accessories such as saddle, bridle etc., until one reaches the destination. In the same way, performance of prescribed rituals are to be observed as accessories to vidya until one attains moksha." The quote is from SMS: p242. The relevant topic is titled, "5 Sarvapeksha Adhikaranam". On SB p785 Ramanuja quotes verses from Gita also:BG 18.5 (yajnya-dana-tapah karma) and BG 18.46 (*yatah pravrtir bhutanam*) to highlight the accessories (5 *Sarvâpeksha Adhikaranam*).

The daily routine of the house holder is likely to make him a pray of *râga* (SS act iii.2) and make him forget the higher purpose of life. He should develop virtues such as *sama* or tranquility, *dama* or control of senses, *uparati* or inner satisfaction, *titiksha* or tolerance and *samahitatva* or equanimity. Refer Brhad. 4.4.23 (6 *ShamadamâdyadhikaraNam*).

Purity in respect of food should be observed. More than the clinical aspect is the source from which food is taken. When unavoidable the rule can be waived only in so far as hunger is quenched. An upâsaka like Ushasti would not even partake water that is left over after drinking by somebody (*uchchhishhtam me pîtam syât-* Chand.

1.10.3). Swamy has recommended Ushasti's example to be followed (RTS 18). The famous prescription for purity: "*âhâra shuddhau sattva shuddhih*" is quoted here. Drinking is prohibited (7 *SarvânnânumatyadhikaraNam*). Yajnyas are permitted since dharmic activities expitiate sin (8 *Vihitatvâdhikaranam*).

The importance of observing ashrama dharma is stressed. According to Manu (2.87) a brahmin loses his character by not doing japa no matter how he engages himself otherwise. See also Prashnopanishad (1.10) the priceless ingriedients of the upâsaka are virtues such as *tapas, brahmâchârya, shraddha* or faith and knowledge of âtma (9 *VidhuradhikaraNam*).

Persons who have committed the murder of a boy or a woman or an act of treason and such of those who are ungrateful are not eligible for lessons on vidya (10 *tadbhûtâdhikaranam*).

In udgita singing is a part of kratu. The singing part is got done with the help of ritviks for a fee. The upâsaka should concern himself only with meditation. However dahara and other vidyas are free from such kind of external service (11 *svâmyadhikaraNam*).

Sage Yajnavalkya tells Kahola (Brhad. 3.5.1): "The Supreme Being lies beyond the pale of hunger, thirst, grief, delusion old age and death. Knowing this Supreme, the Brahmins renounce the desire for sons, wealth and worlds and lead the life of mendicants, taking alms. That which is the desire for sons is the desire for wealth and that which is desire for wealth is desire for the worlds. Both these are indeed desires. Therefore a knower of the Vedas (Brahmana) gaining knowledge, must wish to lead an innocent and child-like life. Having gained child-like innocence and acquiring knowledge, the sadhaka becomes a muni (meditator). Having gained Amouna (*pânditya* and *bâlya*)- that are other than meditation, he becomes a

385

Brahmana" (a realiser of Brahman as depicted in Brhad. 3.5.1)- 12 *Sahakâryantara-vidhi* and 13 *Avishkârâdhikarana*).

तस्माद्ब्राह्मणः पाण्डित्यं निर्विद्य बाल्येन तिष्ठासेत्।

बाल्यं च पाण्डित्यं च निर्विद्याथ मुनिरमौनं च मौनं

च निर्विद्याथ ब्राह्मणः ॥

Upasana is not only undertaken for moksha but it can also be for short term immediate gains such as heavenly bliss, wealth etc. For an illustration, there are four types as per BG 7.16. For effective results, Refer Chand.(1.1.10) : "Vidya and avidya lead to different results. That alone performed with intense concentration, faith and knowledge yields quick results" (14 *Aihika adhikaraNam*).

It is also stated that in the upâsana for moksha, the goal is achieved soon after the completion of meditation, provided there are no obstacles in the form of over-riding prarabdha karma such as an offence to a Brahmavit. Swamy's specific advice- *brahmavidapachâra dûrakam*- should be borne in mind (15 *Mukti-phalâdhikaranam*).

The 15 adhikaraNas in anga pâda (BS III.4) are summarized in AS 424,5. The Advaitis contention that mere knowledge of the meaning (*vâkyârthajnânamâtram*) alone is sufficient is disproved in this pâda. Besides Swamy highlights several glowing features of BS in the verses AS 426 to 431.

13. Sri Bhâshyam Fourth Adhyâya: *phalâdhyâyah*

The contents of this *adhyâya* are dealt with in chapter Nine: "The Doctrine of Parama Purushartha" of Ref 75.

"This chapter is devoted to the discussion of the nature of the supreme goal (*Parama Purushartha*) which is to be attained by the aspirant for moksha after duly observing the prescribed upâsana or meditation on B. In the previous chapter , we have discussed, in detail, all aspects of the sâdhana as enunciated by Badarayana on the authority of the Upanishads. In the present chapter we shall deal with the nature of *phala* or the goal to be attained by upâsana. This will comprise the following four theories, which have a bearing on moksha, the Supreme Goal.

1. The liberation of jîva from bondage caused by karma in the form of *punya* and *pâpa*
2. Utkrânti or the exit of the jîva from the body after liberation.
3. Archiradi-marga or the path through which the liberated jîva marches to the abode of B
4. The status of jîva in the state of mukti

These are the topics which are covered in the last five adhikaraNas of first pâda named Avrttipâda, eleven adhikaraNas of second pâda named Utkranti-pâda, the five adhikaraNas of third pâda named Gati-pâda and six adhikaraNas of the fourth pâda named Mukti-pâda. As moksha is attained only after the death of the upâsaka, it is considered relevent to discuss these subjects in the *Phaladhyâya* ."

SB p808 to889 (eighty two pages): In a single verse AS432 the Swamy establishes the sangati between the third and fourth adhyâyas and in addition the link between the two pairs of the fourth adhyâya. The several advantages (*bahu prayojana pradarshanam*) of phaladhyâya in AS 433.

The Fourth Adhyâya is duly taken up with the delineation of the ideal of spiritual deliverance and perfection. It is a short adhyâyas as much bearing on the question as already come out in the preceding part of the treatise in some way or the other and a pointed presentation of the essentials is of value. In the first pâda (*âvrtti pâda*) the fundamental nature of the meditation on the Supreme Reality is stated for purposes of decisive recapitulation and because meditation in its maturity passes beyond the stage of the means into that of the end itself. Accomplishment of this height of sâdhana results in breaking the chain of past karma and elimination of the fears of the fetters of karma in the future. Only the karma in present operation should work out its momentum. The second and third pâda (*utkrânti pâda* and *gati pâda*) deal with the manner of the passing away of a perfected man or purified soul and eschatology of liberation as expounded in the Upanishads. The last pâda, (*phala pâda*, the shortest pâda) defines the fundamental nature of spiritual liberation for man, which constitutes consummation of Vedântic life.

Thus, we see that the later two adhyâyas of BS expound the Vedântic theory of human perfection and the means there for. The last sutra by its repetition signifies that the whole science of Vedânta wholly revealed in the treatise.

13 Avrtti pâda (BS IV.1)
SB p808-831 (twenty four pages)
There are eleven adhikaraNas (124-134); AS 434-473.

आवृत्ति। आत्मत्वोपासन। प्रतीक। आदित्यादिमति।

आसीन। आप्रयाण। तदधिगम। इतर। अनारब्धकार्य।

अग्निहोत्रादि। इतरक्षपण॥

The first question to be settled is whether meditation is to be performed only once or often and continuously? The VP (6.7.91) clarifies that meditation on Brahman's form should be done continuously without interruption and the mind free from any other thought or desire. "Dhyana or upâsana is a ceaseless remembrance of the Lord, which is likened to the uninterrupted flow of oil (*taila-dhâravad avicchinna smrti santâna rûpa*)." Refer to PNS: page 365 for details. (1 Avrtti adhikaraNam). A number of texts explain the relationship between the Brahman and jîvâtman as one of soul and body. Meditation should be on the indwelling Paramâtman (2 *Atmopâsana- adhikaraNam*).

"Mano brahme iti upâsîtâ"- After all mind is an inert matter belonging to prakrti. How to justify this statement? A king cannot pass for as a servant but the vice versa is possible. Hence mind which is inferior can be meditated upon (3 *pratîkâdhikaranam*).

Sacrifice is fruitful in so far it propitiates a deity. Udgita is considered as a symbol of Aditya and contemplation should be on the latter since it is higher (*utkarsha*) (4 *AdityâdimatyadhikaraNam*).
Gitâchârya recommends sitting posture for dhyana. (BG 6.11,12) "Asana is the physical control of the body by keeping it stiff, symmetrical and straight and thus overcoming the tamasic languor and rajasic restlessness." Refer PNS: page 343 for further details. Shveta 2.10: "Resort to a place such as a cave which is bereft of

wind, which is free from disturbing factors such as fire or noise. The place should be clean and free from pebbles" (5 *Asînâdhikarana*).

Chand. (8.15.1): The contemplation should continue till one's last breath (6 *Aprayânâd adhikaraNam*). The seventh adhikaraNa BS IV.1.(7), is a very important one. Admitting that one has to meditate until the end of one's life, how is it possible that one can expect any result at all considering the mountain of sins one has accumulated from time immemorial past. There is a saying that the sins cannot be destroyed even in aeons and aeons of time. (*nâbhuktam kshîyate karma kalpakoti shatairapi*). Here lies the efficacy of upâsana. It is so great that the meditation (because of the Lord who effects the miracle by camping in the chitta- VP 6.7.74) wipes out the sins of the past. Chand (5.24.3): "Just as the heap of soft fibres of the munja grass put into the fire gets burnt, similarly all sins of the sadhaka who performs the agnihotra knowing this will be burnt." What about the sins which would be committed in the future? The answer is again in the Chand. (4.14.3): "Just as water drops do not stick to lotus leaf, the sins would not stick." According to Andal this applies to Nyasa Vidya (*sharanagati*) also (Tiruppavai 5).

Refer to Rahasya Traya Sara, chapter 20, Niryânâdhikâra. Swamy has quoted this important sutra BS IV.1.13, which is reproduced below:

तदधिगम उत्तरपूर्वाघयोरश्लेषविनाशौ तद्व्यपदेशात्॥

This is the sum and substance of 7 *tadadhigamâdhikarana*.
For one aspiring liberation, even good deeds (*puNya*) are a liability since they stand in the way of moksha. Any karma left unused does not stick, ashlesha (8 *itarâdhikaranam*).

It was mentioned that the sins get destroyed. The question is whether it applies to *sanchita* (past karma) or *ârabdha* (that which has begun to operate.) The sutra 15 states that only sanchita gets destroyed. The very fact that he has to live till the completion of his life, he has to experience the left over karma, if any (9 *anârabdhakâryâdhikaranam*).

Though the sadhaka does not aspire for the fruits of Agnihotra, still he has to perform without any attachment. Prescribed duties should be performed (10 *Agnihotradhikaraṇa*).

Arabdha karma which has started to yield fruits at the beginning of the vidya, cannot be finished in one birth. It has to be experienced till the end of present life and the left overs (if any) in the subsequent life (11 *itarakshapanâdhikaranam*).

The 11 adhikaraNas of BS IV.1 are summarised in AS 474.

14. *utkranti pâda*, BS IV.2

SB p832-49 (eighteen pages). A question arises, why at all the issue of death is to be discussed in this pâda when its proper place should have been in the third adhyâya itself when the jîva's four states- the awakened state, the dream state, the state of deep-dreamless-sleep and the state of unconsciousness or coma- were discussed? The reason for belated consideration is because of the context. There in third adhyâya the main focus was to highlight the oweful state of samsaric existence in the four a/m states, but now the discussion centres around the noble soul, who has come a long way on the road to Brahma prâpti, and here the sadhaka courts death as a fitting finale to his long career of upâsana. The Swamy has devoted five verses (AS 475-9) mainly to provide an over view of the entire BS in a holistic perspective (*samudâyavichârah*). In a soul stirring verse in Sankalpa Suryodaya (verse 26 Act IX), he compares the successful Vidvan to that of a prisoner coming out of the jail- *samsâra karâ kutir*. There are 20 sutras and 11 adhikaraNas in this pâda and many of the adhikaraNas have a solitary sutra whereas the fifth adhikaraNa (*âsrt*) has seven sutras. The adhikaraNas (135-145) are as under:

वाक्। मनः। अध्यक्ष। भूत। आसृत्युपक्रम।

परसंपत्ति। अविभागः। तदोको। रश्मि।

निशा। दक्षिणायन॥

The soul's exit from the body is described in Chand. (6.8.6) and this verse can be considered as the anchor verse for this pâda. *"asya saumya purushhasya vâng manasi sampadyate manah prâNe prâNastejasi tejah parasyâm devatâyam."* "When the purusha dies his speech unites with the mind. The mind gets into prâNa and prâNa gets into tejas and that tejas becomes one with the Supreme Deity." The above order speech uniting with mind etc. is the subject matter for discussion for the adhikaraNas 1,2 and 3. Does 'tejas' includes light only or all the five elements? Going by the principle of quintuplication, all the elements are always mixed up, and tejas is representative of the pancha bhutas (4.*bhûtâdhikaranam*).

Whatever so far described concerns all, irrespective of whether it is the soul of an upâsaka or any jîva exiting the body at the time of death. The special feature as in the case of the upâsaka is mentioned in Kathopanishad (6. 14-16) and Chand. (8.6.6).
When all the karmas get exhausted (*pramuchyante*), the jîva enjoys Brahman here. Such a karma-less state is the sine qua non of immortality when the heart gets freed of its knots (*prabhidyante*). There are 101 nâDis connecting the heart to the head and out of these one vein is very special and is called *brahma nâDi* (also known as *sushumna nâDi*) which is connected to the cerebral region. The soul's exit through this special *nâDi* constitute liberation since there is no more further entry of rebirth.

Brhad. (4.4.6,7 &11): A man resolves according to the desire he wants to achieve. No sooner he exhausts the fruits of his karma, he returns to this life again. On the contrary the man who had no other desire apart from the desire of liberation, the vital airs do not depart from him. The possession of guNashtaka, so assiduously cultivated stand him in good stead to develop Brahma bhava. Though he resides for a short period in this world, his body is as lifeless as the slough of a snake cast away on an anthill. Contrastingly, non-upâsakas go to joyless worlds.

The fifth adhikaraNa, as noted earlier, contain as many as seven sutras (7-13) and this long adhikaraNa is lucidly dealt with in SMS's book (page 266-9). The AS verses 485, 6 are also explained while emphasizing Swamy's views.

There is temporary rest (as during sleep or during the phase of praLaya) for the soul to be in the safe custody of Antaryamin to get rid of fatigue or perhaps a pause before a leap into eternity. (6 parasampatyadhikaraNam). "When the jîva is united with Paramâtman at the time of death, the two cannot be differentiated." The union does not imply merging but the two entities become indistinguishable (7 avibhaga adhikaraNam).

In response to devoted upâsana, the antaryâmin, out of His grace, (hârdânugrhîta) illuminates the particular vein (sushumna nâDi) to enable the jîva to exit through this nâDi and proceed further to the higher abode through archiradi marga(8 tadokodhikaranam).

Chand.(8.6.5) The soul Brahmavit after leaving the body rides on the rays of the sun and reaches Aditya in a moment (9 rashmyanusârâdhikaranam).

Does it mean that those who die in the night do not get moksha? The effect of the blazing sun would persist during the night (IR Cameras function on this principle). For that matter clouds in the day can also obstruct? No object under the sun can escape the influence of the sun (10 nishâdhikaranam).

Given the fact that the Grand Sire Bhishma waited for the arrival of uttarâyana before he let go d his last breath, it would appear that death at uttarayana is a sine qua non for mukti. It is clarified that no such stipulation exists. Regarding this aspect verses from Gita are examined. BG 8. 21,23,24,26 &27. In all these verses only the Kala Abhimani Devata is mentioned and not the times. Gitâchârya has adviced that one should always be focussed in yoga- *sarveshu kaleshu yoga yukto bhava*. "The delay is only so long as there is no release from the body." Hence Dakshinayana is not excluded (11 DakshinayanadhikaraNam).

This pâda (BS IV.2) is summarized in AS 499.

15. *gati* pâda, BS IV.3 SB p850-67 (eighteen pages)
The fiteen sutras of this pâda are spread over five adhikaraNas (146-50).

अर्चिरादि। वायु। वरुण। आतिवाहिकाः। कार्य॥

This pâda concerns with the journey (trajectory) of the liberated soul through ether to Sri Vaikuntam.

"After *utkranti*, the ascent of the jivâtman commences through different realms (lokas) ruled by the celestial beings. There are a few conflicting statements regarding the pathway to moksha. Badarayana therefore discusses this matter and presents the correct theory of *archirâdi m*arga in the five adhikaraNas of this pâda." Commencing with these remarks SMS explains the sub-topics of this adhyâya. What are the conflicting statements?"

Chand.(4.15.5) : "When the upâsaka dies he attains Brahman irrespective of the funeral rites being performed or not. He reaches fire, the first in the *archirâdi marga*." The Kaushitaki and Brhadaranyaka describe the path in a different manner.

Swamy has given the order of celestial deities thus: *jyotis, ahas, shukla paksha, uttarayana, samvatsara, vayu, aditya, chandra, vidyut, varuna, Indra* and *Prajapati* (adhikara sangraha 27).

Chand (4.15.6) The jîva is escorted to Brahma loka by the amânava purushas (4 Ativahika adhikaraNam).

The above statement raises the issue whether the term Brahma denotes the Brahman, the Supreme Being or Chatur-mukha Brahma also named as Hiranyagarbha? According to Badari (a sishya of Badarayana) it is Hiranyagarbha and this view with supporting arguments is expressed in five sutras- *kâryam bâdari asya gati upapatteh*. The term karya is taken to mean Hiranya, a lower deity. This point is also discussed elaborately by PNS page 471: "Following the interpretation of Sutrakara, Ramanuja combats the view of Badari and establishes the truth that *archirâdi gati* is the direct way to mukti, by appeal to reason and revelation. Mukti is not only the direct apprehension of Brahman, but a spiritual pilgrimage to, or the progressive attainment of, Brahma loka... The ascent to the absolute is further described in Paramapâda Sopana, following the Vaikunta gadya and the Kaushitaki upanishad as the entry into the home of the absolute or *divyadesha prâpti*. The soaring self led by the ambassador of eternity at last enters the waters of immortality or Viraja which mark the boundary line between the trancendental sphere of Brahman and the empirical sphere of karman" (5 *kâryâdhikaranam*). AS 517 summarises the pâda BS IV.3.

16. *phala* or *mukti* pâda (BS IV.4)
SB p868-89 (twenty two pages: there are 22 sutras spread over six adhikaraNas 151-156).

संपत्याविभांव। अविभागेनदृष्टत्व। ब्रह्म।

संकल्प। अभाव। जगद्व्यापारवर्जं॥

Chand. (8.12.2): Vayu, lightening, thunder- these do not have a body. Akâsh shines in its natural state. Similarly this âtman attaining the supreme light comes into its own natural form.

The nature of jivâtman in the state of release is discussed in the sutra BS IV.4.1. The *samprasâda* signifies jivâtman in the state of mukti. "*asmât sharirât samutthâya*" means moving out of the final body through mûrdhanya nadi for going through the path of archiradi for the attainment of Brahman.

The marsh or dirt sticking to a diamond is unrecognisable and the shine is blocked. But once the diamond is thoroughly polished, its brilliant lustre is restored. Similarly the soul gets its lustre restored in the liberated state. The diamond example is from Vishnu PurâNa. The reader may turn to page 481 of PNS's book: "The Chândogya text (VIII.3.4) explains mukti as the self realisation of the âtman by self transcendence (*param jyotir upasampadya svena rupena abhinishpadyante*) and the sutra (BS IV.4.1) brings out its full implication."

sampatyâvirbhâvâdhikaranam
Param jyoti means the Supreme Brahman who is adorning the Supreme Abode of Sri Vaikuntam. '*svena rupena*' manifesting with its *gunâshtaka* which are acquired from Brahman.

When the jîva attains Brahman, it realises that it is integrally and inseperably related with Brahman. Hence the jîva enjoys Infinite Bliss along with Brahman. For a detailed discussion on this topic refer to PNS's book page 483: "The sutrakara reconciles all the texts and their truths by the all comprehensive concept of *avibhâga*" (2 *avibhâgena drshtadva adhikaraNam*).

Once again Badarayana resolves the conflict between Jaimini and Audulomi. The former's contention is that the muktâtma possesses *guNashtaka* while the latter maintains that the soul has only intense consiciousness. It is established that there is nothing wrong with the two coexisting and complementing each other. See also the discussion on page 486 of PNS which begins thus. "The next question is the enquiry into the nature of manifestation of intelligence in mukti" (3. *Brahmâdhikaranam*).

The liberated soul is free to do whatever it wants. Two questions arise: Does the jîva fulfills all its desires out of its own will or with some effort as in the case of ordinary individuals? Secondly does the liberated jîva possesses a body and the sense organs to perform the activities? Badarayana answers the questions in the two adhikaraNas- 4 *SamkalpadhikaraNam* and 5 *abhâvâdhikaranam*. Refer to pages 293-6 of SMS.

The issue of freedom is probed to its esoteric depth by PNS between the page 496-502. He ends this chapter (titled Mukti) in these words: "The bliss of Brahman is however irresistible and every Vedântin seeks Ananda as supreme end and aim of life."

We come to the last adhikaraNa. "If the *muktâtma* is capable of creating anything desired by it, the question arises whether it is capable of creating the universe by its samkalpa? The equality of Brahman with jîva is only in respect of experiencing infinite joy (*bhogamatra lingashcha*-sutra 21) but the jîva has absolutely no role to play in the creation and governance of the universe which is entirely in the hands of the Brahman (*jagatvyapara varjam*- sutra 17). It is easily explained with a concrete example familiar to us. The farmer tills the land, and the entire farming operation yields the produce, namely the crops. Every one enjoys the crops such as rice, wheat etc. without going through the trouble of farming and raising the crops. The Brahman is like the farmer. SMS has discussed the issue in pages 297-300 (6 *jagatvyaparavarjadhikaraNa*).

The import of this adhikaraNa is also discussed brilliantly by PNS (page 489): "Ishwara has cosmic rulership and the stability of salvation is the gift of His redemptive will, and it is this *jagatvyâpâra* or universal lordship that marks the difference between the 'âtman' that is the self ruler and Brahman the world-ruler (BS IV.4.17). He also sustains the cosmic, moral and spiritual order and guarantees immortality (*na cha punarâvartate*) to the mumukshu. He plays with the âtman in the world of lîlâ and Brahminizes it in the world of eternity."

AS 551 summarises BS IV.4. A suggestion for further reading: "Attainment of Brahman in salvation"-pages 145 to 157 of the book "The Philosophy of Sadhana" by NSA.

<u>Utility of Brahma Sutras As Highlighted in Rahasya Traya Sara</u>
A true adherent of Ramanuja Darshana should not be ignorant of BS. He should at least have a brief overview of BS. Just as the entire Vedas is the expansion of Mûla Mantra, the latter is also the quintessence of BS. A question may be asked as to how much of BS is useful for those who have adopted Prapatti Marga as the means of Mukti? This question is addressed and answered unambiguously by Vedânta Deshika in the chapter 27 (Mûla Mantra Adhikâra) of Rahasya Traya Sara. But for a solitary pâda viz. 3.3, the whole of BS is useful and hence should be studied. The first two adhyâyas annalyse the nature of Brahman or Parâvara Tattva. (The Supreme Real and the reals subordinate to it) In the third adhyâya, competency (adhikara) and accessories (angas) are stated along with upâya and in the fourth and final adhyâya, the fruit or attainment of goal is explained.

Undoubtedly, the first two and the fourth adhyâyas must be known for anybody desiring mukti irrespective of Bhakti / Prapatti. And the first two pâdas of the third adhyâya, namely, vairâgya pâda (3.1) and Ubhaya linga pâda (3.2) are also meant for any mumukshu since the former deals with the sufferings of samsâra and the latter on the antidote for samsâra are delineated. In the third pâda (3.3) different forms (upâsanas or vidyas) are dealt with and all are not competent to observe any of the 31 Brahma Vidyas. The fourth pâda (3.4) dealing with rites and duties (Varna-Ashrama dharma) is again general meant for any *mumukshu*. The prescribed duties are observed as essential requirement of Upâsana- "*sahakâritvena châ*" (3.4.33) - whereas they are observed as Divine commandments (*vihitatvât-*3.4.32) by the adherents of Prapatti in view of their efficacy in leading a virtuous life or *ujjîvanam*.

A Savant's Experience (Brahmânubhava) of Sri Bhashya
It will be appropriate to end this section on BS with a passage from PNS's book, "The Philosophy of Vishishtâdvaita" (page 415). "The four chapters of the BS reveal the synoptic insight of the Sûtrakâra and are a systematic elucidation of the truth step by step from the first sutra to the last. Each chapter of the Shârîraka Shâstra is not merely a part or unit of the whole and a member of an organic unity, but is itself a complete whole. A fresh insight into the Shâstra is afforded by Mahamahopadhyâya Kapistalam Deshikâchârya in his master thought that every Adhikarana or section is an *anubhava* or intuition of Brahman. What is metaphysically determined as the ultimate ground of all existence is also the supreme end of man's spiritual quest and yields a specific *anubhava* of the divine perfection. Each adhikaraNa aims not merely at logical satisfactoriness or coherence but also at spiritual satisfaction. The synthetic insight corrects the ordinary idea that the BS are a mere theoretic study of Vishishtâdvaita and that the Bhagavad *vishaya* of Nammâzhwar embodies its practical aspect of spiritual experience and confirms the theory that Vishishtâdvaita is Ubhaya Vedânta. It is the supreme

399

merit of the Svamin to have replaced the analytic method by the synthetic, and regarded each adhikaraNa as the spiritual experience of a Bhagavad-guNa or auspicious quality of Bhagavan in the manner of ecstatic outpourings of Nammâzhwar. This chapter furnishes a summary of his exposition, which throws fresh light on the meaning of the term 'philosophy of religion' as it insists on the ultimate unity of philosophy and religion and the supreme truth that the reality is realizable and that what is logically valid is also spiritually valuable. In his *Vyasa-siddhanta-mârtânda* the Swamin shows that each adhikaraNa both proves a philosophic truth and is a spiritual *anubhava* or experience of an attribute of Narayana. In his later work, Adhikarana Ratnamâlâ, Narayana is equated with Srinivasa. The BS consisting of 156 adhikaraNa(s) or sections are valued as 156 gems (Ref 91) of the perfections or kalyana guNas strung together by devotional art. The absolute of the Upanishad is equated with the supreme Narayana, the God of religion, and is finally identified with the Redeemer, Srinivasa.

14. Bhagavad Vishayam

வான்திகழும்சோலைமதிளரங்கர் வண்புகழ்மேல் ★
ஆன்றதமிழ்மறைகளாயிரமும் ★ - என்ற
முதல்தாய்சடகோபன் ★ மொய்ம்பால்வளர்த்த
இதத்தாய்இராமானுசன்.

The above picture shows the display found on a pillar at the temple
Tirupper (incidentally, this tribute was offered by the author's

401

father, Sri Veeravalli Parthasarathy). It is said that Ramanuja was immersed of the padikam (Tiruvai Mozhi 10.8) devoted to this temple. Observing close by, his disciple could decipher the unmistakable hand gestures made in silence. Ramanuja had no hesitation in selecting this disciple to write the commentary (6000) on TM. This event explains the following *tanian* of Bhattar on Ramanuja (*vân tikazhum cholai*). For reference, also see RTS 23 (*inRennaip poruLâkki...*).

Introduction

Ever since the advent of Tiruvai Mozhi several commentaries came to be written on the subject matter of the poem Tiruvai Mozhi by several savants and âchâryas and the entire collection extant on the subject goes by the title Bhagavad Vishayam. Any study should be undertaken under the guidance of a preceptor. The study should begin by paying homage (through *tanians)* to the foremost âchâryas who have been responsible for the guarding and propagation of the moksha dharma, TM. The three most important among them are, Madhura Kavi, Natha Munigal and Tiru Kurugai Piran Pillan. The last mentioned was the direct disciple of Ramanuja. More than a hundred years had elapsed between the time of discovery of Tiruvai Mozhi by Natha Munigal and the birth of Ramanuja. Natha Munigal belongs to the period 824- 924 AD and that of Ramanuja's (1017 - 1137 AD).

In keeping with the hoary tradition, the commemorative Sanskrit verse (*bhaktâmrtam*) of Natha Muni should be recited first followed by the Tamil *tanian* of Madhura Kavi (*tiruvazhuti nâDu*) and then only the third *tanian* in Tamil (*manattâlum*) composed by Natha Munigal, should be recited. For a critical appraisal of commentaries and treatment of tanians in extenso Ref 85.

Natha Munigal: "I offer my obeisance to the outpourings of Shatagopa (*vângmayam* =Tiruvai Mozhi) which serve as nectar to the

402

ears, providing immense pleasure to the listener while conferring whatever benefits one desires in life. Tiruvai Mozhi is verily the sea of Tamil veda, the equivalent of the thousand-branched Sama Veda, inclusive of the famous Chandokhyopanishad" (incidentally the bulk of the aphorisms of Brahma Sutras are culled out from this single source known as Chandokya Upanishad).

Madhura Kavi: "O Mind! Conjure up a pleasant vision of the town Kurugur (also known by the name Tiruvazhuti), the birth-place of Shatagopa, situated on the banks of the holy river, Tamraparani. Reflect on the greatness of the author, who has presented the fathomless Vedas through a garland of verses in chaste Tamil. Let the mind remain ever yoked to the lotus feet of the composer of this *andâdi*."

Natha Muni: "My mind and voice will not hold in respect or praise of anyone who does not connect oneself to the lineage of Kurugur family. Since I am yoked to the lotus feet of Shatakopa, I always remain calm and contended and hardly do I suffer from any want. He takes care of me like father towards his son."

The word 'Bharatha' is symbolic of everything that is orient or Indian. According to Vishnu PurâNa (VP 2.3.1) the term Bharath stands for the Peninsular Subcontinent –the geographical region lying between north of the sea (*uttaram yat samudrasya*) and south of the Himalayas (*himâdreshchaiva dakshiNam*). The word can remind us of the great Emperor Bharata who ruled a whopping 60,000 years before retiring to the Himalayas as a Spiritual Philosopher & Preceptor (Refer 'Bharata Charitra' in VP 2.13). The name can also refer to the famous Bharata Muni who is the founder of the Science of Karnatic Music and Dramaturgy. The word Bharata is composed of three letters –*bha*, *ra* & *tha* respectively representing '*bhâva*', '*râga*' & '*thâla*'. Both, Nammazhwar & Tirumangai Azhwar have made references: '*ragas*' – (*ezhisayin chuvai* (*sapta svaras*)–TM 10.8.8).

403

Anyone familiar with Karnatic music should be aware of what raga means. Natha Munigal popularized and propagated not only Tiruvai Mozhi but the entire 4000 by setting raga to each one of the Tamil Pasurams. Two of his illustrious disciples (Kîzhagattâzhvân and Melagattâzhvân) propagated the Prabandam through musical rendering, in a manner like that of Maharishi Valmiki who propagated Srimad Ramayana through the twins Lava and Kucha, sons of Sadhvi Sita Devi. In the land of Bharata dance & music is the tradition. From Natha Muni the Nalayira Divya Prabandam was passed on to his grandson Alavandar (also known as Yamunâchârya). And keeping this lineage in view the verse in Stotra Ratna (5) - *mâtâ pitâ-* is also recited as a tanian for the commemoration of Alavandar. The disciples of Alavandar were many and through them several rivers of propagators branched off only to get merged in the sea of Ramanuja who is also popularly known as Yatiraja (king among the ascetics). The next tanian *aeinda perum kirti* is offered at the lotus feet of Ramanuja.

A profound thought is brought to bear about commemorating the unique role played by Ramanuja. Just as Devaki's child was brought up by Yashoda, Nammazhwar's brain-child Tiruvâi Mozhi was cherished and nurtured by Ramanuja, like a foster mother (இத்தாய் இராமானுசன்). This conceptualization is not without support. It appears even Nammazhwar had a premonition of the emergence of Ramanuja as purportedly indicated in the *(patikam)*-*kangulum pagalum* and *polika polika*.

The added significance is that each verse in the patikam, *kangulum pagalum,* has the import of each hundred- e.g. the words *cenkayal pâi nîr tiruvarangattâi* appearing in the first verse has the import of the first hundred *Sevâyogyan,* the words *tâmaraikannâ mugil vannâ* occurring in the second verse indicative of the subject matter of the second hundred *atibhogya* and so on. Thus, this patikam (TM 7.2) is the very epitome of the whole Tiruvai Mozhi and what is more is that it is cast in the style of the mother who bemoans the condition of her pitiable daughter afflicted with God-love, and more specifically love for Lord Ranganatha of Sri Rangam. No wonder Ramanuja is assigned the role of the mother as typified in *kangulum pagalum* (Kovil Tiruvai Mozhi).

Once, Ramanuja was found deeply immersed in the divine experience of recalling to his mind a patikam of Tiruvai Mozhi. His joyful experience found expression through an appropriate gesture of hand movement (*abhinaya*) and the disciple watching him close by was quick to discern the movement as prompted by the verse of TM 10.8 (*piditten piravi kedutten*). Ramanuja's joy knew no bounds and embraced the disciple in admiration for the latter's power of observation. "You could decipher it thanks to your being the descendant of Natha Munigal. You are like my son. I want you to write a commentary on Tiruvai Muzhi", said Ramanuja to the disciple who was also named Tirukkurugai Pirân Pillân for being endowed with a deep insight into Tiruvai Mozhi.

The commentary on Tiruvai Mozhi written by Tirukkurugai Piran Pillan is titled as *ârâyirappadi* which literally means a measure of 6000 granthas, of the size of Vishnu PurâNa. A grantha is a unit of reckoning consisting of 32 syllables (*anushhtup*). Though the commentary is written in the medium of Tamil, it is an admixture of Tamil and Sanskrit words, known as manipravâLa. Incidentally it is the smallest and the earliest of the several commentaries extant on Bhagavat vishayam.

The next one 9000 was from Nanjîyar who was an Advaiti turned Visishtadvaitin because of losing a prolonged debate (*vâda biksha*) he had with Parashara Bhattar (elder son of Kûrat âzhvân). The a/m 9000, obviously more elaborate than the 6000, employs more tamil words than Sanskrit in the ratio 5:1 per verse. Nanjîyar had a disciple

Nampillai, who, it appears, lost the palm leaf manuscript, entrusted to him for copying, while swimming across the river Cauvery running in floods. However, he had such a brilliant memory that he rewrote the whole of 9000. Even more remarkable was his profundity that two of his disciples produced two more extended commentaries 36,000 and 24,000. The former one by Vadakku-tiru-vîdi-pillai contains not only all that is in the latter but includes more of the details retained from the utterances of his master- additional details accounting for its bulk and being an exact replica of his master's voice, it earned the reputation of being named as Edu. The author of 24,000 is Periavaccan Pillai who made an additional contribution of providing commentary for all the 4000 verses known as Nalayira Divya Prabandam. His commentary was approved and blessed by his master Nampillai and consequently Periavaccan Pillai earned the celebrity status of being called as King of Commentators, *vyâkyâna chakravarti*. His lucid style adopts Sanskrit words to Tamil in the ratio 2:1 and explains Nanjiyar's commentary (of 9000) by providing clarification to difficult words (Ref 84).

Vâdi-Kesari Azhakiya Manavala cîyar was not only the disciple of Peria-vaccan-pillai but later continued to be the disciple of Pillai's son, Nayinar-acchan-pillai. The Ciyar earned the title Vâdi Kesari for his skills in arguments with Advaitins. His commentary Pannîrâyira Padi (of 12,000) expounds Tiruvai Mozhi from the stand point of Artha-Panchakam.

Vadi Kesari had obviously drawn his inspiration from the tanian of Vangîpurattu Nambi who is said to have rebutted the critics' objection that, Tiruvai Mozhi, a work in Tamil, cannot be accorded the hoary lore status of a Brahma Vidya, for that being the preserve of the time-honoured 'Fourteen Vidyas', which are all in Sanskrit. Any spiritual work should be imbued with the spirit and flavor of the shrutis for acceptance and the tanian of Vangipurattu Nambi projects unequivocally the central theme of TM as being no different from the one outlined in the Harita Samhita, according to which the burden of the song of any of the work belonging to the Vedic-lore should echo the spirit of 'Artha Panchakam' which we have mentioned and explained the verse earlier.

"The Bhagavad Vishaya as well as BS employ the same vedantic method, and use the same spiritual language. The first two chapters of BS determine the nature of the *tattva*, the third defines the *hita* and the fourth deals with the *purushârtha*. In the same way, the first section of the Bhagavad Vishaya is the meditation on the chief tattva or prâpya. The second section describes the hita or *upâya* and the last section the purushârtha or *prâpti*. Thus, the beginning (*upakrama*) as well as the end (*upasamhâra*) is identical in both the systems. The end and aim of Ubhaya Vedânta is summed up in the Upanishad: 'He who knows Brahman attains the Highest.' Just as the whole teaching of BS is summed up in Chatus-sutri', the meaning of the entire TM is epitomized in the four lines of the first verse '*uyarvara*' (page 433 of Ref 43).

See also Artha Panchakam –the fifth poem of Deshika Prabandam. The Divine Couple (Divya Dampati) constitute the Supreme God-Head (மிக்கவிறைநிலையும்). The jivâtmas are the embodied individual souls suffering bondage due to karma. The means of liberation consist in adopting either bhakti or Prapatti route, *mârga*. The stumbling block that stand in the way of spiritual progress are two-fold sins of the individual which have accumulated from the time immemorial past and obstructions to lead spiritual life (*samujjîvanam*). The above aspects constituting the message of the Vedas (artha panchakam) are taught by Nammazhwar through the medium of Tamil, the sound of which is vibrant like the music of lute.

In the "12,000" the ten centuriums of TM are divided into three broad sections- the first four, the middle two and the last four: The first four deal with Paravara-Tattva; the middle two with the methodology viz. siddha / sâddhya upâya. The last four teach the ways and means to get rid of the undesirables thus paving the way for the attainment of the desirable goal.

॥ अनिष्ट निवृत्ति पूर्वक इष्ट प्राप्तिः ॥

We may refer to the recent edition (1989) of "The 12000" published by the author Dr. M. Varadarajan with financial assistance from TTD. A brief extract from the introduction, tells the merits found in 12000: "Though rather brief the commentary contains an explanation of all the words and epithets, which enables the reader to understand easily and appreciate the basic ideas in TM mentioned in other commentaries. He has brought in detail that TM elucidates the Artha Panchaka in the main and the Rahasya Traya."

It is said that Vâdi Kesari's (his period 1242- 1350) other work 'Tattva Dîpam' contain several references to Swami Deshika's works and it appears that the former was elder by more than ten years. All the five commentaries are extolled by the saint Manavâla Mâmunigal (1370-1443) in his poem, Upadesha Ratna Malai (Pillai Lokâchârya, the son of Vadakkutiruvîdi Pillai is considered as the pioneer of Tenkalai school. He is also sometimes referred to as younger pillai to distinguish him from Nampillai who lived earlier and was succeeded by Manavala Mamunigal). The verse eulogizing 'The 12000' is quoted below:

அன்போடழகிய மணவாளச்சீயர்
பின்போரும் கற்றறிந்து பேசுகைக்கா -தம்பெரிய
போதமுடன் மாறன் மறையின்பொருளுரைத்தது
ஏதமில் பன்னீராயிரம்

The Vada kalai Sect

In the biography of Ramanuja there is reference to an incidence explaining the circumstances under which Ramanuja was brought under the benign care of Kidambi Achan thanks to the good offices of Goshthipûrna. The tradition of Kidambi is known as Yatîshvara Mâhânasa Sampradâyam (refer the first verse of Sharanâgati Dîpika) since Kidambi took up the role of a cook to protect the health of Ramunuja whose very life was under the threat of being poisoned.

॥ मान्यं यतीश्वर महानसंसंप्रदायम्॥

He was no ordinary cook but founder of a sect which has earned name and fame over the millennium. In the language of Sri Nigamanta Maha Deshikan, who is the grandest architect of a sampradâya the world has ever known, the aroma emanating from the kitchen has carried forward special flavor and unique taste imparting idioms and phrases that are peculiar only to this tradition, known as Vada kalai. (Paramapâda Sopânam).

எதிவரனார் மடைப்பள்ளி வந்த மணம் எங்கள்
வார்த்தையுள் மன்னியதே.

By far the most distinguishing difference is the status accorded to Lakshmi, as is quite evident in Shri Stuti of Deshika. The Lord and His Consort forming the Divine Couple constitute one single God-Head and they form an inseparable pair, if we go by the all-embracing doctrine of *aprutak siddha*. If the verse 9 of Sri Stuti is any indication the controversy has exercised several minds unnecessarily: some would regard Lakshmi as the ultimate ruler while others attribute the Lordship only to Vishnu and so on. The shrutis declare that the Lord engages Himself in the Divine sport of Creation only to please Lakshmi.

"The Tenkalai is more monotheistic when he denies the dual nature of Infinite and relegates Lakshmi to the level of jîva" (vide page 534

409

of PNS book which lists 18 points of difference between the two sects. In the book "Tenkalaiyum Vadakalaiyum" the author Krishnaswamy Iyengar also begins his discussion with this point of difference in status accorded to Shri."

Vadakalai school's contribution on Bhagavad Vishayam is in no small measure. Apart from Dravidopanishad Sâra and Ratnavali, Deshika is believed to have contributed a massive commentary of size "72,000" (known as Nigama Parimalam) but unfortunately it is lost. Before going in for a detailed study of Deshika's works on the subject it would be worth mentioning the commentaries of âchâryas who came later to Deshika. Ranga Ramanuja Muni, the famous Upanishad Bhashyakarar, wrote a commentary "the 9000" in Sanskrit in response to the request of Kannada speaking devotees of the temple town, Melkote. It appears the commentary though makes repeated references to Sara and Ratnavali does not present an exhaustive account of the poems of Deshika. Portions of the text in the palm leaf manuscript got 'eaten away' by the termites! However, the whole poem was deciphered and reclaimed by Venkatadri and this version was adopted by Sâkshât Swâmy in his commentary "24,000" which is in the manipravâLa style.

The objectionable sections found in the commentaries of Nampillai's successors have been pointed out by Peria Parakalaswami in his commentary "the 11,000" and he has adopted some of the thought trends (yojanas) of Upanishad Bhashyakarar's commentary. (Ref 86) and for english translation Ref 87).

Uttamur has some reservation regarding Vadi Kesari's claim that the whole of TM is structured solely based on Artha Panchakam. We may refer to the two verses 127 &128 of D. Ratnavali in this connection. A host of benefits, apart from Arthapanchakam, are mentioned by Deshika while summing TM in the two verses. For a Prapanna who has performed *âtmasamarpanam* there hardly remains anything to be done or achieved. He would lead a blissful life free of any commitment. He would have no obstacle that is unsurmountable to face in the ensuing future.

While on the topic of means (upâya), a few of Swami's Rahasya works should be recalled here. In Tattvamâtrkâ, for example, the ontological realities of Visishtâdvaita siddhânta are explained or better still defined in 51 pithy sentences one for each of the 51 Parâvara Tattvas. The word *mâtrkâ* refers to the 51 alphabets of Sanskrit starting from 'a' to 'ksha' and tattva broadly denotes the 'Three Fundamental Realities' and hence the title, tattvamatrka. These realities are explained invariably with quotations from Tamil Prabandam and particularly the 23 tattva dealing with the soul's road map of liberation (muktas) containing pâsurams profusely drawn from TM alone. This study would be more rewarding if further supplemented with some more of TM quoted in another of Deshika's Rahasya granta viz. Parama-pâda-sopanam (6).

TM as a Sahasra Nâmâvali
Even the earlier commentators notably the two Pillais, set the trend of condensing the TM into succinct phrases as indicative of the content of the respective set. For example, at the close of the First hundred, the '24,000' sums up each ten of the first hundred as an attribute of the Lord Almighty while Eedu condenses each hundred. But Swami Deshika went further and coined phrases (nâmâvalis) not only for each hundred or each ten but also for every single stanza of TM. Thus, the thousand stanzas of TM are condensed as Sahasra Namavali (Ref 92).

|| यानि नामानि गौणानि विख्यातानि महात्मनः ||

The nâmâvali discovered and realized by Shatakopa should be considered more important than that of the Rishis' who are held in high esteem for being the discoverers of Mantras. The reason for

411

Nammazhwar's supremacy, according to Deshika is that his TM is a special branch of the Vedas (*sarvîya shâkha*), meant for serving everyone without an exception. TM is not a painstaking composition but spontaneous outpouring of what appeared before the saint's inner eye, as Deshika puts it in Paduka Sahasram. Sitting in the cave of the holy tamarind tree he saw the 'olive-branch' and presented it to the blessed people of kali yug through his faithful messenger-cum-disciple Madura Kavi! The cluster of words constituting the branch was propagated through the pleasant aroma of vakula flowers composing the garland which was adorning the *tirumeni* of Nammazhwar.

वर्णस्तोमैर्वकुलसुमनोवासनामुद्वहन्ती

मान्नायां प्रकृतिमपरां संहितां दृष्टवन्तम्।

The strategy Nammazhwar prescribes is an efficacious one specially tailored for the people of kaliyug. No need to go through the time-consuming process of yoga-mârga involving aeons of time- the aspirant must pass through several lives of penance and sacrifice before attaining his desired goal i.e. brahma-prâpti. This strategy (Prapatti) is no different from the one given at the end of Gitopadesha which was revealed by the one and only one Krishna who had a penchant for secrecy either of secret teachings (as a charioteer) or as a wonder-kid secretly stealing butter kept in the high loft (TM 2.3.8)!

குறிக்கொள் ஞானங்களால் எனையூழி செய்தவமும்
கிறிக்கொண்டு இப்பிறப்பே சிலநாளில் எய்தினன் யான்
உறிக்கொண்ட வெண்ணெய்ப்பால் ஒளித்துண்ணுமம்மான்பின்
நெறிக்கொண்ட நெஞ்சனாய்ப்பிறவிதுயர் கடிந்தே.

ॐ देवाय श्रीशाय स्वसिद्धेः करणाय नमः ।

श्रीभगवन्नामदशकम्	திருவாய்மொழி
ॐ सेवायोग्याय नमः	முதற்பத்து
„ अतिभोग्याय नमः	இரண்டாம் பத்து
„ शुभसुभगतनवे नमः	மூன்றும் பத்து
„ सर्वभोग्यातिशायिने नमः	நான்காம் பத்து
„ ध्वस्तद्धेतुदाने नमः	ஐந்தாம் பத்து
„ प्रपदनसुलभाय नमः	ஆறும் பத்து
„ अनिष्टविध्वंसशीलाय नमः	ஏழாம் பத்து
„ भक्तच्छन्दानुवर्तिने नमः	எட்டாம் பத்து
„ निरधिकसुहृदे नमः	ஒன்பதாம் பத்து
„ सत्पदव्यां सहायाय नमः	பத்தாம் பத்து
ॐ श्रीमते नमः	

THE 1000 PITHY PHRASES OF DTR TOGETHER WITH THE ABOVE 10 ARE OFFERED

AS SAHASRANAMA ARCHANA OF THIRUVAIMOZHI IN SANSKRIT.

FOR DETAILS, SEE REF. 92.

Merits in Commentaries

Whenever necessary weightier arguments (based upon authoritative sources) are advanced to counter the views expressed by one or the other of the earlier commentators.

In his commentary on Tiruviruttam, Peria vacacchan Pillai, after weighing the options, preferred to accept the view that Nammazhwar was a samsâri. But this point was once again raised by Peria Parakalaswami in his commentary, "The 11,000"and the said view of Pillai was rejected on the ground of the evidence available in Kurugâpura Mâhâtmyam (vide Bhavishyat PurâNa) in which Kurugûr Shathagopa is spoken of as a Nitya Sûri. It would be demeaning to reduce him to the level of an ordinary samsâri. In Samakhya Paddhati of Paduka Sahasram, Nammazhwar is addressed as Shathajit and this very special name of his is attributed to the fact that even at birth he had extraordinary powers which enabled him to overcome the nascent forces of prakrti (manifesting as *shata vâyu*) which is supposed to impart delusion soon after birth. To put it in another way, not only he was uninfluenced but retained his pristine awareness of Parama Pâdam, from where he was sent on a mission of serving the role of Preceptor of Kali Yuga, to earth.

॥ शठं गूडविप्रियकृतं जयतीति शठजित्॥

Dravidopanishad Sâra

The Dravidopanishad Sâra (DS for short) of Vedânta Deshika presents the essence of TM in 26 verses. The first verse gives the essence of each hundred (starting from *sevâyogyan, atibhogyan* etc.) while the second verse elucidates the master plan or the rationale behind the arrangement of the ten shatakas. The kernel of 20 verses not only present to us the quintessence of each of the ten shatakas of TM but also informs the link in thought with the succeeding shatakam. The last four verses of Sâra deal with the conclusion (Ref 88).

In the second verse of Sara the broad plan of TM is outlined. The first hundred, to repeat, is upâya, the second upeya; the third is common as we said before. The remaining seven shatakams explain upâya and upeya, not in that order as found dealt with in the first two hundreds. The fourth hundred is upeya instead since it is relatively a minor issue to be disposed first. The rationale behind is explained through an example: Suppose two customers, the earlier needing a sword and a customer needing a small needle arrive at a smithy workshop. The blacksmith in the workshop would entertain the needle order first and execute it quickly and then only would take up making of the sword, setting aside the first-cum-first served principle. The upeya aspect is dealt with in 4th and the upâya being an elaborate issue gets dealt with in six shatakams, from 5th to 10th. A mumukshu is made of a sterner stuff. The reader should note that Vedânta Deshika has used the same phrase *vishha madhu*, here in the second verse of Sara as well as RTS 7, *mumukshutvâdhikâra*.

Dravidopanishad Tatparya Ratnavali (DTR)

The DTR is also a work of abridgement but provides insight into each verse of TM. The name Ratnavali implies, the three-fold art of abstracting the essential meaning and significance, of selecting a gem from each pâsuram, and stringing together the gems in the form of artistic garland. Thus, the phrases abstracted are the equivalent of aphorisms (sutras) of BS. The phrases are expressed sequentially in a shloka cast in Srakdhara which literally means garland of flowers, *pâmâlai*.

Of the 130 verses in DTR the first are introductory (*avatârika*), from 11 to 124 devoted to coining phrases for each of the 1000 verses of TM and 125 to 130 are set apart for the conclusion (*nigamanam*). Of the 114 verses comprising the text proper, 10 verses are for epitomizing the shatakams as is done in Sara and the four extras are distributed between 1 for the first and 3 for the fourth decadium. Verses which sum up the shatakams in Ratnavali share a common or identical purpose with those of the ones in DS and the corresponding verse numbers can be paired to facilitate quick reference: 22,3; 33,6; 44,8; 58,10; 69,12; 80,14; 91,16; 102,18; 113,20; and 124,22.

415

Introductory (avatarika) verses of DTR

Saraswati is a generic term applied to speech (*vâk* or *vângmayam*) composed of words, phrases or sentences –in general known as *sârasvatas*. Among all the works in all languages the greatest is Tiruvâi Mozhi (T.M) contributed by Shatagopan for the benefit of the whole mankind (*sâra: sârasvatânâm shaTharipu phaNiti:*). TM serves as a palacial *antahpura* (private quarters for women) for Shanti Devi (*shânti shuddhânta sîmâ*).

Maya binds the people of the world through its three guNas born out of prakriti (*âyâminibhi: svaguNa vitatibhi: bandhayantîm*). This bond is the equivalent of poison caused by snake bite. TM has the power to suck this poison of maya out and free the victim from the sting. In other words, TM helps the people to cross the sea of *samsâra* (*pâram-parîta: bhava jaladhi bhavan manjjanânâm janânâm pâram*). After crossing the sea, TM further guides the soul to come to the vicinity of the Divine Couple (*pratyak prati niyata ramâ sannidhânam*) and show us (*na: pratyakshayet*) the great treasure waiting to be discovered (*nidhânam*).

This first verse of Dramidopanishad Tatparya Ratnavali compares well with the *dhyâna shloka* of Sri Bhâshyam (SB) –*samsârâgni vidîpana vyapagata prâNâtma sanjîvinîm*.

The a/m verse of SB states that Veda Vyasa churned the ocean of Upanishads to extract the essence known as Brahma Sutras. In a similar manner, Swami Deshika churned the Tamil Upanishad (Dravidopanishad) of Shatagopa to extract the essence (*tattallabdhi prasaktai:*) and expressed them in sutra-like Sanskrit phrases. This he did in response to his ardent followers (*vibudhai: arthita:*). He used his knowledge that he obtained from his pûrva-âchârya (sampradayam) as the churning rod (*prajnyakhye mantha-shaile*) and the rope for extraction (*netrayan*) of attributes of Emberuman (*pratita guNa ruchim*) from the ocean of TM (*kalpantha yuna: talpam shaThajid upanishhad dugdha sindhum vimadhnan*). From the churning emerged thousand

416

phrases (*svadu gadha lahari dasha shati nirgatam*). It is not a haphazard heap of diamonds but skillfully composed necklace of immaculate excellence, thanks to the composer. Hence the name 'Ratnâvali'. Lord Narayana is referred to as (*kalpânta yûna:*) which means that He remains ever a youth. By stating that TM served as the bed (*talpam*) for the Lord (of the Milky Ocean), it is indicated that TM represents Dvaya Mantra meant for contemplation. Since diamond provides delightful experience when viewed from different angles TM conveys different messages –it is an eloborate treatise, for example, on the 'Doctrine of Surrender' or '*dîrga sharanagatî*'; it can serve as a manual of '*artha panchakam*' and so on and so forth. Unlike the inert diamonds, these are lively ones (*ratna jatam*) capable of generating new avenues of thought.

The third shloka of DTR has reference to a scene in Maha Bharat (Virata Parva). The females who saw Draupati during her bathing, fell for her beauty lock stock and barrel –totally captivated by her irresistible charm. For enjoyment, they imagined themselves as men and sited her (*pumbhâvam manasâ yayu:*)! Draupati through her beauty stole their hearts (*pânchâlî gâtra shobhâhrta hrdaya vadhû varga pumbhâva nîtya*). In a similar way Nammazhwar turns into a woman as Parangusha Nayaki. She fell for Emberuman who was the darling of Sri Padma Devi, His wife (*patyau praNayini padmâ sahâye*). The Nayaki loses herself to Him (*preyasî pâra-tantriyam*). The Nayaki's consuming love for Him (*muner bhâva bandha prathimnâ*) transformed devotion into love (*bhakti: shrungara vrttya pariNamati*). In this verse, another issue is also sorted out. There are joyous moments when the Azhwar is with Him and during times of depression he loses company or contact with Him. At such sad moments, he sends someone as an envoy. This phenomenon is explained. For a devotee experiencing Him during Yoga, are the joyous moments and sad when the contact is lost. The âchârya acts as a go between or as an envoy to restore yoga (connection). Prior to yoga and after are the depressing moments (*yogât prâk uttarâvastiti: viraha:*). At such moments of

417

seperation the âchâryas come as an envoy (of God) and reconnect the *sâdhaka* to the joyful state of Samadhi (*viraho deshikâ: tatra dûtâ:*).

The first of Nammâzhwar is *Tiruviruttam* of 100 *pâsurams*. In this poem, the Azhwar highlights the woeful life of samsâra and makes an ardent appeal to the Lord to get him freed from karma-bound body which is detrimental to the development of higher consciousness. To overcome the limitations imposed by the body constituted of prakrti, the Lord imparts spiritual knowledge which would eventually develop the awareness of the soul and this is the burden of the song in the second work, Tiruvâciriam. Exposure of knowledge of the soul reveals the soul's absolute dependence on God, the creator. This revelation provides a glimpse of Sri Vaikunta where the Nitya Sûris share their delightful experience with the Lord. The yearning for Sri Vaikunta increases by leaps and bounds for the Azhwar. The Azhwar pours out his cravings to unite with the Lord by talking, thinking and remembering relentlessly about the Lord. All this is the subject matter of Peria Tiruvandadi. The fourth one, Tiruvâi Mozhi, is his magnum opus and in this long poem (which is considered as the equivalent of Sama Veda) he gives the roadmap to achieve Sri Vaikuntam. The essence of Nammâzhwar works as outlined above will be found summarized in Swami Deshika's verse quoted below:

आद्ये स्वीयप्रबन्धे शठजिदभिदधे संसृतेर्दुस्सहत्वं

द्वैतीयीके स्वरूपाद्यखिलमथ हरेरन्वभूत् स्पष्टदृष्टम्।

तार्तीयीके स्वकीयां भगवदनुभवे स्फोरयामास तीव्रां

आशां तुर्ये यथेष्टं भगवदनुभवादाप मुक्तिं शठारिः॥

DTR on the Ten Hundreds of TV
The Upanishads propagate the message that God himself is the means (*upâya*) for the jîvâtma and God himself is the goal to be

aspired for and attained. TM conveys the same message in easy to follow Tamil and hence TM is called Dravidopanishad.

स्वप्राप्तेस्स्वयमेव साधनतया जोघुष्यमाणः श्रुतौ

सत्त्वस्थेषु भजेत सन्निधिमसौ शान्तावधिः शेवधिः ॥

To make the message of TM loud and clear, the ten groups of hundred each constituting the text of TM, project ten attributes of God and taken TM expounds the Dvaya Mantra. We will come to this aspect a little later after explaining the attributes in the respective shatakams.

The first hundred defines and expounds God i.e. Brahmam, as the Supreme Self, who alone is adorable and fit to be worshipped-*sevâyogyan*. What is adorable is also blissful and this is the subject of the 2nd hundred. What is adorable and blissful cannot be formless. The third hundred, therefore, describes the beautiful form, Divya Mangala Vigraha, of the Lord. Thus, it is unambiguously emphasized that the aprâkrta form (*tirumeni* or '*mûrti*', to put it in other equivalent words) is a mandatory requirement for the pursuit of Brahma Prâpti both as upâya and as upeya. The inclusion of *Shubhashrayatvatva* excludes all other non-Visishtadvaitic approaches to Brahma Prâpti.

॥ सेवायोग्योऽतिभोग्यः शुभसुभगतनुः ॥

But the beautiful form should not induce the *âshrita* (bhakta) to seek hedonistic pleasures of *aiswarya* or revel in spiritual form *kaivalya*. Attaining Him is greater than all the goals since succumbing to either Iswarya or kaivalya is bound to result in continuance in bondage. For, Kaivalya, after all, is not eternal but, only a temporary relief from samsâra. The 4th is *sarvabhogyâtishâyî*. He is the means as well as the fruit and thus He is the means for satisfying all requirements that

419

befall in one's life-5th The key to elicit His grace for liberation is the physical act of surrender (Prapatti) to Him-6th.

॥ सर्वभोग्यातिशायी श्रेयस्तद्धेतुदाता प्रपदन सुलभः ॥

Owing to one's past karma, several undesirable things are likely to happen and hinder the Pilgrim's progress. They would get prevented or the effects get annulled thanks to His intervention and benign influence-7th. During the life of the ashrita, several demands would occur in life and at the ashrita's bidding, the Lord fulfills those requirements-8th. But the lord acts in a way that is beneficial to the ashrita like a well wisher or a friend. He would act spontaneously under some pretext without even waiting for a request or a prayer - 9th. He escorts the ashrita through the Archirâti route till the attainment of Eternal Bliss in Sri Vaikunta- 10th. Thus, the sum and substance of TM is explained in those ten pithy phrases of the first verse of Dravidopanishad Sâra.

॥ अनिष्टविध्वंशशीलः भक्तच्छन्दानुवर्ती निरुपधिकसुहृत् सत्पदव्यां सहायः ॥

In this manner, TM conveys the grand message that the Para Brahmam is Himself the prâpaka and prâpya, the upâya and the upeya, all in one. The last four shatakams (7th to 10th) concern with the exposition of namah occurring at the end of Dvaya Mantra. The consensus among all the commentators is that TM unmistakably expounds Dvaya Mantra in all its grandeur and majesty. Sriman Narayana, the God-Head (Para Tattva) occurring in the first half and the second half of the Dvaya Mantra representing respectively the upâya (means) and upeya (goal) constitute the first two hundreds of TM. The word 'charaNau' of the mantra (the part viz. the Feet standing for the whole) is representative of the auspicious form of contemplation-the subject matter of the 3rd shatakam of TM. The dative case ending 'âya' (of NârayaNâya) emphasizes that He alone should be aspired for and not any other goal such as Iswarya or Kaivalya- *ananyaprâpyatva*, 4th shatakam of TM.

Thus, the four centuriums expound the words in the Dvaya which are attached with the word Narayana. The following are the remaining words in Dvaya to be correlated to TM:

॥ शरणं प्रपद्ये नमः ॥

That He confers all auspiciousness to the ashrita, (He is the receptacle of all that is good) is dealt with in the 5th centum-corresponding to the word *sharanam* of Dvaya. By performing the act of surrender himself, Nammazhwar demonstrates the significance of '*prapadye*' in the sixth shatakam. The shatakams 7 to 10 expound the import of *namah* as explained before.

There are several brilliant features structured into TM. They would become self evident as we comprehend the import from the stand point of Tirumandiram, Dvayam, Brahma Vidya, Yoga Shastra or Sharanagati Shastra. It goes without saying that Bhagat Vishayam must be learnt from a preceptor.

TM as an operation Manual of Prapatti Shastra:
The BS speaks at length of Bhakti or Upasana and makes only a passing reference to Prapatti –*tasya cha vasikaranam tac-sharanagatireva*. But TM describes both Bhakti (loving and uninterrupted contemplation) and Prapatti (loving whole-hearted surrender) and shows a marked preference for the latter as it is comparatively easy and open to all, thus providing for the yuga dharma. This central message of Prapatti as the only means of Bhagavat Prâpti is show-cased in TM 6.10.10.

அகலகில்லேன் இறையுமென்று அலர்மேல்மங்கையுறைமார்பா!
நிகரில்புகழாய்! உலகம்மூன்றுடையாய்! என்னையாள்வானே!
நிகரிலமரர்முனிக்கணங்கள் விரும்பும் திருவேங்கடத்தானே!

421

புகலொன்றில்லா அடியேன் உன்னடிக்கீழ் அமர்ந்து புகுந்தேனே.

The above concise text of Prapatti can be translated as follows: "The Lord is infinitely great in knowledge, power, strength, brilliance and the like and is full of mercy and loving kindness. He is the Lord of all the worlds; and is my master. I am His servant and is a fit object of His protection. His has been an interminable round of protective care of souls; I have no other refuge; and have no merit of any kind; and I seek refuge on thy Lotus Feet."

This pâsuram of TM is considered as the equivalent of Dvaya Mantra and the one to one correspondence between the two is as under:

Srimad = *akala killen … mangaiurai mârbâ*
Narayana = *nikaril … thiruvenkataththâne*
charaNau = *unadikkîzh*
sharaNam prapadye = *adiyen amarnthu pugundene pukalonRillâ*
srimate nârâyaNâya namah = The sole object of surrender is only to be for service at His Lotus Feet.

The above-mentioned service (*kainkarya*) is abundantly made clear in TM 3.3.1. This verse is considered as the equivalent of Thirumandiram and dedicated to the Lord of the Seven Hills.

Swami Deshika, in his magnum opus, Rahasya Traya Sara, concludes in the summing up (*nigamana*) chapter in the following words:

தாளிணைக் கீழ் ஒழிவில் காலமெல்லாம் உடனாய் மன்னி
வழுவிலா அடிமை செய்யவேண்டும் நாம் என்ற மனோ ரதத்தின்
படியே ஸர்வ தேச ஸர்வகால ஸர்வாவஸ்தோசித ஸர்வவித கைங்கர்
யங்களையும் பெற்று வாழ்வார்கள்.

The Equivalence of Tiruvâi Mozhi (T.M) and Brahma Sutras (BS)

Nammazhwar conveys the gist of the Shariraka shastra in the very first *padikam* (also called as *dashakam* which means a set of ten veses), nay in the very first verse of Tiruvâi Mozhi. Experiencing Tiruvai Mozhi is like watching the 20-20 cricket match. The opening verse is a sixer indeed. *Uyarvara uyarnalam* suggests that the Azhwar has in his mind the ascending domains of joy described in Anandavalli. The Supreme God-Head is the only one who has the Supreme Bliss under His command and He only can confer that Bliss to us. He is the one who endowed us with indefatiguable intellect for boundless devotion. He is the Lord of the Nitya Sûris and the devas. "O Mind! Offer your obeisance to the effulgent feet of that Lord for getting rid of the griefs of samsâra."

It is difficult to reach Him. The mind may be purified but that will not help much. He is beyond the comprehension of the senses. With the debilitatating equipment we possess He cannot be comprehended at all. Nonetheless the fact remains that this all time great Lord enjoys undiminishing greatness for ever and what is more He is residing in each and everybody's heart. "O Mind! Without losing hope keep worshipping Him who is within you" (2).

There are people who worship other gods because of the difference in their level of intellect and their worship of a particular deity to secure a particular fruit in view. Each deity is entrusted with the power to shower the benefits prayed for. The worship and attainment is governed by the individual's destiny (*vidi vazhi*). Little do they know that everything comes from the ultimate God-Head. The reader may refer to Gita verses 20, 21&22 of the seventh chapter where Gitâchârya explains the mindset of these class of worshippers. The hymn '*ishtâpûtam*' which occurs in '*ambasyapâre*' is quoted for the context.

ஸ்ரீ:

முதற்பத்து

திருவடிக்கீழ்த்தந்தேரவேல பேறென்றறுதியிடுதல்

[1]-ஆந்திருவாய்மொழி - உயர்வறவுயர்நலம்

எம்பெருமான் திருவடிகளிலே நிச்சலுமடிமைசெய்ய
ஆழ்வார் தம் திருவுள்ளத்துக்கு அறிவுறுத்தல்

கலிவிருத்தம்

(பண்—முதிர்ந்தகுறிஞ்சி, தாளம் — ஏழொத்து கமஸ் ராகம் — ஆதிதாளம்)

†† உயர்வறவுயர்நலம் உடையவன் [2]யவனவன் ★
மயர்வறமதிநலம் அருளினன்யவனவன் ★
அயர்வறுமமரர்கள் அதிபதியவனவன் ★
துயரறுசுடரடி தொழுதெழென்மனனே!   1

மனனகமலமற மலர்மிசையெழுதரும் ★
மனனுணர்வளவிலன் பொறியுணர்வவையிலன் ★
இனனுணர்முழுநலம் எதிர்நிகழ்கழிவினும் ★
இனிலனெனனுயிர் மிகுநரையிலனே.   2

இலனதுவுடையனிது எனநினைவரியவன் ★
நிலனிடைவிசும்பிடை உருவினனருவின் ★
புலனொடுபுலனலன் ஒழிவிலன்பரந்த ★ அந்
நலனுடையொருவனை நணுகினம்நாமே.   3

நாமவனிவனுவன் அவளிவளுவளெவள் ★
தாமவரிவருவர் அதுவிதுவுதுவேது ★
வீமவையிலையவுவை அவைநலம்தீங்கவை ★
ஆமவையாயவை ஆய்நின்றவரே.   4

அவரவர்தமதமது அறிவறிவகைவகை ★
அவரவரிறையவர் எனவடியடைவர்கள் ★
அவரவரிறையவர் குறைவிலரிறையவர் ★
அவரவர்விதிவழி அடையநின்றனரே.   5

---

1. இந்தத் திருவாய்மொழி. கோயில் திருவாய் மொழியைச் சேர்ந்தது.
2. எவனவன் என்றும் பாடங்கூறுவர்: மேலும் இப்படியே.

திருவாய்மொழி 601

நின்றனரிருந்தனர் கிடந்தனர்திரிந்திலர்★
நின்றிலரிருந்திலர் கிடந்திலர்திரிந்ததிலர்★
என்றுமொரியல்விளர் எனநினைவரியவர்★
என்றுமொரியல்வொடு நின்றவெந்திடரே. 6

திடவிசும்பெரிவளி நீர்நிலமிவைவெமிசை★
படர்பொருள்முழுவதுமாய் அவையவைதொறும்★
உடல்மிசையுயிரெனக் கரந்தெங்கும்பரந்துளன்★
சுடர்மிகுசுருதியுள் இவையுண்டசுரனே. 7

சுரரறிவருநிலை விண்முதல்முழுவதும்★
வரன்முதலாயவை முழுதுண்டபரபரன்★
புரமொருமூன்றெரித்து அமரர்க்குமறிவியந்து★
அரனயனென உலகழித்தமைத்துளனே. 8

உளனெனெனில் அவனுருவம்இவ்வுருவுகள்★
உளனலெலெனில் அவனருவம்இவ்வருவுகள்★
உளனெனவிலலெனன இவைகுணமுடைமையில்★
உளனிருதகைமையொடு ஒழிவிலன்பரந்தே. 9

பரந்ததண்பரவையுள் நீர்தொறும்பரந்துளன்★
பரந்தவண்டமிதென நிலவிசும்பொழிவற★
கரந்தசிலிடந்தொறும் இடந்திகழ்பொருள்தொறும்★
கரந்தெங்கும்பரந்துளன் இவையுண்டகரனே. 10

††கரவிசும்பெரிவளி நீர்நிலமிவைவெமிசை★
வரனவில்திறல்வலி அளிபொறையாய்நின்ற★
பரனடிமேல் குருகூர்ச்சடகோபன்சொல்★
நிரனிறையாயிரத்து இவைபத்தும்வீடே. 11

அடிவரவு:- உயர் மனன் இலன் நாம் அவர் நின்ற திடசுரர் உளன் பரந்த கர வீடு.

நம்மாழ்வார் திருவடிகளே சரணம்.

[1]2-ஆந்திருவாய்மொழி - வீடுமின்

பக்தியுடன் எம்பெருமானையடைய பிறர்க்கறிவுறுத்தல்

வஞ்சித்துறை

(பண் — முதிர்ந்தகுறிஞ்சி, தாளம் — ஏழொத்து
செந்தருட்டிராகம் — ஆதிதாளம்)

† †வீடுமின் முற்றவும் ★
வீடுசெய்து ★ உம்முயிர்
வீடுடையானிடை ★
[2]வீடு செய்ம்மினே. 1

மின்னின்நிலையில ★
மன்னுயிராக்கைகள் ★
என்னுமிடத்து ★ இறை
உன்னுமின்நீரே. 2

நீர்நுமதென்றிவை ★
வேர்முதல்மாய்த்து ★ இறை
சேர்மின், உயிர்க்கு ★ அதன்
நேர்நிறையில்லே. 3

இல்லதுமுள்ளதும் ★
அல்லதவனுரு ★
எல்லையிலந்நலம் ★
புல்குபற்றற்றே. 4

அற்றதுபற்றெனில் ★
உற்றதுவீடுயிர் ★
செற்றதுமன்னுறில் ★
அற்றிறைபற்றே. 5

பற்றிலனீசனும் ★
முற்றவும் நின்றனன் ★
பற்றிலையாய் ★ அவன்
முற்றிலடங்கே. 6

அடங்கெழில்சம்பத்து ★
அடங்கக்கண்டு ★ ஈசன்
அடங்கெழிலஃதென்று ★
அடங்குகவுள்ளே. 7

உள்ளமுரைசெயல் ★
உள்ளவிம்மூன்றையும் ★
உள்ளிக்கெடுத்து ★ இறை
யுள்ளிலொடுங்கே. 8

ஒடுங்கவவன்கண் ★
ஒடுங்கலுமெல்லாம் ★
விடும் பின்னுமாக்கை ★
விடும்பொழுதெண்ணே. 9

† †எண்பெருக்கந்நலத்து ★
ஒண்பொருளீறில ★
வண்புகழ்நாரணன் ★
திண்கழல்சேரே. 10

† †சேர்த்தடத் ★ தென்குரு
கூர்ச்சடகோபன்சொல் ★
சீர்த்தொடையாயிரத்து ★
ஓர்த்தவிப்பத்தே. 11

அடிவரவு:- வீடு மின் நீர் இல்லது அற்ற பற்று அடங்கு உள்ளம் ஒடுங்க எண் சேர் பத்து.

நம்மாழ்வார் திருவடிகளே சரணம்.

---
1 இது கோயில் திருவாய்மொழி.
2. வீடிசெமினே என்றும் பாடம்.

A convincing explanation is given by our pûrvâchâryas. An unruly son quarels with his mother, leaves the house in a huff and after wandering the whole day, comes to a nearby choultry, late in the night, tired and hungry. The son is fed by the warden, little does the son know that the food has come from his own merciful mother. The ultimate God-Head Sriman Narayana is like the caring mother! In the succeeding two pâsurams 6&7, Nammazhwar waxes lyrical about this Ultimate God-Head as the creator of the universe. The 6th verse proclaims that all the chit and achit are under His command and control. In the 7th pâsuram, Nammazhwar establishes that the ultimate God-Head he is talking about, is none other than the Para Brahmam glorified in the BS / Sri Bhâshyam.

जगदीश्वरयोः शरीरत्मनिबन्धनम्॥

To substantiate this view of the azhwar, Arayirapadi quotes a whopping 48 different texts from the Upanishads and 25 from itihasas and purânas.

Mûla Prakrti, the primordial substance is His creation. The cosmic egg takes its origin from this primordial sustance. All the gods including Chatur Mukha Brahma and Shiva fall within this cosmic egg. To give a concrete example, but for Him, Shiva would have faced defeat in Tripura Samhara. Even the power to destroy has to come from Him. For all intents and purposes, pâsuram 8 is devoted to paratatva nirnaya. Incidentally in TM 4.10 Nammazhwar upholds the supremacy of Sriman Narayana in most forthright terms.

In pâsuram 9 the arguments of the nihilist (shûnya-vâdins) are rebutted. Based on strong supporting documents (druda-pramana) the Azhwar enthusiastically proclaims (pâsuram 10) the omnipresence of Brahman in all the three states- creation, maintenance and dissolution. The more one delves deeper into the ten pâsurams of this decad, the more will be the motivation to know

427

the whole thousand and nearer one gets to the land of Infinite Bliss (*vîdu*).

Vedânta Deshika in his Dravidopanishad Sara and Ratnavali, establishes that Tiruvai Mozhi closely follows the teachings of Veda Vyasa's Brahma Sutra. The first seven pâsurams of Tiruvai Mozhi summarizes the contents of the first adhyâya and in addition includes the first pâda of the second adhyâya. Pasurams 8 & 9 refute rival schools, orthodox and heterodox. The tenth pâsuram epitomizes the contents of the second adhyâya. Thus the first ten pâsurams taken togethet is the essence of the first two adhyâyas of BS- Paramâtman is the Siddhopaya and upeya and also refute rival systems of thought.

The next ten verses of the second decad (TM 1.2) correspond to the first two pâdas of the third adhyâya and also part of the third pâda of the third adhyâya.They expatiate on the central theme that Bhagavad-bhakti presupposes as a necessary preliminary the withdrawal of interest from all other things, for the reason that worldly pleasures are beset with deficiencies. They are trivial, transitory, procured with much painful effort, bring pain in their train, preceed from ignorance of one's true nature and prevent man from realising his higher potentialities. On the contrary, Paramâtma is the abode of inexhaustible auspicious qualities (kalyanaguNa) and wholly free from taints and imperfections (*heyapratyanîka*). The need to cultivate complete detachment to everything other than God (*Bhagavat vyatirikta vastu vairagya*) and to direct our prema to God is stressed in the first stanza of this group (TM 1.2.1). The next verse draws attention to the fact that the self endures through all states, while the body is perishable; and the practice of bhakti is to start here and now. The third stanza enjoins the need for rooting out egotism and acquisitive propensities as they are the cause of man's miseries; and the fourth emphasises that the Lord is free from imperfections of any kind. The following stanza refers to the

428

possible danger of the *upâsaka* getting side tracked in *âtmanubhava*, called kaivalya, and warns him to guard against it. Having dealt with the substance of the First Pâda and also parts of the second upto mukta-adhikaraNa of the Third Adhyâya, the rest of the second pâda commencing from Ubhaya –linga-adhikaraNa is then taken up. Stanzas six to eight teach that we should utilise all our faculties – thought word and deed (*uLLum urai cheyal*) –in the service of the Adorable Lord who loves all alike and is interested in the well being of all. The ninth verse briefly touches upon the fruits of bhakti and the tenth establishes that Sriman Narayana is the supreme object of our prema and reveals the sognificance of the term 'Narayana'.

The ultimate Reality, Narayana, is the source and sustainer (ayana) of all other realities (naras), organically integrated in the Real of reals. It explains the nature of *prapatti-marga*. In the manner of the Upanishadic texts – brahmavit apnoti param; mumukshur vai sharana maham prapadye –the results flowing from the upaya are indicated in order to prompt speedy effort. Thus verses 11 to 20 correspond to the first two pâdas of Third Adhyâya.

To meet the possible objection that the cultivation of *Bhagavad-bhakti* is most difficult, the next batch of ten verses (TM 1.3) assures us that the Lord is easy of access to the bhakta and is inaccessible to others, and is thus *bhakti-yoga sulabha*. Besides saulabhya, the other qualities of the Deity are also mentioned. In the third verse of this group (TM 1.3.3) bhaktimarga, is advocated; and after an elaborate treatment of matters related to this, Shatagopa concludes in TM 10. 4.1. (*chârva tavaneRi*) that bhakti is the primary upaya. The modes of bhakti such as nama sankirtana, Tirumantra japa, namaskara, dhyâna and the like are mentioned. (vide TM 10.5.1). This is reminiscent of –manmana bhava, satatam kirtayantomam –of Gita BG 10.34 & 10. 14).

The performance of duties ralating to one's station in life in an attitude of worship of the divine is enjoined. After thus completing the latter off of the Third Adhyâya, the substance of the Fourth Adhyâya is taken up.

The primary phala, bhagavat prasâda and what follows therefrom, namely bhagavad sakshatkara are mentioned in TM 10.6.1

அருள்பெறுவார் அடியார்தம் அடியனேற்கு ஆழியான்
அருள் தருவான் அமைகின்றான் அது நமதுவிதிவகையே.
இருள்தருமாஞாலத்துள் இனி பிறவி வேண்டேன்
மருளொழிநீ மட ஞ்சே வாட்டாற்றானடிவணங்கே.

In the case of those who feel too impatient to wait till the *prarabda-karma* is spent out, the Lord shows His great eagerness to reveal Himself. TM 10.5.7; 10.6.2, & 10.5.10 and others summarise BS (4.1). The second Pâda (4.2) dealing with *Brahmanadi gagikrt* is summarised in TM (10.6.3) and the following TM (10.7.1) describes the Lord's special interest in those who are steadfast in their devotion to Him. That attainment of moksha follows immediately on dissociation from the body is taught in TM (10.7) and (10.7.9). In stanza TM (10.8.1) it is stated that the Lord Himself makes the devotee think of God during the soul's final departure (*antimasmrti*), even if he failed to take the initiative.

The first two pâdas of the Fourth Adhyâya may be said to constitute one division devoted to the description of the fruits that the prapanna enjoys even when he is still with the body; and the last two pâdas form another division dealing with the bliss experienced from the moment the aspirant relinquishes his body. The subject matter of the Third Pâda speaks of how the spiritual pilgrim is receivedby the *ativâhikas*. What is merely touched upon in BS is elaborated in the verse TM (10.9.1) which sums up the thought of the last pâda dealing with final beatific experience. Having once attained that, there is no return therefrom.

[1]9-ஆந்திருவாய்மொழி - சூழ்விசும்பு

நனிசிறந்த அறிவுபெற்ற ஆழ்வார் திருநாட்டுக்குச் சென்று அடியாரோடு சேர்ந்தமையை அருளிச்செய்தல்

கலிவிருத்தம்

(பண் — கொல்லி, தாளம் — ஏழொத்து கல்யாணிராகம் — அடதாளம்)

†† சூழ்விகம்பணிமுகில் தூரியம்முழக்கின ★
ஆழ்கடலலைதிரை கையெடுத்தாடின ★
ஏழ்பொழிலும் வளமேந்தியென்னப்பன் ★
வாழ்புகழ்நாரணன்தமரைக் கண்டுகந்தே.						1

நாரணன்தமரைக்கண்டுகந்து நல்நீர்முகில் ★
பூரணபொற்குடம் பூரித்ததுஉயர்விண்ணில் ★
நீரணிகடல்கள் நின்றார்த்தன ★ நெடுவரைத்
தோரணம்நிரைத்து எங்கும்தொழுதனருலகே.					2

தொழுதனருலகர்கள் தூபநல்மலர்மழை
பொழிவனர் ★ பூமியன்றளந்தவன்தமர்முன்னே ★
எழுமினென்று இருமருங்கிசைத்தனர்முனிவர்கள் ★
வழியிதுவைகுந்தற்குஎன்று வந்தெதிரே.						3

எதிரெதிரிமையவர் இருப்பிடம்வகுத்தனர் ★
கதிரவரவரவர் கைந்நிரைகாட்டினர் ★
அதிர்குரல்முரசங்கள் அலைகடல்முழக்கொத்த ★
மதுவிரிதுழாய்முடி மாதவன்தமர்க்கே.						4

மாதவன்தமரென்று வாசலில்வானவர் ★
போதுமினெமதிடம் புகுதுகவென்றலும் ★
கீதங்கள்பாடினர் கின்னரர்கெருடர்கள் ★
வேதநல்வாயவர் வேள்வியுள்மடுத்தே.						5

வேள்வியுள்மடுத்தலும் விரைகமழ்நறும்புகை ★
க‍ாங்கள்வலம்புரி கலந்தெங்குமிசைத்தனர் ★
ஆண்மின்கள்வானகம் ஆழியான்தமரென்று ★
வாளொண்கண்மடந்தையர் வாழ்த்தினர்மகிழ்ந்தே.				6

---
1. இது கோயில் திருவாய்மொழி.

மடந்தையர்வாழ்த்தலும் மருதரும்வசுக்களும் ★
தொடர்ந்தெங்கும் தோத்திரஞ்சொல்லினர் ★ தொடுகடல்
கிடந்தவெங்கேசவன் கிளரொளிமணிமுடி ★
குடந்தையெங்கோவலன் குடியடியார்க்கே.   7

குடியடியாரிவர் கோவிந்தன்தனக்கென்று ★
முடியுடைவானவர் முறைமுறையெதிர்கொள்ள ★
கொடியணிநெடுமதின் கோபுரம்குறுகினர் ★
வடிவுடைமாதவன் வைகுந்தம்புகவே.   8

வைகுந்தம்புகுதலும் வாசலில்வானவர் ★
வைகுந்தன்தமர்எமர் எமதிடம்புகுதென்று ★
வைகுந்தத்தமரும் முனிவரும்வியந்தனர் ★
வைகுந்தம்புகுவது மண்ணவர்விதியே.   9

விதிவகைபுகுந்தனரென்று நல்வேதியர் ★
பதியினில்பாங்கினில் பாதங்கள்கழுவினர் ★
நிதியும்நற்சுண்ணமும் நிறைகுடவிளக்கமும் ★
மதிமுகமடந்தையர் ஏந்தினர்வந்தே.   10

†† வந்தவரெதிர்கொள்ள மாமணிமண்டபத்து ★
அந்தமில்பேரின்பத்து அடியரோடிருந்தமை ★
கொந்தலர்பொழில் குருகூர்ச்சடகோபன் ★ சொல்
சந்தங்களாயிரத்து இலைவல்லார்முனிவரே.   11

அடிவரவு:- கூழ் நாரணன் தொழுதனர் எதிர்
மாதவன் வேள்வி மடந்தை குடி
வைகுந்தம் விதி வந்து முனி.

நம்மாழ்வார் திருவடிகளே சரணம்.

Srinivasaya Mangalam

References

श्रीः

श्रीमते रामानुजाय नमः।

श्रीमते निगमान्तमहादेशिकाय नमः॥

1. Arthur MacDonnell: "A history of Sanskrit literature" (First Edition 1900).
2. K.C. Varadachari: Complete Works, Volume 9. (April 2001)
3. Veeravalli Jagannathan: Srimad Bhagavad Gita (Based on Ramanuja's Gita Bhashya).
4. Tom Wolfe: "Sorry, But Your Soul Just Died", Orthodoxy Today.org –commentary on social and moral issues of the day
5. Swami Ranganathananda: "The Message of the Upanishads" See under the titles, "Indian Christianity" and "The Upanishads and Indian Islam".
6. Dr. S. Radhakrishnan: Eastern Religion and Western Thought.
7. "Tolerance or Equalization?" published by Sri Vaisnava Sudarsanam, Trichy.
8. "Conversion, an assault on Truth".
9. NIE28 Dec 2006.
10. ravibhatia28@rediffmail.com.
11. Swami Chinmayananda: Kindle Life –The Joy of Living.
12. Vedârtha Sangraha.
13. Swami Prabhupâda: Teachings of Queen Kunti (an ISKCON publication).

14. D.Ramaswamy Iyengar: "Peeps into Mysticism", 1962. The book is in three parts: "The Mystics", "Mysticism" & "The Peeps".
15. Dr. P Narasimhan: Gleanings from the Sri Bhâshya.
16. K.R. Krishnaswamy: Sri Ramanuja Nootrandhadhi (Meanings in English).
17. Pillaiandadi.
18. Yatiraja Saptati (Sri Poundarikapuram Swami Ashramam Publication).
19. Yamunâchârya: Stotra Ratna.
20. The poem Tirucchanda Viruttam of Tirumazhisai Piran.
21. "Rahasya Traya Sara" of Vedânta Deshika.
22. William J Long: "English Literature: Its history and its significance for the life of the English-speaking world", published in the year 1909.
23. Stephen Knop: "Proof of Vedic Culture's Global Existence", year 2000).
24. Veeravalli Jagannathan: Srimad Valmiki Ramayana: A Brief Study.
25. Weber: "Indian Literature".
26. R.G Bhandarkar: "Date of Patanjali".
27. P.T. Srinivasa Iyengar: History of the Tamils.
28. "PurâNas as sources of history revival" by P.L. Bhargava, Prof. K.S. Srinivasa Raghavan and Dr. N. Mahalingam."
29. Bhagavan Das: Krishna (Bharatiya Vidya Bhavan, 1990).
30. "Indian Antiquary", Bombay, Vol. III, p16, (1874).
31. Kural (Translated into English verses) by Sundaram (Penguin).
32. Guruparampara Saram of Rahasya Traya Sara.
33. Vedânta Deshika's "Sri Sampradaya Parishuddhi".
34. Swami Ramakrishnananda: Life of Sri Ramanuja.
35. Yatiraja Saptati.

36. The consummate artist Kalaijnyar has marvelously show cased this event in his serial "Ramanujar" (this episode was shown on 16 Jan 2017).

37. Dr. S. Venugopalâchârya: World Wide Hindu Culture and Vaishnava Bhakti.

38. Weber: Indian Literature

39. Dr. N.S Anantha Rangachar : "Gems From The Rigveda", 1977

40. R.Ramanujachari on Purusha Suktam.

41. See the introductory part of Bhattar's commentory on Sahasra Namam.

42. This translation in English (four volumes totaling 1300 pages) is from Professor L.S. Seshagiri Rao, Retired Professor of English, of Bangalore University. Refer to the first volume which begins with a lengthy introduction to the story proper.

43. P.N. Srinivasachari: "The Philosophy Of Vishishtâdvaita".

44. Veeravalli Jagannathan: Yoga in Visishtâdvaita.

45. Veeravalli Jagannathan: Manusmrti (Sapthagiri, issues April-July 2006).

46. Wendy Doniger with Brian K. Smith: "The Laws of Manu" (a paperback Penquin Classics, 1991).

47. Kullûkabhatta' s Commentary (in Sanskrit) on "Manusmrti", a Motilal Banarsidass, publication, 2000). Shashi S. Sharma: 'Imagined Manuvad' (Rupa.Co, 2005).

48. S.S. Raghavachar: Ramanuja on the Gita.

49. S.S. Raghavachar: A Synthetic Study of Vedânta.

50. Kapistalam Deśik achariar: Sri Siddhanta-Traya Saṁgrahaḥ by Kapistalam Deśik Achariar.

51. Prof K.S. Narayanâchârya: "The Basic Concepts Of Vishishtâdvaita" 1990.

52. Dr.K.C. V volume 8, page 140, "Post Ramanuja Vishishtâdvaita Philosophy").

53. Books on the life of Ramanyja.

54. Sri S. Krishnaswamy Iyengar: "The Epistemology & Metaphysics of Sri Ramanuja –Vindicated" a booklet of 80 pages published in 1991.

55. "History of Science, Philosophy and Culture in Indian Civilization- Advaita Vedânta, Volume II part 2: D.P. Chattopadhyâya - General Editor, Balasubramanian-distributed by Motilal Banarsidoss. A review appeared in The Hindu dated 9th April 2002 under the caption "Contemporary Classic in Vedânta" and reviewed by Vedamurthy.

56. Prof K.S. Narayanâchârya: Sri Ramanuja on "Tat Tvam Asi & Neti Neti" (1988).

57. George Thibaut.

58. S.S. Raghavachar: Sri Ramanuja on Upanishads.

59. S.S. Raghavachat: Sri Bhashya On The Philosophy of The Brahma-Sutra (1986)

60. See:

    a. S.S. Raghavachar: Vedârtha Sangraha of Sri Ramanuja (RK Math 2002)

    b. Rajagopala Ayyangar: Vedârtha Sangraha of Sri Ramanuja (1956)

61. Vairâgya Panchakam of Deshika .

62. Prof K.S. Narayanâchârya: Tat Tvam Asi & Neti Neti (1989).

63. Sri Bhâshyam: This fully Sanskrit version consisting of the original text along with the commentary named 'Bhashyartha Darpana of Abhinava Desika Sri Uttamur T. Viraraghavâchârya. The book is in two volumes: The first volume consisting of pages numbered from 1 to 438 contains the First Adhyâya alone. The second volume numbered from page 439 to 902 contains the rest of the adhyâya-s viz. Second, Third and the Fourth Adhyâyas. We have followed the page numbers of these two volumes, published by Sri Rangam Srimad Andavan Ashramam.

64. Translation of SB titled "Sukhabodini" in Tamil by Purisai Nadadur Sri Krishnamachariar Swamy is avaible. It ispublished by the Visishtâdvaita Research Centre, Chennai. But for a section of the first adhyâya the translation is complete. The 'Sukhabhodini' has covered only 62 pages of the first adhyâya in four small volumes. The first introductory volume covers upto the page SB p1-12 (the numbers as in Ref 63) . The second volume contains Laghu Purvapaksha and Laghu Siddhanta corresponding to the pages SB p12- 23; The third small volume contains the Maha Purvapaksha, SB p 23-47 and the fourth small volume deal with only a part of Mahasiddhanta SB p48-62 . This last publication of his was in the year 16 Nov 2005. Though the rest of the first adhyâya remains unfinished, he has however completed the rest of the three Adhyâyas. The Second Adhyâya in Tamil is without English translation and was published in 24th Jan 2001. The Third Adhyâya was published in (2.2.1992) and the Fourth Adhyâya in 16.9.1985 containing not only Tamil but English translation as well. The all-inclusive nature of 'Sukhabodhini' and its sweetness is praised in lofty terms thus:

एवमस्यां भाषाटीकायां गहनशास्त्रार्थाः श्रुतप्रकाशिका अधिकरण सारावली चिन्तामणि

भावप्रकाशिका भाष्यार्थदर्पणादि नानाकृतिभ्यः संकलिताःव्याख्यानं च मिलत्सर्वास्वादभूम विभाति।

தேனும் பாலும் நெய்யும் கன்னலும் அமுதும் ஒத்தே

65. References on Tattva Mukta Kalâpa:
   a. Dr. N.S. Anantha Rangâchârya: The Philosophy of Sadhana in Visishtâdvaita.

b. SMS Chari: "Fundamentals of Vishishtâdvaita: A study based on Vedânta Deshika's Tattva-Muktâ-Kalâpa." (First edition 1988)

c. Sri Abhinava Desika Uttamur Veeraraghavachariyar Swami: Tattva Mukta Kalapa and Sarvarta Siddhi with Sanskrit commentaries (1973).

66. Paramata- bhanga of Vedânta Deshika. An excellent edition of this book, by Krishna Tata Deshika (Srirangam Srimad Andavan Ashramam, 2005). It is being continued in Sri Ranganatha Paduka.

67. Shatadushani of Vedânta Deshika.

68. Swami Vireswarananda & Swami Adidevananda: BS according to Ramanuja, a Rama Krishna Ashrama Publication.

69. Vedavalli Narayanan :"The Etymology of Visishtâdvaita"-a study based on Nyaya Parishuddhi of Vedânta Deshika" (2008)

70. Sri S.M. Srinivasachari: "Advaita & Visishtâdvaita".

71. Keshava Aiyangar and Srivatsangachar: Shata dushani (1974). Keshava Aiyangar does acknowledge the book of SMS mentioned earlier in his own inimitable style: "The two far from being repetitive of each other and far from dispensing the need of the other stand in need of each other."

72. From the Chowkhamba Edition of Shatadushani mentioned earlier we get a measure of the length of the vadas, in other words the distribution of pages for the 66 vadas. Vadas 1to 10 occupy 228 pages; vadas 11 to 30 occupy 376 pages; vadas 31 to 42 occupy 347 pages and vadas 43 to 66 occupy 339 pages. Particularly the vadas 15, 37,38 and 39 occupy more than fifty pages in that edition which has Hindi translation of the original Sanskrit gloss Chanda Maruta, mentioned earlier. Incidentally this Hindi translation is the

only translation available for all the 66 vadas The largest among them is the 39th vâda extending over 75 pages.

73. Swami Sunirmalananda:'Insight into Vedânta'- Tattva bodha, a Ramakrishna Math publication).

74. "Yatīndramatadīpika" By Srinivasadasa (A handbook on the Philosophy of Ramanuja. Sanskrit original is translated into English by Swami Adidevananda.

75. S.M.Srinivasachari : "The Philosophy of Visishtâdvaita Vedânta- A study Based on Vedânta Deshika's Adhikarana Saravali". SMS has made a choice of his own and he has selected barely a hundred verses from Adhikarana Sârâvali. The reason adduced by the author: "For this purpose we have confined our attention to the discussion of the selected adhikaraNa(s) that have a direct bearing on the fundamental doctrines of Vishishtâdvaita." The said doctrines are outlined on page xxxvi of Introduction.

76. There are two Sanskrit commentaries on the poem Adhikarana Saravali viz. Adhikarana Chintamani authored by Swamy's son Sri Varadaguru and Sarartha Ratnaprabha written by Abhinavadeshika Uttamur Viraraghavachariar.

77. Presently a Tamil rendering of Adhikarana Sârâvali, authored by Shankapuram Narayana Dasa, is being published serially in Sri Ranganatha Paduka. This publication was started at the turn of the present millennium (2000 AD) and as of now (July 2012), verses up to number AS171 (44 *krtsna prasaktyadhikaraNam* BSII.1.9) have been dealt with. At this rate, it appears that it may take several decades to complete the rest!

78. Veeravalli Jagannathan: "Great Women of Bharata Bhûmi", Sapthagiri Feb 2005.

79. Dr. N.S. Anantha Rangâchârya has written the commentaries on all the Upanishads based on the Upanishad Bhâshyam of Sri Ranga Ramanuja Muni. Principal Upanishads:

439

a. Volume II – Chandogya Upanishad which is an important source book for BS. The main theme of this Upanishad is "*Upasana*".

b. Volume III –Brhadaranyaka Upanishadiggest of all Upanishads. It contains six chapters and of these, the second, third and the fourth chapters are of supreme importance. In the third and fourth chapters the great sage Yagnavalkya teaches the unique characteristics of Paramâtman, the jivâtman and their relationship. This upanishad is the paramount authority in establishing the Antaryamitva of Paramâtman in all other entities. Ramanuja has utilized these Ghataka shrutis in expounding the doctrine of Brahman as characterised by the sentient and non-sentient principles.

80. 40th Pontiff of Ahobila Mutt: Sri Bhashyartha Manipravala Dipika (This work on Sri Bhâshyam was contributed in his purva ashrama) This work was translated into a Tamil commentary by Dr. S.V. Narasimhâcharya titled 'Sri Bhashyartha Dipika' (1989). 44 th Pontiff of Ahobila Mutt: Sri Sutrartha Padya Malika. The earlier work of 40th Pontiff mentioned above was further elaborated for a better graph of the subject. This work was also translated into Tamil by Dr. S.V. Narasimhachariar under the same title 'Sri Bhasyartha Dipika' (1989).

81. Dr T.S.R Narayanâchârya has selected about 60 verses from AS for his lecture and by and large he has restricted himself to the contents of those specific verses mentioned. (the CDs are released by Sri Ramanuja Dasa Audios, Bangalore. Yatiraja @dataone.in).

82. A Tamil commentary on the 78 shlokas of AS pertaining to BS 1.1is available with us. The author of this thought provoking work is not known.

83. "Sudha Rasamanjari" –A volume in Tamil released in the year 1981. Each of the 16 pâdas of Sri Bhâshyam is contributed by a pandit of repute. Editor: Velukkudi K Varadachariar. What is presented in the text is the english translation of Sri Bhashyan III.2 –Ubhaya linga Pâda.

84. Commentary on TM in ten huge volumes contain the following commentaries:
    a. Kurugai Piran Pillan: 6000 padi
    b. Nanjiyar: 9000 padi
    c. Vadi Kesari: Pannirâyira padi
    d. Peria vachchan Pillai: 24000 padi
    e. Vadakku Tiruvidi Pillai: Edu, 36,000 padi. This edition got published under the aegis of Kanchi PB Srinivasachariar Swamy and printed in Kanchi Srinivasa Mudraksha Sala (1915)

85. Publication from 'The Visishtâdvaita Pracharini Sabha' (1975). Commentary on TM (in four volumes) contributed by Sri Uttamur Viraraghavachariar, titled 'Prabandha Raksha'.

86. Publication from Sri Rangam Srimad Andavan Ashramam (1986). The five volumes contain 6000 padi, 24000 padi shabdartha, Dravidopanishad Tatparya Ratnavali. The pontiff, Tirukkudandai Andavan's (Vedânta Ramanuja Mahadeshikan) commentary, 'Bhagavadvishaya Sara' is appended in this edition.

87. Publication from Sri Visishtâdvaita Research Centre, 66 Dr Rangachari Road, Chennai (1994). Commentary in two volumes titled, 'Azhwar Tiruvullum' and besides tamil there is English translation.

88. Uttamur Viraraghavachariar: Dravidopanishad Tatparya Ratnavali and Dravidopanishad Sara (1983).

89. Seventh Centenary Souvenir of Nigamantha Maha Deshikan (30.9.1968). See the article, Prof R. Ramanujachari: Ubhaya Vedânta.

90. Dr.V.Raghavan: Sanskrit Essays on the value of the language and the literature. The Sanskrit Education Society, Chennai, 1972.

91. Sâriraka Adhikarana Archana. All the 156 adhikaranas are cast into the mold of *archana*; the first and the concluding namavalis are: *vichârârha – parabrahmane namah (1)* and *muktasya jagad vyâpâravarja parama sâmya pradâya namah (156)*. Courtesy: Sri Nrsimhapriya Nov 1978.

92. Bhagavan Nâma Sahasram with Dramidopanishad Sâra and Tâtparya Ratnâvali. The 1000 verses of TM are cast in the form of *nâmâvali*. The first one is *om nissîmodyadguNâya namah – uyarvaRa uyarnalam*. The last 1001th is *anubhâvyâya namah (suzhnadanil periya suDar jnâna inbameyo)*. Courtesy: Sri Krishna Sabha Bombay-19, Vaikasi Visakam – 1951.

93. Sri BadarâyaNa Brahma Sutra Sri Bhashyadhikarana Samgati Darpanah – Kalyanapuri (Bangalore). April 1971.

94. *Brahma Sutrangalin Anubhavam* – A.V.Gopalachariar. Sri Komalambha Press, Kumbakonam 1939.

95. His Holiness Sri Rangaramanuja Mahadesikan (Kethândapatti Swami): Shâriraka adhikarana samgati – a brief work (of 25 pages) in Sanskrit. Incidentally, the chief disciple of this Pontiff was an ancestor of ours, Sri Kuththakkudi Sri Kavitarkika Simhachar. The Sanskrit poem Acharya Panchasat by this disciple describes, in awe-inspiring terms, the greatness of Kethandapatti Swami.

96. Sriman Thirupazhanam V. Rajagopala Iyengar: Tiruvaimozhi Saaram. This book in flowing Tamil summarises each stanza of T.M. The whole poem is condensed within a hundred plus pages. The book was appreciated and praised by none other than H.H. Tirukudanthai Andavan himself (1972).

97. Books in excellent printing published in the current century. 97. A massive work (of 900 pages) in Sanskrit on Tattva Mukta Kalapa by pundit K.S.Varadacharya. First edition

442

2004. Publishers: Arsha Grantha Prakashana; 2842, Pampathi road, Jayanagar, Mysore-570014.

98. Chatussutri (600 pages) Dr.V. Vasudeva Thathachariar. Published by Vainavan Kural, L 421, Bharathi Dasan Colony,chennai 600078. First edition 2016.

99. Brahmasutra Sribhashya (which includes the Bhashya of Shruta Prakashika). Book is in 2 vol. and has 2000 pages. Editor Sri Devanathachariya.Published at the instance of H.H. 45th Jeeyar of the Ahobhila Mutt. Narasimhapriya Trust, Year 2006.

100.	Bhagavad Ramanuja Granthamala, The Complete Works of Ramanuja (original text), was released by Srimad Andavan Ashramam as part of commemoration of Millennium Ramanuja (sahasrâbdhi). The celebrations were conducted by His Holiness Srimad Srimushnam Andavan at the newly constructed Ashramam building in Sriperumbudur on May 1, 2017. At the same time, His Holiness Srimad Azhagiyasingar also celebrated at Kanchipuram. For details, see Ranganatha Paduka April and May issues. The nine works of Ramanuja are contained in 2 volumes. The contents of the 1st volume (762 pages) are Sri Vedârtha Sangaraha, Sri Shariraka Mimamsa Bhâshyam, and Sri Vedânta Sara. The second volume contains Sri Vedânta Deepa, Srimad Bhagavad Gita Bhâshyam, Sharanagathi Gadyam, Sriranga Gadyam, Sri Vaikunta Gadyam, Niryagranthah. The special feature of this edition is that the letters are in bold Devanagari fonts. Copies can be acquired from Srirangam Andavan Ashramma 31 Desikacharya Road, Mylapore Chennai-600004.

Made in the USA
Middletown, DE
31 August 2023

37696443R00247